HOMESCHOOLING:
A PATCHWORK OF DAYS

HOMESCHOOLING:
A PATCHWORK OF DAYS
SHARE A DAY WITH 30 HOMESCHOOLING FAMILIES

NANCY LANDE
With 30 Families

WindyCreek Press

WindyCreek Press

First WindyCreek Printing: 1996; Second Printing: 1997; Third Printing: 1999
Most recent printing indicated by the last digit below:
10   9   8   7   6   5   4   3
Library of Congress Cataloging-in-Publication Data
Lande, Nancy 1947-
Homeschooling: A Patchwork of Days
Paperback ISBN 0-9651303-0-4
CIP
SAN 298-9425
Printed in the United States of America

TO FAMILY
The Stronghold of Life

To *my family* with love.
To Gary, my husband, who is my partner in life, thought, memories, parenting, learning. and all else that is meaningful. For our children Brian, Katie, Neil, and Kevin who taught me what a gift it is to be their mother and what a privilege it is to be involved in their learning and growing.

To *all of the families* who participated in this book, who once again stretched their time, jumped into yet another project and opened their homes and lives to help the rest of us along the way.

To *other homeschooling families* who have the common bond of courage and commitment to raise and educate their children at home.

"Train up a child
in the way he should go
and when he is old he will not turn from it."
Psalm 22:6, NIV

"The fruit of the Spirit
is love, joy, peace, patience, kindness,
goodness, faithfulness, gentleness and self-control."
Galations 5:22, NIV

COVER: Photograph by Eric Mitchell
PATCHWORK QUILT: The patches of the quilt that is shown on the book cover were designed by the families who participated in this book. When pieced together, the whole quilt presents a vision of homeschooling that is rich, varied, colorful, energetic, and is sewn together with the common threads of family, love and learning.
QUILTING: Pieced and hand quilted by Barbara Zook.

CONTENTS

FOREWORD
By Susan Richman

Probably all homeschoolers wish they could just take a peek into other homeschooling families' days. How do they do things? How do they move through the day? How do they organize themselves? (Or, is anyone else disorganized like me sometimes?) We meet one another at homeschool support group meetings, we visit one another at our homes, and we talk and talk and it's a wonderful support. But that chance to really see what happens on a real day at someone else's home—that's something we all can only long for.

Nancy Lande's wonderful collection of real days from homeschooling families of all stripes can give us that opportunity. And the title is really apt, as this spectrum of days is almost a crazy quilt of different homeschooling styles and strategies. You will not find identical families all doing the same thing at the same time—instead you'll meet real families who are just as unique as you are and who just don't fit readily fit into categories or stereotypes. There are families with lots of children, or only one or two; families with home businesses or farms, families where Dad goes off to an office job, and families where Mom works outside the home and Dad takes on more of the day-to-day homeschooling. There are families from across the USA and from around the world; families with older teens working on chemistry and algebra and foreign languages, and families with young children enjoying the beginnings of learning about the world in an active way.

With some stories you'll probably feel right at home, and with others you'll probably find yourself saying, "Ah! So that's why I can't do it that way—it's just not us!" And with others you may find yourself saying, "That's what I want to strive for—let me read extra carefully so that I can see just what they are really doing." And if you are a new homeschooler, or just thinking about the possibility, you'll find much here to help you sort out what you might do with your own children. Homeschooling will become more of a grounded reality less just a theory or idea.

.   I know these families probably all learned more about what they do and how they do it by taking part in this worthwhile project—writing up our days makes us be thoughtful when we are usually rushed, makes us reflect and think back and mull over things and see what it all meant. I highly recommend any homeschool families consider writing up a real day like these families have done, maybe every year—it will make a wonderful memory and a great complement to the portfolios of work many of us already keep. And you'll learn more about what you really do.

So enjoy this collection, this quilt of days. Put on some tea, put your feet up, and relax for a while as you are welcomed into some wonderful families' homes. Maybe grab a cozy quilt for your lap, if it's winter like it is here as I write. And remember that the quilt image and this book itself, takes us out of our own little circle of family and gives us the bigger picture of the distinctive pattern that all homeschoolers make together. It's a lovely and varied design.

Susan Richman,
Author of:
Writing From Home
The 3 R's at Home
Math By Kids!
Pennsylvania Homeschoolers

ACKNOWLEDGMENTS

Bob, for his insight
Elva, for her tireless care and support
Susan, for her enthusiasm right from the start
Don, in memory, for his encouragement and faith
Homeschoolers who pave the way for those following

INTRODUCTION

My husband and I watched our older two children gradually lose their spark for learning after attending public school for several years. I had spent a great deal of time and worked hard within the school system to establish programs and to effect change. While some small changes were made, the major improvements we sought for our children would take years at best, and we needed immediate changes. But it's one thing to be unhappy with a situation and quite another to create an alternative.

That summer we heard a lecture by a well-known advocate for home education. Everything he discussed about education rang true and we realized then that homeschooling was the answer for the changes we urgently sought. But, since this idea was so new to us, we wondered how we would find the resources, skills and courage to get started in homeschooling by fall.

We rushed out and bought books about homeschooling, sent for newsletters, found Mary Pride's *Big Book of Home Learning* resource guides and met with other homeschooling parents, hastening to find out how to go about this enterprise of homeschooling.

While the homeschooling parents we contacted were very generous with their time and support and readily showed us their resources, we just couldn't pull the various pieces of information together and visualize what it actually *looked* like or *felt* like to homeschool. I knew that curriculum alone wouldn't produce good teaching or good learning and I wanted to comprehend how the whole process of learning becomes so much more than just the sum of its parts. It seemed especially important to be able to *see* other homeschooling families in action--to be able to sit in and observe *how* they do it. But, lacking the opportunity to be "a fly on the wall" in their homes, we made our decision to homeschool based on our trust that this would be the right thing to do to help our children.

Our first year of homeschooling was one of trial and error, wonderful and wasted purchases, changes in styles and routines, too many group activities, and the growing happiness of our family. We wondered if we had to do what the schools did and do it better. Or could we do something that had no resemblance to "school"? We wondered if we were doing too much, or was it too little? Did we have the energy that homeschooling required? Were we doing it "right"? Would we measure up? We had high academic standards, but would that make enough of a difference to bring back the spark of learning for our children? Since both of us were schooled we knew what *school* looked like, but we had never even seen *home*schooling. Was it simply school-at-home or was it some entirely new concept altogether?

At the end of our first year, after hundreds more hours of readings, phone calls, workshops, tapes, discussions, and now *actual experience*, we had begun to answer some of our questions and to find our own style of home learning, which still continues to evolve.

Early on though, I realized that the kind of book that would have helped us the most just didn't exist. There are many books on homeschooling philosophies, politics, and resources, but I wanted a book like some of the quilting books I have. They don't just list how much fabric to buy and tell you to go ahead and cut and sew the pieces together. The quilting books I like have numerous photographs that show different types of patchwork quilts made by experienced quilt makers and include colorful close-ups of the intricate details, quilting patterns and provide valuable short cuts. This helps to inspire and integrate my own ideas and styles for conceiving new quilting patterns.

My favorite quilts are story quilts, in which each patch illustrates a different person, event, or memory of the individual or family who designed the quilt. I was looking for a book that would depict examples of homeschooling just as clearly, giving us inspiration to create our own style of homeschooling. There are so many ways to homeschool, each wonderful in its own right, that it would have been useful to view a whole homeschooling quilt (made up of all different sorts of patches) when deciding which type of patch to design for ourselves.

Is this book for you? It is if you are considering homeschooling. It is if you are already homeschooling but looking for fresh ideas. It is, even if you don't homeschool but are wishing to have a "close up and personal" view into how other families handle chores, resolve differences, or help to nurture the growth and education of their children. This book offers you the one I wish I could have had. I designed it to bring forth for you an abundance of colors and textures showing what it really looks and feels like to grow and learn together as a family.

After proposing my ideas for this book in homeschooling newsletters, Internet newsgroups, online bulletin boards, to individuals, and by word of mouth, numerous families responded who wished to become a "patch" for the homeschooling "patchwork quilt" I had in mind. Their enthusiasm stemmed from encountering the same disappointment of "the missing book" that I had. They also wished to seize the opportunity to look closely at one of their own days, defining for themselves and for you what it is that they live and believe.

Thirty of these families now share with you a wide variety of styles and experiences of how we homeschool so that you can have the advantage to "observe" us and search for what might be harmonious with your own ideals and style.

In response to pages of my detailed questions, each family sent me a description of one of their real days and, in the manner of a written interview, I wrote back to them and asked dozens of additional questions that would project an even more three-dimensional picture. After they replied yet again, I wove the answers into their original descriptions and often repeated this process two or three times, continually editing as I progressed. I also spoke by telephone to gather more information and to become acquainted with the families. A sampling of the many questions I asked were of this sort: How does your family begin the day? How does everyone wake up—alarm clock, Mom sings or shakes, early risers, sleep as late as you want? How do breakfast and clean-up happen? How do kids get started on their day? What *style* of learning takes place? While you are doing one thing, what are the others doing? How do you settle squabbles, interruptions, or the "I don't want to" response? How do the children interact with each other? How do you teach children of all different ages? What do you do with the little ones? How do you handle irritability, noise, mess or time for yourself? Do you feel inadequate in some areas, proficient in others? How do parents find time to talk, plan, and be together? Do you have outside activities, work, or driving arrangements to make? How does the day end and at what time? What role does *each* parent play in the homeschooling process? What is the weather like on the day you choose and how does it affect your day? Do you live on a remote farm or in an inner city? What is your community setting and reaction to homeschoolers?

I also asked the families to note the resources they used during their day; the books they're reading, their outside activities, and support group opportunities. Because there were so many resources mentioned, it was not possible to list them all in detail. (Most of these resources are listed in the numerous homeschool catalogs now available or in Mary Pride's *Big Book of Home Learning* series, of which there are several volumes that review resources to suit different interests and age levels.) I requested planning or record (log) pages so that you could see various methods of documenting a specific day's events, knowing full well that what is written on record pages is the *what* and not the *how* of the day. Most of us seem always to look for better ways to keep track of our homeschooling activities. Families were given the opportunity to add an UPDATE (over a year later) so that you could experience the process of change in our families.

After choosing resources, the most pressing concerns that families face are about how to pull everything together while navigating through the days, dealing with the temperaments of various family members, their learning styles, values, beliefs and interests. There were even more questions to address. How do we resolve conflicts, struggles, anxieties, ambivalences? How do we handle anger and guilt? How do we manage children who are spontaneous learners or resistant ones? How do we structure time, organization of home, academic work, household chores, meals and laundry? (What is it like to be the principal, teacher, aide, playground monitor, cafeteria director, bus driver, and custodian all at once?) How will our children get together with other children? How does homeschooling affect our marital relationship and decision making? How much do we coach, facilitate, or push? If we could become that "fly on the wall" what would we *truly* see and hear in other homes? That we all wrote about a *real* day is most important because, for many of us who tend to make comparisons and gauge ourselves against what we think is ideal, we often imagine that in everyone else's house there is a "perfect" mother like Ma Ingalls and that all goes smoothly, naturally and cheerfully. But what about the rest of us who fall short of these expectations? Are we the only worriers who lose sleep over the nagging reminders of the imperfections we feel at home? Can we "turn around" a difficult day, or do we hope for a fresh start the following day?

To create a book that was honest and forthright required significant self-revelation from the writers. Because of this, a few families requested that we use only first names or be given the option to use pseudonyms. Photographs and record pages were optional. Some families just didn't have them and others chose to be more private.

As you read, you'll find that some of the days that were described turned out to be days that got off to a late start, had interruptions or unexpected visitors. Sometimes it was chore day. Some children were not thrilled with math or handwriting. Animals and gardens needed to be tended. Some families had spontaneous events that changed the nature of the day. Sometimes the pace was a bit of a whirlwind, and sometimes the learning just kept on going late into the night! Each family member had a role in the construction of their day. There is a portion of every kind of day—some pieces that wouldn't fit into the fabric of your family and others you'd like to tuck away for yourself or start using today!

The thirty distinct quilt patches that are on the cover of this book were designed by the families in this book. The only guideline was the size of the patch. From this blank piece of fabric you can see how the families chose to reflect their interests, activities, personalities, or community. I hope you'll find that the variety of resources, styles, interactions and structures found in our chapters will help you to take a plain piece of fabric and conceive a distinctive patch of your own to add to our homeschool quilt! A homeschool quilt, however, can never be complete as there is always change and other new patches to add. I'd love to hear from you and learn about your own innovations and solutions. Perhaps we will soon piece together another homeschool quilt!

Nancy Lande

E-mail to: WindyCreek@aol.com
Internet Home Page: http://www.windycreek.com

HOMESCHOOLING:
A PATCHWORK OF DAYS

Gary and Nancy
Brian, age 13
Katie, age 11
Neil, age 7
Kevin, age 4

Nancy wrote about the gray and chilling day of January 4, in the verdant suburban outskirts of Philadelphia, Pennsylvania.

THE GIFT OF TIME

Last night we all got to sleep rather late. After the funeral of a friend's young child, our family took time to talk together about her death and the pain and emptiness left behind. It was a hard night for any of us to fall asleep.

Today, a gray and chilling January morning meets us too quickly after our late night. Gary's alarm goes off at 7:20 AM, startling us out of a sound sleep, though we are usually up and about by 7:00 AM. We linger in warmth a few more minutes, then Gary showers and dresses for work. (He works from his office at home—what a bonus for us!) As I am going downstairs to make Gary's breakfast, Kevin and Neil hop out of bed and follow me, bringing their pillows and families of stuffed dogs (a routine these past few weeks).They usually sit together in the easy chair that is in our large kitchen and talk with each other for about a half hour before anyone else wakes up—it is a very special time in their close relationship. After I start Gary's coffee, I take some blueberry muffins out of the freezer to heat up for breakfast before he begins work at 8:00 AM. Yesterday I had planned to bake fresh bread and make strawberry muffins (Neil's turn to pick flavors) but because I spent so much time helping our neighbors, we have muffins from the freezer instead. Once the coffee is started, I squeeze into that same easy chair, with Kevin on my lap and Neil snuggled next to me, and read the library books they have picked out. We read three books before waking up Brian and Katie, giving them a little extra time to catch up on sleep. I read *Now Let Me Fly—The Story of a Slave Family*, by Dolores Johnson and we talk about the strength of a family during all sorts of sorrows and strife (reminding us of our neighbors) and tie it in to the history of slavery. We have been studying the Civil War and watching videos of the Civil War, so they have some idea of what the period was like. Then we read *Something from Nothing*, by Phoebe Gilman which was adapted from a Jewish folk tale. The details in the illustrations particularly catch our attention and create some good discussions, as there is so much of life shown in each illustration. The grandfather in the book had made a special blanket for his grandson and, as it became more and more tattered, he fashioned the fabric into smaller and smaller items, giving us the opportunity to discuss family closeness, thriftiness, and special homemade gifts that have real value in our lives. For the holidays we had all been making homemade gifts for each other, so Kevin and Neil relate the specialness of handmade gifts to our own family experience. Next, we read the story *John Henry*, by Julius Lester, and talk about strength of character as we read, as well as various types of hammers and steam drills, always of interest to our young boys. We are each taken by surprise at John Henry's abrupt death at the end and yet again talk about the death of our neighbor. Neil listens avidly and Kevin seemingly drifts. However, his comments and fine attention to the picture details indicate otherwise.

Even though this day does not begin as early as usual, I decide before breakfast that this will be the day that I will write about. This is a day with no scheduled outside music lessons, field trips, or activities to attend and we can follow our own natural rhythm of a day at home. No particular reason I choose this day, except that I'd been putting it off and it was the "now or never" sort of decision that often follows the start of a new year.

Before we really get started on the journey of our day, let me first describe the *setting* of our day. "Home" is a three story (counting the basement level) house we have owned for twenty years and where our living and learning begin and end each day. We live in the suburbs of Philadelphia where each house is different. There are many small community neighborhoods nestled close by, a wide variety of community resources, and within twenty minutes we can be in Philadelphia by car or train. (The city is rich in history, culture, activity, and diversity so, naturally, we go there often.) Home is where we have over-filled bookshelves in every room, inviting chairs and sofas in which to read and talk, lots of cheerful quilts on beds and walls, a woodworking shop and a well supplied art room in our basement, a kitchen area that is the center of activity where we all gather to cook, bake, can, clean, learn, play, think, and most often—talk. Our living room serves as our main resource room and is often where our children sit down to work quietly. Our backyard backs on ten acres of land that is mostly field, with old growth forest, foliage, wildlife, and a stream to explore.

The use of our rooms continually changes, as does our homeschooling itself. From the beginning of homeschooling, as the children grew to relax and become comfortable working around each other, they quickly found that they all

Brian (13), Katie (11), Neil (7), Kevin (4)

preferred to work in the living room or at the kitchen table. For concentrated focus, they can retire to a quiet corner of the house. The living room has a large informal coffee table for pencils, paper, magazines and the children's record keeping books; and our "project" table (an old plank farm table with benches) is usually stacked high at one end with projects, papers, books, or puzzles. The children sit there for GeoSafari practice, projects, table work or going over material with me and for assembling our homeschool newsletter.

Also in the living room are the piano, violin, cello, and percussion instruments, along with one of our three networked computers, the TV and video machine, CD and stereo equipment, copy machine, and baskets on the floor for well over a hundred library books. Our book shelves hold thousands of books, games, math manipulatives, and things we have forgotten about. In some attempt to organize them, I arranged by them by category: math, science, US and world history, geography, nature, religion, natural resources, Native Americans, language arts, reference, anthologies, homeschooling, foreign languages, foreign literature, humor, modern literature, science fiction, poetry, classics, drama, art, music, math, biography, magazines (*National Geographics, Cobblestone, Odyssey, Stone Soup, Faces, Calliope, etc.*), works published by our children and other children, and puzzle and game shelves. Whew!! We *never* have enough bookshelves!

All around the rest of the house we have assortments of collections: fossils of every imaginable type, petrified wood, shells, rocks, feathers, sea glass, rubber bands (really), pen knives, glass animals, pins, buttons, nature "treasures," key chains, and on and on. (Actually, not until just now did I realize what collectors we are!) We enjoy working outside at the stream, in the backyard, or on our patio when it is warm—unless swarms of bees invade.

We never have enough pencils, the cushions always fall off the sofas and chairs, piles rapidly turn into mounds, and there is usually one lost shoe under some piece of furniture. Within the living room and our kitchen, we have all managed to work both together and somewhat separately at the same time. No one uses a desk, sits up straight, or works in the same place each day. The children each have a handled basket (of the supermarket variety) that holds their work, folders and books (though one of my children recently discovered a new "force" that seems to pull all of this *outside* the basket in a three foot radius and strews it about on the sofas and chairs).

Our home looks well lived in, warm, and has an air of, well . . . clutter. After cleaning the kitchen each evening, we tidy up the rest of the house quickly—sometimes. I'd like to say all the time, but it's just not true. I always feel apologetic for not having "everything in order" but realize that six people busily working at home all day doing various ongoing projects does not lend itself to easy clean ups.

Our children have always enjoyed sharing bedrooms. We find that most of our "bed" rooms are multi-purpose rooms anyway, with a bed being just a place to sleep. One of the bedrooms serves as office/work/sewing/computer/ project room; another has the electronic piano hooked up to one of our

Brian (13), Katie (11), Neil (7), Kevin (4)

computers and also has our amazing Lego drawer—three foot square and almost filled if everything were to be taken apart and tossed back in! The other bedroom houses the costumes, farm and tractors, building blocks and car-and-truck box. The room in where someone might be found depends on *what* they are doing at the moment. Woodworking, painting, crafts, electronics, chemistry and other messy projects the children enjoy are done in our well-lit, semi-finished basement. Anyway, this is the home where we begin our days each morning, kiss our children good night at bedtime, read, talk, learn and spend time together.

Now, back to our morning. After reading stories, it is 8:30 AM and I gently wake up Katie while, in contrast, Kevin awakens Brian by climbing on his bed and playing horsie! We try to begin our activities by 9:00 AM because there is always so much we want to do and it seems that there is never enough time in any one day to do it all. Katie showers first, dresses and I put her hair into a French braid. Brian reads the newspaper and by the time he gets to the comics he shouts with glee that the comic *Calvin and Hobbes* has made it back from a year-long sabbatical. (Brian is a great humorist and loves all types of comedy, comics, satire, and parody.) Katie isn't too hungry and, in fact, there are many days when someone just does not choose to eat breakfast. The three boys and I sit down to our blueberry muffins, look over this week's log pages and talk over basic plans for the day. They are usually at no loss for what they have in mind. I add a few suggestions of my own. We also read aloud bits and pieces of the newspaper that catch our attention.

At this unusually early hour, our doorbell rings and we greet our UPS driver who is delivering a package. As we open it we are delighted, not by the *package*, but by the little packing "worms." While visiting friends recently, we discovered that these "worms" can simply be licked and stuck together to form wonderful "sculptures." You can imagine our delight at being able to sculpt during breakfast. Aside from the white mess scattered all over the kitchen floor, we end up with a cat, a box, a basket, a ladder, a log cabin, a DNA chain and many other whimsical creations, many that are now sitting on the window sill.

Breakfast clean-up and morning chores now. It became apparent this year that the children would busily get caught up in their activities before, or even during, breakfast. They would shower and dress, pick up a book or project . . . and before you knew it, it would be lunch time! The breakfast dishes would sit in the sink (can't say that it bothers me) until then. Since the children have kitchen chores at mealtimes, the breakfast chores just seemed to fall by the wayside. Then, when it came time for lunch chores, the children would insist that breakfast chores be done *first,* before they'd start in on lunch chores! With all that debate, I came up with the perfect solution. Now, *I* do the breakfast dishes, the floor, and wipe off the table. Isn't that a wonderful solution? And I don't even argue with myself! Today I am especially drawn to the broom so that I can quickly get up those static "worms" before they begin to spread throughout the house like in some science fiction movie. Katie and Neil feed our two cats. Brian is in charge of changing the kitty litter. While Neil is finishing up taking

Brian (13), Katie (11), Neil (7), Kevin (4)

the trash and recycle cans to the street, I ask Kevin to go upstairs to "take a dress" (his own expression derived from "take a shower"), but he wishes to wait until Neil is ready also. To solve that, Kevin helps Neil with his chores. Kevin and Neil then go together to get dressed. I never know what clothing to expect from Kevin. Some days when he comes downstairs he is a fireman, a policeman, Captain Picard from *Star Trek—The Next Generation*, Timmy (from *Lassie*) or, most often, an Amish boy—if he's not being himself, that is! Whatever Kevin's interest is in the morning, it shows up in his clothing. Today he is Amish, with black pants, green snap shirt, suspenders, and straw hat, because we often visit the farm of Amish friends. Okay, so now the chores are all finished and the kids are all dressed. Am *I*? Well, no . . . not yet. (This reminds me . . . people often ask pressing questions such as if our children can go to school in their pajamas, have to wear shoes, go to the bathroom when they want, or eat if they're hungry—and *where* do they do "homework"? But they never ask us if the *teacher* is ever in her nightgown!!!)

Two days ago Brian and Katie were invited to join the National Geographic Geography Bee with other homeschoolers in our area who join together for contests, fairs or field trips. They decided to enter—Brian quite willingly and Katie a bit less so, because, on this short notice, they only had *four days* to prepare. We decided that we would change this week's plans and devote extra time to go over Geography and current events, letting some of their more usual studies wait until next week. Since they watch *CNN Newsroom* daily, I know they're up to date on world events. I know that the computer and GeoSafari in the living room will be in constant use today, and as I clean the floor, I wonder who will start up first. It is Katie who grabs the GeoSafari and reviews the countries of Europe, Asia, Africa, the Americas, the Solar System, landmarks, famous monuments and other facts of the world. She and Brian have already memorized the fifty states and capitals and this gives them extra motivation to tackle the rest of the world's countries, capitals, customs, and resources. *All in four days????* Well, they *are* well on their way to a lifelong pursuit of getting to know about the world.

While Katie is doing her geography, Brian sits down at the word processor to work on his story from the vantage point of our male cat, Mickles. This idea began as a family musing and many giggles two days ago. We had gone away for a few days and one of our neighbors and her four-year-old daughter came over twice a day to feed our cats. They stopped by when we returned and told us about some of the cat's antics and what fun it was for them to take care of the cats. We wondered what the *cats* would have told us about *their* experiences while we were gone. Brian would write for "Mickles," Katie would write for "Maggie," and we would get to hear *their* stories! So far, "Maggie" has written a whimsical daily "journal" describing a fearful storm, food preparation, conversations between the two cats, animal friends who came to visit, and a pet party that includes recipes and decorations. Excerpt from Maggie:

Brian (13), Katie (11), Neil (7), Kevin (4)

"My eyes caught hold of a dark gray cloud, my ears caught hold of a loud boom and my spine caught hold of a chill as a pitter patter, pitter-patter sound came down, pounding hard on the roof. I laid down, trying to ignore that horrifying sound. But then Mickles came next to me and comforted me with some soft meows and I fell asleep next to his warmth, with the pitter patter, pitter-patter singing me a song. I woke up about two hours later and there were still those horrid sounds that I so dearly dread. To ease my mind, I went over to the food box and had a bit of kibble and a few licks of that freezing cold water. Then I used the litter box and played with a yellow mouse that has a ball in it so that it makes a playful jingling noise. Of course, that noise had to wake up Mickles and he gave me quite a scolding by batting his paw at me.")

"Mickles" is expounding his philosophical musings and his questions about the universe. He practices "resting" exercises while *his* "pets" are away on vacation! Excerpt from Mickles:

"I ate my fill and went past the small red chair that I enjoy sitting on to look out the window. As I made my way past, I stopped at the kitty litter, only to find Maggie there first. Being in no mood to argue, I took my leave back to the red chair. I hopped on and faced the window. The chilling breeze tickled my nose but otherwise it felt good. I peered up at the sky and stared at the moon with awe as my father had done and my fathers's father before him. It is strange that something that looks as warming as the moon is nothing but coldness. I turned my eyes to another lighted point in the sky and wondered what it was and where it came from. At the same time, I wondered why am I here and where does our future lie? I wondered if it was in the heavens, like a streak of moving light.")

All during the day they keep coming back to work on these stories. I wonder how they so easily come up with creative and fanciful perspectives! They enjoy the flexibility and efficiency of using a word processing program and amicably improve spelling from their ever faithful spell-checker!

Meanwhile, Neil and Kevin are in the kitchen conducting great science experiments with the "worms." Kevin is cutting them up into tiny particles—trying to see if he can get down to the molecular level! (It looks like we have a snow covered kitchen floor.) Neil is putting his "worms" into little cups with cold or hot water to compare how long it takes them to become starchy mush after first incredibly wrinkling up and then shrinking. Neil wants to pour his goo outside onto the patio to see what happens and I make him promise to *clean up* after getting him to hypothesize what could happen when starchy goo hardens on the patio in freezing weather. He decides to leave them outside *in* the cups instead, as he also can now hypothesize what kinds of scrub brushes and elbow grease he would need! Why do I consider the clean-up aspect instead of letting free-spirited investigation take flight? Because we have spent all too many days cleaning up spilled glue, reseeding the lawn, repairing fences and other joyful tasks. This is one of our ambivalences and we're never sure how far to let messy projects go. So I do instill a vision of possible clean-up chores when

Brian (13), Katie (11), Neil (7), Kevin (4)

our children pursue their projects and give them that responsibility. Most of the time. Not as much as I wish. Well . . . sometimes.

Now, as I finally get showered and dressed, they are all well absorbed in their tasks. I have finessed my showering/dressing routine down to fifteen minutes max.

When I return to the kitchen, I find Kevin drawing pictures of "an Amish boy with hair" on a small chalkboard, Neil is still brewing worms—but now in the sink, Katie is finishing another card or two of GeoSafari and Brian is still writing his cat philosophies. I call Katie to the kitchen table after she is finished (yes, the table is now clean for a *very* short time) and review her work with her. Yesterday she never did fill in her learning log, so I have her do it now, as this is a daily responsibility for our children. We discuss which things she really ought to get done today and what she wishes to do today. For all four children, we leave the *when* up to them. We review her ideas for how she will choose to respond to the books she has been reading. (I expect each school age child to do at least ten or twelve book/film responses each year by choosing to react to what they have read by writing essays, poems, satires, new endings, by rendering drawings, or other art work, or whatever suits their fancy. These choices give them many other options of expression than the standard book report format.) Katie wants to write a comparison of two Civil War novels she read called *Look Homeward Hannalee* and *Be Ever Hopeful, Hannalee,* both by Patricia Beatty. They complement our studies of the Civil War era.

Gary and I present history for our children as a large framework of interwoven stories and events that have people, motives, feelings, and often conflicts that link humans to their lands and struggles. Katie has always loved to supplement history with historical fiction. She is trying out a new writing format like that of a "recipe," where she gives the ingredients and instructions that are needed to become an Amish girl, synthesizing what she has read in perhaps two dozen or more books of Amish history, customs, and beliefs. She is an excellent writer and an accomplished poet. She quickly and easily forms a theme and direction for her writings. This was not always so. Both she and Brian used to balk at writing assignments or journal writing when they were in school and when we first started homeschooling three years ago. They now write a lengthy and comprehensive homeschool newsletter every few months, or every "blue moon" as we call it, where they have a chance to publish their writing for family, friends and other schooled and homeschooled friends. Katie and Brian have both had their writings published in national magazines and books. They have found writing to be a real form of expression for their own ideas, humor, wonderment, concerns, and feelings, rather than "assignments" that "have to be turned in."

Next, Katie and I do a lesson together of Dr. Henry Borenson's *Hands-On Equations*, a manipulative and visual way of learning algebraic linear equations. She loves it and looks forward to each new step, while building confidence and competence. She has been trying to write several algebraic story problems but has stumbled into the difficulties of the real-life application of "negative" numbers. I listen to her attempt to develop an algebraic problem

Brian (13), Katie (11), Neil (7), Kevin (4)

involving negative numbers and hear how she is going about it: "Our family has some canvas bags that we use for carrying library books. We *always* put the same amount of books in each bag. Well, last week nothing went right when we went to the library. We ended up forgetting as many books at home as we took back to the library! I carried one bag to the library, Brian carried one bag, Kevin carried one bag but we realized that it was missing all of the books because they fell out at home, and Neil carried five loose books in his arms. When the librarian checked us in, she told us that we still also had two bags worth left at home. How many books do we keep in each bag and how many books *should* we have returned to the library?" She's not sure whether the problem is solvable yet so we work through it and determine the problem spots. We subsequently discuss bank accounts and missing objects and ponder what other ways negative numbers might have real-life application, with Katie setting out to try a better approach. From our earliest days, problem solving has been a central focus of our math learning. The children not only solve problems but write them. It takes a great deal of patience in order to have a well-formed problem that not only makes sense but holds interest. Her trials in this area have led her to correspond directly with Dr. Borenson and she was recently invited to join him for lunch in a nearby city and discuss the difficulties of writing algebraic word problems. These kinds of real life daily interactions are one of the bonuses of home-schooling.

While we are working on this, Neil joins us at the kitchen table and works on the *Miquon Math Lab Orange Book* by himself, solving addition and multiplication problems. (He *loves* math and thinks it's fun and easy!) When he finishes, he independently works on some spelling games, some concepts of zero and reads a story to Kevin from one of the first books he ever read called *First Steps*, an early reader that he loves, published by Pathway. As I watch him work, I think how it is easier for the younger ones to get into a learning routine when they see the older ones at work over the years. It's a natural expectation, and they look forward to the simplest experiments, manipulatives and workbooks with great pride.

Kevin plays with two little trucks at the kitchen table where we are working but has to be told to hush several times as he is obviously having significant muffler trouble and it's hard to do positive and negative x's, numerals, zeros and spelling games (*Boggle*) with roaring trucks rumbling across the table. Since the muffler does not get repaired, we substitute some Legos and have a quieter time. Katie and Neil seem to finish up at about the same time.

Gary has a work break and comes in to visit with us for a few minutes. During the day, he often has a chance at least to peek in on what we're doing. He is always on call for our endless computer problems—he's our in-house computer consultant. Occasionally he will have time to do projects, help smooth out difficult questions, or just spend some time with one of the children. Though I am the one who spends most of the day with the children, Gary fully supports our homeschooling with his input, guidance, supplies, field trips, computer support, financial backing for our family, and his constant love for all of us. We

Brian (13), Katie (11), Neil (7), Kevin (4)

all clearly value his gifts of devotion, insight and sense of purpose. He guides us to keep on track, hears our frustrations, helps us find solutions, and always comes up with the most wonderful resources. His being home with us allows us much freedom to come and go, not to mention the joy of his company. It was important to Gary and me, even before we started our family, that Gary would choose to work at home so that he would be an integral part of our family life, being a father who is a visible role model and who is available to his children.

After Gary returns to his office, I call Brian to the kitchen table to join Katie and me so that we can practice solving *Math Olympiads* story problems (designed for third to sixth graders, and really quite challenging) together and then talk over our individual strategies. Problem solving was very difficult when we first started homeschooling and something they had not previously had experience with in school. Familiarizing our children with many strategies to solve problems of all types was, and still is, an important focus of our curriculum. The children now find pertinent and unusual problems to be enjoyable and can readily find resourceful strategies to solve them. I work right along with them and we each discuss the strategy we have chosen for any given problem. Additionally, they use the *Figure It Out—Thinking Like a Math Problem Solver* books. Brian and Katie are working in book 6 and Neil is in book 2. Problem solving strategies are wonderful thinking tools that really stretch the mind! We have recently formed a small *MathCounts* team with a few other homeschoolers. We meet once or twice a month to work on solving math problems as a group, eventually preparing for timed individual and team competitions in problem solving. The February *MathCounts* contest is for seventh and eighth graders, but the children have enjoyed the practices so much that they have decided to meet all year round, even though they won't be in the contest until next year.

While the three of us are still together at the table, we spend a short time on E. D. Hirsch's *What Your 5th Grader Needs to Know*, going over the economic and religious motives of the age of European exploration in the 1400's. We follow the trail of Spanish, Portuguese and Dutch explorers until we enter the age of slave trade. They both have many excellent questions that we look up, discuss and relate to other topics. We leave off here, knowing that we will be heading into further studies of the American South, the Civil War, slavery and Reconstruction in the following weeks. We then look over the library books we have selected on these issues and they choose books to read this week.

One of the earliest resource decisions Gary and I made in homeschooling was to use the E. D. Hirsch Cultural Literacy series because of its commitment to a "core curriculum" of knowledge. We found this series to be of such excellent quality that we started our older children in the first grade book and worked our way up. The concepts are well synthesized and get to the essential strands of what underlies each "story" in history, art, science or literature. We use the book as a launching point for further studies, and I feel that beginning at the first book for almost any age is beneficial as the

Brian (13), Katie (11), Neil (7), Kevin (4)

information spirals around and around, fleshing in more each time until the information is like an old friend. Brian and Katie are concurrently reading the ten volume series *History of US*, by Joy Hakim. These books discuss the historical foundation of the United States through biographical anecdotes, original resources, art and cultural events, and with the author's engaging style that seems to keep them reading right along in the series. Between the Hirsch series, Hakim's books and our own historical resources, we expose our children to many views of historical events. We have exciting conversations and make many connections to literature, art, philosophy, current events and our own life experiences.

It is now about 11:30 AM and it won't be long until lunch. The children and I join together to munch on a few unsalted pretzels and some orange juice, and decide to practice French *before* lunch rather than after, like we usually do. We have just picked up working on French again after a two year absence and use the *Learnables* audio tapes and picture books. We renewed our studies of French at the request of the children this time after we attended a "French supper" where there were French foods and the conversation was only in French. After realizing they could merely ask for bread and cheese to be passed, they saw the gastronomical advantage of learning a language for real!! We listen to the tapes together, stop the tape machine to announce silly sentences of our own like "the dog bumps into the banana" or "the doctor puts his shirt on the apple" and I have great fun listening to my children proclaim sweetly "Bonjour, Maman" or "Merci, Maman" throughout the day. Kevin, who is sitting in my lap, moves away from the table after a while and looks at some library books before taking out some domino-like blocks to build a long and twisty road through the kitchen. Neil eventually leaves to play with the toy barn and farm animals in the room he shares with Kevin upstairs. Kevin ultimately joins Neil, calling out "Au revoir, Maman." I realize that he too was absorbing the lessons! The two boys come back downstairs in about twenty minutes and go outside to dig deeper into the almost waist deep hole at their "construction site" even though the ground is practically frozen by now. (They have built a crane and have a compost-making "business" there.) I am surprised at how motivated Brian and Katie are about French, as two years ago it was like pulling teeth when it was *my* idea. We dropped French then, figuring that they'd learn it when they saw the need for it or wanted to. Now, we really have great fun and it proves that sometimes the best strategy is timing and waiting for something to be *their* idea—a "teachable moment."

While Kevin and Neil are happy at their construction site, we continue playing through the French lessons, spending even more time than we had intended until now it is 12:30 PM. Brian and Katie make up some tuna salad, I peel some carrots, Brian searches for salsa (which he will put on almost anything), Neil gets out the juice, Kevin gathers the cups, and we all whip out the paper plates. Washing dishes three times a day is not a high priority for our time. Paper plates at lunch are an ecological concession we have made in light of our tight time commitment to learning. We have some help with heavy

Brian (13), Katie (11), Neil (7), Kevin (4)

housework, which leaves us with chores of straightening up, doing dishes, laundry, and putting away all the clutter we create each day. We welcome a lighter load of lunch dishes!

Gary now joins us for lunch. All through the morning he had come to see what we'd been doing during his short work breaks and he now catches up with the latest events that everyone is bursting to relate. We tell silly knock-knock jokes, discuss the documentary we saw this week— *How the West Was Lost* about Native Americans, we look at Kevin's drawings and computer art from sometime this morning and wonder what else he and Neil will end up doing with those "worms." Usually, we watch and discuss *CNN Newsroom* during lunch, but not today, unless we find time later on. While we're eating, Katie reminds me that we had planned to read *Romeo and Juliet* and asks when we will. We had already read *Julius Caesar, King Lear* and *Hamlet* and thought we would like something a little lighter from Shakespeare. I think I know where the book is so I jump in while the opportunity is ripe and begin to read. We really get caught up in the story and the beauty of the language and have some lively discussions about teens, courtship, fate, and how comedy can turn to tragedy. Neil seems to understand and enjoy the play. Kevin falls asleep on the easy chair in the kitchen and I cover him with a blanket. We decide that we'd all like to see the *Romeo and Juliet* play on video and we plan for me to go to the library later with Neil and Kevin to check it out for our evening activity. Most evenings the children practice their instruments, read, watch an educational video, play games, talk, or just spend time with us. Tonight, Shakespeare it will be!

After we finish lunch and reading the play, Brian clears the table and puts the food away, Katie puts the dishes into the dishwasher, Neil sweeps the floor and Kevin puts away the toys after he wakes up. The water and kibble for the cats are checked. I straighten up the living room and organize Neil's materials for his afternoon work.

A few afternoons each week Brian and I take a twenty minute brisk walk and combine exercise with conversation, but I can tell by our busy day that this afternoon won't be one of them. After a shorter than usual outdoor play break, the children get back to their activities. Katie chooses to add on to her now three-page typed (Katie and Brian type effortlessly and Neil is learning) letter to her friend. She next works on her "Maggie" cat story. This takes quite a bit of time as she is really involved in her writing today. She may decide to show me her writing after she spell-checks and edits it, or perhaps wait until another day.

Brian now goes to the computer with Gary where they search for software covering geography. Gary is continually teaching them how to use the computer for research. Between the Internet and other online services, they come up with about five different programs that go over geography, current events around the world and even happily find a theoretical physics program in which Brian is extremely interested. (Physics is one of his favorite subjects.) Computer work takes up most of the afternoon for Brian and he has not yet had a chance to do his lesson in *Saxon Algebra 1*, which he enjoys, or a lesson in

Brian (13), Katie (11), Neil (7), Kevin (4)

Balanced Science 1, a British high school text, which he *really* likes. He sets his own pace for these subjects and works primarily alone on them (his choice), asking for help only if he needs it. I help him with math reasoning if necessary. Gary usually goes over science or history with Brian when he is searching for underlying theory or synthesis.

Because Katie is still writing, she also has not had time to do her daily *Saxon 76* lesson or read and take notes from her nature book *Naming Nature—A Seasonal Guide for the Amateur Naturalist*, by Mary Blocksma or to practice outlining skills using the book *Secrets of a Wildlife Watcher* by Jim Arnosky. These tasks combine her keen interest in nature and note-taking skills. (I have always found that outlining is a valuable tool for note-taking, organizing, and thinking, and it is something that I will eventually make sure that all of our children will use automatically when writing lengthy papers.)

Now it's midafternoon and my time to spend with Kevin and Neil. Neil writes a sentence about "bread, milk, eggs, and fruit" and we playfully try to take the food words off his page and eat them! He and Kevin then have the idea to take out some magazines and search for and cut out pictures of those foods, then glue them on to colored papers. They help each other and are pleased with their results. Neil decides he does not want to do a chapter in his Pathway reader *Days Go By* just now but wishes to read the whole Dick and Jane book that he enjoys instead. This book is much easier but he gains pleasure and confidence when he reads it to Kevin. So, we do that with all of us bundled again on the easy chair and giggle about all the funny situations the story kids get into. Father helps Dick, Jane and Sally to make wooden boats that they paint (though the red boat does fall into the yellow paint can!) and Neil decides that he will make a wooden boat also. (He is very adept at woodworking and owns his own hand saw and electric drill, along with his own tool box and hand tools. Kevin watches every move that Neil makes and learns woodworking by watching him.) After reading, Neil solves problems in his *Figure It Out* book 2 and in *Math By Kids!* by Susan Richman. Several of his (and his sibling's) problems were published in *Math By Kids!* and he enjoys doing the problems of other children that he knows. I love to watch him and see how he finds solutions in his own unique manner.

Neil loves maps and volunteers to show Kevin the seven continents and works on learning the names of the seas and oceans. While enjoying the map, we talk together about Spanish explorers who left the southern continent and moved north to the Mississippi River looking for gold. Finding none, they figured the land was *good for nothing* and left. (He says this reminds him of the book *Something from Nothing* that we read this morning and mulls over the two different phrases—*good for nothing* and *something from nothing*.) English explorers came later and we discuss Virginia Dare, the first English baby born in America and ponder what could have happened to her settlement, causing them to all disappear. Neil imagined what he would have done and seen if he'd grown up to be the first settler born in Virginia and had lived to tell about it. We also read *Peter Rabbit* and Kevin wants to hear it a second time. Neil is able to complete his first grade work in about one and a half hours on most days and so

Brian (13), Katie (11), Neil (7), Kevin (4)

has the rest of the day to plan out for himself.

Since it's about 4:00 PM now, I decide to take Neil and Kevin to the library to pick up the *Romeo and Juliet* video tape while Brian and Katie keep up their busy day. (Another benefit of Gary working at home is the flexibility it gives me to go out and take one or more children along, leaving the others at home, etc.) While we are gone, Brian keeps working on geography and later practices saxophone, clarinet, music theory, and composition. Brian is very serious about jazz (and music in general) and has been studying since he was eight years old. Gary takes him into Philadelphia each Saturday afternoon to rehearse with his jazz ensemble and to a music lesson. He also has another music teacher and spends another two hours each week studying composition, rhythm, improvisation and saxophone with him. Music is a central area of pursuit for Brian and it wins the prize for our largest homeschooling expense! There are many parallels between jazz and homeschooling—both require mastery of the basics before the fun of improvisation and creativity can occur with smoothness and depth.

During the same time, Katie takes about a half hour to practice piano from the *Suzuki* Book 2. She was well on her way in her violin studies but within this past month has begun work on the piano. She is working at great speed, as her years of music lessons have prepared her well for a new instrument that combines all of her interests in music.

When she is through practicing, she sits back at the computer and works on a poem she had begun last month. She is pleased with her corrections and hands me her poem to read when I return home:

FADED YELLOW

Slow summer days pass
Barely moving in mother's wood rocker
My faded yellow dress sticks to flesh
Like flies caught in maple syrup
Too hot to concentrate
Too hot to move
Weakened by humidity
I gaze beyond wavy curtains of heat
And dream . . . .

Brian and Katie work together on geography at the computer with Gary, as he has some free time this afternoon. After that, he ends up spending hours on a computer systems problem he found. It's hard to believe just how much time is required to keep our three computers up and running, since they are used from early morning to late at night by six people. Afterward, he takes care of some paperwork from his office.

Brian has a little bit of time to log onto the Internet to research about dogs. He has an abiding interest and love of dogs and is researching different

Brian (13), Katie (11), Neil (7), Kevin (4)

breeds, health issues, breeders, animal psychology and veterinary science. He has filled a three inch binder with information he collected and organized from on-line bulletin boards, e-mail, home pages, and research areas. He has obtained many excellent answers to his questions and the respect of several breeders. His notebook of research is an example of the synthesis of the skills he has learned these past few years from computer communication, note taking, research skills, writing, curiosity, thoroughness, and media reference. He has read dozens of books, synthesized much information, and has corresponded with people all over the country. Hopefully, this will be the year that he finally gets a dog.

While the three of us are at the library, Neil reads a chapter from *Days Go By* (because he *likes* to read it at the library table), we pick out a few more books then realize it is almost 6:00 PM! We hurry home and on the way back pick up some fresh baked bread to go with the spaghetti, marinara sauce and salad that I will quickly make when we get back home. Many days the children love to cook dinner, but I know how busy they've been today and how late it's gotten. Katie is an especially good baker and is disappointed that she doesn't have enough time to make a pie for dessert as she had planned. So many days it gets too late to do something that we had hoped to do. Today is one of those very active and productive ones . . . a nice feeling.

Brian and Katie are still working when we arrive back home, so I make the salad and get dinner ready. (Our children always have the option of having a bowl of cereal and yogurt at dinner if I am serving a meal that they really don't like, but this doesn't happen too often.) Neil and Kevin set the table, clean the toys (boots and coats) off the floor—after too many distractions and reminders from me—and set out the water glasses. Dad is called to the table and we all sit down together at 6:30 PM to hold hands and take a moment together to appreciate the gifts life has brought us. While the meal that took thirty minutes to prepare disappears in fifteen minutes, we discuss the rest of the day's activities, laugh a lot, listen to each other's highlights and hurry along our dinner so that we can watch the video from the library. Katie clears the table, cleans the stovetop and counters, and puts the food away. Brian loads the dishwasher, washes and dries pots and plastic containers and cleans the sink. I run upstairs to the "quiet" computer to work on this book for a little while, only to be interrupted by Katie telling me that Kevin and Neil are lying on the kitchen floor, playing and laughing, so that she can't vacuum the floor—they haven't picked up all of the toys and are *just playing!* I call them upstairs and tell them to please pick things up off of the floor or they will be in charge of vacuuming it themselves. (Actually, I realize while I write this, that I don't have to raise my voice very much any more! A few well chosen reminders and a steady gaze are often enough of a correction. Gary and I have worked very hard to train the children to respect and listen to their parents.) All is well again and while I continue with my work, Kevin and Neil put on their pajamas, brush their teeth and straighten up their room . . . slooooowly, talking and laughing all the while. I stop after about ten minutes more of my work and help them clean up the rest of their room. All during this time, Gary is on the phone *again* with technical support,

Brian (13), Katie (11), Neil (7), Kevin (4)

trying to find out why the spell-checker on our word processing program is not working. The children moan and groan when it doesn't work. The technical support person has never heard of this particular problem. Gary thinks he's figured out how to fix the situation, but will give it more attention tomorrow. He is persistent and creative in solving problems. His style of persistence and enormous self-motivation is a model for us all.

We then all head downstairs to discuss *Romeo and Juliet* a bit before watching the video. (While we were at the library, Kevin picked out *Pinocchio* as a more suitable video for him to watch in another room while the rest of us watch the first hour or so of *Romeo and Juliet.)*

At 9:00 PM (an hour later than usual, for the second day in a row—we may be sorry tomorrow . . . .), Neil and Kevin get ready to go to bed and say good night. Kevin fusses (yep, *too* tired!) that he wants to see the end of "Pinocchio." I tell him he can finish tomorrow, but that's no substitute for *now!* I pick up his stuffed snowman and *The Snowman* by Raymond Briggs and start talking about when and where we would build his snowman when the snow finally comes this winter. This nicely distracts him and we have a peaceful good night after all. Bedtime is usually very routine: pajamas on, dirty clothes in laundry, brush teeth, bathroom, cup of water, fluoride tablet and into bed. Favorite books or gadgets are put at the foot of their beds and we all come in to hug good night and share a few last words. After actively busy days, all of our children gladly go to bed, occasionally even *asking* to go to sleep!

The rest of us watch more of *Romeo and Juliet* until about 9:45 PM. Bedtime for Brian and Katie is usually 10:00 PM with up to an hour or so to read, but you know how it is . . . . We decide to watch the rest of the video tomorrow and they fill in their daily logs that barely begin to document the fullness of their actual day. Their logs document each subject area and also specific topics or projects of the week and on the back is a place to note books, films, projects or trips they take. Gary goes over the children's logs with them as a way to review the day with each child to keep in touch with their daily activities and to keep them accountable for their learning. I see by glancing at their log sheets that sometime during the day, Katie and Brian each managed to fulfill their requirement to read two library books per day. The choices for Katie were *Tough Choices A Story of the Viet Nam War*, by Nancy Antle and *The Oregon Trail* by R. Conrad Stein. Brian read *The Civil War—"A House Divided"* by Zachary Kent and *Focus on Coal* by Theodore Roland-Entwistle. They keep track of their reading list on the back side of their daily log sheets.

As we are doing this, I am reminded by my log book notation that we had never started up our battery experiment that we *vowed* to begin today. As a research project that will be published in the National Student Research Center's annual journal in the spring, Brian and Katie had decided to design a system that would test the battery life of different brands of batteries and determine their cost effectiveness. Since we go through so many batteries in our house, this would indeed be very worthwhile information for us. It took many, many hours, with

Brian (13), Katie (11), Neil (7), Kevin (4)

the help of a neighbor, to design a circuit using a photoelectric cell, a relay, a transformer, and an hour meter to measure the exact length of time that each brand of battery functions in a flashlight. After weeks of work we were all set up and ready to go, their information chart was ready, and all that had to be done was to start it. But *where* was the flashlight??? Along with pencils, we have a black hole in our house that also sucks up flashlights and one sock at a time. We search the house for the flashlight and finally do find it. So, at 10:00 PM we start our experiment running, making still further hypotheses about what we might find out. It is now that I recall that I was going to write about this day and ask everyone to think back to what we have done. We all talk at once and laugh over some of the day's events. I hurriedly write down the topics now, knowing I will remember the small details after that. By tomorrow it will be ancient history.

We say good night to Brian and Katie. Tonight's late hour will afford them just a few minutes to read. Often they are each involved in several books at once. Katie is reading *Cheaper By the Dozen*, by Frank B. Gilbreth, Jr. and *The Last Silk Dress* (a Civil War novel) by Ann Rinaldi. Brian is reading *Cosmos* by Carl Sagan, *Don Quixote* by Cervantes and *Dave Barry Slept Here*, by none other than Dave Barry. Usually Gary and I go upstairs to talk together, read, do some computer work off-line or on-line and watch the taped national news before going to sleep at about 11:30 PM. It is our regular time to be together, just the two of us, and we value our evenings together dearly. This is also the time we make changes or adjustments in our homeschooling plans. We are continually fine tuning and changing resources or strategies. (Together, we do our major planning for the year in the summer but continually enjoy the flexibility to make changes.) But tonight I decide that I *really should* just sit down and write up our day before I actually *do* forget it. So, here it is now—almost 1:30 AM and *way* past my bedtime—but there is only so much quiet time to sit down and write this. Maybe since we all go to sleep late tonight, we'll all sleep late tomorrow . . . or maybe not. No way to tell.

A day like today is really nice because we didn't have to go anywhere. We didn't go to the 4-H farm to do chores for the pigs we help raise or to study veterinary science, nor to music lessons, to civic association meetings, to do errands, to doctor or dental appointments. Today, we went only to the library which is our second favorite place next to being home. The librarians are our true facilitators in locating unusual and hard to find materials. Our days at home are valued, as is our time together. Many of our days are more relaxed than this one was. The sudden announcement of the upcoming Geography Bee certainly shifted us into high gear early in the day. Spontaneously reading and watching the video of *Romeo and Juliet* also added unplanned hours to our schedule. You could say we are on the busy end of the spectrum of homeschooling families —our days are packed! Although I missed spending time with my husband this evening, all of us went happily to sleep after a very full day of learning, playing, working, laughing, and living, with thoughts from the previous evening reminding us of how grateful we are to be with each other. Homeschooling has given us the gift of time to live our lives together and the time to *be*.

Brian (13), Katie (11), Neil (7), Kevin (4)

KATHERINE → Weekly Planning and Learning Log   WEEK # 28, Jan 2-Jan 8

This week: French, Newsletter, Cultural Literacy

READING
M T W Th F S S   Novel-- Daily
M T W Th F S S   2 Library Books Daily
M T W Th F S S   Magazine, *Stone Soup*
M T W Th F S S   Newspaper-Daily

Last Silk Dress, Cheaper by the Dozen
READ + DISCUSS
Reading ROMEO + JULIET
+ ESSAY

LANGUAGE ARTS
M T W Th F S S   Write article, book resp.
M T W Th F S S   Poem, Story, Essay *cat story*
M T W Th F S S   Wordly Wise # 15
M T W Th F S S   Spelling, Editing, Gram.
M T W Th F S S   French Learnables # 3
M T W Th F S S   French Workbook
M T W Th F S S   E-Mail, Letter to Molly
M T W Th F S S   "Wishbone"
Faded yellow
Book Response, Watkins Thank You's
- hopscotch   Stone soup
Cats, Famous writing Newmoon

MATH
M T W Th F S S   Saxon 65: test 105,-6,-7
M T W Th F S S   Borenson Algebra 17, 18
M T W Th F S S   Figure It Out P. 30
M T W Th F S S   "Olympiads"
M T W Th F S S   Dyna Math, CD-ROM
M T W Th F S S   Project, game, puzzle

Math By Kids!, DynaMath, 3-D Jigsaw

SCIENCE, HEALTH, SAFETY
M T W Th F S S   *Geology*
M T W Th F S S   Multimedia Cats CD
M T W Th F S S   Science Reading
M T W Th F S S   Experiment *Battery*
M T W Th F S S   Health, Safety
M T W Th F S S   Nutrition, Cooking, Bake
M T W Th F S S   4-H Pigs, Vet Sci
M T W Th F S S   Nature and notes
M T W Th F S S   Museum, Trip
M T W Th F S S   Current Health, Contact
M T W Th F S S   Video, Computer, CD
M T W Th F S S   "Bill Nye," Newton's Ap.
M T W Th F S S   Family Skills
M T W Th F S S   Home Skills

January Nature & notes, "Bees" Nova
on Prodigy (Matter & Energy), Battery
Research project, continue.

Planets, cube, things

SOCIAL STUDIES
NEWS
M T W Th F S S   CNN Newsroom
M T W Th F S S   World Vision
M T W Th F S S   ABC, TV Magazine

HISTORY
M T W Th F S S   *History of US* Book 5
M T W Th F S S   *World History Homework*
M T W Th F S S   Bible History--Sam-King
M T W Th F S S   Cobblestone, Faces
M T W Th F S S   Natl. Geo Article
European Explor. of US, Slavery
Oregon trail, Europe, Indians
GEOGRAPHY
M T W Th F S S   National Geo, CD-ROM
M T W Th F S S   GeoSafari, CD-ROM
M T W Th F S S   *Maps Skills*
Nat'l Geo on Prodigy (Europe, Spain, 7
Wonders of World, Paris, London,
Leningrad, Italy, Germany

CIVICS
M T W Th F S S   Economics, Money
M T W Th F S S   Gov't, Constitution, Law

MEDIA
M T W Th F S S   Computer
M T W Th F S S   Video, CD-ROM
M T W Th F S S   Seminar, Speaker
M T W Th F S S   Museum, Exhibit, Trip

MUSIC
M T W Th F S S   Listen, Appreciation, CD
M T W Th F S S   History, Read
M T W Th F S S   Sing,Conc., violin, piano
music lesson
ART
M T W Th F S S   Project
M T W Th F S S   Read, Biography
M T W Th F S S   Exhibit, Museum
M T W Th F S S   History, CD, TV
Hist: Th. Cole, Handmade gifts, Sewing
build with worms

PHYSICAL EDUCATION
M T W Th F S S   Fitness Walking, 2 miles
M T W Th F S S   Bike, Games
M T W Th F S S   Field and Stream Club
M T W Th F S S   Play Outside

PROJECTS:
"Worms," Battery, Drama

SHAKESPEAR'S _ FAMILY DISCUSSION
ROMEO & JULIET

READING LOG (Title and Author)

Tough Choice by Nancy Antle - Viet Nam War
The Oregon trail by R. Conrad Stien
Sibling Rivalry by Elaine Landau
Childrens Homer
Turn homeward Hannalee by Patritca Beatty
Be Ever hopeful Hannalee by Patritca Beatty
A day in the life of the Amish
A quilt in time
Letters of a woman homesteader by Elinor Stewart
Beautiful land by Nancy Antle
Stone Soup
Heidi by Johannah Spyri
My first Cat by Rosmaire Hausherr
My first puppy by Rosmaire Hausherr
Now let me fly by Dolores Johnson
Copper toed boot

VIDEOS, SERIES, FILMS, COMPUTER CD

How the West was lost - PBS
Romeo and Juliet - Video

FIELD TRIPS, ACTIVITIES, PROJECTS

Helped set up & help at funeral party
Geography project
read about many mental & physical disabilities

Brian (13), Katie (11), Neil (7), Kevin (4)

HOW OUR HOMESCHOOL JOURNEY BEGAN:

Once we decided to take our children out of school, it was important to us to make a positive transition from school to homeschool. Since Brian and Katie were socialized in the ways of school, we could not simply begin to homeschool with a clean slate. Our first task was to steer them away from their previous schooling habits and help them to form new ones. Those first months, I got spiral notebooks for Brian, Katie, and Neil, and made a list of daily activities appropriate for each of them with a check-off box next to each item. I made the entries as different from school as I could imagine, in order to stir up their enthusiasm and break the old set of expectations and assumptions. The building of a new structure was very important for all of us. We rapidly saw that our children didn't like total freedom (they got grumpy) nor total structure. They loved to have expectations they could meet with the freedom to approach them in their own manner, while still having time to explore their interests. I created scavenger hunts through our resource books in all areas of the house, sent them around the neighborhood to find and draw a cactus or a spider web. We got an old shoe box that became a treasure chest for unusual nature finds. I sent them scurrying to the dictionary, had them calculating household math problems, and gave them brain teasers. They learned to use the computer to send mail to friends, to research questions, to invent a newsletter, to enter contests, and to participate online with other groups of children around the world. Gary bought some historical stamps and set them on a race through the community to search out the history of the stamps and find out *how* the postal service selected them. They used the yellow pages, made phone calls, used maps, laughed, and enjoyed the variety and the challenges. They were pleased to check off the assignment boxes at the end of the day. I wrote them messages and they wrote me back. They got used to our home and community resources and learned where to find things.

Our home became a rich and familiar place once again. They read *hundreds* of books. As always, they had zillions of questions—you know, the kind that are hard to answer and you're not even sure if there is a good answer, the kind where you say "Gee, I don't know, we'll have to look into that—it's a *good* question." They hated writing a journal, loved jumping mental hurdles, and got used to being teammates rather than competing as aliens from different grades. They remembered how to apply themselves towards meaningful goals that were a challenge, rather than do busy work. They got used to each other's noises and fidgets, found comfortable places to work, worked at their own quick paces (finally!), and truly loved the idea of homeschooling. We maintained standards of excellence and mastery throughout, but since they had meaningful and interesting work, they were more willing to do some of the things we asked of them that were less desirable. They had choice and responsibility! They were accountable and enthused! They loved it!

We kept Neil's assignments based on his interests, while at the same time working on phonics, reading, writing and math skills, and I read and read to him from books of all types. I usually spent an hour to an hour and a half to

Brian (13), Katie (11), Neil (7), Kevin (4)

accomplish those basics with him. He and Kevin spent hours playing together spontaneously and creatively, both indoors and outside. We felt that play time was a vital aspect of their growth. Kevin enjoyed joining our activities and wanted real work of his own, so I found interesting problem-solving and thinking-skills sticker books for him and helped him to create his own cut-and-paste books. We also gave him magazines and read him stories. We provided him with ropes, shovels, and full access to all of our art and woodworking supplies (with supervision, of course!). Sometimes he'd want to come up on my lap and sit with me while I was typing at the computer or working with the other children. He was able to take a nap if and when he was tired and would do so anywhere he found himself at the time!

By September, after only eight short weeks of our homeschool experiment, we were all convinced that homeschooling was what our family needed. In the process of formulating our goals and objectives for the coming year, we realized that we had to first question *all of our previous assumptions about education.* We questioned not only *what* to teach, but *how* to teach and *why* it was important. We didn't just go out and find English, history or math books. We thought about *why* it was important to learn history in the first place, what *purpose* history served in our children's lives, and what we hoped the end results would be. Should we have them memorize important dates, eras and people, or should we find causes and connections to the present and future? After we considered *what* we wanted them to know in history, we then decided *how* we would go about teaching it. Our resources followed our goals. It was not easy for us to break away from the familiar school model of covering separate subjects in separate ways with any sense of comfort, but we continued to settle in and find a way to find and integrate goals and resources. The only textbooks we selected were for math and in other areas we selected original source materials and literature. Since Brian and Katie were already excellent students, we didn't have to work too hard on the academic content but had to focus on the *process* of learning and applying effort. It was necessary for us to think ahead to the qualities we hoped our children would possess as they reached adulthood, and to work backward from there, instilling the necessary training.

We knew we had to come back together and restructure our family. We needed to help our children strengthen their values, to make our expectations of them clear, and to help their characters flourish into loving and responsible people. We wanted them to learn that man is not the measure—that it's important to see ourselves with perspective in the larger picture of life.

As with ourselves, we knew our children would benefit from periods of privacy, solitude and calm. They would need a chance for honest, serious, unhurried talk, joking, playing, tenderness, sympathy and comfort. We wanted to help them see things from many points of view while keeping Truth at the center.

We all had our work cut out! These goals were a tall order for a family who never even dreamed of homeschooling before, but we really thought that, together, we could make it work. Not that there wouldn't be setbacks, failed

Brian (13), Katie (11), Neil (7), Kevin (4)

attempts, frustrations, and anxiety about whether we were doing the right thing. Not that we wouldn't be uneasy wondering if our children would be missing something by *not* being in school. Not that we wouldn't feel uncomfortable if we didn't teach what the schools did each year. Could we *really* have the freedom and joy that others homeschoolers alluded to?

We created an environment in our home that made accessible wonderful books and resources; art supplies of all kinds; wood, gardening and electronic equipment; investigative tools like magnifying glasses, binoculars, microscopes, cameras, astronomy and chemistry equipment, reference materials, computers, and most importantly we made ourselves available.

We created experiences that would nurture in our children the ability to ask questions, define problems, take risks, experiment, determine the relevant from the useless, explore the process of building conclusions, work creatively toward solutions and communicate effectively. We helped them to learn the *satisfaction* of mastery of a task or subject. We also recognized that each of our children was distinct in personality, learning style, and interests. We believed that they needed individualized curricula, where they could go at their own pace to follow their capacities and to learn from life's experiences.

All of these goals and expectations required levels of flexibility that we didn't always have. Our conclusions sometimes clashed, our communications got heated, and our frustrations sometimes let loose. In the long run, we knew that it was us, as parents, who had authority and responsibility. Our children learned in those earlier days that, though they had opportunities to question, we were the ones who ultimately made important decisions. These boundaries freed them to take risks and explore. Our consistency and follow-through helped keep tempers in order. Since we have never allowed physical fighting and tolerate very little arguing, we had little down time. Quiet time with a good book for the grumpy one usually turned things around. If we were all getting a little snappy, it was time to look at the cause of it. Maybe we were in a rut, something was not at the correct skill level, or perhaps we lost sight of *why* we were homeschooling. Gary and I tried to figure out the cause of the problems and then fix them. Sometimes it was better to switch tracks altogether for a little while. What we really had to do was learn to live together again and not just function as a way-station where children make short stops between school and visiting friends.

Our spiral books grew into a stack, the children raced through academics (except for little spots here and there), and the spiral books gradually transformed into log books where each child eventually recorded his or her own activities. What we had envisioned was now coming true! The children have input and accountability about their studies, readings, extra pursuits, chores and use of their time. Gary and I serve as their facilitators and encouragers.

Now, Brian has time enough to create political comics, pursue veterinary medicine, play music with young and old friends, and read hundreds of books each year. Katie writes, bakes, keeps up long-distance friendships, makes scrapbooks, writes poetry and reads stacks of historical fiction. When her interest in reading was focused on real people who spent long, hard lives farming

Brian (13), Katie (11), Neil (7), Kevin (4)

or ranching, we assumed the responsibility of helping her search for books that would excite her interest. We were delighted to find a series of seven autobiographical books by Ralph Moody. When these became her favorite books in the world and when there were none left to read, we searched until we found books by Willa Cather that satisfied her.

Neil uses our lumber and tools to put together all sorts of ladders, shelves, boxes, sleds and other fanciful projects. We make sure he has the supplies and lumber he needs. He likes to be a banker and exchange paper money for coins, search for different types of coins, and sort and roll pennies, nickels, dimes and quarters. He likes to climb, dig, ride his bike and swim. He can choose to read *Charlotte's Web* instead of *Little House on the Prairie* if he likes.

Kevin pursues "careers" passionately. After seeing the film *Squanto*, Kevin became interested in exploring the Native American culture; cutting out photos, watching films, asking questions, picking out books, putting on war paint, making bow and arrows, and learning history and tribal differences in clothing, shelter, and gathering of food. We help him to gather leather scraps, make clothing, fashion a quiver, search for feathers and encourage his interest to delve ever deeper. He likes to "collect" stamps (though he mostly likes taking them off the envelopes!) so we save our envelopes for him. He and Neil spend much time together and have not been taught boundaries between learning and playing.

Our children need time to follow their pursuits, small and large. Brian, for example, no longer wishes to be an astronaut or a military officer, but we certainly had encouraged him to delve into these interests. He went to Space Camp, read and wrote about planets, stars, quarks, black holes and the physics of space, and seemed to read every book on war, weaponry and military strategies. Now he wants to be a veterinarian, and he has worked out an internship where he is actively involved in diagnosing, treating and caring for animals at a veterinary clinic.

We are presently living what we had only imagined and hoped for at the beginning. For us, homeschooling has always been year round, where learning is a part of family life and where spontaneous time for trips and activities shares in importance with academic study. In the summer we become more physically active with lots of swimming, biking, walking, and playing. We think ahead to what we each will want to focus on in the fall. We have other seasonal differences, too. During fall, we rake piles upon piles of leaves, look at the foliage, order a few new materials, rearrange our resources, and gradually move back indoors to settle into projects. The children pick up their math and history books more often and at a certain point, we realize we're full swing into our studies. During winter, we leave plenty of time for sledding and snow activities. All of us even *like* to shovel snow and look forward to blizzards! We hunker down to prepare for *Math Olympiads*, our *MathCounts* team, The National Geographic Geography Bee, Global Challenge (a current events competition), prepare our science research for the National Student Research Center's annual

Brian (13), Katie (11), Neil (7), Kevin (4)

journal, or get ready for different writing contests. Then, in spring, we finish up all (most?) of our projects, clean the yard, work in the garden, enjoy the outdoors and finish our yearly portfolios before we have our end-of-the-year homeschool evaluations.

Homeschooling for us only *begins* at home, because we use the world-at-large as our classroom. At the drop of a hat we are off to watch or even help municipal workers or repairmen, to explore a cave, visit a science laboratory or take a trip. Our children now have a business where they care for neighbors' pets midday. Social interactions of all kinds are important. We see our neighbors and our community as venues of education that provide opportunities for friendships, teachings, tutorials, apprenticeships, and discussions in all major areas of our living and learning. Brian and Katie have both attended college seminars, help us with office work, speak to authors, researchers, and inventors. Neil and Kevin create worlds and explore their surroundings from digging below the ground to climbing high in the trees. Over the years our children have participated in karate, baseball, basketball, soccer, swim lessons, music lessons, 4-H Club, animal training, bands and orchestras, and homeschool groups for writing, nature, art, and math. They currently help out and visit relatives and neighbors, meet with friends, play with older and younger children. They are able to converse easily with people of all different ages.

We spend a great deal of time discussing world news, geography, or historical beginnings of current events. We read newspapers, magazines, and journals; watch documentaries on history, anthropology, nature, and science; and explore world trade and resources. We have delved into jazz, the life of the Amish, the countries of the Middle East, and both grand and dreadful periods of history. Exposure to the various peoples, traditions, languages, art, music, and literature helps them to see themselves in a larger perspective and as truly responsible individuals. We try to keep connecting the past to the present, the people to the land, and cause to effect. They ask questions and we encourage them to continue questioning. Increasingly both younger boys and Gary and I ask questions of Brian and Katie and they are the ones who come up with "answers."

REFLECTIONS:
Now that we're in our fourth year of homeschooling and can look back to our beginnings with a little perspective, I can relate some lessons we've learned the hard way (is there really any other way?). The first big one is about *anxiety*. At our lowest points we've worried that we should put our children back in school, thinking they might be better off there. Sometimes we probably expected too much from us all, feeling pressure to prove that we could teach our children at home, and that our ideas about what we wanted for our children really could be accomplished. We worried about purchases and where to put everything.

In the long run, I think anxiety comes hand-in-hand with homeschooling, because each of us is really like a pioneer trying to settle into

Brian (13), Katie (11), Neil (7), Kevin (4)

unknown territories without being able to "assume" that the "experts" are taking care of educating our children. Our first year took the prize for high anxiety, but it did lessen with time as we attempted and succeeded at numerous and varied experiences. We got used to anxiety's nagging presence, and gradually, we let it just rest in the corner for a while. I've made the mistake of trying to "look good," and tried to prove myself. I've caught myself going down the wrong track. But now when I put the whole picture together, I realize that I no longer worry so much, that I do trust myself and my children, that we have found our natural rhythms and we have all built up confidence. We work together well and our children are blossoming.

I've also gotten to know during these years that the impatience of the children often triggers my own. As with many other children, they like answers to questions right now, want to find a lost item right now, want help on a problem right now, and always want to eat right now. Years of reinforcing and practicing patience are now paying off. At the beginning of the two years it took me to work on this book, I remember the number of times I had to say "not now" or "wait until later" or "sorry, I can't just yet." Teaching them to wait, to be aware that I am occupied, to realize that I am on the phone, that I'm working with one of the other children, or in the middle of writing this book has required a great deal of forbearance from all of us. But the rewards I see are significantly higher levels of patience, more independent study and some very creative menus (the children are preparing wonderful meals when I'm occupied). The older two are taking more responsibility for their younger brothers' work, their projects and in answering their questions. The time I've spent working on this book has really taught us all some valuable lessons, patience, responsibility and skills that might have taken much longer to achieve otherwise.

Throughout the years we hear the same questions over and over again that reflect people's curiosity and concerns: How do you have the energy, patience or ability to stay at home all day with your children? When do you have any time for yourself? How do your children get socialization? How do you get your children to listen to you? What about your marriage and what is the role of your spouse in homeschooling? How do you organize all of the materials relating to homeschooling? How do you set up chores? How do you structure your time? Will your children be academically prepared for college? How has homeschooling affected your family?

How do you have the energy, patience or ability to stay at home all day with children? This question is a composite of several other concerns: Don't you need the stimulation of other adults? Can a parent really find satisfaction as an individual by staying home all day? How do you maintain your "identity"? Do you miss having a career? How do you feel about being a "housewife"? Don't you feel helpless and unsure of yourself?

Certainly many families cannot survive economically without two incomes, but currently too many people are defined by their career. The value of being a full-time parent has lost most of its former status. I consciously chose to give up my career as an artist to be a wife and mother who rears her children and

Brian (13), Katie (11), Neil (7), Kevin (4)

guides their learning at home. For me, the most important, complex and creative career of all is preparing to send four well-grown and well-prepared children out into the world as productive young adults. Being a "keeper at home" has rewards for me far beyond title or status. It is a responsibility I've grown to cherish. I have found that the energy and curiosity of my children stimulates a great deal of thought and creativity in me. Since Gary works at home, I also have his adult companionship during the day. From following my children's and my own interests, I have many opportunities to communicate with other adults. Through writing this book I have had the pleasure of interacting with numerous homeschooling parents, and I have the convenience of communicating online with other adults. I have set aside time each week to spend with other adults or attend classes. Many of the people I get to know are connected with my children's activities. There are many homeschooling groups that get together to share activities and support, both for children and parents. Granted many of us homeschooling parents fall into bed at night tired from a long day. Homeschooling is hard work but is also interesting, demanding, and requires a myriad of skills, and it is where we daily get to see the fruits of our work. Many days I get caught up in learning and *gain* energy.

Patience with ourselves and our children takes time to train and build, and I think there's no way around that, but it's so worthwhile. Learning to wait and to set boundaries that are suited to us and our children helps to keep the day under control.

Parents don't need to be trained in teaching—they need mostly to be fond of learning! I was concerned about being a mother and a "teacher" at the same time because of what a huge responsibility it is to oversee our children's education and character development, setting up structure and self-discipline. Each year, though, I become more relaxed, more confident in myself and in my children, and more sure of our original homeschool convictions. Our days are creative, energetic, interactive, and I find it extremely satisfying to be in the company of my children. Each day brings new prospects, challenges, surprises, and masteries that build my identity, as well as my children's. It becomes even more meaningful to me to grow along *with* my children.

When do you have any time for yourself? Especially in the evenings, after dinner, I feel that I need to retreat upstairs for a little bit of quiet, away from noise and activity. I have interests of my own that I am able to pursue because my children have learned how to be quite independent in their daily learning. I like to read, sew, paint, sculpt, write, and have time to talk with Gary. Often, it is my own interest that triggers someone else to come up close and investigate what I am doing. Katie has pursued sewing, baking, and gardening after spending time with me while I'm working on those things. Neil watches me in my woodworking shop (I used to make fine furniture) and has a keen interest in woodworking. All of the children, like us, enjoy reading and watching films and gladly join us in those pleasures. We often work together in close company with each person doing something different. I weave in and out of their studies, checking in on their progress, asking if they have any questions. I can arrange to

Brian (13), Katie (11), Neil (7), Kevin (4)

attend seminars or events, especially now that Brian and Katie are old enough to supervise at home for a while. These past two years my family has generously supported the time needed for me to write this book, to explore my own ideas about homeschooling more fully, and to be able to give something back to the homeschooling community by writing this book.

How do your children get socialization? This is often the first question that people ask. When I hear this question, it isn't clear whether people are asking about being "social" (having pleasant and cooperative companionship with others) or about "socialization." Our children are out in the community a great deal and interact with people of all ages almost every day. They are very comfortable in any age group. They are levelheaded, form friendships, and cooperate in group settings. Since we spend so much time pursuing their interests which take us outside our home setting, they are often actively engaging with other people in the real world. They communicate by phone, with neighbors, through seminars they attend, with mentors, online, and with their own family members.

If people actually do mean "socialization" (the process of acquiring habits and beliefs, and training people to fit into a social environment), then that is one of the reasons we decided to take them out of school in the first place. We see it as *our* role to train our children in values and beliefs and not the responsibility of school or peers.

How do you get your children to listen to you? Before there can be any teaching, a respectful environment must be created with a clear sense of authority and recognized boundaries. Whining and complaining cannot be accepted as a norm. I don't mean to say that there are never complaints or whining, but that they don't prevail. We all have moments of annoyance, misunderstanding, and irritability and we must tolerate those moments without too much fuss about it. I have learned, and my children have learned, how to apologize easily and readily. I think it's a very important thing for our children to know that we make mistakes and can recognize them enough to send forth an apology and make amends. It allows them the freedom to make mistakes and know that they too can apologize. We must also take the time to analyze our children's complaints—are they justified? Is it something that *must* be done, or is it an *option*? Were we off track? Is that child sick or too tired? As our children learn to respond to our authority, they will at the same time learn how to foster authority as they stride toward adulthood. They learn to listen with respect and thoughtfulness.

What about your marriage and what is the role of your spouse in homeschooling? Having a spouse who gives support, encouragement, relief time, and a listening ear has been incredibly valuable for me. With Gary, I can reaffirm our educational goals, review our methods, give and get inspiration. The two of us mutually decided to homeschool, and working together so closely around the focus of our family has definitely served to strengthen our marriage. *Together* we take joy in participating in the learning and experiences of our children, sharing their activities, most often learning and growing ourselves.

Brian (13), Katie (11), Neil (7), Kevin (4)

Yes, time is tight, but because of that, we usually learn to do our best to make the most of being together and to make each hour worthwhile. When we have time alone, we can *talk and talk*, share our interests, go on short outings, get some of our work done, and enjoy each other's company. We go out alone each week. Homeschooling can be pursued as a single parent or when one or both parents must travel or work very long hours. Not all homeschooling spouses need be as involved as Gary, but support and encouragement are important!

How do you organize all of the materials related to homeschooling? Issues of organization pervade homeschooling—organization of materials, the home itself and especially organization of time. For me, these can *all* be a problem, but over the years I have greatly improved organization out of the necessity that comes from the six of us working, learning and living together. I have lost too many things, missed too many appointments, stayed up too late or slept too long. I have been overwhelmed at times with piles of papers/mail/books and have not been able to find a consistent way to use files.

For various resources, I have learned to use boxes. I keep our portfolio materials in a box, my receipts, catalogs, homeschooling information, miscellaneous items all in separate boxes. Each box has a place and all I have to do is toss things into the right box. It is much more my style to sift through a pile of papers in a box than to pull out separate files. I like to organize for a *reason*, such as putting together our portfolios for end-of-the-year evaluations, receiving a shipment of new books, or having a family stay with us (sound familiar?). But that's me and it works better for me this way. Now I do have some files I actually use, but they are mostly for completed projects that I no longer need at my fingertips. I like to have our ongoing work out and available in my boxes.

Sporadically, I thoroughly reorganize my home and all of our books, media, office machines and resources. That has been enough to keep our "stuff" organized, except of course, for all those pencils. And I know I've bought about a dozen tape dispensers, but where is even one of them right now? Anyone observing us knows that on occasion we get clean clothes directly out of the dryer rather than out of the closet! I've learned not to feel a failure when our work and play take precedence over tidiness. Also, I've learned to use my answering machine so that I don't need to stop working with my children unless it's an important call. Then, I return calls when convenient.

How do you set up chores? It's important to us that our children be responsible for *their* home and think of it as *their* home. Chores take years of constant training and reinforcement to run effectively. Each child in our family is shown exactly what a task requires and is helped through it for a while before being left to do it alone. A list is posted on the refrigerator with complete instructions. Brian, Katie and Neil rotate kitchen chores monthly. From the age of two, small chores are expected, even if as simple as putting out napkins at mealtime. We try to divide chores evenly and according to ability. One child clears off the table before dinner, sets the table, helps with cooking, and straightens up the living room after dinner. Another child clears the table after

Brian (13), Katie (11), Neil (7), Kevin (4)

dinner, puts away left over food, cleans the counters and floors and straightens up the pantry/laundry room. The third child washes and dries dishes. Kevin is in charge of picking up large items off the floor, the patio, and his and Neil's bedroom. These chores shift depending whether it is lunch or dinner time. I clean up after breakfast. We try to get all of the laundry done in one day, otherwise the ones who need clean clothes run their own wash, fold and put it away. Extra tasks, such as watering the garden, washing the car, shoveling snow, or other seasonal necessities are assigned at the time. Gary and I strive to have the children do what they see needs to be done without being asked, and this really does improve with age!

How do you structure your time? Time has probably been the most difficult to organize because it *takes time* to know how it's best to *use time.* When we first started homeschooling, I felt we needed to join every group around so that we wouldn't miss out on anything and would be sure the children had social contacts. I realized that we always seemed to have to stop midstream in work at home in order to go off to a group. We all felt frustrated. This was not our rhythm, so after a while, we dropped many group activities. At the beginning, I was up until midnight every night, preparing assignments, checking record keeping, planning ahead. This now runs smoothly and almost seamlessly. We currently try to schedule most of our time at home, especially in the mornings, when I work with the younger boys. Brian and Katie spend most of the day on their studies. After lunch, we usually plan our "group" type of home activities such as French, history, and news. We still go to 4-H, jazz ensemble, MathCounts group, music lessons, internships, etc., but we enjoy spending most of our time at home at our own natural rhythm, which I would call a "relaxed fast pace."

It is an amusing challenge to see how efficiently we can use our time. We do mental math, sing and listen to music or story tapes while in the car, we watch PBS or the news while exercising on the treadmill, we read while waiting at medical appointments. We draw or make up stories while waiting for the train . . . there are just so many ways we have learned to make good, enjoyable use of time. And we use the whole day, from the time we wake up until the time we go to sleep, diving into life and learning, never seeming to have enough time for all that we want to do.

Will your children be academically prepared for college? We are committed to preparing our children to be competent and to have options of all kinds. Certainly one of the basic options is to go to college. Though I have commented on many issues other than homeschool academics, it was for that primary concern that we first left school and began to homeschool. One of the great benefits of learning at home is that our children are able to move at their own rate and master subject matter in both a breadth and depth that is often not possible at schools. Our children are getting a highly individualized, rigorous, and demanding education. As parents, we hold them to very high standards and help them to reach their potentials. We are able to focus on the *process* of learning and on each child's developing character. Complaints, impatience, and

Brian (13), Katie (11), Neil (7), Kevin (4)

irritability turn into *opportunities* to learn and build character. Since all four of our children are expected to spend some independent time on their studies, they must become always more self-directed and diligent. High academic expectations lead to persistence, accuracy, motivation, self-esteem and confidence. Keeping our home in order requires responsibility, obedience, and cooperation. Being with each other teaches loyalty, faithfulness, nurturance, love and caring. All of these are skills that prepare them not only for college, but for lifelong pursuits of all kinds. Brian looks forward with confidence to the college courses he will start taking this year. We feel that education is the means to enhance life, rather than the end goal.

How has homeschooling affected your family? Though we first started homeschooling primarily for academic reasons, we immediately found that with everyone at home our family became closer, happier, and more active. We hadn't even realized what a gift it would be to "have our family back," since we hadn't realized the effects of our children leaving each day to go their separate ways at school. We presently share in the pleasures of each other's interests and successes and in the disappointments of failed attempts or difficult endeavors. Our children have the opportunity to find their personal ways of thinking, learning, relating, and dressing that are not dependent on peer pressure. Because they all have the room to find out who they naturally are, we are a family composed of strong characters who care about themselves, each other and those around us.

Choosing to educate our children at home is a responsibility and a challenge that we tackle with as much skill, humor, creativity, enjoyment and flexibility as possible. We encourage our children to experience the joys of discovery and caring. We have found homeschooling fosters a cohesive family with a foundation firm enough to give each of us the strength, courage, and insight to reach the fulfillment of our purpose.

Brian (13), Katie (11), Neil (7), Kevin (4)

UPDATE:

Follow-up of our day over one year later: Radio Shack D alkaline batteries were top rated in our science battery project; Katie's poem "Faded Yellow" won first prize in a national contest; Brian won the local level of the Geography Bee contest; Neil now reads chapter books silently; and Kevin is beginning to read. We took a trip to French-speaking Québec and found our gastronomy much improved!

This past year we have since added three more kittens and *finally* a dog to our family. This sounds like it could be a disaster, but it has been quite an opportunity for us. The children take full responsibility for the animals. This means that they have read dozens of books on cat and dog care, diseases, treatments, behavior, and other related necessities. Brian is reading comprehensive books such as Ettinger's *Textbook of Veterinary Internal Medicine*, the Merck *Veterinary Manual*, and magazines such as *Veterinary Medicine* and *Vet Economics*. Brian has read all of James Herriot's books and all our children enjoy watching the BBC series *All Creatures Great and Small*. Katie takes care of all five cats, including feeding, changing litter boxes, making sure they have collars on, and that they eventually come *down* out of the trees. Brian has responsibility for our dog and feeds, walks, trains, cleans up, and plays with her. Of course our younger boys also help out with the pets and all of us like to go on walks and play with the animals. Walking the dog has led to meeting many other dogs and their owners in the neighborhood and Brian and Katie, by chatting with the owners, have gradually built up a pet sitting business

Brian (13), Katie (11), Neil (7), Kevin (4)

and are pleased to have the both responsibility and the income.

Brian is interning with our veterinarians each week and his hours there have gradually stretched into a full day. The vets are very encouraging, helpful, humorous and generous with their knowledge and time. It is a wonderful experience for Brian. Through the Boy Scouts, he is working toward becoming an Eagle Scout. He also was delighted to learn that he was the first place winner for his grade in the national current events contest *Global Challenge*.

Katie's interest in cats has grown. She is concentrating her studies on feline issues of breeding, health and caretaking and will soon attend a university-sponsored Feline Symposium. She enthusiastically reads anything and everything about cats. She is reading Cleveland Amory's *The Cat Who Came For Christmas, The Cat and the Curmudgeon,* and *The Best Cat Ever.* She also enjoys Desmond Morris' *Catwatching,* James Herriot's *Cat Stories,* and Bruce Fogle's *The Cat's Mind.* She pours over *Cat Fancy* and *Cat World* magazines.

Katie has designed and sewn a quilt entirely on her own. She drew out her design with crayons on grid paper, selected the fabric from my huge collection of quilting cottons, pieced them together by machine, and hand stitched the quilting design. This all took planning and patience. She has also made her first dress. She developed her own system of organization for her weekly studies and projects, and enjoys writing long letters to her friends. Katie wrote this poem the day of our music teacher's sudden death, remembering how he'd toss his jacket onto our couch before going to the piano:

THE COAT

the coat on the couch
once a week
brought joy to our eyes
music to our hearts

Sunday it came
cold with the season
warming our home
coat and couch were one

suddenly gone
coldness closed hearts
sadness watered cheeks
anger toward life

dirt shoveled over
coat and couch became two
saying goodbye
without knowing it true

Brian (13), Katie (11), Neil (7), Kevin (4)

> loving ceased
> no longer alive
> faith ran away
> with tears in her eyes
>
> teeth clenched tight
> coat floated toward heaven
> cheeks light with sorrow
> flesh burned with rage
>
> coat and all
> died from eyes
> loving it stayed
> in the hearts carrying stone

Neil has blossomed into a real reader and, thanks to his grasp of phonics, can write anything he wants, so long as the reader also has a good grasp of phonics! He sees spelling as a game and is always challenging himself to "guess a word." It is delightful to see Neil develop an integration of concepts in math. He solves complicated real life problems in his head, like "If I earn $2 a day, five days a week, for a month, and then give Kevin $3 for helping me, I will end up with $37 at the end of the month." It only takes him a second mentally to jump to the answer and they are mostly based on real computations that are required just by living in the real world. He plays easily with multiplication, fractions, comparisons and the real life tasks of his woodworking. He and Kevin watch *Hometime,* which shows how to build and repair homes as they exercise on the treadmill and put the information to work in their building projects!

Neil was one of ten children picked as international winners of the Time-Warner *Visions of Mars* art contest. His drawing is commercially available on the *Vision of Mars* CD-ROM, by Virtual Reality Laboratories, Inc. This CD-ROM will be launched by Russia and landed on the surface of Mars by two Mars landers. We were really excited for him!

Because Kevin is so industrious, he too is learning phonics and is just beginning to sprout his reading and writing wings. He follows after his older siblings and keeps busy all day with Cuisenaire rods and other manipulatives, drawing, using the computer, and just playing and learning more about firemen, fire trucks, fire stations, fire equipment, and fire articles in the newspaper. He wants to be a fireman when he grows up and I have promised to get him a Dalmatian puppy when he gets there. These are very important topics to Kevin and he keeps a folder of fire safety pamphlets, fire pictures, news articles, and other fire related references. He has fire CDs, videos, books, and library references.

Gary continues to be our ever-present guide, taking the children on field trips and giving me the much needed time and quiet to work on this book. He is my anchor and proceeds to work hard earning the living that enables us all to

Brian (13), Katie (11), Neil (7), Kevin (4)

pursue our goals.

 With everyone's gracious (most of the time) support, I have managed to put in the time required to write this book between all of our other activities. I have stretched my own patience by dealing with computer programs that don't do exactly what I want them to do, by meeting time deadlines, and by needing to tell a child just one more time to "please wait a minute until I'm finished." All of this, though, has brought rewards far above what I would have imagined.

 Our family keeps growing stronger together and individually. We keep finding better ways to do things, finding more things we enjoy doing, more opportunities to make life meaningful, and better ways to make use of our gift of time. We wish the same for you and your family!

ANOTHER UPDATE:

 It is now three years after our last UPDATE . Our family took a giant leap and moved to a log home in the Rocky Mountains of Montana. Since Brian took college biology at age 14, both he (now 17) and Katie (now 15) took more and more courses and are now full-time university Honors students. Brian is a junior majoring in philosophy and psychology, while Katie is a sophomore majoring in media and theater arts. They both experience college as a natural transition and an exciting continuation of homeschooling.

 Brian became an Eagle Scout and is Junior Scout Master. He worked with our vet for a few years and decided it really wasn't the career he wanted. Katie is a volunteer intern at our Senator's office this summer and cares for neighbors' horses and dogs. At this time, Neil is determined to visit the moon or Mars—one way or another! Kevin is interested in history, the military, and criminal justice. He *still* wants to be a police officer. Neil hopes to become an Eagle Scout within the year (at age 12), and Kevin is a Webelos looking forward to his first year of real summer Scout camp. The Boy Scout camping experiences in the Rockies have been the highlight of *all* seasons of the year. All four children ski and can hardly get enough of it. Gary continues to work at home as an executive consultant, teaches at the university, and is our all-around dependable ranch hand. I'm having my first solo art exhibit (view on our web page) in a Montana gallery and am working on a new book of homeschooling "days" with updates from the families in this book and many new families.

 We now have two Scottish Highland year-old heifers, Hazel and Tess. This opens up a whole new world of investigation, curiosity, learning, and pleasure. Our Lab, Tucker, had a litter of 12 puppies almost two years ago. Breeding was an extensive learning experience that added Quinn and Razzberry to our home. Theo and Grace are our cat companions and mousers.

 As we reflect on our many years of homeschooling, we realize that developing our own comfortable homeschool style has required us to define our values and convictions and to articulate them three-dimensionally on a daily basis. Life and homeschooling have become a continuous circle with no beginning or ending. We have an ever growing appreciation for our gift of time.

Brian (13), Katie (11), Neil (7), Kevin (4)

Joseph and Barb
Matthew, age 7
Nick, age 5

Barb wrote about this day of October 1, when the weather was still nice at their home, near the middle of the small, rural town of Derry, Pennsylvania.

PAPER RAILROAD

I would like to begin by saying that for the last two years I was a strict "workbook" style teacher. I have two boys, Matthew and Nicolas, and this was *definitely* not the style of teaching they liked. But still I struggled on, determined to make it work. Then, near the end of last year, I just stopped and got rid of all the workbooks and texts, deciding to try unit studies at the beginning of this year. Matt and Nick are both a grade ahead of their peers so I did not feel guilty for ending school before it's time.

What brought about the change in my teaching attitude from workbooks to unit studies? Maybe the remembrance of my boys cringing when they saw a workbook approaching or having them cry themselves through several pages of boring, mundane work that I thought they just had to complete! I think I'll contribute my attitude towards being a new homeschooling mom, wanting to have something to "show" that the boys were progressing, and maybe just a little laziness on my part. After all, it doesn't take much thought to get out a workbook and fill in the blanks, whereas unit studies require thought and creativity on the part of the teacher.

I also sold the school desks and moved school into the dining room. I wanted school to be combined with family living and not banished to a certain room. I do have an old swivel chalkboard (six feet across) in the dining room now and educational posters all over the walls. Anyone entering our house is sure to know we homeschool!

I also had sweatshirts made with an embroidery sewing machine that

Each sweatshirt has a corresponding picture. I had these made so the boys can wear them and not feel ashamed or embarrassed because they are schooled at home. It has worked and they tell everyone all about their school. I also refuse to hide my children inside during public school hours. What I do is legal. I take my children out the most during public school hours to avoid crowds. The boys are very good at answering the question "Why Aren't You In School, Young Man?" from what I expect are well-meaning people. We sometimes have school under a gazebo on the square in the middle of town, and the boys play outside.

So we began this year, full steam ahead, with unit studies. I must say that it is easier (so far) than what I thought it would be. Yes, I must go to the library and pick out books relating to our topic, but I was already going to the library every other week anyway. Also, our family was truly blessed when the area library opened a resource center. For two weeks you may borrow telescopes, microscopes, human body kits, music instrument kits, records, complete math curriculum, reproducible workbooks, and the list goes on and on. I now have thousands of unit studies at my fingertips with all the "hands-on" activities that make learning fun. And the best part is all the money I am saving now because I do not have to buy all the materials needed, I just go the library and "borrow" them.

Once I decided to try unit studies, I planned *how* I would teach one month in advance. I decided on three-week studies of one main topic. For example, in September we studied mammals. I planned this to coincide with the zoo letting children enter for free until the end of that month. So, we finished up our unit study on mammals with a trip to the zoo. It was great fun and there were no crowds since all the children were in public school. We went through the zoo twice and were never hurried. We even got to hear the lion roar several times!

Anyway, I plan my school year several months in advance. I know that in October we will be studying the human body. Since the local hospital is offering tours of the emergency room and hospital rooms to children for free, I thought this was a nice way to end the unit study.

Between October and November we will be studying creation and dinosaurs. The study will be ending with a trip to the Natural History Museum, as the boys earned free passes this summer from reading books.

In November, I know we will be studying the Pilgrims and Colonial America, with the study ending with a Thanksgiving meal and presents being opened. (We open presents at Thanksgiving instead of Christmas. Wonderful!)

I begin the planning a few months in advance. I do not know what we will be studying in December yet. I am waiting to see what trip happens to come our way.

I must say that I am beginning to enjoy teaching more now that I have changed learning styles. I cannot remember much from my early education as I did all workbooks. I did not want my children to have that same thing happen to them. Most of all, I think learning should be fun but should have some structure and order to it.

I still have the boys complete some workbooks, such as handwriting

Matthew (7), Nick (5)

(we are using the Getty/Dubay *Italic Handwriting* series). We also use math workbooks. We use the math program *Moving With Math*. Some of the pages in each workbook are worked through for each grade, and then when those are finished, you work those same workbooks, but do the other sheets that were not completed for the next grade level. This allows the child to actually see how he had advanced and improved

We also use *The Bible Study Guide for All Ages* for our bible study. They receive work with timeliness, maps and reading. This company has now begun to sell accompanying worksheets to coincide with each lesson. I did not want to go back to my old style of teaching, but these worksheets are colorful and marvelous. The boys love them! We always begin our day with the Bible and take two days per lesson. This insures that we will not "burn out" on these worksheets.

I decided not to use any kind of ready-made language arts curriculum but I do use *Learning Grammar Through Writing*. I have Matt write a sentence or small paragraph on some of the unit study activities we do. I must say that this part of the learning phase seems a little vague to me. After all, shouldn't Matt be doing mindless exercises in nouns, verbs, adverbs, and adjectives over and over again? Then I tell myself, "*No*," but I wonder if I am doing enough in this area. Matt does *not* enjoy writing. Until I find a writing program that's more his style, I will allow him to dictate stories to me as I type them (I never knew learning to touch type in high school would come in so handy!) The stories that Matt and Nick come up with are amazing! But if they had to write them, I doubt if those stories would ever surface.

For reading, I have the boys read lots and lots of books. I keep a written report of all the books they read. The goal for Matthew this year (third grade) is to read 200 or more books. This summer both he and his brother were in the library summer reading club. Matt read 167 books and Nick read 118. I do censor what they read but they pick out sensible books on their own. My youngest told me this summer that he wanted to read only non-fiction books, as they were real stories and not made up. I had a very hard time getting him to read something other than books on animals or trains.

For art I use whatever I have on hand. No structure here. It all ties in with the unit study.

For current events, I use the *God's World* papers. We read and discuss the articles and that's it. On Friday we have a modified day of school. We sort through any papers that were completed throughout the week and file them. School is out for the day.

For physical education, I have the boys go over to the high school track. They walk around the track with me, and then run a 100 meter dash. We record their times and then at the end of each month we make a graph of their times. It inspires them to run faster.

For science, geography, social studies, health, and history, I am using the local library and some reproducible worksheets. The boys seem to like these worksheets as opposed to workbooks. There are not as many and they are fun!

Matthew (7), Nick (5)

For music I use the series *Our Musical Friends*, by Christian Education Music Publishers. Although this series uses workbooks, we only have it once a week, and it comes with a tape. The teacher on the tape makes it so much fun that the boys actually cheer when they know they will have music. I have also supplemented this course by borrowing a xylophone and chime bells from the library when we were learning the names of the notes. Even though I played a clarinet during some of my school years, I am learning more than I ever had in school, and we are only on book two!

We also practice Spanish twice a week. We listen to tapes of songs and have memorized over twenty. We play Spanish bingo games and other fun games that were made with paper and pen.

I would like to note that my boys hate coloring. I usually let them skip instructions that say color this or that. To me that is busy work. Instead, they draw and draw and draw. They have an unlimited supply of scrap paper which I get from my workplace. (Yes, this is one parent that works part time outside the home.) I may come home to find page after page of paper taped together down the hallway with a train engine and boxcars on each page. Or the solar system or digestive system all drawn out with labels and all! I think this sort of art is very creative and not as inhibiting as coloring.

One drawback to homeschooling is that the boys want to play between classes. I do not start my day of schooling until 10:00 AM and we usually end around 2:00 PM. I have begun to limit toys out of the toy closet until after school. There are times when I do allow it though, such as when Matt needs one-on-one work, or vice versa. I do limit TV time. No cable in this house. Only three PBS shows are allowed—*no cartoons*! I think this one thing (limited TV) is what has contributed to the boys' imagination and creativity! We do watch certain videos though.

I have opened my journal (I use "The Home School Journal"—which is easy to use) and picked out a day—September 16:

10:00 AM: Bible Study
Read Genesis 39. Time-line work on worksheets. Only three questions. Sang song, "If The Skies Above You Are Grey." (We sing along with a tape.) Drew pictures of the story we read. Worked on Memloc verse John 15:13. (I love Memloc. We learn to memorize a new Bible verse each week.)

10:46 AM: Spanish
No break between these two subjects. Listened to side one of the *Phonetic Funky* tape. We also listened to the *Teach Me Spanish* tape. Learned names of common farm animals in Spanish by playing a card game. The boys get rowdy while playing this game and are told they will lose a *Choreganizer* mom-money (more about *Choreganizers* after lunch) if they do not get off the table and settle down! This works immediately since they work hard for dad-dollars and mom-money.

11:15 AM: A short break while I prepare for math.

11:30 AM: Math

Completed pages six and seven of *Using Models to Learn Multiplication*. With this course Matthew used base ten blocks to learn addition, subtraction, multiplication and division. Nice hands-on approach. Also completed a small review page. Matt works on math facts using *Learning Wrap-Ups* and various math games on our computer. I used to spend a lot of time coaxing through a lesson and it was *frustrating*!! I felt that the page had to be completed or I was a failure! But now that my teaching style has completely changed, I do not coax, yell, or yes . . . even scream anymore. As I look back now, I see how he needed to do some hands-on math and actually "see" how the math concepts worked. For me it looked so simple, $3 + 2 = 5$. But not to Matt. I would get so upset when he would not complete his dutiful two pages of math. Now, we use *Moving With Math*. The difference is amazing. Since I never went over multiplication or division with him until my teaching ways changed and we began to use *Moving With Math*, I was very uneasy about even trying multiplication and division. But, Matt has breezed right through both of them!!! I am thrilled. He has had to use basic addition and subtraction to master multiplication and division and he never realized it!!

In the workbook days I used to push my child to learn by bribing, yelling, and threats. I sometimes felt that I might have been too extreme. I do not do this as much now. There is no reason to, since our way of schooling has changed and will continue to change. I think I felt pressured into making sure my homeschooled child was way ahead of his public schooled peers so that I could "prove" myself to others. But I found that no one in the neighborhood really cared and my boys suffered so. (Thankfully, they are very forgiving and resilient!)

I may push for the child's attention during a class if he begins to giggle for no apparent reason or begins singing so that no one can hear themselves think and I may actually say, "Sit up, quit singing, listen to your brother read." Sometimes disciplining is necessary, but as they get older it is less and less. Nick is active and will talk, sing, hum, or tap even as he sits at the table reading. He is very outgoing and will go outside to talk to the birds if he cannot find an audience in the house. He also will sneak his cat upstairs into the house and talk to her for hours if I let him.

(When the boys were smaller, if I was working alone with Matt, I had Nick watch a video or do simple workbooks. I never had an actual infant or toddler when I first began homeschooling. Nick was already three when I began to teach Matt. Also, by the age of four Nick could read at a first to second grade level, so he joined school with us.)

For Nick, I work on basic addition and subtraction. He loves the *Wrap-Ups* and especially the computer. He has been on it from the age of two and amazes us with what he can do! If I have a question about what to do on the computer, I find myself sometimes turning to ask him (a *five* year old!!) instead

Matthew (7), Nick (5)

of reading the manual.

12:30 PM: Lunch and Chore Time.
Our family now uses *Choreganizers* by Noble Publishing Associates. It has changed the way the housework gets finished around here. We have a small house that gets cluttered very fast. I found myself doing all the chores and this is ridiculous! Children should help. There is no need for the mother to do the major portion of the housework if she has children four years old and up.

Choreganizers has a nifty chart for children to hang pictures of their chores onto for the day. As the chores are completed, they are put into a pocket on this chart. Even children who cannot read can do these, as the pictures tell it all. So, when the boys wake up, their chores are already displayed for the day. At the end of the day, I will give out mom-money (fake dollar bills with a mom's face) for chores completed on one of their charts. Also, dad-dollars (fake money with a dad's face) are given if all chores were completed on the dad-dollar chore chart. If the chores are not completed, then the corresponding money is taken away. Then the chores for the next day are posted that night. On Sunday, I open the chore store, where the play money they earned can buy them candy (this is about the only time they will receive candy), Match Box cars, special trips for French fries and so on. Some of the chores for mom-dollars are: make the bed, brush teeth and hair, clean bedroom, take garbage to composter, take cans to recycle bins. Now, the dad-dollar chores take more time, only two per day are posted along with four or five mom-money chores. Some dad-dollar chores are vacuum and clean interior of car, dust, put loads of laundry in the washer, clean a kitchen cupboard, wash cellar steps, clean appliance fronts, etc. To have a dad-dollar taken away when they have behaved poorly, truly makes an impact, since they see how hard they have worked for that piece of money. Plus, the dad-dollars earn the best toys and candy from the chore store!!

1:30 PM: Physical Education
Drove over to the track. Completed a half mile walk and a 100 meter dash. We were chased off the track when a high school class came out and began using the track. We then walked on the cinder jogging path which encircles the high school, middle school and elementary.

2:30 PM: Free time while I recover from the walk!

3:00 PM: Unit Study on Mammals
I counted today's work as science and reading. Okay, it's past my normal time to end school. This used to worry me and make me frantic, but since I do not have to go to work this evening, I am much calmer about it.

Next, we all took turns reading from an old fifth grade A Beka science book. Read chapter 25. It was about canines. We then completed a fun worksheet on mammals and matched pictures to names of mammals. Matt next did silent reading from a book called *Mark Trails Books of Animals* and read three chapters

Matthew (7), Nick (5)

(small chapters). The boys began cutting out pictures of mammals from old nature magazines in preparation for a poster depicting a collage of mammals.

4:00 PM: Handwriting

Matt completed page four of the *Italic* series, Book C. I keep trying to stress the importance of staying above the bottom line to Matt. Nick completed page four from Book B. He is left handed and seems very challenged with trying to write legibly. I point out that all he will have to do is trace the letters, but in the end, I cannot understand half of what is on the paper!! I do not push though. Well, at least I *try* not to. I do recognize their weak and their strong points and reward my children for work well done. I give hugs, play games with them, or pass out stickers or "brag tags." (Brag tags are large stickers in which I write what the child did that was special. He wears it all day.)

That's it for this school day. It may seem rather laid back. Some days I wonder if I am teaching enough. But then I look at the neighbor's children who come over and see their attitudes and how, at the third grade level, they cannot do basic math or even read what I consider first grade material.

Let me say that I do *not* like the situation of having to both work part time *and* homeschool, as it pulls me away from the family and rushes me around all the time. But I must work right now to help support the family so I might as well make the best of it. I work part time at a K-Mart store. I mostly work the 5:00-9:00 PM shift. Although now, one week out of every three, I can work 10:00 PM to 4:00 AM. I like this shift better since I am there for the boys during the day and they do not even realize that I am gone during the night. My husband is home with them. During the week that I work the midnight shift, he is working the day shift as a 911 Dispatcher. The other two weeks he is on the midnight shift while I work the day!! Sounds like a revolving door!! I average fifteen-twenty hours a week at K-Mart now. But I only teach Monday through Thursday, with Friday being a modified day. I also use Saturdays to catch up on certain subjects if I missed them earlier in the week. My husband is all for homeschooling. I am trying to include him in more of the learning, though as of today, he has worked thirty days straight and some of those days are twelve hour days! Sometimes when I have to work outside the home in the morning, I leave him with a basic outline of what has to be done in schooling for that morning. He does it, but not on a regular basis. This is hard for me sometimes, as I feel all I do is homeschool, housework, go to work, then sleep and repeat the process all over again the next day.

As far as community support towards homeschooling, the school board seems to be very kind to homeschoolers and will let them participate in sports and extracurricular activities with the public school children, if they so desire. I have no such desire at this time. I am not part of any homeschool group. I have a bumper sticker in my window that tells everyone who looks that we homeschool. I take my boys out with me during school hours as much as possible. When school is out, we are usually home. I do not seem to get as many questions now as I used to. I can remember shocked looks I would get when I told someone I

Matthew (7), Nick (5)

homeschool. Now, when someone finds out I homeschool I receive one of three responses (and some of these answers have come from actual school teachers!):

1. That's wonderful. I have an aunt (niece, uncle, etc.) who homeschools.
2. Good for you! If I could raise my children all over again, I would do the same. The schools nowadays are just awful!
3. I am glad to see you take an active part in your child's education. I admire your courage and wish more parents would do the same with their children.

Teaching styles and learning styles *do* change. Our way of home-schooling is constantly evolving. Even now, I may do things differently than I did two weeks ago. For instance, I have made a "puppet theater" from a cardboard box, scrap material, and hot glue. I will now use this to reinforce learning by having the boys put on a show about what they are learning. I think this newest technique by our family will greatly enhance and help them retain what they have learned. Also, our schooling continues to become more relaxed. I keep a journal open at the table during the school day so I can record as much as possible.

I, like many others, was a little intimidated when reading homeschool magazines that had readers writing in about how far ahead their child was or what fantastic things their children do. I sort of felt like they must all be "little geniuses" but I have now learned (and am still learning) not to compare other children with my owns sons. Children are to be raised as the parents see fit. They are all different and those differences need to be recognized.

Some days of schooling are better than others. Not all days work out the way I imagine they should. Sometimes I am frustrated and other times elated. I am learning different ways to teach and as I learn, my teaching changes. I do hope to have more children very soon, and that will change our schooling, too!

No matter how hard or trying homeschooling may get, I will *never* allow my children into a public school system. You may have noticed that I have been blessed with two wonderful boys, and I am reaffirmed in the belief that for *this* family, homeschooling works!

Matthew (7), Nick (5)

	Subject: Bible	Subject: Writing/Music	Subject: Math	Subject: Listening Skills
73° (cloudy) ⑤ⒹⓉ(W)ⓉⒻⓈ 9/26	Read Gen. 41: 1-36 Discussion followed. Sang song 'God Is So Good'. Worked 2 pages of worksheets.	Completed page 6 of Italic Handwriting. Listened to tape. Completed pgs. 54 and 55 of 'Fun with Our Musical Friends'. Letter notes, F, A, C, E	Completed page 23 of moving with Math. Completed review sheet. Worked with subtraction flash cards as a review.	Completed lessons 5 and 6. Matt loves these listening skills. Today he got the worksheet all correct!
75° Windy ⑤(M)ⓌⓉⒻⓈ DATE: 9/27	Subject: Bible/Geo. Reviewed yesterday's story. Sang songs. Played 'Match' Bible People'. Finished worksheet which included map work.	Subject: Spanish Sang from side 1 of Spanish tape. Played a Spanish language game by having only Spanish being spoke for 5 minutes at the table.	Subject: Listening Skills Completed lessons 7 and 8 of Learning To Listen in the Classroom. Matt received a perfect score.	Subject: Math Reviewed basic multiplication facts of X 2's, 3's. Used worksheets to reinforce this. Also began with a maintenance review of previous skills learned.
64° ⑤(M)ⓉⓉⒻⓈ DATE: 9/28	Subject: Bible Read Gen. 41 Completed 2 pages of worksheets. Fun. ☺ Sang - 'The Wise Man Built His House Upon the Rock'. Used sign language to help 'sing' this song. Memory work.	Subject: Writing/Spelling Completed page 7 of Italic Handwriting. Spelled words that pertain to transportation examples: jet- ice skats kayak - Ilana.	Subject: Listening Skills Physical Ed. Completed lessons 9 and 10. This completes Level A- now Matt progresses to level B. P.E. Rode bicycles for 1 mile.	Subject: Math/Computer Completed page 13 of Using 'Models for multiplication. Took over 1 hour for this page - as Matt was using patterns to solve the problems. Worked with 'Math Champ' on computer.
60° ⑤(M)ⓉⓌ(T)ⒻⓈ DATE: 9/29	Subject: Bible/Geo. Reviewed Gen. 41. Completed map work of Egypt on Bible Worksheet. Finished worksheet. Mem-lok verse work.	Subject: Spanish Listened to the tape: Fonetica Funky. Played Spanish number bingo, color bingo and food bingo. This is a fun way to learn Spanish words! ☺	Subject: Math Completed maintenance review. Completed pg. 13 once again to review what was learned yesterday. Completed page 14 of Using Models. Glued that page to heavy paper to use as a multiplication table later.	Subject: Health Discussed and completed worksheets on safety rules to keep our bodies safe. Gave instruction about strangers + reviewed our fire drill in the home. (In these drills, the alarm is set off and the boys actually go out the window up to their delegated safe spots.)
70° ⑤(M)ⓉⓌ(T)Ⓢ DATE: 9/30	Subject: Reading/L. Arts Read God's World newspaper on current events. Circled all verbs in article entitled 'Moose On The Loose'.	Subject: Review Sorted through weeks worth of completed papers. Decided what to keep + what not to keep. Reviewed all we learned as we looked over papers.	Subject: Listening Skills Completed lessons 13 - 14. These lessons are now getting more complicated, as the background noises get louder + the instructions are more complicated.	Subject: Health Practiced manners in a restaurant. Attended a fancy restaurant + practiced good social manners.

This chart is from *The Home Schooler's Journal*, published by Fergnus Services.
This chart is from The Home Schooler's Journal, published by Fergnus Services.

Matthew (7), Nick (5)

UPDATE:

I now work full time with the U. S. Postal Service! I sit in front of a computer terminal with 800 other employees and process live images of mail pieces. I do not come home tired anymore since I am sitting the whole time. The only drawback is the long drive—I have to drive an hour each way to get to work. So we have decided to move closer to my work. I work the afternoon shift so the boys can still be watched by their father while I go to work. Sometimes we have to use a sitter (another homeschool mother) about four days a month. Many people ask me why I would want to work and homeschool. The answer is that by taking on this job, it has doubled our income and taken us off the "just-above-poverty" income guidelines. Also, I still get to see and teach my children for a major portion of the day. If they had been going to public school I would never see then.

When Matthew took his state mandated testing for third grade, he scored in the 99th percentile in all subjects except science (though that was very high also)! I was surprised because I was worried that his scores would be low since everyone tells me that working and homeschooling don't mix. But now I have a piece of paper that shows this not to be true.

My husband has taken up schooling the boys (when I cannot) on a regular basis. He no longer needs to work such long hours. This is especially good timing because we just found out we're expecting our third child!

Matthew (7), Nick (5)

Ed and Jane
Anna, age 9
Anthony, age 5

Jane wrote this on drizzly August 5, a Saturday at their rural farm in East Ryegate, Vermont.

THINGS MAKE SENSE

Today is a drizzly Saturday. Although Saturdays and summer days are not traditional school days, they aren't very different from other days in our schedule except that Saturday means we have Dad at home.

This particular day I woke up sometime between 6:00 and 6:30 AM. Ed had already gone out to the barn to do chores. We raise beef and sheep and also have a dairy cow, four dogs, two cats and various pigs and chickens, depending on the time of year. This affects our daily schedule much more than anything else! At 6:45 AM I went upstairs to wake Anna and remind her of the Saturday morning story on National Public Radio. It was her decision whether to get up or not, I just wanted her to have the opportunity. Both she and her brother Anthony soon bounced down the stairs and when Ed came in from the barn, we all had scrambled eggs, bacon and toast together.

Anna finished breakfast in time to cuddle up to the radio speaker for the story—we get very poor radio reception and listening is *not* a passive activity! Afterwards, she went to the barn to get her pony ready for riding, giving Anthony a lead-line ride before getting on herself. I had finished washing dishes by then and went out to watch her ride and to help her. It is difficult for her to visualize and then execute the circles and angles that I ask her to do while she is riding. I have seen this in other kids her age so I think it's a developmental skill which will right itself in time. Meanwhile, I tried to help her by having her understand certain concepts. In order to ride to a small jump in a straight line (essential for successful jumping), I told her that she needed to pick a "spot" and ride straight toward it. She showed me that she could ride in a straight line toward the spot from anywhere and not necessarily even hit the jump! Oh yeah, I reminded myself, the shortest distance between *two* points . . . . Okay, we also needed to pick a point for her to turn for the jump and connect it with the spot to ride toward and bingo, she got to the fence with her pony at a right angle to the fence . . .GEOMETRY! We discussed bending, curved lines, straight lines, speed and momentum, and the correlation between a sharp angle and slowing speed. After an hour, the pony, the rider, and Mom were well exercised and further educated.

At that point, Anthony yelled down that a friend had called (although I ran most of the way up the hill before finding out that the person was *not* still on the phone waiting for me). On my way into the house I picked all the ripe broccoli from the garden and put it to soak while I returned the call. The kids came in for a snack and then I read a library book to Anthony. ("Will you read to me first since Anna's chapters take so long?") I had read a horsemanship manual chapter to Anna while she cleaned her tack on the porch.

I had just enough time to cut the broccoli up before lunch. Ed came in and joined us for sandwiches. Anthony was excused from the table early (I can't honestly remember why, but he frequently flies or drives or forklifts his food, even with repeated warnings that this is *not* proper table manners).

Afterwards I froze the broccoli and washed dishes while the kids wrote thank you notes for birthday presents. These were a combination of pictures and writing; Anthony spelling out parts of his and dictating the rest to me, and Anna practicing her new cursive of which she is so proud.

When they were done, Anna went to the computer and Anthony discovered a workbook on numbers that he had forgotten about. I mostly juggled back and forth between them, answering questions and making suggestions. Anna created a page full of Venn diagrams, which she thinks are great fun. She made it a puzzle by drawing the forms and will try to fill in appropriate categories (and set members) at a later time. We'll go to our annual family reunion at the end of the month and Anna loves to collect things like that for entertainment on the four-hour drive. I showed Anthony what the intended directions for his chosen workbook pages were, then he decided how he would do them. ("Anthony, do you know you put those number stickers on upside down?" "No, they're not Mom, you just turn the book upside down to read them.")

At 3:00 PM, they both went to work with hammers and nails in the garage. Anna built herself an easel out of scrap lumber and then Anthony asked her to draw a picture of him. She did and presented it to him. His reply was, "Not very pretty Anna—I don't want it." She came in and confided to me that her feelings had been hurt. However, she said she had made up her mind to ignore him if he bothered her that day, so that is what she did. (She did make a journal type entry of the incident on the back of the paper and stowed it away with other drawings.)

Anthony joined me while I dug some potatoes for dinner and I made a

Anna (9), Anthony (5)

point of telling him that he had hurt Anna's feelings and asked him to try to be more polite in the future. He agreed but his attention was focused on finding potatoes under the earth. I, too, have always loved finding them, so I understood his fascination.

Back in the house, I made some zucchini bread and put it in the oven before heading out to the barn with everyone for chores. Anna took care of her pony while I fed and watered lambs, dogs, and sheep. Ed finished up some work with the tractor and fed the steers and the dairy cow. Anthony tagged along with each of us in turn and then climbed on a parked tractor for a trip into the imaginary future.

Before leaving the barn, I asked Anna if she wanted to go see the movie *Apollo 13* with me that night. I had thought it looked interesting and Anna has only been to the movies twice, both times at a drive-in where we didn't have to worry about her preschool brother's behavior. She responded that she wasn't really interested in space that much and didn't want to have to stay up late because she'd be tired the next day. What's that theory about kids with no TV not being able to make sound judgments about such forms of entertainment when it is available? Doesn't seem to hold in this house. At 5:00 PM it is "pick-up" time and both kids put away the day's worth of toys, projects and clothing that have been scattered around the house. On good days, they scurry and help each other; on bad days they grumble and I have to point out every little item or they don't "see" them. Luckily most days fall somewhere in between. This day took a turn for the negative when Anthony picked up a splinter. It looked to me like the type that would need to work its way out (although my own father believed he could dig any splinter out!) but Anna saved the day by making a successful attempt at it. Anthony was very grateful (and obviously thought much more of *her* than *me* for a while).

Dinner was at 6:00 PM and afterwards the kids cleared their dishes (with several reminders for Anthony) and got teeth brushed and washed up before reading time. Ed read a chapter of a *Hardy Boys* book to Anna; I hate the things, but he and Anna get a real kick out of them. I read some *Little House in the Big Woods* to Anthony and took him up to bed. Anna read some science magazines to herself for a while before going upstairs and then read some more in bed before going to sleep.

As days go, I guess this one was as typical as any. Although I do not have to keep a daily log for the state or district, I do occasionally jot down things that I know will interest them in my year-end evaluation. On this day I mentioned the "geometry" lesson, even though Anna had never heard the word during the day and would have been baffled if she had been questioned on what she learned about geometry. Other things I have noted this month include swim lessons earlier in the month, her daily riding, the historical fiction books we have read together, the trip to the local museum, the special talk on owls given at our local library, the fiction and non-fiction books she has chosen to read to herself from the library, etc.

Our schedules revolve around the seasons and the animals. We may not have the variety of museums, classes, and opportunities that a city offers (although for a rural area, there is a lot) but we feel that is more than made up for by the real experiences that exist with the land, the garden, and the animals.

We each fit in other things that we like to do as we see fit. The kids both choose their activities, the books and magazines that they read and we read to them, and how they spend their time. We do make suggestions, picking books off library or bookstore shelves and point out activities we think they would enjoy although they may have no experience with them. I did ask them to write the thank-you notes, but they've both been doing that ever since they could hold a block crayon, and I got no more resistance than if I had reminded them to say thank you to someone.

This is our form of unschooling. I certainly have had, and probably always will have, my fears about the looseness of it. Will they really learn all they need this way? So far, experience has shown absolutely yes. When I review professional curricula that I borrow from others in order to do my yearly plan, I find that many of the topics are already of interest to Anna, and therefore I am confident that we will cover them (and we do) without my forcing anything. It's the depth with which we are able to cover them, the other things we are also able to cover, and the still-remaining "free" time that Anna has that impress me. And of course, the lack of resistance, since she is not forced to do anything which she doesn't want to. I did my brief piece with a curriculum when she was in first grade and both of us were miserable. She has responsibilities: genuine responsibilities of caring for animals, helping us with house and farm chores, as well as being an older sister. These are things that make sense and are rewarding simply by doing them: a happy pony, serving food that she has made herself, and a hug from a little brother.

Multiplication tables are the first thing she has run into that just need to be memorized and aren't particularly interesting on their own. We have played games, found patterns, and done other things that she has enjoyed and have given her a good sense of multiplication, but there are still those facts to be learned. I grit my teeth and try not to say, "These have to be learned by such and such a date." She knows she needs to learn them because we have explained it, and she sees us use math. When I remind her, she works on them and is slowly learning them.

Anthony is a very different type of learner and is interested in very different things. He is very independent and focuses intently on things, as long as they are things that interest him. I think self-directed learning might be the only way he will ever learn anything—he just can't concentrate at will (at this age anyway). I may go crazy while he ignores many things in order to focus on one, but I hope he will eventually hit them all if I leave him alone and just do my job of finding things to tempt him with as I do with Anna.

Our kids "socialize" with others at a weekly homeschooling group during which the kids are free to do as they wish. Sometimes they play schoolyard type games, sometimes they play word games, and sometimes they sit and talk. Parents frequently suggest special activities such as a cooperative

Anna (9), Anthony (5)

math game, a drama instructor, or science experiments. If the kids want to (usually), we do them. If they aren't interested, we don't waste our time, money and energy organizing it.

They also socialize with other kids when they invite them over or go to other houses. And of course, they are able to socialize with adult friends, grandparents, cousins, and townspeople on many days and in many ways.

We do not have to keep our kids busy; they do that just fine on their own. Anna is a very people-oriented person, so she loves to be around us and/or anyone else who is here. She does not ask "what can I do?" and only wants to talk and be a part of whatever anyone else is doing. This is a big part of her actual learning style—bouncing ideas, opinions, and dreams off of others and hearing the same. Luckily, she can now also use books in this fashion, lightening the load on her parents' ears.

Anthony, on the other hand, can spend hours on his own—building with Legos, driving his toy cars, drawing or walking through the woods and fields, examining flowers and bugs.

We evaluate it all as we go and we'll change things if we need to. In the meantime, we're thankful that there isn't too much typical around here.

Anna (9), Anthony (5)

UPDATE:

Nothing of significance has changed here. Of course, the lambs have grown, another set has been born, the calves have been weaned, and we've added another dog and another pony. Anthony is trying to read and it's not dull, that's for sure!

Anna (9), Anthony (5)

Chuck and Nancy
Noah, age 14
Jesse, age 12
Joel, age 10
A.J., age 6

Written by Nancy, Joel, Jesse, Noah and Chuck during different months from
the small Harley-Davidson city of York, Pennsylvania

BUILDING CASTLES

All summer I wondered which type of day we should choose to
describe as typical. There are those laid-back and fun-filled summer days, when
we work on big projects (like the doll that Joel made to look like his younger
brother, or the model of Narnia he created, or the rainy days we all spent
working on Jesse's stamp collection). There are the easing-into-routine
September days, when I'm sick with allergies and we slowly get into the swing
of things. There are our busy Mondays, when we do most of our out-of-home
activities, since that is the only day I know I'll have a car. Thursdays, we teach
American Sign Language classes in our home (that involves lesson preparation,
rearranging the house to make room for both the class and the play space for
younger children, teaching two different classes, eating lunch with the whole
group between classes, and the big clean-up after everyone leaves).

Our December days are filled with geography activities, as we do the
Geography Awareness Week activities (a month late, of course) and prepare for
the National Geographic Geography Bee. December days are also brightened by
Christmas preparations, as we memorize advent hymns, bake cookies, make
gingerbread houses, act out a favorite book entitled *Haffertee's First Christmas*,
sing carols around the angel chimes, etc. During December we also play
Colombian games, in honor of one of our children who is from Colombia. These
games are guaranteed to make adults go crazy, but are an important part of our

family tradition. Later in December, we celebrate Kwanzaa with the traditional items, principles and feast. During Kwanzaa we enjoy reading African folk tales or stories with specifically African-American themes. Then there's that special school day on New Years Eve when we all bundle up and go downtown for First Night. There we hear African storytelling, enjoy a Latin jazz band, listen to the Junior Symphony and end the night with a rousing gospel group. Quite a school day.

In January, we drop almost everything else and throw ourselves into preparing for our homeschool group's International Fair. We study a country by reading folk tales, historical fiction, biographies, history and geography books, art books, etc. We listen to that country's music. We eat a feast of traditional foods related to our country (and yes, the kids always complain about trying the unusual foods). We make maps, models of famous buildings, calendars explaining holidays and traditions, and crafts (such as Persian rugs and marbled paper when we studied Iran, Matreshka nesting dolls and Ukrainian Pysanky eggs when we studied Russia). After many project-filled weeks, we put together our display. At the International Fair, we enjoy everyone's displays and sample traditional foods of each country represented.

Typical of those cold, snowed-in, or we've-all-got-the-flu days of February might be a day when we all curl up in our warm water bed and read *The Hobbit* or *A Tale of Two Cities* or *Treasures of the Snow*. The younger children lie on the floor and draw. Our animal lover holds a dog or cat while listening. Our oldest son does calculus problems while he listens, but seems able to give both activities full attention. (It took me years to understand that it is difficult for Noah to "pay attention" to one task at a time. Recently I've allowed him to shoot hoops while we practiced Spanish verb conjugations, or read physics while he played clarinet. I finally understand that he really can pay attention better if I let his extra energy spill over into some second activity. He's been telling me for years that it takes a lot more energy to sit still than to move.) Sometimes we have passed an entire day pleasantly reading a book, before seeing that same story performed on stage that evening.

March days are something like our January days, except our emphasis is on preparing for our group's Project Fair. Each child prepares a few different projects. This event is another highlight of our homeschool year. During April, we push hard to wrap up loose ends, finish up projects, etc. In May, as I begin my end-of-the-year reflection and evaluation, I usually find one or two areas that we've brushed over too lightly. May school days focus on those areas. For example, we spent most of last May doing science experiments and art projects.

Throughout the year there are field trips: to the Symphony Orchestra and the National Aquarium one day, on a paddle-wheel boat ride on the Susquehanna River followed by an afternoon at the Museum of Scientific Discovery another day, or a week-long trip to Florida for the Deaf Church's Basketball Tournament. Then there are those weeks when my husband and I work together out of town. At those times our schedule is so demanding that we usually can't take the boys, so they stay with different families. They get to see a

Noah (14), Jesse (12), Joel (10), A.J. (6)

slice of life in another homeschool family. All of us enjoy these little vacations from our usually intense interactions here at home.

So, everyday around here really is different. Maybe that's why the kids ask us each night, "What are we doing tomorrow?" Sometimes unexpected things pop up—some that would be labeled surprises, others that would be called crises. But, that's all part of the learning process, here in our family.

We had fun going through last year's logs and choosing days to write about. Each of our three older boys chose a different type of day to describe. Notes [*in italics*] are my added comments.

Now, I'm having misgivings . . . . Maybe we should have described a day when we had Math Olympiads here or when we went to another family's home for Writing Club. Or we could have told about the days when my husband takes off work and he and the boys spend the entire day building and painting to make the set for the upcoming play at the local children's theater. Or a day when Joel crowds our house with kids and costumes, background scenes and props, to rehearse a play he has written and plans to perform on stage at a local church (pastored by a homeschooler who is willing to lend the building to encourage such creative endeavors). Maybe I should have described a day when we actually accomplished everything we planned to—except I didn't find a day like that in my log and can't recall a single such ideal day in the past decade of home-schooling.

I could have told about the day after we studied simple machines, when Joel lowered the rabbits down from the balcony in a pink basket, using a pulley he made by himself. And I had thought he wasn't even paying attention to the previous day's science lesson! Then there was that dreary December day when one of the rabbits escaped from our balcony, so I had to climb onto our neighbor's second floor roof, in the pouring rain, to retrieve the wandering pet. That certainly disturbed our normal routine.

Anyhow, despite our misgivings, we settled on a few sample school days. This exercise of writing about our homeschool day seems to be a small picture of our broader homeschool program: lots of decisions, some misgivings, plowing on in spite of it all, and enjoying every minute of it—almost.

OUR HOUSEKEEPING ROUTINES:

I often make dinner in the morning. I usually let the children sleep until 8:00 AM (or even one or two hours later, if they have been sick or are tired because of being at the theater until late with performances or rehearsals). That gives me time in the morning to tackle something—that night's dinner, the weekly cleaning, writing a letter, etc. I normally listen to a tape of a sermon while I work, so I can nurture my soul's happiness in God while I order our home. Often we have many tapes to listen to as we prepare to interpret a conference or translate a video series. These quiet morning hours are my best times to listen to God's Word.

In the summer I almost always make dinner before the children get up. I love getting all the household chores done early, freeing us to spend the day outside or at the city pool. A few leisurely days like that give me a real break and help me feel ready to dive into another school year.

During the boys' baseball season, we eat dinner around 2:00 PM, enjoy the boys' evening baseball games then eat a snack of fruit and popcorn together before bed. This seems to fit their baseball schedule well.

I sit down with our calendar once a week and plan meals according to how much time I have to cook that day. That way I know if the children have to be at soccer practice at 6:00 PM (which means a quick meal) or if no one goes out until chess club at 7:00 PM (which means a little extra time for a little fancier meal—like adding bread and salad with our spaghetti or muffins with our crockpot soup!). I plan the menu and write the grocery list; Chuck does the grocery shopping (and often takes the younger two boys). I normally cook dinner, with Chuck jumping in to help toward the end. If I am out in the afternoon and wasn't able to cook dinner in the morning, Chuck cooks. (Since we only have one car I can only take the boys to a homeschool activity if Chuck is home working in his office.)

There are a few dishes (lasagna, eggplant Parmesan, etc.. . . .) that I always make in huge batches so I can freeze six extra casseroles. It's great to be able to pull a nice meal out of the freezer when guests arrive on a busy day.

While I'm describing household routines, let me tell you how we keep our home somewhat clean. I wipe up in the bathroom every morning and evening. The kitchen gets put in order after every meal, often with the help of one of the boys. Everything gets straightened up all day long. I used to take everything the boys left out and keep it for a day or two. It didn't take long before they learned to clean up after everything they did. Once a week I clean the kitchen more thoroughly and wash the kitchen floor. I also vacuum and dust the living room and dining room. Noah and Jesse vacuum two rooms each on our second floor. They check each other's vacuuming, then the one who checked must re-vacuum if I find any dirt when I come through. That makes our checkers extra diligent.

Once a month, we stop all our school work until we get the house more thoroughly clean. I dust, wash floors and vacuum everything on the first floor (kitchen, dining room, living room and hallway). Noah, Jesse and I thoroughly dust their room, the three stairways, the second and third floor halls, Chuck's office and the schoolroom. Joel thoroughly dusts and vacuums his room. I do our bedroom and the bathroom. Chuck tackles the basement and the outside porches. A.J. cleans up the yard. So, the whole house is clean from top to bottom, once a month.

Once a year, right after I wrap up our schoolwork for the year, I tear into every nook and cranny. I reorganize every closet and redesign our home to better fit our lifestyle. I think about each child's interests and how we can better use our space to let them pursue those interests. Last year, that meant taking the single shelf of art supplies (that had been adequate for Noah and Jesse) and arranging an entire closet of art supplies for Joel. One year's spring cleaning involved making room for a stage Chuck built for Joel. Joel has spent thousands

Noah (14), Jesse (12), Joel (10), A.J. (6)

of hours writing and producing plays and choreographing dances to be performed on his stage. While I do this spring cleaning, I get rid of hundreds of items that we don't really need. I reevaluate every item and the use of every household space. Afterward, life runs more smoothly because our home is set up according to our needs (not according to where I threw the paints on some busy day three years ago).

Our program has gotten more school-like as Noah and Jesse have grown older. When they were younger, they did a lot of hands-on activities: turning the backyard into a miniature golf course, archeological digs for artifacts in the yard, panning for gold in the creek, feeding the ducks at the pond, building rockets, etc. As they've gotten older, they have begun to use more concentrated materials, like textbooks. (They still use a lot of library books. We have about sixty in our home right now.)

What we've written here doesn't define our homeschool program. It is very different today from what it was a decade ago. It will be different next year. Our program is fluid, constantly changing to meet the needs of our four boys and our lifestyle. Every change in our ministry, every development in the boys' lives, every step in our marriage, every new glimpse of God's beauty—these and a hundred other factors daily shape our homeschooling.

JOEL'S DAY, in July:

After breakfast, I played a computer game called *Lemonade* with Jesse. [*Lemonade is a game in which players set up stands and sell lemonade. After reading the day's weather forecast, the players must decide how much lemonade to make, how many advertising signs to invest in and what to charge for their lemonade. Their profits rise and fall according to the weather patterns and the wisdom of their decisions.*] Then we had worship time. We read Bible verses about God being our refuge and fortress. We learned the song *A Mighty Fortress is Our God.*

Then I read books to Mom for our summer reading program at the library. Every time I read five more books, I get a prize, like a free goldfish or a free personal pan pizza at Pizza Hut.

After lunch, we started building our castle in our basement. We made it from cardboard boxes we found at a kitchen appliance store. Our castle had a keep in the middle. There was a ladder inside the keep so we could climb up and look out the high window. We could shoot arrows out of the keep window. It had turrets and a drawbridge. About ten kids could fit inside our castle. We painted it all silver.

We went to the city pool. We swam and went down the fast water slide. During the lifeguard break, we played cards.

We came home and ate dinner. After dinner, we went bike riding at the fairgrounds near our house.

We got ready for bed and listened to Mom read *Prince Caspian*. While I listened to the story, I colored many pictures I had drawn for making an animated film.

Noah (14), Jesse (12), Joel (10), A.J. (6)

JESSE'S DAY, one day in December:

Hi! I'm Jesse and I'm here to tell you about a school day. My day went like this:

8:00 AM: "Jesse, you'd better get out of bed. You've got first shower today," Mom calls. "Oh, all right," I groan as I get up and get clean clothes for the day.

8:15 AM: It's my turn in the shower.

8:30-9:00 AM: For breakfast I have a Shacklee protein smoothy and vitamins. Then I get straight to work. First Noah listens to a tape from the series *Surprised by Suffering*, by R. C. Sproul, while I read the Bible.

9:00-9:15 AM: I walk the dog, clean the kitty litter, and brush the animals.

9:15-10:00 AM: Now it's time for Family Worship: singing and praying.

10:00-10:30 AM: For math, I do worksheets for my MathCounts team.

10:30-11:00 AM: I play recorder and drums for music. I practice drums because the Middle School Christmas program is in a few weeks.

11:00-11:45 AM: I start questions from the book *Where on Earth?* as preparation for the National Geographic Geography Bee, which is coming up soon. Noah and I make bridges with skill sticks, string, scissors, tape, etc. This is a physics, engineering, and creativity project, since the point is to find a design that can support the most weight in pennies. We have to clean up the mess in our room before we can eat lunch.

11:45-12:15 PM: I read a chapter in my A Beka science book and plan my science activity for this month. (I plan to build a constellation viewer, so have to gather the materials and list the things Dad needs to buy.)

12:15-1:00 PM: For lunch I made broiled fajita shells with cheese for my younger brothers and me.

1:00-1:30 PM: I'm doing a book of logic games and puzzles, etc.

1:30-2:15 PM: I work in my civics activity book. Also, Mom, Noah and I work on projects from the Geography Awareness Week packet, while Joel and A.J. play with play-dough. We learn about the Colorado River and all the places where people take out water from it for various cities. Then we play a geography game called *On Assignment.*

2:15-2:45 PM: For writing, I wrote this (boring).

2:45-3:15 PM: I made authentic Czech boxes during project time, using a kit brought to us by a Peace Corps Volunteer we've been writing to.

3:15-5:30 PM: During some free time, I play with my friend Nick. We play football in our living room.

5:30-6:00 PM: We have left over lasagna, salad, and bread for dinner.

6:00-8:00 PM: We go to theater practice. The play we're working on now is called *A Fairy Tale Times Two*, which uses characters from *Cinderella* and *The Emperor's New Clothes*. My dad and Noah are in the play too. Tonight we are learning how to waltz.

8:00-9:00 PM: I read *Bridge to Terabithia*, by Katherine Paterson.

9:00-9:30 PM: Mom and Dad are reading through the Bible with us. We're up to Isaiah.

Bed time.

Noah (14), Jesse (12), Joel (10), A.J. (6)

[In this family, several of us are project-and-idea people who like blasting our way through a year's worth of science in one month, and working on a project night and day for two straight weeks. Jesse, however, likes to approach subjects in small bits each day. With Jesse's help, I planned monthly checklists outlining what Jesse needed to accomplish each month. Then, week by week and day by day, Jesse and I break those monthly goals into manageable chunks.]

NOAH'S DAY, Spring:

"Time to get up," I hear my mom shout. I think, "Another day already," and roll over. "Come on, Noah," says Mom. "I'm coming," I answer as I drag myself out of bed. Today is Monday, and Mondays at our house are crazy. While I shower and drink my protein shake, my mother and my brother, Joel, get ready for my brother's art class. My dad and I go to the local high school to check my math work. This year we borrowed my math books from the school district. I do the work at home and check it with the math teacher at the school.

When I get home, I start my school work. First I read my Bible study. Jesse is reading in his Bible. After that we play our instruments. Today I am playing clarinet and Jesse is playing the drums. Some days we play recorders instead.

For math, I could do either Geometry or Algebra 2. I would like to finish both of them this year, as well as Trigonometry. I decide on Geometry. I read a chapter and do that test. I normally get a good score; if I don't, I must do the chapter over again and do another test. I used to have to do every other practice question and, for every one I missed, I had to do an extra problem. This year I finally talked Mom into letting me spend one or two days per chapter.

My mom just got back. We run downstairs and I grab a book. Mom wants us to help get stuff ready for Spanish and pack our lunches. I do this while reading. "Put that book down!" Mom shouts.

We drive to the Y.M.C.A. where Dad, Joel, and A.J. get off. My dad is going to play basketball. Then we hurry to Spanish class.

I go to the elementary class where I teach Spanish during the student lunch break. We talk with our Spanish teacher (in Spanish, of course) and read a book of Spanish stories. Then I talk to a friend from the theater, before going to a Spanish class for homeschoolers. Jesse and I are in the advanced class. My mom is teaching the intermediate class. In our class, we are debating how poor countries and rich countries should work together. Of course, we do all this in Spanish, which is how it gets difficult.

At 4:40 PM we rush home and grab some soup and bread. While we were gone, Dad and my brothers took a bus home from the Y.M.C.A. Dad mowed the lawn and worked in his office. Jesse goes to MathCounts. I go when I don't have rehearsals, but tonight I take off for the theater, where I am Templeton in *Charlotte's Web*.

When I get home, I brush my teeth. Then I get into bed. My mom comes in to go over tomorrow's school day with us. She asks me to clean my room. My dad reads the Bible to us and prays for us. Then I read *A Connecticut*

Noah (14), Jesse (12), Joel (10), A.J. (6)

Yankee in King Arthur's Court. I am reading this because Mark Twain (actually I think this book was written under the name Samuel Clemens) lived during the period of history that we are studying. Each year we study a different period of history. Last year we studied the years from the reconstruction of the South to the early 1900's. I choose half of my books and Mom chooses the other half. Then I alternate reading one of my books and one of hers. The "school" ones (that my mom chooses) are normally literature or historical fiction. I choose books on interesting things like math, science or computers.

My brother is going to sleep now, so we turn out the big room light (actually, it isn't that bright anymore because only one of the three bulbs is working) and I turn on my reading lamp. I finally finish that book (it took me nearly a week because it was almost a thousand pages long). I can now start *my* book. It is called *Calculus the Easy Way*. I find the math I do in school is simple, so I like to study ahead on my own.

It is time for me to turn off my light. I turn it off (after I finish the chapter, of course) and lie in bed thinking. I think about everything I can for about an hour before I finally doze off.

CHUCK'S DAY:

When I went to bed last night, I noticed that my foot was a little bit sore. But I couldn't find anything wrong with it. This morning, I wake up to find that I have a splinter causing a lot of pain. Nancy and I spend a good bit of time getting it out, which pushes us behind schedule. I jump into the shower, get dressed and run downstairs. Just enough time to make my breakfast. I debate whether I have time to get out everyone's vitamins. I know that I have already put Nancy behind schedule, so decide to go ahead. I run downstairs and move a load of wash into the dryer, and then take off for a day of work.

I am leaving myself just enough time to get there right on time. I usually like to get to interpreting jobs early. But this is a weekly assignment, so I know the ropes. [*Chuck interprets from American Sign Language into English and vice versa. Half of his work time is in ministry, interpreting conferences that Deaf people want to attend, interpreting business matters for Deaf churches, interpreting when Deaf preachers preach to hearing congregations, etc. Interested churches and individuals send donations which provide half of our salary. The other half of Chuck's work is his own interpreting business: interpreting in businesses, universities, government offices, courts, etc. His schedule varies greatly day by day and week by week. Every once in a while, he is home for a whole week. Once he was overseas for three weeks. Sometimes he leaves home at 5:30 AM and arrives home at 7:00 PM; other times he only has a two hour assignment in the afternoon. (Note: People who identify themselves as belonging to the cultural group of Deaf people and who use American Sign Language, use a capital "D" to identify their people group. They also prefer the term Deaf to the phrase hearing people made up—Hearing Impaired. Some papers use the word D/deaf to include both the culturally Deaf who use ASL and deaf people who use signed English that is more closely linked to the hearing*] *world.)]*

The first meeting I was to interpret is canceled, so I read from *Desiring God* by John Piper. During lunch break, I listen to tapes of a seminar that I will be interpreting next month. I also run a few errands (the drug store for allergy medicine, etc.). I remember to pray for Nancy. The afternoon work goes smoothly and I start for home, only to find a detour due to new road construction. I stop at the copy store to make copies, the pet store for cat food, and the building store for some home maintenance stuff. I make a deposit at the bank and head home.

To be honest, I never know what to expect when I get home. Homeschooling four boys, while being actively involved in ministry, along with all the other things that go with life in the United States, results in a lot to do and a lot of uncertainty as to what a given day will hold. I wonder how the day went for Nancy. Nancy is extremely creative and has a higher energy level than anyone I know. She is an idea person. Most people (including me) wouldn't try to accomplish as much in a week as she does in a day. So, I walk in the house wondering what state the house will be in, but more importantly, what state Nancy will be in. Our life is such that you don't know what will come next, like a roller coaster. We could round the corner to find a pleasant ride to the finish line, or to see one more 180° drop, ending in a full loop.

Well, it turns out to be the latter. It was a tough day, so dinner isn't ready and the evening plans are drawing near. I see the look of frazzledness in Nancy's eyes, give her a quick hug and kiss (quick for her sake), look on the weekly menu and dive right into cooking the taco meat and cutting up the vegetables. As the meat cooks, I run upstairs to strip the younger boys' beds, run downstairs, sort the laundry and put in a load. The tacos are ready and I call everyone for dinner. Of course, I have to call several of the boys a second, third, fourth??? time.

Finally, everyone's hands are washed and Nancy and I are taking taco orders. We sit down, pray and dive into our meal.

As we eat, Nancy and I tell each other about our days. My minor frustrations seem mild compared to her day. Tonight, Nancy will have to clean up dinner because Jesse and I have to go to soccer practice. Jesse's coach backed out a week before the season was to start, so I volunteered to take over. I have a lot of coaching experience, but none of it in soccer. But, since I usually go to practice and games with the boys, I figured I could handle it. I checked out several soccer books from the library and dove into it. Before taking off, I put in another load of wash. Noah comes along to soccer to help out, while Joel and A.J. head off to the playground on the other side of the park.

After practice, Nancy works with the older boys while I put the last load in the washer and fold clean laundry. I run up to my office to listen to my answering machine. There is a whole list of messages that will have to be returned the next day. I go through the mail—mostly bills and junk.

I put the sheets on the younger two boys' beds and supervise their bedtime routine. I read them their Bible story book, pray for them, tell them what will happen the next day, give them each a hug, a kiss and an "I love you," and find out what I can do to cut down on Nancy's end-of-the-day straightening up.

Nancy finishes with the older boys. I read them the Bible, pray for them, give them hugs and turn out the light. Nancy makes a phone call, while I put away the laundry.

We get ready for bed and fall exhausted into bed. We like to get to bed by 10:00 PM so that we will have time to talk and pray (and possibly read) before catching a few hours of sleep. We didn't make it tonight. Actually, we didn't come close. It's 11:30 PM. That doesn't stop us from talking. It seldom does. We have been married for almost seventeen years and hardly a night has gone by that we haven't spent an hour (or sometimes several hours) talking. This is one of the things that has held our marriage together.

We have committed ourselves to homeschooling four very different children. To do so, we have had to make many sacrifices. Putting the boys in school might seem easier, but would force us to sacrifice what we are unwilling to sacrifice: strong and active involvement in the lives of our children. To accomplish this, we have decided that I will be the primary "bread winner," while Nancy will be the primary teacher and "housekeeper." There is not enough time in the day, however, for her to do all that is necessary for both of these jobs. So, I do the grocery shopping (usually taking the younger two boys, so that Nancy can focus on the other two, or get something else done), all the laundry, clean the bathroom, and jump in where necessary with cooking, meal clean-up, and whatever else needs to be done.

While helping with household routines is an important duty, I think that the most important role that a homeschooling father can assume is that of nurturing his wife. One aspect of this is helping her to maintain perspective. It is easy to get overwhelmed by the nitty-gritty of life and homeschooling. It is easy to forget why you are doing it in the first place. As a father, I can observe what is going on, listen to Nancy's struggles and frustrations, and remind her once again that what she is doing is worth it. While we don't see the effects on our children *each* day, we know that it will benefit them in the long run. When she is worried that our children might be missing something that they would be learning at the public school, because of our unit-type approach to learning, I can remind her that she really doesn't believe that. Maybe they don't know the date 1620, but they understand how America came to be. They understand what it was like for the Native Americans, as well as for the newcomers. After I've listened to Nancy, she's ready for my input and encouragement. Then she feels ready to face another demanding day and enthusiastically pursue our calling to teach our children at home.

Noah (14), Jesse (12), Joel (10), A.J. (6)

DAY #	July, 1993 (Joel's day)	Sept. '94 (Jesse's-1)	December '93 (Jesse's-2)	Monday - Spring '93 (Noah)
BIBLE + WORSHIP	Study on God as refuge & fortress Praise time	No - Tabletalk Bible study Je - Family Worship	No - Surprised By Suffering Je - Bible; Romans	Je - Bible; Psalms
MATH	Lemonade	- USAMTS problems No - Calculus @ York College Je - MathCounts Worksheets	Design bridges to hold maximum weight. Use only the materials listed in activity guide	No - Check Alg 2 & Geom. work @ high school No - Geometry Ch. 10 Je - MathCounts
WRITING		No - Write-up team project during Calculus Je - Write "Home School Day"		(I write this sideways to show that it took most of our day)
READING	Rd. to me; You'll Soon Grow into them, Titch; Word Birds Hats Rd aloud book; Prince Caspian	Je - Geog. book No - Dragon's Gate, by Yep & Internet for Dummies		No - Comp. Yankees... Calculus-Early Alg Je - Hardy Boys;
SPANISH + ASL				SPANISH at Christian School of York; teaching class on chinese read/translate
MUSIC		Jesse - Recorder & Drum practice	Je - Drums No - Clarinet lesson	No - Clarinet Je - Drum
UNIT: SCIENCE/ SOCIAL STUDIES/ ART	Build / Paint huge castle Draw pictures for animated film	Je - Plan experiment. Gather materials List any needed materials Je - Civics CAAP book - Begin timeline; list historical events you might want to study Je - Make Czech boxes	Geography Awareness Week activities - "Diverting the Colorado" Geog. game "On Assignment"	Je - Drum
P.E.	Swimming Biking	Make plate design Je - soccer	Learn to waltz	
OTHER	Noah - CHEMISTRY at CTY program →	Je - Logic problems No - York Little Theater	York Little Theater	No - YLT (York Little Theater)

Noah (14), Jesse (12), Joel (10), A.J. (6)

UPDATE:

While Chuck worked in New Mexico for seven weeks this summer interpreting lectures, the boys and I enjoyed a leisurely homeschooling routine out West. I had such fun teaching and running a quiet home, without our usual distractions and outside activities.

We spent several weeks, both before and after Chuck's summer job, camping in national parks throughout the West. It was a hands-on homeschool adventure. For geography, we hiked in alpine meadows, rocky beaches, colorful deserts and rugged canyons. For science, we watched whales, coyotes, pikas, moose, golden eagles, big horn sheep, and many other animals. We viewed many interesting geological features. For physical education, the boys swam with seals and sea lions, went white water rafting, and fought wild river currents. For safety education, we dodged bubonic plague-carrying rodents, walked carefully when approaching precipices or crossing glaciers, thoroughly extinguished our fires and gave bison the right of way. We read dozens of great books while driving 15,000 miles. We picked fresh blackberries, watched shooting stars, built driftwood fires, and got stuck in a cramped tunnel of a dark cave. All summer, we reveled in the beauty of God's creation and the glory of His character.

Meanwhile, living and learning goes on now that we are back home: Noah is delving into the history of philosophy, Jesse is keeping up with

Noah (14), Jesse (12), Joel (10), A.J. (6)

chemistry and geometry, and the older boys are improving their Spanish without my help. I spend most of my day working one-on-one with Joel. A.J. enjoys lots of time to play with his older brothers and work on the computer. Noah and Jesse have been helping A.J. with his reading and math. Noah, Jesse and I are studying post-World War II history. Jesse, Joel and A.J. have begun a unit on Brazil—our country for this year. There's a rain forest montage growing in the dining room!

This year, we have a second car, which means I have spent a lot of time driving to new activities. This has been an adjustment, but we're all getting used to packing lunches and car activities. We have slipped into a fairly smooth weekly routine. This coming semester, Noah hopes to take more courses at a nearby university. He will, however, consolidate his schedule by choosing courses that meet only on certain days, giving us time to do all day science field trips on another day.

Last year's main adjustment was getting used to the older boys' increased evening activities. We learned to transport the boys to and fro, while still maintaining our evening routines with the younger boys. Who knows what adjustments next year will bring. With God's empowering us, we trust that next year will be another opportunity to delight in God and enjoy our family relationships.

Noah (14), Jesse (12), Joel (10), A.J. (6)

John and Penny
Johnny, age 9
Jenny, age 5

Penny described this rainy and windy day in February from the wee historic
town of Dunblane, Scotland.

WE'RE DOING IT OTHERWISE

First, I'll tell you about us. We are, in order of age, Penny, John,
Johnny, and Jenny. Johnny attended school for six weeks, just before his fifth
birthday. It was not a success. He had been reading fluently for over a year, and
the type of number work he was expected to do was the sort of stuff he'd
enjoyed doing at eighteen months: sorting, counting, putting the appropriate
plastic number against the set—that sort of thing, and he was bored. We took
him out of school just before his fifth birthday. We have never even considered
sending Jenny to school.

Johnny and Jenny adore each other and do almost everything together.
This, of course, would be impossible if they were at school. They do fall out
sometimes and must learn to deal with each other.

We are vegans and are committed to human and animal rights. John
teaches Religious and Moral Education in a high school in Dundee, about fifty
miles from here. We could live closer to his work, but this is his home town and
we all love it here. Our home is a tiny, stonebuilt, terraced cottage (which is part
of a 200 year old weaver's cottage, which used to have a thatched roof) with a
front door that opens out onto the street. Our street used to be a separate village
but is now part of Dunblane. It's a narrow street, with mostly 18th and 19th
century cottages. Behind our house is a field with a couple of horses and behind
that are the Laigh Hills, which are reached by walking fifty yards down the
street, turning into a short lane and we're there. A burn runs through them and
comes out in the River Allan, which runs through the far end of the Laigh Hills.

Dunblane is an historic wee town, officially a city because it has a cathedral. There have been iron age settlements here—the Romans were here, there is a medieval cathedral, and the remains of the medieval Bishop's Palace. Long ago Bonnie Prince Charlie lodged in Dunblane and some of his troops hid in a house where friends of ours now live. From a house in Dunblane (now demolished), a serving girl poured hot oil from an upstairs window in an attempt to kill the Duke of Cumberland, but missed him and got his horse, who promptly threw the Duke into the mud. The girl managed to escape! It's the perfect place to live for such a history-loving family as we are! Also, within easy traveling distance are Stirling and Edinburgh, each with a castle, bags of history, art galleries, museums and book shops! Do you get the impression we love living here?

We have two mongrel dogs, four cats and a pond with three goldfish and, at the last count, ten toads. (And judging by the way they were behaving, we're going to have an awful lot more toads fairly soon!)

I sell Dorling Kindersley (D.K.) books and recruit other people to sell them, too. This means that I get wonderful books at cost price and also earn money without having to do a nine-to-five job. I also look after the house and take responsibility for the children's education, which is semi-structured.

We have maths workbooks (*Ginn Maths*), but we also use maths about the house, use maths computer games, play maths board games, etc. (for example, *Monopoly, Yahtzee,* and *Rummikub*). We've also been enjoying Susan Richman's *Math by Kids!* It has really inspired *my* kids to make up their own sums. I have recently bought her book, *Writing from Home,* and it is doing the same thing for their writing. Jenny has a reading scheme (Oxford *Reading Tree,* which she loves) but we do all sorts of other reading activities and have several thousand books.

The children write diaries and stories and Johnny has three penpals: two in Australia (he took an interest in Australia and we arranged for the children of two of my Australian cousins to correspond with him) and one home-educated girl who lives nearby but whom we haven't had a chance to meet yet.

We study history and at the moment are on the Romans in Britain—we live near part of the Antonine Wall and various Roman camps, but we also visit castles and discuss anything historical that comes up, no matter what period. We're making a time line so that all the periods we talk about can fit into place.

We study nature and science—science experiments can come from one of our D.K. books or may arise because something has come up in conversation. We also study world religions, geography, English grammar, cookery, play lots of board games and computer adventure games together, paint, draw, sew, do various crafts . . . .

We listen to a lot of music—coincidentally, I had just typed the word "music" when Jenny called to me to ask me to put on the CD of Tchaikovsky's *Album for the Young.* We listen to baroque, romantic classical, opera, Scottish folk and fiddle music, thirties and forties popular songs, and the Beatles. We sing *a lot,* particularly Johnny.

Johnny (9), Jenny (5)

We discuss anything and everything! Often, when Johnny and I are doing some reading together, Jenny will be playing nearby and we're amazed when she makes a comment on what we've been saying or discusses a point we've made, usually without even looking up from her dolls!

We try to do two to three hours formal work most days, but if something crops up, like an unexpected visit, a chance to go somewhere interesting, or a great game that has to be played out in full, then the lessons are left for a bit until a more convenient time, usually either later that day or the next day. We visit museums and art galleries and we have a small garden where John and Johnny are planning to create a fruit and vegetable plot this spring. The children are members of the Young Ornithologists Club.

Some of the children's friends go to school, some don't. They visit and are visited by the home-educated ones at various times and the school ones after 3.30 PM, at weekends and when the teachers are having an "in-service day."

Things don't always go smoothly. Sometimes the children don't want to start lessons when I think they should. We usually start with a story, chosen by each of us in turn, to ease them in gently. They actually enjoy their lessons, it's just the thought of starting sometimes. I have been known to threaten them with school on very bad days. It always works, but I feel bad about doing it.

Actually, the more I see and hear of schools (I used to be a primary school teacher and I see schools when I'm out selling books), the surer I am that we're doing the right thing. The children have a great deal of freedom but they're also getting a much better education than their friends who go to school and, very important to us, we're able to be together most of the time. We're not always in the same room. The children often disappear for hours at a time to play in their room, but we're always near each other, available for talk, comfort, cuddles.

We met a friend in the supermarket, recently, and she looked at Johnny and Jenny and said, "I'm glad my two are at school!" I'm glad my two aren't. Together with their Daddy, they're my best friends.

A DAY IN OUR LIFE, 16th February:

The alarm goes off at 5.30 AM. "Set it for another ten minutes," mutters a sleepy voice at my side and I turn over in surprise to see John beside me. Usually, when I wake up in the morning, it's Johnny who's there, having come through to us in the middle of the night. When he does this, John takes his pillows and goes through to the children's room because we find it hard to sleep with three of us crammed into our double bed (British double beds aren't as big as American ones). When I get over my surprise, I set the alarm for 5.40 AM and we lie there, cuddled up, for an unexpected bonus of ten minutes, together in the warmth, before we have to get up.

Because of inconvenient train times, John has to leave the house just after 6.00 AM for an hour's train journey. When he reaches Dundee he has half an hour's climb up a very steep hill to the High School. He arrives there an hour early, but the next train would make him ten minutes late. We look forward to not setting the alarm clock at weekends, especially in the winter!

The alarm rings again, I switch it off and John and I go downstairs. I let the dogs out into the back garden, make John's breakfast and pack his lunch while he gets washed and dressed. After he's eaten, I wave him off to work, refill my hot water bottle and go back to bed. At first, I used to stay up and work about the house until the children woke up, but I found I was falling asleep halfway through the morning, which was no use to anyone, so now I don't even try. The trouble is, I'm reasonably awake by now so I usually just lie and think about all the things I have to do.

At 7.00 AM I switch on my bedside light and pick up my book. I'll read until 7.30 AM and then get up. At 8.00 AM I'm still reading! I'm enjoying my book so much and my hot water bottle feels so good . . . . Then I hear voices from the children's room. Johnny and Jenny are awake and talking to each other. They both come through and we all cuddle up together in bed. I tell them that I had meant to get up half an hour ago, but I'm enjoying my book so much that I couldn't stop reading. I tell them that it's a children's book about a girl who was evacuated to the United Stated during the War and how difficult she finds it to fit back in England when she returns home, and how she misses her American family and thinks of America as "back home." Jenny then becomes sad, thinking about the house we used to live in. I remind her that there are two good friends who live in the street where we now live. I also mention how close we are to the Laigh Hills (a large area of wild, common land behind our house.) We didn't take the decision to move here without consulting the children and they were thrilled with the move, but Jenny sometimes becomes sentimental over times past.

The dogs start barking so I rush downstairs to see what's happening. It's only the bin-men (trash men) putting our week's supply of black polyethylene bags through the letter box. At least it's got me out of bed!

Then, having dressed, I go back upstairs and get Jenny's clean clothes out for her. While the children are getting dressed, I phone in an order to Dorling Kindersley. While I'm on the phone, I notice some cat sick on the sitting room floor so as soon as the call is over, I clean up the sick and disinfect the floor. Then I start to make bread and put it to rise, prepare breakfast and feed the animals. By the time my porridge is ready, Johnny and Jenny have finished their breakfast. Johnny is sitting by the fire reading *Winnie the Pooh* and Jenny is playing with her press-and-peel Victorian kitchen, making up a story about the people in it. They both chat to me about what they're doing while I eat my porridge. Then, having finished his chapter, Johnny joins Jenny at the table and they both act out a story with the Victorian kitchen people.

I put the bread in the oven. The children continue to play while I tidy up, wash dishes and sweep floors. As soon as the bread comes out of the oven, we get on our coats and welly boots (galoshes) and take the dogs for a walk in the Laigh Hills. It begins to rain, so we put up our hoods and splash on through the puddles. We admire the colours of the moss and lichen on the dry stane dyke (dry stone wall) running beside us. I remind them how dry stane dykes are made

Johnny (9), Jenny (5)

and tell them that they could be built far out in the countryside from stones that were lying in the fields, without having to transport cement, water or sand to where you were building. Surprisingly, I haven't really thought this out before, but I often find that, when I'm telling the children about something, or when they ask about something, it all seems to fall into place in my mind and I think, "Now why didn't I think of it that way before?"

Jenny is playing a "Celtic" game (there is believed to have been a Celtic hillfort in the Laigh Hills about 2,000 years ago and we "did" the Celts for history last year). She's telling a story about them as she walks and deliberately puts in anachronisms like plastic and cement and bus stops. Then she says, "Ah! That gives the game away!" I tell the children that these are called anachronisms and explain what the word literally means. Soon after, Jenny skips by me and I hear her laughingly muttering, "All those achromisms!"

As we squelch through thick mud on the way back to the house, we discuss what the climate would be like in a country where they built mud huts to live in. We talk about using the most available material: snow in the far north, wood in Scandinavia, etc. We realise that this is the same principle as building dry stane dykes.

When we arrive home, we all have some warm bread and fruit spread and I read a *Milly Molly Mandy* story. Then Jenny does some sums from her maths workbook. It involves filling in the missing numbers in sums where a dog's dirty paw has supposedly obliterated them. Having two dogs who very often have *very* dirty paws, she thinks this is highly amusing and works at them happily. Meantime, Johnny and I look up more "chrono-" words and see how they all have something to do with time, because it comes from the Greek word "khronos" which translates into English as "time."

Johnny then does his maths for today on the computer with a maths game. It involves mental addition, subtraction, multiplication, division, and averages. He asks me what median is. I tell him, but ask him to look it up in the dictionary, in case I'm wrong. I'm right!

Jenny has finished her maths and we go over to the couch and sit cuddled up together while we read a page from her reading book. She then plays with her peg doll and toy castle and listens with half an ear while Johnny and I read about Roman roads (the Romans were around these parts, too!) We then watch a schools television programme I taped some time ago, about the Romans. Johnny then consults some books and writes about Roman roads for his history project book.

While he's doing this, I go and heat up the soup I made yesterday and Jenny writes out my shopping list for me. She uses sound writing with which she is *very* confident, but which is not always decipherable to the uninitiated, especially when she often pronounces words in a way which is all her own. Her shopping list reads:

Miock (milk—soya, of course)
Leflits (leaflets—about the growth rate of children. We're doing a
    project about our bodies and the health visitor said she would leave

Johnny (9), Jenny (5)

some leaflets for us at the doctor's surgery)
Porjots (porridge oats)
Larbry (library)

We all sit down for lunch and have our fairly common battle about whether they want to eat the soup or not. As a special favour to me (!) Johnny eats all of his. Jenny touches her spoon to her mouth and says she doesn't like it. She eats some bread. I tell the children about an article I was reading while waiting for the soup to heat up. (I have to admit to snatching every possible opportunity to read!) The article was about Shakespeare's plays and the fact that all the parts, in Shakespeare's time, were played by men and boys. We already knew that, of course, but I tell them that this article said that there were two particularly good boy actors at the time—one tall and fair, the other smaller and dark, so Shakespeare often wrote parts suitable for them. I also remind the children that in Shakespeare's plays, quite often the "girls" dressed up as young men, as that made it easier for the boys to act naturally. Johnny says, "That's the opposite of *The Marriage of Figaro*, isn't it?" (where the young page, Cherubino, is acted/sung by a soprano and, during the course of the opera, dresses as a woman).

As a family, we became interested in opera only a couple of years ago, when we all watched a TV programme called *Harry Enfield's Guide to Opera*. I would read the subtitles out to Jenny and I also explained to them both what was happening. They loved it and have taken great pleasure, ever since, in listening to opera. One day when we were in the library, Jenny (then aged four) recognised a picture on a CD as similar to a scene from the TV programme. "Look, Mummy!" she called out in her little piping voice. "*The Drinking Song from La Traviata!*"

After lunch, the sound of rain lashing against the window and the wind howling down the chimney makes us decide to at least postpone our visit down the town. Jenny and I mix up some salt dough and I teach her to knead. I tell her she can make some rolls, someday soon. She's thrilled. We take the salt dough upstairs to our classroom/playroom and we all sit together and do some salt dough modeling. Johnny goes off after a while and does his "silent reading," while Jenny and I continue for a while.

The weather has calmed down a lot, so I put our creations in the oven (very low) and we get ready to go out (a lot later than intended). We decide just to go to the library, but by the time we get there it's after 3.30 PM and the schools are out. It is very busy and noisy and I make a mental note to try to get there during school hours in the future. Johnny, as usual, is quite happy to sit and look at the younger children's books while I pick out some books for him, and ask him what he thinks. I hear Jenny introducing herself to a little girl who is sitting at a table, colouring in a picture with felt pens. Soon Jenny is colouring in too. Felt pens are a bit of a treat for her as we don't use them at home because they are not biodegradable. The children agree with the principle, but Jenny enjoys using them when she gets the chance!

When we arrive home, the children go upstairs to their room to play.

Johnny (9), Jenny (5)

They often spend hours acting out stories together. I prepare dinner and tape the football news from the radio for John, who's a keen football (soccer) fan. He arrives home at 5.45 PM to a chorus of excited barks from the dogs. He comes through to the kitchen and is just about to kiss me "hello" when the children erupt into the room, screaming "Daddy! ! !" at the tops of their voices. Soon we are all joining in a big, family cuddle.

We sit down to dinner together (this meal of chickpeas in tomato sauce on brown rice, followed by fruit salad, meets with the children's approval so they eat heartily) and talk about what we've been doing today. The children love to hear about all the funny things John has said to his pupils. Johnny tells John that he was telling my parents the other day about a cartoon that featured a Yankee dog who finds himself in the verandah of a "Southern Gentleman's" house and how my father had asked him if he knew anything about the American Civil War. Johnny had said, "Yes. Mummy told me." We talk some more about the American Civil War. Jenny tells us that she hates hearing about people dying, and we talk about the horror of war and how it affects families.

After tea, John and I watch the Scottish news on television while the children sit at the table and draw. Then we settle down for our bedtime story. At the moment it's *The Foxbusters* by Dick King-Smith, a favourite author of ours. The chapter begins by describing an early morning scene, and I notice that Johnny is humming, quietly. I'm getting a bit tired and ratty by now, so I snap, "Are you listening to this story or do you just want to sing?" Johnny looks aggrieved and says, "But that's what they always have for the background music when it's a daybreak scene." He hums it for us again. I forget my bad temper. Johnny actually has a beautiful voice and has always had perfect pitch, even when he was tiny. "You're right!" I exclaim. "Now, what *is* that? Is it from *The Planets*?" "No, it's Tchaikovsky, isn't it?" asks John. We look at Johnny. "*Dawn*, William Tell," he informs us. I then read the chapter, and we discuss it as I go.

The children then have a shower/bath, brush their teeth, and go up to their room to play/read in bed. We used to try to get them to sleep earlier, but they were never ready, and I would spend half of my precious evening lying beside Jenny, trying to get her to settle down. Now we let them sleep when they're ready, on condition that they spend the time upstairs. I must have *some* time without children around. I tell them that I'm going out to a school tomorrow to sell books and so my parents will be looking after them. I tell them that it's the Episcopalian School in Dunblane. Johnny asks me what "Episcopalian" means. I ask him if he remembers Henry VIII. "The one with all the wives?" he asks. I tell him about Catherine of Aragon and go on to say that Henry wanted a divorce so that he could marry Anne Boleyn, but that the Pope wouldn't give him permission to divorce her, so Henry decided that *he* would be the head of the Church—and the Episcopalian Church was born! Johnny wants to hear about all the other wives, too. While I'm telling him, Jenny calls over to tell me what she's playing with. As soon as she stops, "Go on!" says Johnny urgently. I go on. Once his thirst for historical information is satisfied, for the time being,

Johnny (9), Jenny (5)

I go downstairs and John and I chat together and read. We don't do the dinner dishes. I'll do them in the morning. This is our time for relaxing.

At 10.00 AM we start to get ready for bed. We see to the animals, lock up, get washed, etc. I take longer than John, and when I go up, he's in bed and almost asleep. I go in to the children to kiss them "goodnight" and settle them down to sleep. Jenny likes me to lie beside her and sing lullabies before I go over to Johnny and lie beside him for a wee while. Tonight, however, they're in the middle of a story that Johnny's making up and telling Jenny. I tell them that it's time they went to sleep, as Daddy and I will soon be asleep. They say that they'll "put themselves down to sleep" as soon as the story's finished.

I climb into bed, kiss John "goodnight," set the alarm for 5.30 AM, turn off my bedside light and settle down to sleep. The last thing I hear from the children's room is Johnny singing lullabies to Jenny.

Not all our days follow this pattern. Some days we do much more formal work, some days we do none at all. Some days the children watch a lot of television, some days when the weather's nice, we take a picnic lunch and spend most of the day on the Laigh Hills with the dogs, paddling in the burns and acting out stories (a lot of our history lessons about Celtic people happened this way). Some days we have friends visiting. But always we delight in the fact that we can choose how to spend our days. One recent morning I was sitting by the fire, cuddling Jenny on my lap. I happened to look at the clock and noticed that it was 9.50 AM and I thought how if Jenny went to school (in Scotland children start in the August nearest their fifth birthday) she would be sitting, not on my knee, but at a desk, with thirty other children and someone who wasn't her Mummy. I know what we both preferred!

When it snows a lot, we take our sledge out and enjoy the snow. My parents visit often. They wouldn't be able to see nearly so much of the children if they were only available outside school hours.

About record keeping in Scotland: we don't have to have permission to home educate. It is the parents' responsibility to make sure that their child(ren) get(s) an education, "either at school or otherwise." We're doing it otherwise! When we took Johnny out of school, we were visited once but then we moved to another region and that was that! No more visits! I feel *very* lucky when I read what some of you in the U.S.A. have to deal with. Usually I keep records for our own benefit. I have a looseleaf book with subject dividers. Firstly, I list all the books and other resources we use for that particular subject. Then I list any associated activities. Finally, I have a heading, "Impromptu discussions and activities" and here I report anything interesting that we've discussed "out of the blue" or any interest that just came up and we followed it through. There's always LOTS under this heading!

My entries for "Impromptu discussions and activities" for today were:
English:
    Discussed book I was reading, *Back Home* by Michelle Majorian.
        Outlined plot to children and discussed with them the different
        picture painted of boarding schools in this book,

Johnny (9), Jenny (5)

compared with "boarding school" books I read as a child. Discussed play on words in the title.

Jenny making up "Celtic" stories and deliberately putting in anachronisms. Told them the word "anachronism" and what it literally means. Later, Johnny looked up various "chrono-" words in the dictionary: chronometer, chronological, etc. and we discussed their root.

Johnny looked up "median" in the dictionary, to confirm my definition of it.

Told children about an article I read about young boys taking the part of females in Shakespeare's plays. Told them that there were two boys, one tall and fair, the other small and dark, who were very good actors and for whom Shakespeare often wrote parts. Johnny said that this was the opposite of the situation in *The Marriage of Figaro* (Cherubino).

Environmental Studies:

Told children about evacuees during the Second World War.

Discussed dry stane dykes and why they were a good way of building walls in the country.

Discussed how homes in different parts of the world are built using suitable and readily available materials.

Discussed the American Civil War, its causes and effects.

Discussed war, in general.

Discussed the origins of the Episcopalian Church. Talked about Henry VIII and his wives; the dissolution of the monasteries.

Discussed the part of Cherubino in *The Marriage of Figaro* being acted/sung by a soprano.

Johnny hummed several bars from *Dawn*, from William Tell. Identified it as music that was often used as a background for scenes taking place in the early morning and told us where it came from.

The other things that the children did, like maths workbook, maths computer program, reading book, reading and writing about the Romans are not entered individually each time. They are covered under the main headings for Maths, History, etc., where I list projects undertaken, books used, other resources, etc. This way I don't have to labouriously write in each time, e.g. page ** of maths workbook; read pages ** to ** of *The Romans in Britain,* and so on. If anyone does ever check what we've been doing, s/he will be shown the books themselves, in their entirety, so individual pages don't need to be logged. Also, this helps to disguise the fact that some days we do no formal (or informal!) work at all! I don't date my entries in the log, just list them under school terms. During the day, I jot down headings to remind me of what we've done, e.g. *Back Home*. Dry stane dykes. Mud huts. Anachronisms. Then, when I get the chance, I write up the activity/discussion in full.

How is our home educating accepted? Well, our families are very supportive. My mother reckons that her (only) two grandchildren are far too

Johnny (9), Jenny (5)

clever for school anyway! Our friends are also very supportive. Several of them say that they wish that they could keep their children at home, but can't for various reasons: single parents having to go out to work, clash of temperament with child(ren), that sort of thing. They often tell me horror stories about school, other children, teachers, methods, and so on. Others, who *don't* wish they could keep their children at home, think I'm very brave!

We have had some marked lack of support from a couple of people whose own children have gone through the school system and who seem to take it as a personal attack that our children are being taught at home. If it was good enough for *their* children, what makes *ours* so special? sort of attitude. Someone asked me recently if Johnny was still being taught at home. "Oh, yes!" I smiled. "Oh, dear!" she replied. But I have found people like that to be in the minority.

To the people we know now, it's an established fact that both children are educated at home. Interest and support sometimes comes from unexpected quarters, too. We used to meet regularly an old lady on a bus we took into Stirling. She commented, one day, in a friendly way, on the fact that the children weren't at school and I told her that I taught them at home. She was interested and said that she'd read an article in her Sunday paper about a boy who was educated at home. Next time we met her on the bus, she gave me the article which she'd cut out of the paper for me.

We're so glad that we've taken the decision to home educate. We don't know whether or not the children will want to go to secondary school. At the moment, they certainly have no intentions of going to school. At least, unlike most children, they have a choice.

Johnny (9), Jenny (5)

UPDATE:

I had mentioned Johnny going to the library and sitting looking at the younger children's books while I chose some books for him. I wanted him to be more interested in choosing his own books, but repeated urgings of, "Come on, darling, don't you want to choose some books for yourself?" had no effect. Then I hit on a plan! Johnny has kept a book of book reviews for some time now and he loves reading it over in his leisure moments (like when I've asked him if he'd like to review another book he's just read!) So far it had been in the form of questions and answers: Name, author, illustrator, publisher? What is the book about? Did you enjoy it? Why? What was your favourite bit? Now I suggested that his book reviews could be in narrative style. I told him the sort of thing I meant and he was keen on the idea. I wrote a check-list of points to be covered and we stuck it on the inside back cover of his jotter. This is the checklist: Where did the book come from? e.g. bookshop, library, jumble sale, charity shop, borrowed from friend. Who chose it? Why? Have we read other books by the same author? Did you enjoy them? Why? Was this book similar to or different from the author's other books? Would you like to read more books by the same author? What did you think of the illustrations? What was this book about? Did you enjoy it? Why? Do you know anyone else who has enjoyed this book and/or someone who would enjoy this book? After Johnny had written a few book reviews along these lines, I drew his attention to the fact that they all said, "Mummy chose this book because we like this author," or "Mummy's read it herself and enjoyed it," or "Mummy heard about the book and thought we'd like it," that sort of thing. "Wouldn't it be good if you could sometimes write, 'I chose this book because . . . .?'" I asked. He agreed! So, now when we go to the library he chooses his own books and has been really enjoying his choices.

Every evening now we have "booky time." I read the latest chapter of the bedtime story and then we all four settle down for about half an hour of silent reading together. Johnny reads books that he has chosen himself. I'm really pleased that it worked out so well.

Because of our constant financial difficulties (the down side of home education) we have had to take in a lodger, so our classroom/playroom is no more and lessons are now done in the sitting room. But the best thing to happen this year was that Jenny became a fluent reader! She now reads anything she can get her hands on and it gives her so much pleasure. (As I was writing this, I looked across at her and she was reading the summary on the first page of the novel I'm reading at the moment!)

Johnny (9), Jenny (5)

John and Pauline
Andrea, age 18
Jonathan, age 16
Emily, age 13
Susanna , age 5

Pauline wrote about this sunny day of February 9, when there was snow on the ground at their twelve acre home in rural Fleetwood, Pennsylvania.

TWELVE YEARS, ONE AT A TIME

We live in a rural area on twelve acres, with a creek, a marsh and woods where the children have had many afternoons of fun. Between us and the road there is a series of two-acre lots from which have come neighborhood friends. When our three older children were younger, our home seemed to be the center of activity, and in the evening and during vacations the neighborhood children often congregated at our place. As the neighbor children became teenagers, they seemed to go their own way, or moved away, and so for awhile the neighborhood was fairly quiet. Recently, however, children Susanna's age have been finding their way here, and it seems like we are reliving history by having children here most days after public school lets out. The neighbors for the most part are very accepting of our homeschooling and some of the children have even wished that I could teach them.

John works in the heating industry as a technician in the research and development laboratory. He is my support person in homeschooling, and I often "bounce" concerns, ideas, and questions off him. He actually was convinced about this whole homeschooling journey before I was. Since the children have reached the higher grades, he handles almost all their questions in the higher math and sciences. Last year when Andrea studied chemistry, he was her sole tutor. Since chemistry was his major in college, he loved getting into the material again.

We first heard of homeschooling on the *Focus on the Family* radio program where Dr. James Dobson was discussing homeschooling with Dr. Raymond Moore. After reading about it, we started homeschooling Andrea in first grade.

THURSDAY, FEBRUARY 9, sunny with snow on the ground:

Our household begins stirring when, between 5:00-5:30 AM, John rises to stoke the wood stove and prepares to leave for work. The hall light and the clanking of the metal grates in the stove begin to draw the rest of the family out of their deepest sleep. Normally, I rise at 6:00 AM but today when I open my eyes, it is 6:25 AM. Oops—a late start! I kiss John goodbye and wake Andrea and Jonathan right away (they also normally rise at 6:00). Each of us has the hour from 6-7:00 AM to dress, straighten our bedrooms, have our personal devotions, and memorize scripture.

In the kitchen, at 7:05 AM, I try quickly to write some correspondence before the children come down for breakfast.

Andrea and Jonathan show up at 7:15 AM and do "*double time.*" Andrea reads *World* magazine while eating, and Jonathan (between bites of breakfast) experiments chipping a rock Indian-style. He is doing research for a paper on Indian arrowhead making techniques. I suggest to him that he stand away from the table so that we do not end up eating the rock chips. When Jonathan gets "into" a project, he eats, sleeps, and drinks it!

By this time, Emily and Susanna have come for breakfast, with Susanna proudly announcing that she is dressed and her bed is made. The younger girls' wake-up time is a bit more flexible than the older two children.

Breakfast is self-help style. The table is set the night before and the children help themselves to homemade granola or rolled oats, bread for toasting, and fruit. After breakfast, but before 8:00 AM, chores must be done. Andrea cleans up breakfast, including washing and drying dishes; Jonathan burns the trash and gives the bathroom sink its daily shine; and Emily feeds and waters Brisa (the dog) as well as makes sure the porch is tidied up. Today she lingers by the cook stove with her book (*Ellie* by Mary Borntrager) before braving the cold outdoors. I'm reminded by my eager five-year old, "Mommy, it's 8:00!"

This year, for the first time in our twelve years of homeschooling we actually have a written time schedule. This schedule is mainly for *my* benefit, to avoid unending decisions as to "who comes next." It was always a source of tension for me when all the children clamored at the same time for help in their studies, each hoping to finish their schoolwork before lunch. Although they increasingly worked independently as they grew older, there were still subject areas where we worked together. A schedule has relieved most of this problem. The children each arrange their own school work around this schedule:

  8:00- 8:45 AM: Susanna
  8:45- 9:00 AM: Work break for Mother
  9:00-10:00 AM: Jonathan—geometry
10:00-10:15 AM: Work break for Mother

Andrea (18), Jonathan (16), Emily (13), Susanna (5)

10:15-11:00 AM: Emily—science and history
11:00-11:15 AM: Work break for Mother
11:15-11:30 AM: Andrea—Spanish
11:30-11:45 AM: Jonathan and Emily—Spanish
11:45-12:00 PM: Lunch preparation
12:00- 1:00 PM: Lunch and read aloud
 1:00- 2:00 PM: Andrea and Jon—literature and writing

Susanna gets my first hour of school time. Today we write a get well card for a sick friend. While she works on the card I get dishes out for making bread. The card takes the larger portion of our time and we finish by reading a chapter in a new book from our church library, *Walking with Jesus* by Meyer. I do not have a structured curriculum for Susanna's kindergarten year, but she is learning to read phonetically (A Beka *Little Books*) and is able to read short vowel words and simple sentences. She also enjoys reading an old Dick and Jane pre-primer, one of many books purchased at yard sales. Emily enjoys teaching Susanna simple math facts. We also use *Big Backyard* and *Weekly Reader* for a springboard into other subjects. Our trip to the public library is a highlight of Susanna's week.

Today, during the 8:00 AM hour, Andrea works in math (*Saxon Advanced Mathematics*), Jonathan writes out a list of sources for his ten-page research paper to mail to our writing instructor and practices the piano. Emily finishes feeding Brisa, gets her hair brushed, searches for a pencil (yes, homeschool children do lose pencils!) and begins her math (*Saxon Algebra 1/2*).

At 9:00 AM I call Jonathan for geometry (A Beka). After reviewing new concepts, he studies and takes a quiz while I start making bread. The days on which Jonathan takes a quiz or test allow me extra time for household chores, otherwise Jonathan and I work a solid hour through theorems and proofs (actually one of my favorite subjects).

During the 9:00 AM hour, Andrea finishes her math problems, begins anatomy (development of central nervous system and of the ventricles), and also studies for a history test on law and order. For her senior year she is studying American government (A Beka). Since she will be of voting age this year, this seemed like a good year to study government processes. Emily continues math, moves on to vocabulary (*Wordly Wise*, Educators Publishing Service) and then returns to the second set of ten math problems. We found that Emily did better in her math if she split her thirty math problems into three sets of ten each and interspersed other school work between the sets. This was the first year that we used *Wordly Wise* and also *Reading Comprehension* both from EPS, for Emily as well as Jonathan. Both children comment from time to time about words they find in the real world to which they have been exposed in their vocabulary lessons. Jonathan finds *Wordly Wise* more beneficial than other vocabulary books he has used in earlier grades.

Between geometry and Emily's time slot I walk the mail to the mailbox at the end of the lane. It is nice to get outdoors and clear my brain. Sometimes Susanna walks with me but today I go alone. Susanna generally occupies herself

Andrea (18), Jonathan (16), Emily (13), Susanna (5)

quite well during our "school routine." It is common to hear her humming, singing, or chattering to herself in imaginary play or as she "putters around." Today during geometry Susanna was taking restaurant orders and then served us all "tea." I try to take time when working with the older children to answer her questions or help her begin an activity. She especially enjoys the responsibility of real work. Some days there are little jobs I assign her that help me along with housework, such as hanging small items of laundry on the clothes rack to dry next to the cook stove, emptying wastebaskets, helping me with baking, etc. She most enjoys jobs she has never done before.

Today my 10:00-10:15 AM work break lasts longer than it should because I need to mix the yeast sponge (which by this time has risen much more than adequately) with the remaining bread ingredients and knead the dough. Also, Andrea and I have discussed how we would go about calculating her GPA in preparation for scholarship application. I have been fairly traditional in my grading, with a percentage score on tests, and then averaging for a final grade (A, B, etc.). For the grade point average I took her final grades of each subject for grades 9-12. In high school, I try to keep fairly good records for the children's high school transcript. I don't know how much credibility they hold for colleges, but we were asked to provide grades for Andrea's college application. We feel it is important for the children to learn how to take tests and study for tests, so we are pretty "traditional" in testing and grading.

It is 10:40 AM before I begin working with Emily and just as we begin, Susanna tells me that I will be really surprised to see what she did on the computer. Of course I want to see the surprise, so I take about thirty seconds to go look. She proudly displays a list of ten to fifteen simple words, which Emily had dictated to her to spell.

Actually, it is rather good that Emily and I are beginning late because, by this time, Jonathan has finished practicing the piano. He has scheduled one half hour of his practice time right after geometry and the sound level is rather high. Sometimes Emily and I retreat to an upstairs bedroom, but today we are at the kitchen table, where I usually work with the children. We generally read Emily's science and history together, and if we have time, her literature as well. Right now we are studying the earth's atmosphere, and World War I and II. As we are working together, Jonathan is studying old world history and Andrea is taking an American government test.

Today Andrea and I begin Spanish at 11:30 AM and work for fifteen minutes. When Andrea was in tenth grade we started at ground level with *Learnables I and II* and *Basic Structures I*. This year we are working our way through *Berlitz Self-Teacher Spanish* and will finish the year with *Basic Structures II*. *Basic Structures* gives the written text to vocabulary found in *Learnables I* and *II*. I personally found it helpful to see what I had been saying—but then I think I am a visual learner!

Just as the Spanish session ends there is a knock on the door and we welcome a surprise visit from Grandma. Jonathan and Emily's Spanish lesson is set aside for today and we invite Grandma to have lunch with us. We begin

Andrea (18), Jonathan (16), Emily (13), Susanna (5)

visiting while I get the bread dough rolled out and formed into loaves and the girls prepare lunch. There is always so much to tell Grandma and it is nice to get to share details about the many happenings of our days at home together. The children enjoy having another person take notice of their homeschool endeavors and listen to some of their activities. Today Grandma comes with a few treats—purchases for the children from a trip she and Grandpa had just taken.

Lunch time normally lasts till around 1:00 PM and ends with a read-aloud time. Right now I'm reading to the children *The Walk West* by Peter and Barbara Jenkins. I read while the children clear the lunch table, then I wash dishes. Today, though, we chat with Grandma.

The afternoons are more flexible than the mornings. I have combined Andrea and Jonathan's literature courses in the interest of promoting more discussions. Right now we are reading *Macbeth*. If Emily has not already read her daily literature assignment, she and I do it together at this time also. Throughout their school years, from elementary on up, I have chosen to use a literature anthology because it exposes the children to many types of writing and to subjects which they might not have chosen on their own. More than once the excerpt found in the anthology was the stimulus for them to search out the complete book.

Andrea and Jonathan spend one or two hours each afternoon working on their research paper. Andrea's paper is on the Oregon Trail. She has been interested in pioneering ever since the *Little House* books by Laura Ingalls Wilder, and more recently became absorbed in the Oregon Trail and its travelers. Jonathan has always, it seems, been interested in Indian arrowheads and artifacts, and in recent months has become increasingly curious about how the Indians actually chipped the arrowheads. Both children found wonderful resources for their papers at the university library about seven miles away.

Andrea and Jonathan have been fortunate to be able to participate in two writing courses by a homeschool father and pastor who is an excellent writer and communicator, and who also enjoys relating to young people. The big plus for these courses is that all the assignments, examples, lessons and corrections are sent through the mail, thus not necessitating travel time. He also was available to them on the phone. I think the best thing that happened in Andrea and Jonathan's writing was that they learned to write concisely. The way they write now sounds much better than before. This course was a definite plus to our curriculum.

Emily enjoys afternoons to read and work on creative projects. She enjoys science experiments and crafts and often comes up with original creations for her own pleasure or to share as gifts. She is also becoming skilled on the computer.

Besides these activities, towards the end of the week, one of the afternoon activities includes cleaning the house. None of us really enjoys this, but we all work together and in one or two hours the house is relatively dust free and pleasantly orderly. We work hard through the week to keep it tidy and generally we are fairly successful, but with five people living here all day, there

Andrea (18), Jonathan (16), Emily (13), Susanna (5)

are the inevitable items that must be returned to their proper storage places.

Today, as we are cleaning, I get a phone call that takes about twenty minutes, but the children, anxious to get finished, keep at their work and I rejoin them later. We get finished in time for Andrea's 3:00 PM flute lesson.

The children are looking forward to getting outdoors to sled in the snow. We have had very little this year so this is a special treat. I watch them from the kitchen window as I prepare supper for tonight, trying a new recipe. I do not do "once-a-month" cooking, but I do plan a month's menus at one time. It saves a great deal of thought each day about what to cook for the evening meal. Sometimes I switch one night's menu for another, but there are enough meals planned for the entire month, and I can shop in bulk or take advantage of specials. The family enjoys trying new recipes, and it keeps me on my toes in preparing better quality meals, rather than the "quickie" meals that are chosen at the last minute and squeezed into the end of a busy day.

John arrives home at 4:30 PM and it is nice to have him nearby again. The evening meal together offers us time to talk and swap stories of the day's activities. If the children have had questions from school work that they want to ask John, these topics are often discussed at the table. This evening after the meal John helps Andrea with algebra problems.

During the evening each of us pursues various activities of his or her own choosing. Evenings, when the entire family is at home, we often have another read-aloud time; John reads from the Bible, and we pray together before going to bed.

Susanna does not generally have a nap anymore, so she is tuckered out by 6:45-7:00 PM, and I like her to be in bed by 7:30. After she is cleaned up and dressed for bed, I read to her for about fifteen minutes. Then she is tucked in. At bedtime the older children often linger in each other's bedrooms talking, seemingly hesitant to end the day, and I'll have to remind them to get to bed. They like to read a bit before sleeping, but their lights are usually out by around 9:30 PM.

My last job today is packing John's lunch for tomorrow and setting the table for breakfast. Then it is off to bed, where John and I read a book or favorite magazine. As my eyes are closing, I take a few minutes to think back on how we have taken one year at a time. We've thought about the future, but didn't try to plan out every little detail. It is extremely rewarding to see our first child graduate this year—and it blesses our hearts to see our children mature and become responsible, trustworthy young adults. We truly are beginning to reap the benefits of all the years of training, teaching, and nurturing. We give thanks to God for His grace to our family through these "just twelve years"

A NOTE FROM ANDREA:

As I helped record the events of this day in our home, I was amazed at how much activity there was. The minute-by-minute account I kept totaled more than eight pages!

Two unusual occurrences of the day were the visitors we had and a lack

Andrea (18), Jonathan (16), Emily (13), Susanna (5)

of phone calls.

Personally, I enjoyed the day a lot (as I do most days), but decided it is easier simply to live the day than to record the events as they happen!

Feb 6-10

	Monday	Tuesday	Wednesday
ANDREA Math	Lesson 38 1-13 Accured by Bulletin	The Color of els Exhib Enable... House p. 351-354	Lesson 39 1-15 Factorable Trig Equations
History	p. 343-350, United States Army	p. 343-350 on Tone Li Sammy	p. 351-354 p 355-61 Navy, Marine Air force Coast Guard
Science	Plate 113 Anatomy of a Synapse	Plate 114-115 Reversed Reflex area Reflex Ending	Plate 116-117 Nervous System Organization Development of CNS
Spanish	p. 179-180 Lesson 28	Lesson 28 Questions 1-10	Lesson 28 Question 11-20 Lesson 39 p. 183-184
Computers	Creative writing a word computer		Begin Work on research paper
Jonathan Andrea & Jonathan Literature	MacBeth Act II Scene II	MacBeth Act II Scene III	MacBeth Act II Scene IV
Geometry	3.10 Common Tangents Ex. 7-10 3.11 Intersecting Circles	Ex. 3.11 #2 3.12 Concentric Circles #1-7	3.13 Measurements of Args in a circle 7 # 8-13
History	Answer 7-27	ANSWER QUESTIONS	ANSWER QUESTIONS 1-12
Science	Answer questions 1-6	STUDY for Quiz ANSWER QUESTIONS 1-10	STUDY 88% QUIZ 116-120
Vocabulary	Word List 17 Ex. 17A	Ex. 17B	Ex. 17C
Reading Comprehension	Selection 18	"Symbolic Logic"	
Jonathan & Emily Spanish	—	Leccion 7 Ejercicios 6-11	Leccion 7 Ejercicios 12-15
EMILY Literature	p. 364-374 Narcissa Whitman ✓	p. 375-377 Narcissa Whitman ✓	p. 380-384 Child Pioneer ✓
Grammar	Pronouns p. 100 ✓	Pronoun Subjects ✓ p. 101	Pronoun Subjects ✓ p. 102
Math	Lesson 79 Formats of Equations ✓	Lesson 80 TEST Algebraic phrases ✓	Lesson 81 Trichotomy ✓
History	Study	Study	TEST ✓
Science	—		
Vocabulary	Crossword Puzzle p. 95	Crossword Puzzle ✓ p. 95	Word List 16 Ex. 16A ✓
Reading Comprehension	Selection 21	"An interesting	Language"
...	Draw Cross section	Draw ... endings	Characters ✓

Andrea (18), Jonathan (16), Emily (13), Susanna (5)

UPDATE:
      This year has been considerably different since Andrea has gone to college. The maturing process continues as the children who are still at home have assumed greater responsibilities. Andrea has completed her first semester, and, with satisfaction, we see that homeschooling excellently prepares students for college.

Andrea (18), Jonathan (16), Emily (13), Susanna (5)

Brendan and Sharon
Katy, age 12
Colleen, age 7
Ethan, age 5
Eamon, age 1

Brendan described this cloudy and cool April 26 day from their bedroom community that is surrounded by farmland in Papillion, Nebraska.

TEACHER DIDN'T SHAVE TODAY!

When I first wondered whether I would be interested in writing this chapter, it was an enthusiastic "Yes!" But my enthusiasm dimmed and my thoughts changed to such things as, "Do I really want people to know that my wife, Sharon, had to drag me kicking and screaming (almost literally) into homeschooling?" "Do I want people to know that I sometimes (frequently) wonder how I am doing and how the kids are doing?" "Do I really think anyone cares what I, a stay-at-home father, really do with my kids?" The answers to all of these was a simple "yes." I am now an enthusiastic supporter of homeschooling and believe that this is a growing national need.

Our oldest child, now twelve years old, is Kathleen, a.k.a. Katy or Katy Rose—unless she is in trouble, then it is very definitely Kathleen. (This doesn't happen very often, but it does happen.) Sharon adopted Katy from Bogota, Colombia. I was asked to help translate some documents into Spanish for her and to help Sharon make some calls to Colombia during the long wait to adopt Katy. After Katy arrived at the Air Force Base where Sharon and I were assigned, I sort of hung around a lot—babysitting, reading to Katy, speaking Spanish, and trying to teach Sharon a little bit of Spanish. All in all, I had a great time being an "uncle." I continued to avoid Sharon, who out-ranked me at the time, except if it meant babysitting or spending time with Katy. Of course, this all changed when Sharon proposed that January. I accepted her proposal and we got married.

We were married the next May, with Katy as the flower-girl, ring-bearer and unofficial entertainment provider. She did a great job and had a fun time skipping down the aisle afterwards. Our family grew two years later when Colleen Bridget was born. She is now a seven-year-old with big dimples.

We moved to Montana to work in a group home. And our family grew again two years later, when Ethan David was born. By the way, if anybody knows the final score of the New York Yankees game against the Kansas City Royals on July 4, 1990, I would appreciate knowing. Ethan made his appearance right in the middle of the game and I still don't know who won. (Kids have incredible timing, don't they!) Ethan is now an energetic four-year-old.

I quit working full-time outside of the home a few months after Ethan's birth, after my wife had been hired by the Air National Guard to be a plans officer and a navigator on air refueling tankers. I had spent the six months before I quit working as a Bilingual Child Protection Investigator for the Department of Children and Family Services. When I quit working, we had Katy Rose in a very good Catholic school and the two others, Colleen and Ethan, at home. My days were spent chasing Colleen around the house, toting Ethan around on my back, doing household chores, planting a garden and generally enjoying life. I thoroughly enjoyed the freedom (more or less) of being at home, although I hardly considered myself unemployed. Even with the two children at home I had time to do things I enjoyed: I indulged in my love of cooking, tried (failed) to write a book about being a stay-at-home parent, took some courses towards a master's degree, and read a lot of history (especially church), biography, and fiction.

I also stayed busy as an Air Force Reserve officer. I was assigned to an Air Lift Group until last year. I am now in a different position with an active duty unit. Because I was an intelligence officer, I kept busy learning the job and helping to write briefings. I had been an active duty officer for six years, but only briefly had I been an intelligence officer. All in all, being in the Reserve part time was a nice break from working outside the home all of the time and something I enjoyed.

Sharon came up with the idea of homeschooling after talking with a Reservist friend of ours. I did not want to because I had the same doubts as so many others do: I can't teach my kids; they need social interaction; the Catholic school Katy is in is outstanding; I enjoy having the kids at home, but I enjoy the break I get having Katy Rose gone part of the day, especially the quiet when Ethan and Colleen are napping. So, there are a lot of issues to resolve.

I was finally convinced that homeschooling would be a good idea, so we then tackled the next set of doubts: What program should we use? How should we schedule the day? What about Ethan and Colleen? What type of support will I need/want and what will be available? Will I get any time for myself?

Sharon, in a methodical manner, went out and started buying books. First she bought Mary Pride's *The Big Book of Home Learning*. She had the

Katy (12), Colleen (7), Ethan (5), Eamon (1)

responsibility to review the books and narrow the choice of programs down to a manageable two or three. Obviously, I was willing to homeschool, but I was still not an enthusiastic supporter of the idea.

Sharon narrowed the curriculum selections to Seton Hall, Covenant Home, and Calvert. And she talked me into going to a conference sponsored by Seton Hall. She also talked me into visiting the Covenant Home bookstore. And she ordered information from Calvert. (She is very thorough when she decides to really do something!)

Finally, we settled on Covenant Home. I liked the ideas of a Christian homeschool program and of having outside grading and help, but only for the few occasions when my children might be mildly recalcitrant.

Once all of the decisions were made, it came time to start the work. Katy is a very easy-going child and seemed to enjoy the attention she received during the first year. I, on the other hand, continued to be full of doubts and was not comfortable that first year at all. Katy was in fourth grade then and worked hard. Katy is a bright child who wants to learn, but she is an aural learner. She does best when she reads material out loud or has it read to her. This became especially obvious when she had to do her reading comprehension work. When she read it silently her scores went down, when she read it aloud two or three times her grades went up.

Katy continued in some of her activities outside our home, including 4-H, the Children's Choir and, of course, church. She also managed to see several of her friends from the Catholic school she had been in, so socialization was hardly a problem—except for *me*.

We also started Colleen slowly on Covenant Home's kindergarten work during that first year. She was another big part of the reason I agreed to home school. I worried that the schools would not be able to educate her as well as she deserved. On the other hand, she is very bright and wants to learn. We were able to create a routine of fifteen minutes work, with a ten or fifteen minute break before returning to work, which fit her learning style. We continue this routine to this day, although with shorter breaks and twenty minute or longer work periods.

Our school year was interrupted in December when I became involved in Operation Restore Hope and was sent to Africa for two months. Fortunately, our babysitter kept Katy on track very well and Katy was just a few lessons behind by the time I returned months later. By the time I left, once again, for Somalia, she was almost completely finished with all of her fourth grade school work and we were ready to go on to fifth grade once I returned.

That summer proved to be a very busy summer for the entire family. First, I was in Mogadishu from June through September. The United States was providing support to United Nations' forces bringing food and some order to the country, but we were not universally accepted. Although the job I was doing was easy, the frequent attacks at night were difficult, not just for the people there but for the people at home who watched the nightly news. I tried to call home after the attacks to let everybody know I was okay, but that was not always possible.

Katy (12), Colleen (7), Ethan (5), Eamon (1)

Second, Sharon had decided that she was going to go back to school to get her degree as a Physician Assistant. This meant moving.

Oh, did I mention that Sharon told me the day before I left that she was pregnant? This fact didn't sink in until I arrived in Germany, called her at work, and asked her if she had said something about being pregnant. So Sharon did all of the moving and house hunting and looking for the babysitter and all of the other stuff associated with moving, while suffering from morning sickness.

Eamon Grant was born that March. We hope to adopt some more children after Sharon has settled in with her new career. After all, Sharon wants twelve children—there's something to be said for working outside the home!

Needless to say, our school year started late. Once I returned, I still had to get things organized around the house and find the homeschool materials so we could get Katy started on fifth grade and Colleen working further along on kindergarten. One of the most important things we had to decide on was a church. There are a lot of churches in the area, but we wanted a small congregation where we would not feel lost among the multitudes.

Katy finally got started on fifth grade work in late September and Colleen continued kindergarten in early October. Both girls used the Covenant Home program. This late start put the girls behind the curve, as far as I was concerned, and meant that they had to work hard to catch up.

Colleen, meanwhile, zipped through her work quickly and was ready for more, so we finished her scheduled work and got going on some extra work in preparation for the first grade. I also had Ethan to deal with who, although only two years old, wanted to participate, with his sisters. So we started him on learning the alphabet and how to count and several other things to get him ready for kindergarten.

Near the end of that school year Sharon and I decided that we would start the children on a different program the next year, so we decided to use the Calvert Home School program. Calvert, like many homeschool programs, has a reputation for being very good and having high academic standards, plus the ease of being accepted by all fifty states. This was a major concern for us because Sharon had been accepted to a Physician Assistant program and had earned a National Health Service Corps scholarship, which meant she could be sent anywhere in the country in her service to the NHS. So we ordered the complete Calvert program for Katy's sixth grade and Colleen's first grade, including the video materials and French for Katy.

Our one concern with Calvert, which is a great program and does teach values very well, was specific religious education. I decided that the best thing to do would be to use the Baltimore Catechism that I had grown up with, and supplement it with the Baltimore Catechism Bible Education program. Between these educational programs and Sunday school, we believe our children get the very good Christian education we want them to have.

This school year also started late as I once again went overseas, this time to Saudi Arabia. We got going in early October with Katy, following a week later with Colleen.

Katy (12), Colleen (7), Ethan (5), Eamon (1)

Colleen is working hard and completing her work fast. Keeping her on track is not a problem, unless Eamon has a stinky diaper or Ethan has decided to join in the fun of learning. Ethan is eager to learn, so he sits in on many of Colleen's lessons, although I have him do other things while Colleen is doing workbook problems.

This, in short, is the history of the Morning Star Homeschool.

As to a normal school day—we really do have a few, maybe once in a while . . . at least twice each year. With Sharon in school, our normal school days start very early. Sharon usually is gone by 8:15 AM, but she gets Eamon up, cuddles him for a little while and dresses him. Katy is usually up at about 6:30 AM so she can get an early start to her day, which includes walking the dog—her big responsibility every morning. Katy also has to empty the dishwasher and make sure the kitchen and counters are neat and the table ready for school work. The latter is a problem because I let Ethan and Colleen sleep late (they are both night-owls, as are Sharon and I) and the cats generally do not drag them out of bed until 8:30 AM.

For our day, which was April 26, I decided to keep a detailed log, rather than the abbreviated calendar and personal diary I normally use to keep track of things. A lot of people keep logs of the daily activities, but I prefer just to make notes in my calendar, then update my diary. I update the diary once or twice each day, depending on how much time I have. So here goes:

6:00 AM:

Sharon has to leave early today for her clinical consultations and training, so she is up and ready to go.

6:30 AM:

Katy's alarm is sounding loud and clear from her room in the basement, and a few minutes later I hear her in the bathroom across the hall from my bedroom.

7:00 AM:

Sharon leaves and Eamon wails. I really hate early mornings, but get out of bed to warm a bottle for him. While he drains the first of many, I shower (I decided to be a bum and not shave).

7:15 AM:

Katy is back home and emptying the dishwasher while I get Eamon out of his crib and change and dress him. Fortunately, the coffee is ready and I pour a strong cup of Ethiopian coffee.

7:30 AM:

Katy continues her chores and I start reading the newspaper while holding Eamon. He enjoys his early morning cuddles, but his constant, "Ma ma

Katy (12), Colleen (7), Ethan (5), Eamon (1)

ma ma ma," tells me that he prefers Sharon's cuddles at this time of day.

7:45 AM:

Katy and Eamon are both eating. Katy feeds herself while Eamon and I share a bowl of oatmeal and baby food (great stuff, especially if it's apricots).

8:00 AM:

Sorry, Eamon, it's time to get Katy started on her school work. First I put you down to scream for a few minutes until you notice the cat, then you go off and chase poor Rusty. A few minutes of reading from *The Diary of Anne Frank* and a selection from Bill Bennett's *Book of Virtues,* then Katy gets her spelling and we start the day with the ten words in the lesson. None wrong, so you can go on to math.

8:20 AM:

Math. Katy has to finish the lesson she started the day before. We spend a few minutes reviewing how to add fractions with different denominators. Then Katy has to finish the problems for the lesson. She finished about half of the work in forty-five minutes, so she only has eleven problems to work on. Eamon is cheerfully chasing the cats, who have smartly jumped up onto the couch, out of his reach.

8:45 AM:

We have just finished grading Katy's math, only one problem wrong, so that's a great day. Time to get her going on reading. She reads the story out loud while I warm up another bottle for Eamon, who is now trashing the living room. Colleen and Ethan are waking up, I can hear their thumps through the wall between the kitchen and their room. Neither is a morning person, so I better go head off the grumps before they get going at each other.

9:00 AM:

Katy has finished *Reading for Meaning*. I have asked her to change a diaper while I supervise Ethan and Colleen doing their checklists. Chores are a very important part of the day in our house. Each of the children has a checklist, which isn't a problem with Katy as she can read. Colleen and Ethan, though, still don't read very well so we have had to compromise on checklists. I typed the chores required (brush teeth, make bed, check laundry, feed cats), while Sharon drew some pictures to match the chores. They all have some morning chores to finish before breakfast. Today Ethan forgets to brush his teeth, he eats the toothpaste instead, so I have to help him brush them. Colleen says she doesn't have any underwear, but I have just finished about six loads of laundry and did not see any. The search is on while I get a new load of whites in the wash! Eamon starts crying while I am downstairs. Too bad, kid. I don't want your sister to walk around in dirty clothes all day. (Although that might be a good lesson in being careful when she changes at night.)

Katy (12), Colleen (7), Ethan (5), Eamon (1)

9:30 AM:

Colleen and Ethan are ready for breakfast; yogurt, vitamins and cranberry juice today. Eamon toddles around and Katy is back reading—this time some chapters in *Theras and his Town*. Everything as smooth as a country road.

9:45 AM:

Ethan wants to practice his letters so he gets some attention before Colleen. Meanwhile, Colleen has to pick up the disaster zone, better known as our play room. Why do children always get out every toy and game in the closet instead of the one or two they are using at any given time? Eamon is sitting on my lap while I say a word and Ethan tells me what letter it starts with. He's getting pretty good at this, especially when he can see the word by using his "letter-case." This is a great game that looks like a briefcase in which someone has sewn all the letters of the alphabet and put objects into the small pouch that has each letter.

10:00 AM:

A break for me! I am a news-a-holic, so I turn on *CNN* to watch the latest. Normally this is when the daily destruction of the playroom begins. Katy likes to go down to her bedroom and listen to one of her tapes. I restrict radio listening because I do not like what is played on most radio stations. I do listen to a couple of stations that play classical and jazz, while Sharon enjoys country, so Katy listens to them with us.

10:15 AM:

Back to work. Eamon and Ethan are actually playing quietly (more or less) in the living room, so it's Colleen's turn for lessons. First, I have to get Katy started on drawing, then remind Colleen the rules for school: Sit still and pay attention; ask any questions about the lesson, but not about other things (like what is for lunch); sharpen your pencils before you sit down; and, put the pencil down when you aren't using it. Math is first.

10:45 AM:

I wash Eamon's hands and face. Colleen wants to do more math, but reading and other subjects come first. Katy is finished, so I get her going on composition. I work with her on neatness and handwriting.

11:15 AM:

Katy is working on science now and there is a cacophony of noises in our home. Katy and Colleen are at the kitchen table, both reading aloud, Ethan is in the back of the house playing with Eamon's toy piano (I really don't like the creative geniuses who came up with this noise-maker), while Eamon's stomach is growling and he is beginning to squawk. Oh boy, I forgot the laundry. Whites into the dryer.

Katy (12), Colleen (7), Ethan (5), Eamon (1)

11:30 AM:

Katy has finished her lessons for the day and has done very well! So she gets the privilege of feeding Eamon. Ethan has now joined Colleen and me on the couch as I read a story. Colleen has worked for about twenty-five minutes without getting distracted and fidgety, a new record.

12:00 Lunch:

I'm in a hurry, so it's Spaghetti-O's for the children. I'll just have some chunks of cheddar cheese with some mustard. Not a very healthy diet, but today seems busier than usual, mainly because I am tired from getting up earlier than usual.

12:30 PM:

Eamon has fallen asleep on the living room floor, so I gently carry him into his crib. The three older children are walking the dog—a few minutes to myself. It's a cloudy, cool day, but no rain, so the big three are gone for about thirty minutes. Peace and quiet. Some very pleasant classical music on a local public radio station and some time to read the magazines that arrived while I was gone earlier this month for the Reserve. (I assign the work straight from the lesson book and our babysitter is great about supervising and helping Katy if she needs help. If not for our great babysitters, past and present, I doubt that I would be able to continue in the Reserve as the school year would be much more disjointed than it already is.)

1:15 PM:

Ethan is in bed, Colleen is in the play room reading, and Katy and I are spending some time reviewing vocabulary for history and science. Next—more history review to see if she has actually learned the material or if she has just read it to say she is done.

1:45 PM:

I get a break almost every day, so I go lie down and read some fiction for a while. Colleen has fallen asleep, which does not surprise me because she had a long two weeks while I was gone and she always seems to take several days to catch up on her sleep after I get back. Ethan snores, but I have some jazz on and ignore him.

3:30 PM:

I fell asleep! Eamon, Ethan and Colleen are still asleep, so I have to get them up too. I wonder if they are fighting off the strep throat that Sharon has and, if so, if that is why they are so tired. Katy has continued to review the lessons I assigned her while I was gone, but she is ready for a break. I did not mean for her to spend all that time reviewing. Oops. Good girl, though, as she obviously has learned a lot of the material this time.

Katy (12), Colleen (7), Ethan (5), Eamon (1)

4:00 PM:

Ethan and Colleen are playing in the back room, Katy is feeding Eamon and I'm getting dinner ready. Colleen requested "naked spaghetti" so I am cooking spaghetti with garbanzos. (This is a variation of the "Spaghetti and Lentils" in *The Vegetarian Cookbook*.) The onions get chopped, garlic is crushed and the oil is heated. By the way, does anybody know when Sharon will be home tonight? *All Things Considered* is on public radio, so I am getting the news for the day while I cook. Of course, I can't hear much of it because there is a lot of noise from children playing or doing their "volunteers" or whatever. I am actually tuning the kids out for a little while because I need to get dinner done.

5:00 PM:

Katy has volunteered to bathe Eamon, so he is happily splashing away. Colleen and Ethan are fighting about who made the mess and who has to clean it up (they both *did* and they both *DO*). I am drinking some decaf coffee and listening to the news still. The mail came late, so I am actually ignoring the coffee and the news and reading a letter from a friend still assigned to Saudi Arabia (*wow*, he just got promoted).

5:25 PM:

Oh, Sharon will be home around 6:00 PM so she can take Colleen and Ethan to Daisies and Rainbows, respectively, at the church. It's time to feed the children and get Colleen and Ethan ready to go.

6:00 PM:

Sharon still isn't home (maybe she forgot it's Wednesday). Colleen is changing her clothes, which I have to stop her from doing because she tries to change three or four times each day. Ethan is still playing with his spaghetti and Eamon is . . . . Well, what can you expect of a thirteen month old chow- hound? He's a mess. Hey, I forgot the laundry again. I'll fold it later.

6:10 PM:

Sharon is finally home, which sets Eamon off. He wants to be picked up and carried around whenever she gets home. (Eamon is normally a very happy child and a lot of fun to be with, but having Sharon gone so much seems to throw his universe out of alignment and he demands attention until he thinks it is safe, once again.) Ethan is done, but needs to be hosed down. Colleen has put the clothes she had on earlier back on, but needs to be told to put the clean clothes away. Katy is loading the dishwasher.

6:30 PM:

Sharon has taken all of the children with her, so I have a couple of hours of peace and quiet. While Colleen and Ethan are at church, Sharon decides to take Katy and Eamon to the library. I am going to spend some time on the computer typing some work for Sharon—maybe I should go through the P.A.

Katy (12), Colleen (7), Ethan (5), Eamon (1)

program after Sharon is done?!

This day is a fairly normal one around here. Some of the things that are different than usual include Sharon's early departure, her early return and my nap. Sharon usually leaves at about 8:15 AM and gets home between 8:00 and 10:00 PM. I usually lie down, but seldom fall asleep. It turned out that Colleen, Ethan, Eamon and I were all fighting off strep throat, which probably made us so tired. For another thing, I don't usually forget the laundry. And, finally, the girls worked extra on this day, although I did not tell them that I was keeping a detailed log.

One other way this was not normal, and a very important factor: the children each get some time to use the computer most days—we have three. We have a lot of educational games that they can select from, and the rule is they must do something educational before playing any of the mindless games. Ethan, especially, loves the early learning games and is always asking for more computer time. Katy and Colleen like the educational games as well, but would rather play some of the mindless games that I have loaded on to the hard drive for them. (I don't set as good an example as I probably should, because I don't use my computer for much beyond our finances and typing things like this or the Psalms for church. The rest of my computer time is either spent scanning the Internet or playing games like *Scrabble*.)

We have a couple of different bedtime routines, depending upon Sharon. If she is staying late to study, I read to the children or play (Eamon loves having me sit on the floor so he can crawl all over me) or supervise showers and clean up with them until 8:00 PM, then put the three little ones to bed. Katy usually spends some time after dinner cleaning up the kitchen, then practicing her piano or choral music. Katy also has to walk the dog, so she generally gets little time from me after dinner.

If Sharon is home, she spends time reading, playing, supervising showers, or helping Katy and Colleen with science experiments. Sharon is very good at science, while I admit to being less than thrilled about the subject, so we try to time each experiment to a night when Sharon will be home and can help. On these nights the children are generally in bed by 8:30 or 9:00 PM, so Sharon hits the books and I usually collapse into my recliner and read. I subscribe to eleven magazines, including four cooking magazines, so I usually have a lot of reading to catch up on. If I am not reading, I spend some time on the computer or writing menus and a shopping list, or just being a couch potato (I usually have the news or CSPAN or a channel like A&E or The Learning Channel on, no matter what I am doing). Most nights I wind up doing some typing for Sharon or editing some work I have done earlier. Another thing I do most nights is watch *Star Trek*. Ethan and Colleen love watching this with me, although Colleen has to stay in bed on school nights. Ethan gets some cuddles and joins me in raiding the refrigerator, so this is a pleasant end to our evenings, even if I have seen all the episodes at least ten times.

Sharon and I seldom get much time together, at least during the week, but we do try. Most Friday nights we drop the children off at a babysitter

Katy (12), Colleen (7), Ethan (5), Eamon (1)

and then we just spend the time together. Having a medical student and a (mostly) unemployed daddy in the home means we don't have a lot of money to spend, but we have a few very inexpensive Vietnamese, Greek, and Mexican restaurants we enjoy going to. We also enjoy going to a local mall, getting some coffee, then just walking around. Some nights after we have just come home, Sharon has hit the books while I "surfed the Internet." (I like surfing and have found some interesting medical stuff for Sharon on various "gophers.")

Sharon and I have also had the babysitter keep the children for a weekend while we go away for a couple of days. And we use the excuse of my trips to the Air Force Base for her to fly there to meet me and we stay overnight, then return the next day. These breaks are very important to us because we see so little of each other most of the time. And next year will be worse, once Sharon starts her clinical rotations and has to travel to some of the sites she will be assigned to!

Finally, one of the drawbacks of being a stay-at-home homeschooling parent is that I sometimes feel I am constantly being a disciplinarian, with little or no time for fun with the children. So, to let the children know that I do know how to have fun and how to be a fun daddy, I try to take each of them out, alone, once in a while. During the winter I try to take them to a local mall to walk around or browse through the bookstore (and let them pick out a book) and then go to eat. Now that spring is here, and to satisfy my craving for some baseball, I get to take them to see either the Kansas City Royals' triple-A affiliate, the Omaha Royals, or to the College World Series. We have some baseball fans, besides myself, in the family, so this is a good and inexpensive way to have some special time with each of the children. I also try to take them to the children's museum or the zoo. I enjoy these outings, but I don't do enough of them with the children. (My New Years' resolutions included taking them out more often, but that was the same resolution I made each of the last two years.) To help me be more fun this year, Sharon bought me an early Father's Day present: a bicycle. I now ride with the older children, when weather permits, and I'll be taking Eamon along once Sharon (the family mechanic and wood-worker) fixes his trailer. (Believe it or not, I actually tried to put the trailer together myself, but hurt my elbow, so I asked Sharon to do it. That was over a month ago, but I'm not complaining too loudly. . . *yet!*)

One of the questions I frequently answer has to do with being a stay-at-home father. This is a very difficult question to answer because there are many factors at work here. I generally enjoy being at home with the children, but I look forward to my breaks from the children when I am gone for the Air Force Reserve, which generally requires that I go to the Air Force Base for a week or so every month or so. I would encourage any father who wants to stay at home to do so, but to keep some outside interests alive (this also applies to all mothers who decide to stay at home). Get involved in a computer group or find a community activity that you can volunteer to help with. Keeping an outside interest provides a challenge that goes beyond being at home. Teaching first or sixth grade is challenging, but is hardly a lot of intellectual/mental stimulation.

Katy (12), Colleen (7), Ethan (5), Eamon (1)

Keeping an outside interest provides lots of mental stimulation. Aside from being active as a Reservist, I belong to the local computer users group and keep very active at church. If you do keep busy with outside interests and plan on being gone for short or extended periods of time, it is critical to find a great babysitter or two. We have two who are great at keeping the girls on track when I am gone. I feel comfortable assigning the girls work, rather than just having them review material they have already studied.

I have learned several great academic and household ideas from discussions in our homeschool support group, and I have enjoyed the activities the group frequently has. One of the things I needed some help with was keeping everything straight, trying to teach two children formally and another informally, while keeping the fourth happy, too. We followed one suggestion to let the children work whenever they get up and going in the morning, instead of getting the children up and pushing them before they are ready to work. This has worked out very well because Katy gets to work quickly in the morning, then her attention tapers off around lunch time, while Colleen is a night owl.

Beside the group we belong to, I have seen a growing acceptance of homeschooling and seldom feel any need to explain our decision to homeschool to people. Many people I have talked to seem to accept it, although sometimes as a novelty because *I* am doing the homeschooling instead of Sharon. Many of the people I have talked to believe that homeschooling is a good idea, and several have expressed an interest in it, including a few fathers who have said they would prefer to be at home with their children.

I must, however, be completely honest: be prepared, whether you are a stay-at-home mother or father, for a lot of questions. And, especially for fathers, be prepared for a lot of derogatory comments. I have heard a lot of comments along the line of, "Well, we know who puts the pants on in that family." (Actually, Sharon and I both do. She wears jeans to classes and nice slacks to clinicals. I wear shorts and sweatpants most of the time at home.) Questioning another person's masculinity/femininity seems to be a pastime for a lot of people. I just ignore those comments or make a typically flippant comment like, "Well, I've never been pregnant, but Sharon has." Also be prepared to answer questions about why *you*, the *father*, are staying home. People have made comments about my intellect, education and employability. (I have a BA in sociology and I was employed my entire adult life, including up to three jobs at a time while I was in college, until I *voluntarily* quit!) A thick skin and a sense of humor are two of the most important characteristics needed.

One of the most important reasons we are homeschooling, and part of the values we are trying to teach our children, is to teach responsibility and hard work. Except for Eamon, the children have chores and responsibilities around the house. More important than just requiring that the children accomplish the chores, each of the children has do some "volunteers" every day. Having the children at home gives them each some time to learn how working together gets things done.

One of the problems with having each of the children volunteer

Katy (12), Colleen (7), Ethan (5), Eamon (1)

everyday, though, is figuring out *what* they can do. Katy started out doing the easiest things she could do (throw away the lint from the dryer, bring the hamper back up to the bedroom), while Ethan and Colleen wanted to be *really* helpful (wash the windows, cook dinner). I finally decided that a list of things to do, appropriate for each child, was important. So, I sat down with each one and we came up with a list. Katy now has to do things like vacuum the living room carpet (which has her dog's hair on it), empty the kitchen trash, sweep the basement, vacuum the stairs. Colleen now has a list that has things like bringing Eamon's laundry upstairs and putting it away, emptying the garbage can in the bathroom or the playroom, changing Eamon's sheets. Ethan now gets to do things like dust (he loves this, but I am afraid to put anything on my table after he is done), take hangers to the laundry room, pick up Eamon's toys in the living room. Eamon gets to be himself and trash all the work the others have done! Oh, a final thing about chores: do them or you don't get dessert.

And when everyone decides that pitching in to get things done requires too much effort on their part, I go on strike. I have actually done this just twice and only after trying to get everybody to help out more. Because I just had my second strike a few weeks ago, I'll give a brief background: I hurt my elbow doing some typing for Sharon (she could give the fancy medical term for it, but suffice it to say, it's tennis elbow, but worse). I continued doing things (like teaching, cooking, laundry, driving to church, piano lessons, chorus, homeschool group meetings, changing the beds, baby's diapers, light bulbs, shoveling the snow) but I asked the children to do more as well, like vacuuming and sweeping—chores they normally do not have to do.The children did these things, but I noticed a grumpy attitude. This grumpiness meant things were not done as well as they could have been and people forgot to do some of their required chores. But what got to me was a decline in the level of courtesy and a rise in bickering. The "You did it," "No, you did it," level increased. So I went on strike. School continued, but Katy had to make lunch. Laundry continued, but Katy and Colleen and Sharon had to fold or hang their own. Dinner was made, but no more "restaurant style" meals (Sharon's words about my cooking). Hot dogs, meatloaf, Shake and Bake chicken instead of Jamaican steamed chicken with gungo peas and rice and Jamaican coleslaw or Saudi Arabian Lamb with Tahini and spinach with eggs. Sharon had to come home early instead of staying late to study, and I disappeared into my office in the basement, turned on the computer and a CD and shut out the chaos upstairs. It worked, but use this tactic sparingly to make a point only when all else fails!

Katy (12), Colleen (7), Ethan (5), Eamon (1)

UPDATE:

I am now teaching a third child and having to control number four, who really wants to be involved in the learning, although he does not speak yet. And, finally, Sharon is doing her clinical rotations all over town and the state, so we don't see her too much.

Katy (12), Colleen (7), Ethan (5), Eamon (1)

Casey and Nancy
Ian, age 8
Caleb, age 5

Nancy described the day of May 15, in the bloom of spring, from their old
farmhouse in the wooded hills about seven miles outside the college town of
Bloomington, Indiana.

NEVER O'CLOCK

My husband Casey and I both had very bad experiences in public
schools and therefore have a strong commitment to homeschool our two sons.
But we also are under some financial pressure and feel we both need to work
outside the home, at least for a while.

Our solution was to arrange our working hours so that we would be
able to share childcare responsibilities. Unlike most homeschooling families, I
am the primary wage earner. I have a master's degree in clinical psychology and
currently do psychological testing at a private psychiatric hospital. Casey is an
artist and has been rather successful, but his income from artwork is sporadic.
He recently took a steady, full-time job at the hospital where I work. He is a
program specialist, day-to-day caregiver for the adolescents who are longterm
residents.

We have about two acres of land, partly wooded with a little creek that
runs through. We live about seven miles from town in an old farm house. We
have our resources spread all around the house and the kids choose to work
everywhere and anywhere but like to work outside best of all, even in the winter.
Our "curriculum" is mostly science-based, and we do a *lot* of nature study all
year round.Our neighbors think we're a curiosity because of our home-
school/work lifestyle and they generally mind their own business. We have a
wonderful support group here that organizes lots of group activities, such as a
science fair and various field trips.

HOW IT WORKS:

I usually get up at 6:00 AM and go to work while the rest of the family is asleep. Casey and the boys wake up sometime between 8 and 9:00 AM and start taking care of things around home. The boys help their dad fill bird feeders, do yard work, clean house, and feed the dog, cat, and fish. Then they usually go for a nature walk through our almost two acre yard, part of which we are converting to a bird sanctuary. They check which wildflowers are in bloom; identify wild herbs; check on the inhabitants of our various nesting boxes, including the bathouse; and hike up the wooded hills nearby to see how the trees, mammals, and birds are doing. All of this we write down as science in our daily homeschooling log.

The nesting boxes were all made by Casey and the boys, giving them valuable skills in measuring and woodworking. They also learn why a house for a piliated woodpecker is filled with sawdust (so the piliateds can fulfill their instinctive desire to excavate the nesting site) and why you leave the inside of the bathouse very rough (so the little brown bats have a toehold when hanging inside).

If Casey has an order for his artwork, the boys help by packing the items for shipping. They routinely tag along when Casey delivers the finished product or buys supplies. They see how earning money requires several steps. Ian, our older boy, often travels with Casey to art fairs and helps him set up the displays and sell the artwork, about which he has become very knowledgeable. He gets paid for labor connected with the business (which he promptly spends on new Lego blocks!).

If Casey is working at the hospital, he comes by my office with the kids at about 2:30 PM so he can start his shift at 3:00 PM. I take the boys with me at that point, whether to go grocery shopping, to the park, to baseball practice, choir practice, or home. I am fortunate that I can take some of my work home. The boys have learned to respect Mama's "word work" on the computer, especially if I promise I will play a board game with them at a certain time. I do a lot of games with them and count it as school. *Yahtzee*, for example, is an excellent math game. Ian is now regularly trouncing me at *Where in the U.S.A. Is Carmen Sandiego?* (the board game). I have also taught Ian to play *Blackjack* and bet using play money. Far from creating a gambler, he was impressed with how easy it is to lose large sums of money, and how his money would be better invested in something lasting (like Legos).

I do the formal instruction, what little we do, in reading and math. I also keep the daily activity log. Generally, however, we just let learning occur. Philosophically, we are unschoolers, who believe in letting learning occur in an organic fashion while going about our daily lives. If one of the boys expresses a special interest in something (for Caleb, it was bluebirds and cardinals; for Ian, knights and castles) we make a point of looking up materials at the library. We also watch science shows on TV, from *NOVA* to *Bill Nye the Science Guy* and *The Magic Schoolbus.*

The tag team parenting has not been easy, but it is working. One

Ian (8), Caleb (5)

problem is that my sleeping schedule is out of sync with the rest of the family. Casey likes to have the boys awake when he comes home at about midnight. The boys refer to themselves as "nocturnals" who like to go to bed at "never o'clock." Casey's work is emotionally demanding so sometimes he wants to talk to me for a while. Mama, however, gets up at 6:00 AM. This means that I am often running on a sleep deficit, and some afternoons I will stick a video in the VCR (not necessarily an educational one) and ask the boys not to wake me until it's over or the house catches on fire, whichever comes first!

Also, because I can't always fit everything I need to do at work between 7:30 AM and 2:30 PM, we have decided to hire a babysitter two days a week, four hours per day, so that I can schedule outpatients after work or after school. The boys weren't too happy about this idea, but they are helping us interview sitters and daycare homes, and therefore feel a certain amount of control in this process.

In summary, it *is* possible to be a two-income, two-jobs-outside-the-home homeschooling family, but it is not easy. If you tag-team childcare, as we do, it becomes harder to schedule family together time or time for the parents to be a couple alone together. Casey was an assistant baseball coach last year, but so far has missed all of Ian's games and practices this summer. He hopes to trade a few shifts so he can come to some of the games. If you need to arrange childcare, be sure your provider is sympathetic to homeschooling. And try to get enough family time, marriage time, and sleep!

UPDATE:

Casey is now working full time at home on his artwork and homeschooling with the boys. Business has picked up, so he quit his day (evening) job. I am still working full time outside the home. I work twelve-hour days on Mondays, Wednesdays, and Fridays, 9:00 AM to 9:00 PM. On Saturdays I work a four hour day, 8:00 AM to noon. This benefits my employer, because I can schedule outpatients in the early evenings three nights a week. It helps me because even if my work day stretches to 10:30 PM or later (as it does at times), I still have all day on Tuesday, Thursday, and Sunday when I don't go to the hospital at all. It's a very eccentric schedule but it allows me to do concentrated homeschooling with my children on those days. It enables us to do *really neat* things like going to museums and libraries on off-peak hours.

We've also recently started to raise homing pigeons and show pigeons. Show pigeons are bred for their looks alone, so the children are learning genetics, care taking, and showing skills. We're in the training process right now for the homers. Although the behavior is instinctual, it helps them to be taken out short distances, then progressively longer distances, and in all compass directions. Next summer we will be entering them in races.

Casey likes being the stay-at-home dad and that we can do things as a family on weekdays. We're still pretty unstructured, doing things as they happen and letting the kids figure out their own curriculum. Of course, my house is perpetually a mess. We have determined our priorities in a very conscious

Ian (8), Caleb (5)

fashion. I've heard it said that no one on his or her deathbed has ever said, "I wish I had spent more time at work [or cleaning the house]!"

And my little "nocturnals," a year older now, *still* like to go to bed at "never o'clock."

Log sheet--selected days.

Saturday, July 8, 1995. SCIENCE: Read in the book Opt from the library, which is all about optical illusions. We did the illusions and also read the explanations of why the illusions have the effects that they do. Some were easier to see than others. HISTORY: Went to see Apollo 13 at the theatre today as a family. The boys were fascinated by the story. We talked a lot about how the people on the ground helped the people in the spacecraft, and how serious the problems had been.
7

Saturday, July 15, 1995. SCIENCE: Bill Nye the Science Guy today, about Momentum and other aspects of energy. Invited their neighbor friend Jay to watch with them, which he did. ART: Worked on the dollhouse and doll house furniture for the 4-H fair arts and crafts project.
8

Saturday, July 22, 1995. SCIENCE: Billy Nye the Science Guy was about reptiles today. MATH: Played Yahtzee. Ian worked on addition skills in his head, used a multiplication chart which was provided for him to figure the upper section, and used a calculator.
10

Sunday, July 23, 1995. SCIENCE: (1) Reading Rainbow, which was about storms of various kinds. The kids were especially impressed with hurricanes. (2) Magic School Bus, about desert ecosystems. GEOGRAPHY: Played "Where in the U.S.A. is Carmen Sandiego?" board game by our modified rules. Ian did good map work, especially. Also discussed the concept of a bay, with which he was not familiar. MATH: Worked with flashcards today, doing basic addition facts. I made him a deal that if he got a card correct twice, he could darken in the number on the math facts chart he had made previously, which was all in pencil. He liked being able to see his progress. READING: Watched Storytime today. John Goodman was on reading two stories. We talked about the different voices he made for different characters.
11

Monday, July 24, 1995: PHYSICAL EDUCATION: Went to the swimming pool today; worked with Ian on floating and kicking skills. I demonstrated various floats for him, and also tried to coach him on how to relax enough to float. LIFE SKILLS: Had some lessons on money today at the county fair. Ian used several of his own quarters, probably about $3.00 worth, to play a gambling game to win a large ball. We then talked about how all that money was spent, with nothing to show. Discussed how gambling is not like buying something--how you might spend money and get nothing. He decided against playing the duck game for that reason. He also chose a nice ring to wear (gold-plated), with money that he had. READING: Without my coaching, Ian went around the fair, trying to figure out the various signs. Did other "environmental reading" such as on cereal boxes and such at home. SCIENCE: I asked Ian to figure out why there were so many fans in the sheep barn, as compared to the other livestock areas at the fair. He correctly figured out that it was because the sheep have to be keep especially cool because of their wool.
12

Saturday, July 29, 1995. READING: Worked on Hooked on Phonics today, the ending two consonant sounds like "sp" and "lk." He did very well. SCIENCE: Bill Nye the Science Guy was about the atmosphere today.

Ian (8), Caleb (5)

Clifton and Edris
Jason, age 13
Tracy, age 11

Edris described the hot and balmy day of August 22, where they live in a small hillside development in the suburbs of Reading, Pennsylvania.

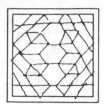

HECTIC BUT ORDERLY

When we started homeschooling almost ten years ago, there were many "typical" days. The children were only six and four years old at that time. There were no allergy shots, orthodontist visits, piano lessons, or support groups to lead. Since then, life has taken on a different outlook. Our day usually begins at 5:00 or 6:00 AM. This depends on how early my husband Clifton has to be at work. Today we woke up at 6:00 AM to the music on the radio.

At approximately 6:35 AM Clifton left for his twenty minute commute to work where he programs Numerical Control machines for a small machine shop. Instead of having my quiet time, I scurried off to the school room to see that everything was ready for another busy week. Our school room is a converted one-car garage that is attached to our house. One side is taken up with book-shelves that are bulging with books, and my desk and chair. On the opposite side are our silent teachers—posters on the wall, a filing cabinet, our computer, a long work table where the children work most of the time, and some storage for curriculum and other school supplies. The children's beanbag chairs are on the floor in front of the bookshelves where they sometimes work. At any given time both children can be found working in any room of the house including the schoolroom. We sometimes use the patio when the weather is warm.

By 7:00 AM the children were awakened by their alarm clocks. This is usually my cue to head directly to the bathroom.

By 7:30 AM we were all dressed and ready for breakfast, which consisted of cold cereal. Oh yes, there were the complaints of Tracy as to why she had to eat cold cereal again. My response was simply, "That's what we eat on Mondays." (She now prepares her own breakfast that never includes cold cereal.) With breakfast over, the children did their chores while I put the finishing touches on our Bible lesson for the day. Jason made his bed and emptied the trash, while Tracy loaded the dishwasher. Tracy had already made her bed and swept the entrance in our tiny hallway. At 8:15 AM Tracy entered the schoolroom and started her science. She has been working through her first LIFEPAC from Alpha Omega. This is a workbook format that includes critical thinking, not just rote memory lessons. The year's work consists of ten workbooks that are not designed for self-study, but include minimal parental involvement. Tracy usually reads her assignment and comes to me to discuss it or test her understanding of the material. I also quiz her before any tests, and her science experiments are always done with my supervision. This year she is in sixth grade but I have tailored her science so she is using some LIFEPACS from both fifth and sixth grades. History was her second subject of choice. Greenleaf's *History for the Thoughtful Child* has really been a hit with Tracy. Our study has been on Egypt so she eagerly read about deserts from an Usborne book. A brief discussion followed, with me learning as much as Tracy did. About half an hour was spent on her math lesson from *Saxon 76*. Then came her spelling using the Rod and Staff text. After she grumbled about having to write the answers (without much sympathy from me), she settled back and did her work. Tracy has always been homeschooled and writing has always been an issue. My over-used line is, "You can and you will."

At about the time Tracy started spelling, Jason completed his chores and his breakfast and was ready to start his academic work. Instead of stopping Tracy so we could do Bible, I allowed Jason to choose a subject. He decided to begin with one of his favorites—science, using *Earth Science for Christian Schools* by BJU (Bob Jones University). At the eighth grade level, Jason is working independently most of the time. He then sat at the computer where he did a chapter summary for health. He is using *Let's Be Healthy* by A Beka. I was then able to sit with Jason for a few minutes to review some grammar rules from *Learning Language Arts Through Writing*, a grammar handbook. During this time, the ever-intruding phone rang three or four different times. Thanks to our answering machine, I did not have to answer the phone. Jason then moved on to his first Saxon math test for the year. He is using *Saxon Algebra 1/2*. He then read two chapters from *The Land of Fair Play* by Christian Liberty Press.

Lunchtime had arrived, so the stereo was tuned to a local station for our almost daily diet of Rush Limbaugh while I prepared the meal. After lunch Jason did the dishes and restored order to the kitchen.

Meanwhile, Tracy was back in the schoolroom wrestling with her spelling. With that completed, she asked if she could do calligraphy. My negative answer plunged us into another, "Why can't I ever do what I want to do?" episode. My typical response has been, "You don't know what's best for you." My response has something to do with the fact that I know her well. So, instead, Tracy agreed to work with me from her *Learning Language Arts*

Jason (13), Tracy (11)

Through Literature text. We enjoyed a Tennyson poem that she later wrote in prose.

For different reasons, and at various times, the children balk at doing certain assignments. I am usually steadfast in my requests unless they can show me why the assignment is unnecessary. Yes, I sometimes second guess myself, and that's the reason why I do leave some room for negotiating some assignments, though this is rarely done.

As soon as Jason was finished cleaning the kitchen he asked permission to play his newest computer game. After questioning the merits of such a venture, I decided that I could use a break, so he played for a while. We returned refreshed and ready to do Bible, which should have been done in the morning before any other subjects. Remember, I said we do not have a typical day! After Bible and prayer time, I read aloud from *Whatever Happened to Justice?* Latin was our last subject and we used *First Latin*.

It was 3:00 PM and our day was far from over. The children played outside while I prepared some chicken for supper. Then we hurried off to the store in search of a scientific calculator, shoes for Jason, and fabric for church dresses for Tracy. After about three hours and aching feet, we returned home. By this time Clifton had been home for two hours. Supper was hastily cooked and eaten. At 9:45 PM the children were finished cleaning the kitchen and were ready for bed. Due to the late hour, we did not have our family reading from *Unlocking the Mysteries of Creation*.

I almost forgot—those phone calls were returned before our shopping trip. I helped a new homeschooler decipher her new curriculum and answered questions about Thursday School (our local support group). My day ended at about 11:00 PM. Obviously, I did not do any housework, but some days are like that. We won't mention the basket of laundry almost three feet high waiting to be ironed or the stenciling supplies laying on the coffee table. My ambitious project of stenciling the dining and living rooms may even happen this year!

My days are not usually problem-free. Our children argue about the things your children argue about. Since we have a boy and a girl, there are the typical differences in how they view things, which are sometimes comical. Tracy's emotions seem to be involved in most decisions, and she is more involved in deeper relationships. She is witty and keeps our family laughing. Suppertime at our house is filled with laughter. Jason, on the other hand, tends to be more practical and is content to be a loner. He is much more comfortable discussing anything factual. They also learn differently. My ambitious plans to place both of them in the same mold backfired. Tracy is a spontaneous learner. She prefers to learn by doing and dislikes workbooks. Tracy remembers general information, while Jason is much more analytic. After listening to a speaker, if Tracy is asked specific questions, she may not be able to answer. However, she could tell you how many times the speaker ended his sentences with prepositions. Jason's ability to recall details sometimes baffles me. He prefers to follow a schedule and does great with traditional school curriculum. This is not to say that he does not learn any other way, but this is his preference. He is also

Jason (13), Tracy (11)

motivated to learn on his own. He reads avidly in various subject areas.

I had attempted to teach Tracy as if she was her brother. I used to become very frustrated when she could not recall details from her reading. It was obvious that Tracy did not learn like Jason, but I was insistent in putting her into his mold. I did not want to purchase two separate curricula because of the obvious cost. It also would be easier to work with Tracy since I would have already been familiar with the material. There was also a hesitancy to use appropriate material with Tracy because my learning style is more like Jason's. My security was using textbooks. I attended Debra Bell's "Blueprint for Success" seminar, which reiterated the very idea I was fighting—tailor the curriculum to suit the child's learning style.

Even though my days are hectic, they are mostly orderly. The children have assignment sheets that Clifton designed on the computer. This enables them to move on to another project or subject if I am busy, without asking what they should do next. Or worse yet, accomplish nothing because they did not know what to do. This assignment sheet puts the responsibility where it belongs—with the children. The children do start their school work without being told or even if I am busy doing something else.

I like to say that we are structured but flexible. With two of us wearing braces and receiving allergy shots, each week has its share of trips to the doctor's office. Tracy also takes piano lessons each Tuesday morning and we belong to a local support group. Our family is also busy at our church with different ministries. I sometimes become discouraged when my "to do" list grows longer than I would like. There are also those days when I would prefer to crochet or read a good book that is not related to school. But I see the children are growing up fast. This is my constant reminder that God has given these children to us for a time to be good stewards.

Clifton is not as involved with the actual teaching of the children as I am. Homeschooling would, however, be extremely difficult without his help. He encourages me when I become overwhelmed and discouraged. Without his help, I would not have my minimal computer skills that help me immensely. The log and assignment sheets are Clifton's projects. As extra security, I compose most of the children's tests and any worksheets when Clifton is at home—he has rescued the computer from me on several occasions. His ability to organize has been a tremendous help to me. In other words, Clifton is the mind behind most of what I do.

We live in a small townhouse, nestled on a hillside in a suburb of Reading, Pennsylvania. Even though there are many children in our development, our children spend most of their free time with only one or two playmates. The parents and children in our neighborhood respond positively to the fact that our family homeschools. Some children have even voiced that they wish they could be homeschooled, while others complain that they would not want to be at home with their mothers.

We have always had a good working relationship with our local school district. I have seen a growing respect for homeschoolers as the district realized

Jason (13), Tracy (11)

that some of us are committed to persevering through junior high and high school. In my experiences so far in homeschooling the children, I know that the only constant is the love of my Father. My greatest encourager, other than Clifton, is the Word of God.

Jason (13), Tracy (11)

Frank and Sandi
Brianna, age 16
Christian, age 10
Svetlana, age 5
(and now Dmitri, age 8)

Sixteen-year-old Brianna wrote about a cold and snowy day in April, from their wooded mountainside home in Eagle River, Alaska

UNCOMMONLY FLEXIBLE

Our family lives high up on a mountain, a mile off the main road in the woods of Eagle River, Alaska, with seven horses, five cats, three dogs, two fish aquariums, and a gerbil. Our family consists of: Frank and Sandi (parents, both in their late 40s), me—Brianna or "Breezy," Christian, and Svetlana, whom we adopted in November last year from Russia. She is adapting extremely well. She had spent all of her life in an orphanage. We are also in the process of adopting another brother, eight-year-old Dmitri, from the (former Soviet) Republic of Georgia, and a thirteen-year-old sister, Elena (from Moscow, Russia).

Before I launch into telling you about a "typical" day, let me give a briefing on what each member of my family is like. In reality, there is no such thing as a *typical* day at our house. We do not keep a daily log, and we have constant interruptions in our schedule, and nothing ever goes as planned.I suppose I shouldn't say never, but we rarely have a day that isn't blessed by various and sundry "emergencies." We are uncommonly flexible.

My dad is an Emergency Room Physician, who works long, extremely erratic hours: days, nights, mids, and anything in between, with some of each kind of shift scattered throughout every month. He is firm but loving, giving, compassionate, outgoing, likes to please, and is fairly laid back and calm. He is brilliant and learns things quickly. He is a computer fanatic and also loves fly-fishing. He spends his spare time, what little he has, working on the computer, getting hay, hauling manure away, and snowplowing our road. He is also an expert on Creation Science and has taught all over the world on the differences between Creation and Evolution. He has spent many years researching the various versions of the Bible, and is a staunch believer in the authenticity and accuracy of the King James Version. Dad has been totally supportive of our family homeschooling, right from the beginning, eleven or twelve years ago when he believed that it was a God-given responsibility to teach children at home. Alaska has a law that states that anyone living more than two miles from a public or private school, or more than two miles from a bus stop, doesn't have to send their children to school. We easily fall into that category.

My mom is loving, compassionate, generous, thoughtful, perceptive, sympathetic, very affectionate, hospitable, a hard worker, a faithful friend, a good listener, often impatient, and (though easily stressed) is mellowing with age. She likes horseback riding, playing with her dogs, taking care of her family, homeschooling, reading, learning how to have a meek and quiet spirit, and doing anything with her children. She enjoys playing, and is a committed homemaker. Her greatest desire is to be a godly wife and mother, and she gets easily frustrated with herself when she doesn't live up to her expectations. One of her virtues is that she is able to admit when she has been wrong. Since she is so aware of her own weaknesses and imperfections, she realizes the rest of us deserve equal understanding. Mom writes out assignments for Christian when he needs them, but he pretty much knows how much he has to accomplish each day on his own. I do all my own planning after a general conference with Mom at the beginning of the year and once in a while thereafter.

I have almost exactly the same qualities as my mom, plus a few of my dad's, and I am the most laid back in the family. I tend to be the peace-maker because I don't get easily angered. I love horses and cats, working with young children, and singing. I spend my spare time riding and training horses, reading, playing with my cats, writing stories and poetry, learning how to sew, cooking, singing, playing the piano, and giving horseback riding lessons. In school work, my favorite subjects are English and foreign languages—Latin and Russian. I used to think I'd like to be a math teacher, until I got to algebra. Science is my least favorite subject. Curriculum-wise, I have used a variety of resources, mostly BJU (Bob Jones University) and A Beka. We have been homeschooled all our lives because of our family convictions, and I have changed curricula many times. We have tried Hewitt Research Foundation materials, PACES, KONOS, and Alpha Omega. As a matter of fact, I spent three years in fifth grade, because we kept changing curricula, and Mom was afraid I'd miss something if I didn't go through each of the books I'd not yet read from each of the different publishers. She eventually relaxed and decided to let me choose which Christian publisher to use for each subject. At that point, Mom was working with me full time in each of my subjects. We would start school at 9:00 AM, take one break for lunch and one for dinner and finish at 10:00-11:00 PM! We decided that this was too much work, but we finished out my second year of

Brianna (16), Christian (10), Svetlana (5)

fifth grade in BJU anyway.

Last summer, I tried to "catch up" by doing two complete grades.I'm now in high school, finally, and use ninth through eleventh grade curriculum. At the moment, I am using ACE eleventh grade, PACES for English, *Artes Latinae* for Latin, several different audio Russian tapes, *Saxon Algebra 1*, and BJU for history and science. This school year found me doing a ninth grade correspondence course through Hewitt Educational Resources. I completed the first quarter and got all A's except for history. We decided that, due to a lot of changes in our lives and the number of hours required, this course was not for us. I am taking Russian as another foreign language using the *Berlitz* Russian program and am also taking sewing lessons from a neighbor for home economics. We learned an important lesson from doing fifth grade for three years: *never* do a grade more than once unless you flunk it the first time!!

When Dmitri and Elena arrive, I will be helping Mom homeschool them. I look forward to being a homemaker, and plan on having a courting relationship first, with my parents choosing a husband for me.

Christian is thoughtful, kind, helpful, affectionate, energetic, literal, and can get frustrated easily. He, too, is an adopted brother, born in Anchorage, Alaska, who became part of our family at one day of age, as a result of my dad's involvement in starting a Crisis Pregnancy Center in our city over ten years ago. He is interested in a number of sports, is planning on playing the recorder and trumpet, is highly artistic, and likes anything to do with military operations, planes, trucks, and cars. One of his favorite pastimes is to help Dad with all the roadwork year-round, and the bulldozing of snow during our long winters. Because of his exceptional neatness and precise handwriting, he has recently been asked to be the calligrapher for a fly tying business. His favorite school subjects are history/geography and science, and he is a whiz at both. He uses predominantly BJU materials, and has just switched from *Saxon Math* to Alpha Omega, which he finds easier to understand. Christian and I have both participated in a homeschool choir, homeschool volleyball, basketball, soccer, and softball clinics throughout the year. We attend AWANA clubs at church, where I am a Leader-in-Training, and we've both been on the Bible Quizzing Teams. We are active in the Longrider's Legend 4-H Horse Club on Tuesday nights. In the past, we have played on Boys' and Girls' Club and local soccer teams in the summers. This spring Christian will be playing on a Little League Baseball team for the first time.

Svetlana (Svyetta) is a petite, really sweet, smart, gregarious girl, who loves animals and is very sensitive when anyone is hurt or upset. She is remarkably strong physically, for her age, as well as strong-willed, loves horseback riding, and even enjoys cleaning up horse manure!! Svyetta has loved being part of our family since the day she arrived, thinks it's great to be an "Amereecan," and tells everyone she meets that she speaks "Ingleesh." Although she loves all animals and because she is so energetic, she can be rough with them. She likes helping around the house and barn, singing, "playing" the piano, and going to her jump-rope/footwork/exercise class. She

Brianna (16), Christian (10), Svetlana (5)

is quite agile so Mom plans to get her involved in gymnastics, someday . . . when life slows down. Now that you know a little about my family, come and join me for a "typical" day at our house.

5:30 AM:
          Svyetta and I share a room, and I am awakened by "la la la la . . . " in a high pitched, loud, off key, little voice. "Svyetta, shhh; please be quiet; I'm trying to sleep," I mumble groggily.

5:40 AM:
          "La la la la LA LA LA LA." "Svyetta, *please,* be quiet."

5:50 AM:
          Dad wakes up and gets ready for work. He is quiet and doesn't wake anyone up, except Mom, who is a light sleeper.

6:00 AM:
          "BARREESY!!! (Breezy) Go potty!" (I have to go to the bathroom.) "All right, go, but please, be quiet." All the lights go on and she thuds noisily into the bathroom. She plops back in bed, and after another half-hour of "singing," she falls asleep. I sigh with relief and try to go back to sleep.

6:20 AM:
          Dad leaves for work.

8:00 AM:
          "MEEEOOWW." I'm startled awake by my cat's (Sweetie Pie or S.P.) scream. "Svyetta, what are you doing?" "Nothing." "Yes you are. Now leave the cat alone and get dressed."

8:15 AM:
          Mom and Christian get up and start their morning chores. We have cold cereal (Wheat Chex, Raisin Bran, Mueslix, Cheerios, etc.), and milk, most of the time. We also alternate with eggs and toast or hot cereal (oatmeal, Cream of Wheat, or 7 Grain). Christian feeds the three dogs, lets them outside, and puts their dog beds in the family room; they have been sleeping in the laundry room all night. He gets dressed, brushes his hair, and makes his bed. Then he heads off to get his schoolwork started as quickly as he can. He likes to see how early in the day he can complete his assignments, so that he can play! I sometimes help Svyetta get dressed and then do my hair.

8:30 AM:
          I've just finished getting dressed and doing my chores when Svyetta comes barreling in from playing in the family room. "Barreesy, brekaveetch!" (breakfast). "Ask nicely, Svyetta." "May I please have brekaveetch?" "Much

Brianna (16), Christian (10), Svetlana (5)

better. Yes, you may." Mom and I get breakfast and we all start eating.

8:50 AM:
Mom is homeschooling Christian with BJU English, grade four, and Alpha Omega math, grades four and five. Mom continues correcting his English and math and helps him with whatever he doesn't understand. Mom had started all this soon after she arose. Svyetta is still eating, and I'm cleaning up the kitchen. I glance at the table, when I hear a spoon drop on the floor. "Svyetta, don't feed your breakfast to the dogs. Get down and clear your dishes." "Yes Barreesy." "That's a good girl. Don't forget to brush your teeth when you're done."

9:00 AM:
My family sits down on the living-room couch for devotions ("lotions," as Svetlana calls it)—Bible reading and prayer.

9:30 AM:
"Barreesy horcheech?" "Yes, I'm going to feed the horses." "Barreesy barrrum, barrrum?" "No, I'm not going riding. I'm just feeding them." "Oh. Svyetta horcheech?" "No, you get to stay and help Mom." "SVYETTA, HORCHEECH!!!!!" I sigh and head down to the barn.

9:35 AM:
Mom and Christian are doing math, Christian's least favorite subject. "Okay, Christian, I've corrected your math, and there are a couple of problems that you didn't do just right. Look them over and see if you understand everything that I marked wrong," Mom says cheerfully. "MOM!" Christian shouts a few minutes later. I don't understand this problem. "Christian, don't yell. I'm folding the laundry.If you need help, come here." Christian brings his math book to Mom and she explains the problem. "I still don't understand," grumbles Christian. "I know it's frustrating, but you will have things that are difficult throughout your whole life. Even when you are an adult, you still make mistakes and have to make corrections. Schoolwork is just preparing you for when you have a job." Christian calms down and goes back to his math corrections.

10:15 AM:
I come in the door from feeding the horses and the three barn cats, and Svyetta comes down the stairs. "Hi Barreesy!" "Hi Svyetta. How are you? What do you have in your mouth?" Silence. . . . "Show me. Where did you get the gum?" "Garrabeech" (garbage). "Svyetta, FOO (her Russian word for yuck) that's dirty! Yuck!" "Gude (good), Barreesy!" "Neeeyet! (an exaggerated form of "no" in Russian), FOO! Throw it out, Svyetta."

Brianna (16), Christian (10), Svetlana (5)

12:00 PM:
   I'm doing my Latin (in our bedroom, where I usually do schoolwork) and Svyetta is "fixing" my hair. "Hilarem datorem diliget Deus" (God loves a cheerful giver) I repeat after my Latin tape.

1:00 PM:
   I'm just finishing my math for the day. "The cube root of 212 is. . . ." I usually do my schoolwork independently. If I have a question about English, I ask Mom. If I have a question about science, I ask Dad. When I have trouble with math, I ask Mom first. If she doesn't know how to work out the problem, I wait until I can ask my dad. Mom usually goes over my work and tells me what things need correcting. "Barreesy, hungarry." In other words, "I want lunch *now!*"   "I have two more math problems and then I'll fix lunch."

1:30 PM:
   We get through lunch without any major problems.   Normally, it is my job to make lunch.   Once in a while, when I am in the middle of something important in school, such as taking a test, Mom or Christian will make lunch for me.   Dad usually fixes his own breakfast, (a combination of three or four different bran cereals) and lunch (a sandwich or Mexican burritos that he can heat up at the hospital) the night before he is going to work.   I (or Mom or Christian) fix meat, cheese, lettuce, and tomato or peanut butter and jelly sandwiches and sometimes soup. At other times, we will have soup with muffins or croissants, carrot sticks, tomato slices, and Tillamook cheddar cheese slices. We also make up some kind of juice. If Christian isn't making lunch, he does BJU fourth grade history or science, Steck-Vaughn *Critical Thinking Skills* or spelling words Mom has written out for him from words he has misspelled in his writings. He also reads *God's World Newspaper* or *Discovery Magazine* (a Creation Science-based magazine). After lunch, Mom goes back to schooling my brother.

2:00 PM:
   "Svyetta go outside?" "I don't know. Ask Mom." "Mom I don't know." (Where's Mom?) "In the school room (dining room) with Christian."

2:05 PM:
   Mom has said Svyetta may go outside, so she dons her snow gear and hurries out to play in the snow with the dogs. "Remember to stay next to the house," Mom calls out as Svyetta rushes out the door.

2:30 PM:
   "Mom," I ask, "have you seen Svyetta outside lately?" "No," she replies. "I've been concentrating on Christian's English corrections." I pull on my boots and tromp outside. "Wow, it's cold. I think I need my coat and

Brianna (16), Christian (10), Svetlana (5)

mittens." I get them on and go searching for my "lost" sister. I find her over the bank, on the other side of the driveway, where she likes to slide, and I play with her for a little while. All of a sudden, I notice that she is missing a mitten. "Where's your mitten?" "Meeetin I don't know." We trudge all over the snow-covered yard, trying to find the mitten.

3:00 PM:

We give up searching and go inside. I get back to my school work and Svyetta goes to do her "kool" and/or play with Mom and Christian.

4:30 PM:

Christian and I finish school, and I go down to the barn to train my horses while Christian and Svyetta play outside, so mom can have some temporary peace and quiet.

7:00 PM:

I come back up from the barn and get cleaned up. Christian and Svyetta have also just come in. Christian then heads to his room to read.

7:15 PM:

Mom and I start making dinner. "Svyetta holp?" (help).Mom or I make dinner and sometimes we make it together. If we do it together, we each pick a couple of things to cook. For example, Mom will cook the meat and vegetable and I'll fix the salad and the rice, potatoes, or noodles. I almost always do the salad. Christian sets the table and feeds the dogs.

7:50 PM:

"PAAAH-OP!!!!" Svyetta yells, as my dad comes home from work. She jumps off her step-stool and knocks the open sugar container onto the floor in her hurry to greet her beloved "Pop."

9:00 PM:

The kitchen has been cleaned by the family, and Mom gives Svyetta a bath while I feed the horses.

9:30 PM:

I come back from the barn and get ready for bed. I pick up Kalee (our kitten) and put her in the bathroom where she sleeps at night.

10:00 PM:

Most of us are ready for bed, and our family prays together; then Svyetta and I climb into bed, exhausted. I pick up my old cat, S.P., and bring her up on the top bunk to sleep with me. I pull the pillow over my head and turn on my classical music, preparing myself for the nightly "la la" concert, starring Svyetta. Mom, Dad, and Christian read together and then go to sleep between

Brianna (16), Christian (10), Svetlana (5)

eleven and midnight.

10:30 PM.

I gingerly pull my head out from under my pillow and listen. It's quiet for the first time since 5:30 AM. I eventually fall asleep, dreaming of Svyetta getting voice lessons!

UPDATE from Sandi:

I broke my back falling off my horse less than a month after our new eight-year-old son, Dmitri, arrived from the (former Soviet) Republic of Georgia; so, we are way behind in everything. Breezy had a quick course in Home Management 101 and 102, combined with an instant family! Praise the Lord, she has her driver's license and is a capable young lady. She literally took over the household. I was flat on my back, at home, for about five and a half weeks. My meager, but valiant, contribution to the family was to try to homeschool the three youngest from bed, which worked out pretty well but we still fell behind.

I am now up and about, wearing a back support, not allowed to lift over ten pounds, not allowed to bend over, and cannot participate in sports of any

Brianna (16), Christian (10), Svetlana (5)

kind for a few more months. Since this is my third horse "incident" this summer, we felt the Lord was giving us a clear sign that I was to stop riding—Frank wants a wife in one piece; so, we are trying to sell off all but two of our now eight horses. We have only sold one so far—not many people are interested in buying horses at this time of year in Alaska, with the long, cold, dark winter ahead. It will probably be spring before we get any more takers.

Breezy was accepted into a literature program about two weeks ago. We are delighted for her and, of course, proud parents. They do one-on-one tutoring by mail and by phone, with various assignments over a two year period, at the end of which time they guarantee that you will have some sort of manuscript: book, article, or whatever your goal, ready to go to a publisher. We are so happy for Breezy!

Brianna (16), Christian (10), Svetlana (5)

Louise Louise and Gregg
Stuart, age 10
Katie, age 8
Martha, age 6
Sarah, age 6
Lydia, age 5
Virginia, age 3
Oliver, 4 months

Louise wrote this on December 12, which was a nice day, not too cold, and there was no snow on the ground at their farm in the heart of apple country in Gardners, Pennsylvania.

NOTHING IS EVER CONSTANT

Our family consists of my husband Gregg, myself, and our seven children: Stuart, Katie, Martha and Sarah (twins), Lydia, Virginia and Oliver.

We live on a small farm in Pennsylvania. We raise subsistence agriculture, have a crafts business and do homeschool consulting and evaluations. My son is the farmer and produce manager. My daughters help with our craft business. I also give private piano instruction as well. Gregg is an aspiring teacher, but presently works as a truck driver.

Subsistenceagriculture, for us, is almost six acres of intensive gardening and livestock. We grow just about everything we eat. We have several different gardens and around the edges of our house are herbs and teas. Just beyond them are grape arbors and year round gardens. Our orchard has apple, peach, cherry, and walnut trees, and bee hives are in the lower section of the orchard. All around the back are pasture areas for our goats (which we milk) and steers—for selling and for meat. We have geese that range the pasture areas. My son raised two of them one year and every year they hatch about a dozen goslings. So we eat them or sell them all year long. We have chickens in their own yard for eating and eggs and we raise turkeys and hogs for eating and sale. Right now there are three hogs, one of which we will sell to pay for the other two.

My children have rabbits in the barn loft. Now this is purely their business. My son is feverishly "breeding" rabbits now and marking up his calendar so he and the girls will have bunnies just the right size for Easter sales. Stuart is usually very good at these things and each year he makes a good bit of money on his sales. He has acquired a reputation among rabbit buyers in our area. He usually has every rabbit sold within two days after he puts up his sign. Stuart owns the buck and he charges the girls a servicing fee. They breed and sell all summer, but they make the most money in the spring. Stuart has a checking account to buy feed and has made investments with his money in bonds and mutual funds. Katie buys feed and reinvests in other livestock. (She doesn't quite have as much money as Stuart does.) My children have really acquired a knowledge, not just of gardening, but also marketing and sales. Additionally, we sell lots of pumpkins, gourds, and Indian corn in the fall. These things sell well at craft shows.

Gregg is not directly involved in planning or executing our homeschool. He is very supportive of it and enjoys hearing about things when he is home. He does do some mind bender type problems that we can't seem to "get." He also is a good sounding board and supporter when things aren't going quite the way I planned. For instance, when I started my twins in a phonics program, they were so different. Sarah was quick and remembered everything, whereas Martha took more time. Gregg and I discussed the situation. He gave me ideas and encouraged me to analyze each girl separately—not to compare (which isn't easy with twins). I began teaching each of them separately. I divided Martha's "sitting time" into morning and afternoon. This has worked well and now I can have them work together sometimes. I have since increased Martha's sitting time in the morning and have slowly cut out the afternoon time and she is doing better.

Gregg is also very generous about buying school "materials." He trusts me to make those decisions and he knows I try not to be too extravagant. Our school materials include a few textbooks (*Bob Jones University Bible* and *Saxon Math*), several workbooks (Spanish, Greek and *Wordly Wise*, with many resource books, art books, music books, crafts and hundreds of good reading books for all ages. I enjoy telling this story: One time when the community library was having a special speaker, we went there. The librarian was very kind. She introduced herself and began to show us the different books and reading level sections. One of my twins, who was five at the time, said rather loudly, "Mommy, are these the only books here? We have more books than this at home!" It was true.

I tend to follow Charlotte Mason's educational objectives. I plan a few necessary lessons. I provide many good books and have lots of materials available for creative expression. My children love to create and I always have shoe boxes of beads, pompoms, paint, brushes, pastels, chalk, paper, scissors, glue, glitter, cloth, etc. I also help them maintain personal outdoor gardens and

Stuart (10), Katie (8), Martha & Sarah (6), Lydia (5), Virginia (3), Oliver (3mo.)

indoor aquariums, terrariums and house plants, shell collections, feather collections, and birds's nest collections and displays. Each of my four older children can play the piano (my son has cerebral palsy and his left-side is not functional, but he understands music). Stuart plays the harmonica and a lap harp. Katie plays recorder and all of them play the handbells. I provide music suitable for their ages and ability levels (all types—classical, hymns, Christmas, and ragtime). I also maintain a large tape library of various composers. I probably spend about $600-$700 each school year on school materials. My husband is agreeable and willing that I continue to add to our collections.

Our schedule for meals is probably different from most. We eat breakfast at 7:00 AM. Stuart usually gets all necessities ready since the girls and I are tied up combing hair. It usually takes about a half hour to braid their hair. Each girl tries to comb out her own hair and I just braid it. Our biggest task is finding their hair bands. Each girl has at least waist length hair and Sarah and Katie can just about sit on theirs.

Lunch is our big meal of the day. I usually plan the previous day what I want to have for lunch, but sometimes I forget. That is why we had a whole hog made into bologna. I tried the "once a month" cooking plan one time but it did not work for us. Our family is so large that I never had enough pans and bowls to do all the cooking and baking at one time. I bake at least two and sometimes four loaves of bread a day. Stuart and Katie cook on Fridays—I let them create something from scratch. The twins and Lydia do all the dishes (drying and putting away). Our evening meal is called "tea" or snack. We eat light foods—biscuits, breads, fruit, tea, and small sandwiches. Usually the children prepare this themselves and clean up since there are very few dishes. Sometimes they create a very formal "tea" with napkins, etc. Other times, especially in the summer, they get it over with as quickly as possible.

Our bed time ritual begins around 7:00 PM. Each child gets washed up or showered, depending on where and what they have been doing. Oliver is usually very fussy at this time, so everyone takes turns playing with him. We put on his favorite tape of Vivaldi's *Four Seasons* to keep him happy. At about 8:00 PM we put him in his crib to "rest" while we read stories. We begin with Stuart or Katie reading two "little" books to Virginia and Lydia. Then I read four chapter books. Right now it is several verses by A. A. Milne, one chapter of *Farmer Boy* by Laura Ingalls Wilder. (I have been reading this series for the last six years. Every two years I start over again because a younger child is ready to hear it for the first time.) Usually after these two books, Lydia and Virginia head off to bed. Then I read a chapter of *Tom Sawyer* by Mark Twain and lastly five pages of *Little Lord Fauntleroy*, by Burnett. Then it is between 8:30 and 9:00 PM. The twins go to bed. Then Stuart and Katie can read, play games, or play a computer game until 9:00 PM.

Thursday is game night. Then we sit down after tea and play games until bedtime. We always play *The Orchard Game* for the little girls. Each child has a special favorite. Some favorites are *The Farming Game, 24, Mad Dash, Where in the World?, Stratego,* and *Dutch Blitz.*

Stuart (10), Katie (8), Martha & Sarah (6), Lydia (5), Virginia (3), Oliver (3mo.)

Nothing is ever constant. What I do this year may change next year. I sometimes wish for more time. There are so many field trips to take, contests to enter, books to read, plans to make, projects to do, languages to learn. (Not because I feel that we have to get it all done, but because it is fun and challenging.) I want our children to see that there is satisfaction in learning and accomplishment.

A DAY AT OUR HOUSE, December 12:

I got up at 3:30 AM this morning. This is the usual time when Gregg leaves for work. My husband taught for three years at a Christian school fifteen years ago. He really wishes to teach in public school. I think he looks at it as a mission field, but so far, he has not been able to get a job. I am not sure if it is his age (thirty-six) or his conservative views on education, discipline, etc. So, for now, he drives a truck for a dairy. He works four very long days but at least there are only four of them. My husband enjoys science (which is the area of his teaching certification) and he has written several unit studies for junior high science courses. He has "tested" them out with several homeschool students. He would love to try it out with school students as well.

I start the stove and do my exercises (twenty sit-ups, fifty leg lifts, and stretching). Then I go to the school room to "find" my desk after two days of absence. I find several business letters. They get filed in the lower right desk drawer. I also find two *Saxon Math* lessons from last week, check them and file them in the proper child's folder for the day. I get all materials out that I need for today.

It is 4:30 PM. I head to the family room to add some more wood to the stove and start cutting out flannel for a bathrobe. It will be a Christmas present for Stuart. I am thankful that the craft shows are over for the fall. I began thinking about craft shows two years ago when my mother started losing interest in her job. She was feeling low about her job and the aging process. So, to rejuvenate her interest in life, I suggested a craft show. She always enjoyed crocheting and sewing so I helped her with some quilting projects. I have always done custom quilting but now I make smaller items for shows, like table cloths, runners, placemats, miniatures, wall hangings, etc. My mother caught the spirit. She goes to all the shows and she usually takes one or two of my children, who are helpers. They help her to set up and replenish items that sell. It gives each child some personal time with Grandma. My mother loves to chat with the other vendors. Our craft business has grown tremendously. My mother also sells from her home and my father discovered a long neglected talent for pen and ink drawing. He has sold several wildlife drawings, and he now has a commission with the Pennsylvania Historical Commission for historic trains from the Pennsylvania Railroad. He has also sold drawings for Harley-Davidson motorcycles. This has given them both new life and vitality since their retirement time is approaching quickly. Now I should have a little more time for other projects.

At 5:00 AM I listen to the *Christian Science Monitor*. At 5:30 AM I go

Stuart (10), Katie (8), Martha & Sarah (6), Lydia (5), Virginia (3), Oliver (3mo.)

upstairs to wake Oliver for his morning feeding. By 6:00 AM I have gotten everyone up and I am in the barn feeding, haying, and watering our pigs, goats and steers.

By 6:30 AM I am back in the house and the girls are dressed. I do all of the girls' hair in braids and then we eat cooked cereal.

We sit down to have devotions. I try to make this a relaxed time. We use Bob Jones University (BJU) Bible materials. First we go through Stuart's lesson on the crucifixion and prophecy concerning it. Stuart recites Isaiah 9:6,7. We review his catechism and sing *What Child Is This?*, one verse. Then Katie has a lesson on honesty—about Gehazi, Elisha's servant. She recites Luke 2: 8-14 with Sarah and also recites Psalm 100. She reviews her catechisms and then we sing *I Was a Wandering Sheep*. Next, the girls have a Bible story on Ruth and Boaz. We sing a few songs and Sarah and Martha recite Psalm 100. Our devotion time can last an hour sometimes, but I enjoy the Bible study, the singing, and the catechism reviews. Then we practice our handbell songs: *The First Noel* and *Angels We Have Heard on High*. We will be doing these songs next week at a nursing home. I start teaching a new song, *Kum Bah Yah*. This is more difficult because of three part harmony. Katie picks it up quickly. Stuart is okay, but Martha and Sarah don't seem to get it together. Soon Stuart and Katie are fussing at the girls so I say, "Let's just put the bells aside for a while."

Stuart and I sit down to practice a Spanish dialogue from *Spanish Living Language*. We are reviewing Lesson 39 this week. Stuart (after two years of Spanish) has a pretty good accent and a fair vocabulary. I read the final quiz in the book to him. I read each question in Spanish and he is supposed to respond in Spanish. He always knows the correct answer, but he has a difficult time expressing it in Spanish. Then we sit down to "do another state." Every Monday we read about another state from the National Geographic book called *Our Fifty States*. Today I first quiz him on all the capitals of previous states. He knows most of them. Then we look at South Carolina. As I am reading to him about the Low Country and Charleston, I remember that I have two books on architecture and lifestyle in Antebellum Low Country Plantations. I ask him to follow me to the library and I look for the two books for him. I finally find them and show him a few interesting pictures. I go to get Oliver while Stuart and Katie pour through these books. Katie had been reading all this time from *Abraham Lincoln--Childhood of Famous Americans*.

After Oliver is fed and down, I begin some school work with the girls. Martha reads through the Phonics Charts 10-16 in the *Blue-Backed Speller* from A Beka. Sarah reads from an old reader about Dick, Jane, and Sally. They love the antics of Sally and Spot. Martha circles some phonics rules on a piece of paper and divides words into syllables while Sarah reads from the first grade *God's World* publication. She reads fluently and smoothly. Martha is struggling on some words. So I give Sarah some words to circle and divide while I work with Martha. Martha is bright but her concentration skills can be weak so I try to always have them each doing something different to avoid comparison and to encourage Martha to learn to concentrate and think. Martha finishes and I give

Stuart (10), Katie (8), Martha & Sarah (6), Lydia (5), Virginia (3), Oliver (3mo.)

her a problem-solver from Creative Publications. I read the problem to her and she tries to work it out. Stuart is reading *Brady* by Jean Fritz. Katie reads two chapters of *Abraham Lincoln*. Then she reads several articles in a *God's World* newspaper. Now she is back again and sees the "Backpack" section of writings by children in the *Pennsylvania Homeschooler* lying on the desk and asks to read it. Oh no! The phone is ringing and it's Grandma. Oliver went back to bed and since this could be a long call, I tell the girls to go play.

While I am talking, I start cutting sausage and potatoes for lunch. Half an hour later I hang up. At least lunch is ready and the first load of wash is dried and folded. The second load is in the machine. Now where was I? Oh yes, the girls' school work. I call them back. Now Martha reads from her reader and Sarah begins her *Saxon* lesson. I use *Saxon Math 2* for her and she begins on lesson 44. She reads a calendar and writes the date. She then tells me the date two days ago and two days from now. She says the months, tells me the fifth month, the month before September and the month after May. Then she writes the date while Martha does her math page. Martha is using *Saxon Math 1*. Today she is reviewing a worksheet. Sarah finishes a continuing shape pattern, she writes the time to the hour and half hour and she writes number sentences for the number 12. Martha reads from her *God's World* newspaper. Katie appears to have me explain her *Saxon* lesson. She is using *Saxon 54* and is on lesson 68 which is on multiplying 3-digit numbers by 1-digit numbers. She heads up to her desk to work. Stuart has been reading *Brady, Low Country Plantations, God's World*, and *National Geographic*. He also heads upstairs to begin his *Saxon* lesson. He is using *Saxon 65* and he is on lesson 78. He is usually quite diligent about his work and works independently.

Martha is finished with her work and I send her out to play with Lydia and Virginia. They have all the dolls and play clothes out in the playroom.

Sarah is working on her *Saxon* lesson using a balance and measuring weights. She enjoys math and does quite well. She does a fact sheet of combinations and a worksheet, then she does a problem-solver also. We are finished with our work. Stuart and Virginia have been in to inquire about lunch.

I announce lunch. Everyone helps set the table, cut bread, fill cups. We eat sausage, potatoes and orange slices and for dessert the kids eat cookies. After lunch Stuart heads back to other projects—coloring with colored pencils in a wildlife book and finishing a worksheet page from a book about the office of the presidency. Stuart is very interested in politics and political offices. He enjoys reading about presidents, officials, etc.

Katie practices her piano lessons and she organizes the girls (Lydia, Virginia, Martha, and Sarah) into a choir and Christmas program. Katie directs and the girls sing, play duets on the piano and recite scriptures and poetry. I sit down to write and read the mail. At 2:00 PM I tell the girls to go out and do their chores while I feed Oliver, finish the last load of wash and start putting it away. I get out "good" dresses for the girls.

At 3:00 PM I tell them to hurry up since we are going away. Now we have a very hectic time as I get Oliver dressed, wash up the little girls, tell the

Stuart (10), Katie (8), Martha & Sarah (6), Lydia (5), Virginia (3), Oliver (3mo.)

rest to get washed and get dressed. Then I do all their braids again. Now we are getting coats, hats, etc. and I make sure to get money. Finally everyone is in the van. Katie wants to get some gummy bears, so she goes back in for them. I can't find my keys (not unusual) and Stuart and I search frantically. Finally, we find them on top of the piano and are all set. I am only about five minutes late. This is very good! Now we head toward town and also Grandma's house. When we arrive at Grandma's, I feed Oliver again while the kids play. My parents will watch Oliver while we go to the play, *The Best Christmas Pageant Ever.* York is very busy with holiday and rush hour traffic. We arrive at the theater about a half hour before the doors open. I pay for our tickets and we look at pictures from the play. We read the book *The Best Christmas Pageant Ever* last year, so everyone has the idea of the play. Finally the doors open. We choose our seats. Virginia wants to sit with me and I am afraid she will be sleeping before the play is over. Once the play begins, the kids are enthralled. They always enjoy plays. The part where Imogene, as Mary, cries is very touching and Stuart is trying not to cry. Afterwards, Katie asks about being in a play. She wants to be one of the actors. I tell her that we will look around for a play to try out for at a performing arts center. Now we are headed back to pick up Oliver and go home.

When we arrive home, Daddy is still not back, so we get ready for bed. I feed Oliver and wait for Gregg. Finally at 10:00 PM he gets home. He eats while we talk over our day's activities. Then he showers and we go to bed and set the alarm for 3:30 AM so we can begin again!

Stuart (10), Katie (8), Martha & Sarah (6), Lydia (5), Virginia (3), Oliver (3mo.)

Dec 11 - 18

Katie   days of credit 5

Weekly Log Sheet

Reading
(M)-(T)-(W)-(R)-(F)-S-S reading in long book _Maggie at the Elms, Teddy Roosevelt_
M-(T)-W-(R)-(F)-S-S reading magazine article _U. Ranger Rick, Cobblestone_
M-T-W-R-F-S-S read aloud_____
M-T-W-R-F-S-S reading poetry_____

Speiling
(M)-(T)-(W)-(R)-(F)-S-S language lesson _Wordly Wise List 16_
M-(T)-(W)-R-F-S-S proofreading articles, reviews, stories _Diary for Outlook_
M-T-W-R-(T)-S-S spelling games (Spelling Demons, Oh Scrud, hangman,
                scrabble)
M-T-W-R-F-S-S cyclo-teacher

Writing   Specials _Math Olympiad Tues (1 right)_
M-T-W-R-F-S-S writing book reviews   _Geography Bee Fri._
M-(T)-(W)-(R)-F-S-S creative writing - _Diary_
M-T-W-R-F-S-S poetry
M-T-(W)-(R)-(F)-S-S newsletter - _addresses v Christmas Cards_

Math
(M)-(T)-(W)-(R)-F-S-S practical lessons/review _Saxon Les 28, 29, 30, test_
(M)-T-W-R-F-S-S math games _Computer_
(M)-(T)-(W)-(R)-(F)-S-S Problem-solving Figure It Out_X_Problem-solver___
M-(T)-W-R-F-S-S graphs, tables, Geometry _Right Angles_

Science
M-T-(W)-R-F-S-S Unit _Blood & Guts_ Activity _Artificial Lung_
M-(T)-W-(R)-F-S-S Readings _Ranger Rick_

History/Geography
M-T-W-(R)-(F)-S-S Reading book _Teddy Roosevelt_
M-T-W-R-(F)-S-S reading magazine _Cobblestone_
M-T-(W)-(R)-F-S-S map study _Color me in Atlas_
M-T-W-R-(F)-S-S time line additions _Teddy Roosevelt_
M-T-W-R-F-S-S projects_____
M-T-W-R-F-S-S government study

Health/Fire Safety
M-T-(W)-R-F-S-S articles/books _Blood & Guts_

Physical Education
(M)-(T)-(W)-(R)-(F)-S-S jogging, walking, active play, _stretching_ _hockey in garage,_
                riding bike in the attic

Music   Art
M-T-W-R-F-S-S music theory/game   M-T-W-R-F-S-S lesson
(M)-(T)-(W)-(R)-(F)-S-S singing/instrument practice   M-T-W-R-(F)-S-S other
                piano v recorder
Spanish   _Felicity Craft Book_
M-T-W-R-F-S-S vocab   _hoop games_
(M)-(T)-(W)-(R)-F-S-S tapes _Span Living language_
                Les 13

Jim and Ann
Dana, age 4
Brian, age 20 months

Ann wrote about the cold and gloomy day of December 14, when there was snow on the ground at their academic town in the Midwest.

SCRAPPING THE SCHEDULE

THE SETTING:
We have a small house with a large room for playing and reading together. We do our art work and writing at the kitchen table. Our community has lots of musical, artistic and intellectual opportunities, which we enjoy.

THE DAY:
Join us for a real, but not ideal, preschool day in our home.

It is 9:30 AM and my children are watching *Sesame Street* while I am half-asleep on the sofa next to them. My husband, Jim, has already left for work (He has a flexible yet demanding schedule in Christian ministry, and we share a strong commitment to homeschooling.) I opted for extra sleep rather than the 7:30 AM family breakfast we had planned, and now I must pay the price. No shower this morning unless I want to stick my twenty-month-old son in his crib while I take one! It is hard to feel positive when I start my day this way. It is not the ideal morning I had in mind when I first began homeschooling.

I flick the television set off, and the kids are disappointed. They love the TV. We limit the amount and content of what they watch (we don't want them watching commercials) so that they usually watch Disney videos and PBS. I think they would watch TV all day if they were allowed to do so! To temper their disappointment, I try to inject some energy into my voice as I tell them that we must get dressed and start our day.

Our morning routine begins, two hours later than I had planned. Getting the kids dressed and ready is a challenge for me, partly because of my daughter Dana's special needs. She is four, very bright and talkative and has a muscle disease that leaves her with less strength than others her age. She walks, but falls frequently and cannot get up without support from a person or stationary object. I need to be with her, giving assistance while she dresses and uses the bathroom. This morning, Brian wants attention while I am caring for Dana, and Dana wants me to talk to her, also giving her my full attention! Hampered by the sluggish feeling that I haven't been able to shake off as of yet, I snap at Dana crossly. I immediately feel like a terrible mother—a homeschooling failure!

By 10:15 AM the kids are dressed, but their hair is uncombed. I have to decide between nutrition and grooming at this point, and nutrition wins out. The only problem is that we have very little breakfast food in the house! A pint of milk in the fridge and several nearly empty cereal boxes in the cupboard do nothing to arouse my menu-planning creativity. And the kitchen is not an inviting place to prepare a meal today, either! Although we *do* get a decent breakfast fixed after scrounging up the clean dishes to put it on, I am feeling very discouraged.

At 10:45 AM, the kids' hair is combed and I am dressed, *finally!* Although my gray sweatshirt and matching sweatpants over white gym socks and Birkenstocks hardly make me look like the Supermom I'd like to be, I am determined to salvage this day. The kids and I choose a book, and we begin to read. When the phone rings, I let the answering machine get it. We read several different books before Brian's attention span runs out. He likes to be read to, and so does his sister. They enjoy nursery rhymes, Dr. Seuss and other books that I consider to be good children's literature, but they also like Sesame Street books and a series of Disney books that are little more than summaries of Disney's movie plots. We all enjoy trips to the library during which we all check out many different books that are new to us, but today we are enjoying our old favorites, *Green Eggs and Ham*, *Goodnight Moon*, a Mother Goose collection, and *The Grouchy Ladybug*.

After reading, I decide to do some housework while the kids play together. I only get about four minutes to load the dishwasher before the kids need me to come and solve a dispute. Dana needs some assistance standing, so I deal with that, too, before returning to my work. After she has another fall, she needs some extra attention, so I sit and tell her a story. She loves to hear me make up stories about Thumbelina, fairies or other characters. She usually helps create the stories by correcting me when I choose a plot line she doesn't like! After the story, I run back to the dishwasher to try to stuff it full before I am needed again.

By 11:15 AM I'd really like some time to myself, but the kids want me to play with them. I oblige with some wrestling and a bit of chasing. It is hard for me to fight off the urge to straighten their toys instead of playing. But I know that when the kids are older I will have bittersweet longings for the days when I was their favorite playmate, so I continue the games and ignore the clutter.

Dana (4), Brian (20 mo.)

At 11:30 AM I ask the kids to clean up some of the toys. Dana holds a bag and Brian bends down to pick up the toys and put them in the bag. They are working well together, and I feel proud of them. Brian doesn't mind bending over to reach things that his sister cannot reach, and Dana accepts her share of the work without complaining that it is too hard for her. Although they don't finish the whole job, I praise them for it and we all go off to the kitchen for a snack.

As we eat, I think about our day so far. I don't feel like such a failure anymore. We have had a great time reading and playing together, and the kids have worked together well. I am glad that the kids are home with me sharing these experiences, rather than being away at day care or preschool. But I wonder why I felt so bad about our day a couple of hours ago. Could it be that my expectations of myself are too high?

After more play, housework and reading, it is time for a late lunch. The kids help me in little ways as I set the table and prepare the food. Brian brings the plastic cups to the table, Dana carries the spoons. We pray, eat and talk. They help a bit with clean-up, by carrying used napkins to the trash and pushing their chairs under the table. Brian goes down for his nap easily, which is a recent development. He used to cry quite a bit when I put him down, although he was very tired and needed the sleep. Dana doesn't sleep, but plays quietly in her room, as she does for an hour each afternoon. Now I have time for some more reflection about my expectations.

When we started homeschooling, I imagined I would strive for perfection and come close to the mark! While I was under this delusion, I made the following rather humorous schedule:

7:00 AM Ride exercise bike, take shower, dress
7:30 AM Breakfast with family, Jim leads devotions
7:50 AM Dress kids
8:00 AM Kids watch Mr. Rogers, I clean kitchen
8:30 AM Kids free play
9:00 AM Kids play outside
9:15 AM Play with kids outside
9:45 AM Read to kids
10:15 AM Snack
10:30 AM Arts and Crafts
10:50 AM Dana—quiet reading time; Brian—private time with me
11:05 AM Physical Therapy for Dana (at home with me)
11:20 AM Clean-up time
11:30 AM Kids help me make lunch
12:00 Noon Lunch—school day over

After reading over this silly list a few times, I consider tearing it up and throwing the whole thing away. I mean, I'm never going to look at the clock and say "Okay, kids, it's 11:05! Time to stop playing with Brian and start the

Dana (4), Brian (20 mo.)

physical therapy!"

But instead of throwing out all of my expectations with the schedule, I decide to try to look at what we do each week instead of each day. All of our days don't start out as slowly as this one did, and instead of letting a tough day get me down, I want to look at seven days and see what we have accomplished. If we get up on time four out of five days, get the physical therapy exercises done five times, read almost every day and get out the art supplies five times, then I will consider it a good week. But this by-the-minute scheduling is just not natural or necessary for us. I won't feel like a failure because I don't follow such a schedule.

Now that the day is over, and I have scrapped the schedule that was hampering me, I should explain a few things about my family. When we first started homeschooling,I was attracted to the idea of family-centered life as opposed to life where the children are separated from their parents in what I feel is an unnatural way. I also hated some of the things that the public schools try to teach students about morality and truth. Jim and I believe that our kids will get a better education and become better thinkers at home than they would if they went to public school. We plan to continue homeschooling, reassessing our plans yearly as God guides us.

Jim and I spend our evenings together, playing with the kids and getting them off to bed, unless Jim has to work. He is a great dad who takes the morning or afternoon off if he has to work at night, just so that he can spend time with the family. I cherish my evening hours because I can finish all of the things that I haven't been able to get done during the day, or I can collapse on the sofa with a book or with the TV on.

Our children usually spend a good part of the day at the kitchen table coloring, cutting and pasting. They enjoy being allowed to make whatever they want to make, instead of having to copy a project that I have done beforehand as an example. I have found that their creativity grows more delightful each day with this free-structured approach.

I allow them similar freedom in choosing what we study. They choose the topics and we go to the library and check out books about those topics. Once we spent two weeks reading about bats. To this day, Dana remembers what a mammal is because I read to her that bats are the only flying mammal in the world. (Once, when in a conversation with her grandmother on the phone, she announced this interesting "bat fact," and now all of Grandma's friends are aware of this particular bat distinction!) The kids both point out any picture of bats that they see in a book or on TV.

I continue to try to put to death the "perfect homeschooling mom" who lives in my imagination. I pray about it, try to keep connected with friends who help me maintain a good perspective and I remind myself often that nobody is perfect. That "perfect mom" is the only one who could follow all of my schedules and complete all my "to-do" lists. Instead of trying to be her, I want to be myself and enjoy my children each day.

Dana (4), Brian (20 mo.)

UPDATE:

It took me a long time, but I finally realized that I was just too tired from trying to be everything for my kids—teacher, mother, physical therapist, etc. We get much more help around here now. We have two new therapists who help us by coming to our home twice a week and working with Dana. Their help has increased Dana's independence considerably, and lightened my load. I also set up a "kid-exchange" with a good friend—I take her two boys on Friday afternoons and she takes my kids on Monday afternoons. This gives me some time just for myself. (I used to only have time to myself when the kids were sleeping, so I stayed up late and ended up exhausted in the morning.) Jim now leads the family devotions over dinner instead of breakfast, and I don't even try to get up at 7:00 AM! I have learned that it is okay to seek outside support systems while we homeschool. It has made a great difference for our family. And I'm still really glad we "scrapped the schedule"!

Dana (4), Brian (20 mo.)

Keith and Cindy
Kendra, age 11
Jonathan, age 10
Tessha, age 8
Aneka, age 3
(and now Anna)

Cindy described this cold day, late in December, from their mobile home between suburban and rural Mechanicsburg, Pennsylvania.

LOTS OF SCHEDULES

We have been homeschooling since Kendra's birth. Our decision to homeschool was based on the fact that neither Keith nor I were pleased with our own educational process. We wanted to give our children a better opportunity and felt that we could best do that by educating them at home. We live in a mobile home in the rural area of Mechanicsburg. Keith is an automotive technician working in a family business that has been in existence for over thirty years.

Over the past six years we have run the gamut in homeschooling. A change in Keith's work schedule now has Keith off by 4:00 PM Mondays and Fridays and 5:00 PM on Wednesdays. Thus, Tuesdays and Thursdays are the only late nights and they are only to 6:00 PM! How could I get school and supper done by four in the afternoon?

After much prayer, God directed me that the key to successful homeschooling was to have and follow a schedule. Now, I've made *lots* of schedules before. They usually last two to four weeks, then fizzle out due to an exhausted mother. Would this be any different? But in obedience to God's direction, I wrote up a schedule. We've been with a "schedule" for four months and, with God's help, it is working.

We've learned not to be a slave to our schedule, but also not to drop it at the slightest excuse. We are learning flexibility, availability, promptness, attentiveness, etc. As time evolves and the needs of the family and individuals change, so does our schedule.

PAST SCHOOL ROUTINE:

My kids *hate* the heat. I insisted if they stayed inside during summer we would do school. They said, "Fine with us. It's cooler in here!" Thus began our six year routine. We began June 1 and ran to August 31, six days a week, doing *all* academic subjects. Then September 1 to November 30 we merely did reading, math and writing. In December we took a break from books. Baking, gift making and field trips were more than enough to gather fifteen to twenty days of school. We would generally finish school by February 28 (remember we went six days a week, and sometimes even seven). Then, from March to May they had off for spring break, rather than summer break. I loved having history, science and health every day for three months. It was tough, along with other academics and our summer schedule, but the intensity of study brought good results and equaled approximately twice the same work that would have been spread throughout the entire school year! I created my own health study based on the desires of the kids. If they wanted to study the nervous system, I used home and public library resources to create a three month lesson plan, complete with tests, quizzes and games. Our history was biography readings—we love history and reading biographies is a great way to learn it. Now science was a problem. I have always hated science and still don't really like it. The combination of *The Backyard Scientist* and other experiment-oriented books was our mainstream for three years.

PRESENT SCHOOL ROUTINE:

We have five weeks of school and the sixth week is off. This will likely be a year-round schedule. It's my first year of doing this and I'm still experimenting with it. As long as the "off" week truly is an "off" week for Mom, I'll probably keep it this way. Four of the five weeks are with Advanced Training Institute International (ATII) *Wisdom Books*. The first week is academics along with a theme song, worksheet, character quality worksheet, and a meditation worksheet. Every *Wisdom Book* has a theme song (hymn). We learn about its history, the author, composer, how the hymn relates to the passage being studied and the major concept being studied for that *Wisdom Book*. Every *Wisdom Book* has a character quality. We work on the worksheet which applies the character quality to the hymn being learned; we learn of its complete definition, synonyms and antonyms of the word, and who did and did not demonstrate the character quality in Scripture. Lastly, we try to list ways we can show this quality to God and others in our daily lives. The most important step is the meditation worksheet. Through a seven-step process we examine what the *Wisdom Books* passage really means in light of the original Greek, etc. We then paraphrase the verse in our own words to summarize its true meaning and then apply it to our

Kendra (11), Jonathan (10), Tessha (8), Aneka (3)

lives. The key to keeping diligent students during the five weeks is the agreement we have made. Any child *consistently* found being uncooperative loses his week off. I have not had any candidates yet! I truly believe knowing *exactly* what I expect of them and for how long has made the days go from ?????!!!!! to *almost* peaceful and quiet (ha, ha).

In addition to ATII, we supplement areas with *Miquon Math Lab Materials; Saxon* 76 and 65; *Easy Grammar;* creative writing with *Writing Brainstorms* by Becky Daniel; the Laura Ingalls Wilder series and workbook; the *Anne of Green Gables* series; public library use; public school spellers; A Beka *Writing with Phonics II;* piano and recorder books; drawing books; *Reading Music with Your Musical Friends, Fun with Your Musical Friends, Enjoying Music with Your Musical Friends; Time* and *Learning About Money* by Frank S. Schaefer; *Character Sketches* Volumes I, II, III published by Institute for Basic Life Principles; and *Keyboarding Skills*—all grades, by Diana Hanbury King.

Setting up a regular schedule and being disciplined has taken some experimentation. Well, what have been the results, you ask? Many! The first response of my children was, "This is great! Now we know what we are going to do, for how long, and when we will do it!" Obviously, there was prior lack of direction since I never seemed to do the same sequence twice in a row. My kids really enjoy getting up early now, knowing it allows more free time. I discovered they were becoming rather independent and needed me less. This enables me to have much more free time. Kendra and Jon's math lessons sometimes take them forty-five to seventy-five minutes to do. So they work until finished with the lesson and then move on to next subject. They can all be done with all academics in three hours. So our day begins something like this:

5:00 AM:
  The kids rise, dress, and make their beds.

5:30-6:15 AM:
  They meet with Dad in the living room and Dad does one resource of the *Wisdom Book.*

6:15 AM:
  Dad leaves for work.

6:15-6:45 AM:
  The kids do devotions and memorization work. We begin with personal daily devotions (although each child uses a different devotional guide, all must read the assigned chapter of Psalms and Proverbs given the morning before. In addition, fifteen minutes is given for meditation on assigned scripture. Presently we are learning Matthew, Chapters 5, 6, 7. As a family, we join in the living room for oral reading of five chapters of Psalms and one chapter of Proverbs. These are read to find God's wisdom for our day and lives. This is then followed by approximately five chapters of Bible reading. We are trying to

Kendra (11), Jonathan (10), Tessha (8), Aneka (3)

read through the Bible this year. My kids know many Bible stories, but few facts.

6:45-? AM:

The kids do academics until they are finished. The next hour and a half or so are spent in *Wisdom Book* studies. This changes from week to week, as two resources are covered per week. Each booklet is finished in four weeks. *Wisdom Book Parent Guide Planner* includes projects and/or particular applications to enforce the objectives the parents have selected for the children in that particular resource. We often take turns reading and discussing the contents of a particular week's resource over a three to five day period. Wisdom Booklet studies cover:
1. Linguistics: This covers the subjects of languages, grammar, vocabulary, and communication. Linguistics is covered by generally three resources. The first is varied month to month, the second is *Power Through Precision* (vocabulary work), and the third is called *Insights through Investigation* (Greek study).
2. History: This covers archaeology, geography, prophecy, music, art and literature.
3. Science: This covers chemistry, biology, astronomy, geology, physics, and mathematics. Additionally, there is a resource known as *Authority Through Accuracy* which is lots of mathematics application.
4. Law: This covers government, economics, and logic.
5. Medicine: This covers subjects of health, nutrition, behavior, and counseling.

Breakfast:

We eat breakfast late so as to get as much done before my three year old rises. Each child is in charge of cleaning his own dishes. This holds true for all meals and snacks.

After breakfast:

This is our time for phonics. I am training my eleven-year-old to begin instruction with the ten- and eight-year-old. We are presently using the *Christ Centered Curriculum*. It complements our *Wisdom Book* studies very well.

After Wisdom studies and phonics:

After all three children do these together, we go to separate "classes." The older ones always teach the younger ones. Say for example, Tessha has a problem with math. She first goes to Jon. If he is unable to help at the time, she goes to Kendra and last to Mom. This would be ideal if done regularly. That is our goal. I often retort, "Ask your sister (brother) to help."

6:00 PM:

Because the kids get up so early, they also go to bed quite early too! By 6:00 PM dinner is cleaned up, everyone brushes teeth, changes into pajamas,

Kendra (11), Jonathan (10), Tessha (8), Aneka (3)

turns their bed down and rejoins Dad for evening Wisdom Search.

7:00-7:30 PM:
    When Wisdom Search is completed, off to bed! At bedtime, I kiss and hug everyone (as he/she lies *in* bed). Then Daddy enters. He listens to their day, concerns, etc. Then he prays for each child.

7:30-8:00 PM:
    Everyone is snuggled and asleep. Keith rises at 4-4:30 PM and is wiped out by this time. We usually go to bed by 8-9:00 PM ourselves. For Keith and I, our times together are in snatches here and there. Often, as Keith "tucks me in," he does with me as he does with the children. I soon fall fast asleep while he showers. By now, everyone is snuggled and asleep.

    There is no "average" or "normal" way to homeschool. As varied as are the children and the families they represent, so are the homeschooling methods.

THOUGHTS ABOUT HOMESCHOOLING DADS:
    Keith plays an important role, often not publicly appreciated. Regarding his participation in homeschooling (with the ATII program), we plan together monthly what we will elaborate on, using the parent guideplanners. In other words, if we're studying the Macabee Revolt, we can elaborate with further research into Jewish history. Keith has always taught music. He (and his whole family who are of Mennonite stock) is very gifted in singing and does well with music in general (I know zip and sing off-key). He teaches Monday and Wednesday evenings for forty-five minutes, juggling two different kids at two different levels on one of those nights. He is very supportive of homeschooling. There's a lot of opposition out there. Even those who think it is great for elementary, really put on the clamps at secondary—a level we are now entering.
    Homeschooling isn't easy—nor is it impossible! A husband who is the sole bread winner has a great responsibility in that fact alone. My husband's willingness to be such enables me to stay at home and teach. This *is* important; this *is* support. It entails a lot of sacrificing of the extras that a second paycheck could offer. Lots of men won't go *that* far today.
    Such a dad (sole bread winner) doesn't need condemnation because he isn't teaching Junior algebra and Suzuki music. Now if he *can*, let him! If he can't (due to time restrictions, work schedule and lack of confidence in his own teaching ability), let him support with his love and encouragement for the kids and Mom.
    He can support me by asking kids what they learned that day and *expecting* a *complete* answer. He can give me an occasional break or take the kids to a freebie for the day (my husband and kids know the museums and parks like the palm of their hands—they go so often). He asks me out to eat for the

Kendra (11), Jonathan (10), Tessha (8), Aneka (3)

quiet and tries to plan a weekend alone for us about twice a year. Sometimes it is away, sometimes it is at home. It's nice and I do look forward to it. I'm sure with a nursing baby coming soon, we'll need to make a few changes on this issue. There are many ways to support and encourage wives besides just the teaching end of it.

KEEPING HOUSE:

I like order—in my day and my life. Being home full time with four kids and a dog can make any home a mess. In our home everything has a place and everything is (or should be) in its place. Since they were little, my kids learned to take out one toy at a time then replace it where it belongs before getting another. This blessing began during my third pregnancy. I experienced such intense back pain that any bending, sitting, walking, *any* activity brought tears. My doctor said to do no lifting, (I had an eighteen-month-old and a three-year-old), no vacuuming, no stooping to pick up toys (yeh, right—we'll just pretend the carpet pattern is "toys of yesterday"), etc. But the fruit is shown eight years later. Thank you, Lord!

My kids help with housework. They've been doing so for two years. This was my husband's idea. My house is always "neat" because all things are in their place. But it is seldom "clean." After two months or more of grubby toilets, filthy carpets and slimy bathtubs, it got to me. So every Saturday I showed and told Keith how I liked a task done and he, in his ever-patient tone, showed the kids. We set up an allowance/chore chart. As with a job, there were bonus fees and vacation fees. However, an undone chore had a penalty percentage subtracted from the allowance. That child then paid from his remaining allowance to the individual who completed his chore (often Mom). We didn't have to do this very often. However, after two years, this idea got to be a pain. Why? The constant, "But cleaning the toilet is Kendra's job," or "Do I get paid extra for this?" got under my skin. We now work as a family. It has been nine months and no one has a set job to do. We all work as the supervisor (me!) deems necessary and where it is deemed necessary. Even the three-year-old feather dusts furniture, folds all of Daddy's hankies, empties the silverware basket of the dishwasher, bangs erasers, shakes bathroom rugs, helps strip beds on Saturday, makes her bed daily and is learning (via our eight-year-old) how to clean toilets. We start 'em young!

ABOUT SOCIALIZATION:

We are much involved in support groups and social experiences. Let me name a few over the years: Piano lessons; group piano lessons; practice with the Pennsylvania Suzuki Association; involvement in state competitions; recitals; gym classes; gymnastics; swimming classes; vacation Bible school; summer camp; church; Sunday school; children's church; field trips; ATIA (Advanced Training Institute of America) week in Tennessee; Regional convention of ATIA; sign language course; overnight guests of friends and cousins; family events with grandparents, or with extended family; our own church-supported

Kendra (11), Jonathan (10), Tessha (8), Aneka (3)

homeschool support ministry (it meets monthly with a day's schedule of events and this gives the moms a day off), and many, many more.

ABOUT RECORD KEEPING:
Documenting homeschooling and socialization can be challenging. Last year I stapled a group of sheets—one for every subject, including "socialization." Since it is so important to folks, I document it with photos. In my log, I don't count socializing time unless a "learning event" is involved such as globe studies, piano lessons, or sign language study, etc. As any item fits into a subject, I record it on these sheets of documentation. Before this, every year was a struggle to recall what resources I used. This has been a great help for me.

Within my log I record hours (for ATII) and days (for my district). I've always counted days. This year I tried something different. I found we hit the hours way before the days and it wasn't that hard to do either! When I see how much time can be put into a day and *still* get housework, etc. done, I'm amazed!

To help my family, we mark "PMS" week on the calendar in red. That week I only do the required minimum. My frustration level is so low then, I try to take on no extra activities, errands or school hours. This helps me plan better and my kids understand.

As my kids grow so will their goals. I'm not foolish enough to believe I can do it all. Nor am I going to worry about tomorrow. After all, Matthew 6:34 says it well, "Therefore, do not worry about tomorrow, for tomorrow will worry about itself. Each day has enough trouble of its own."

I know I'm the best teacher for *my* kids because I know them so well. I know the strings of privilege to pull (such as a late sleeper not rising and coming to school late two mornings in a row—he missed the surprise blueberry muffins for breakfast and he's never purposely done this again!). We never question our ability to teach our kids to wave "bye-bye," play patty-cake, talk, walk, sing, say "thank you," etc. Yet we all tend to be intimidated with teaching academics. Why? It really isn't different, just a different level of instruction. Just giving our sincere best is all that's needed, along with lots of love.

As parents, we are teachers daily! Whether we homeschool or send our children to school, we are teaching them with our responses and examples. Effort and perseverance, even in an area we feel inadequate, speaks volumes. It shows character and that is far more valuable than straight A's in a subject. Our child may never need geometry for his life occupation. But if we taught him perseverance and faithfulness, those character qualities cover every area of life and job options.

In closing, when I review the past six years of homeschooling I see seven lessons that have definitely helped me ride through bad days:
1. I *am* doing the right thing.
2. I *can't* do it on my own.
3. I *am* the best teacher for *my* kids.
4. I start simple—only what's required (beginning school only at the state's legally required time)

Kendra (11), Jonathan (10), Tessha (8), Aneka (3)

5. I read aloud as much as possible.
6. I let the older teach the younger as much as possible.
7. I concentrate on the early years with reading only. Once they've
   learned to read, everything else is A PIECE OF CAKE!!!

UPDATE:
        We were very regimented with our schedule and then Anna arrived.
She was born at home on Labor Day. The Lord has used her to teach us all
flexibility. We still get all the work done but we take time to stop and play with
the baby, feed her, and change her. She has taught us primarily how to set our
priorities and find the middle ground between no schedule at all and a military
regiment. We now are more reasonable and flexible with our priorities.

Kendra (11), Jonathan (10), Tessha (8), Aneka (3)

Time	M	Tu	W	Th	F	S
5:30 to 6:15		Kids Rise at 5:30 6:15				Weekly Cleaning:
6:30 to 7:30	Kids will from the bible Colleen: Meditation,		He rises with Pa	He rises with Pa	He rises with Pa	Memorize
7:30 to 8:00	Wisdom Search	Wisdom Search	devotions/discipleship	need God rises, do chores/dishes	Boys Laundry	Study
8:00 to 9:00	Wisdom Book	Locate and solve for piano lessons	Wisdom Search	Wisdom Search	Wisdom Search	Bricklon detail
9:00 to 10:30	Wisdom Book	Kendra - Piano Lesson	Wisdom Book	Wisdom Book	Wisdom Bank	Divison detail
10:30 to 11:15	Breakfast	Wisdom Book	Wisdom Book	Wisdom Book	Wisdom Book	Get to church
11:15 to 11:45	Phonics	Wisdom Book	Breakfast	Breakfast	Breakfast	Upon completion
11:45 to 12:15	Kendra - Piano	Kendra - Math	Phonics	Phonics	Kendra - Math	the above
12:15 to 12:45	Kendra - Mail	Kendra - Typing	Kendra - Math	Kendra - Piano	Kendra - SSR	Help
12:45 to 1:15	Kendra - Playtime	Lunch Break	Kendra - SSR / Playtime	Kendra - Mail / Spelling	Kendra - Piano / Spelling	Dan's Hospitality
1:15 to 1:45	Lunch Break	Grammar / Phonics	Lunch Break	Kendra - Mail / Spelling	Lunch Break	Family
1:45 to 2:00	Kendra - Break		Lunch Break	Lunch Break	Water to pigs	
2:00 to 2:45	Grammar	Grammar	Kendra - Break / penmanship	Kendra - Break	Laundry/Straighten	
2:45 to 3:30	Afternoon Break	Afternoon Break	Afternoon Break	Grammar	Afternoon Break	
3:30 to 6:00	Dinner Preparations	Dinner Preparations	Dinner Prep/Chores	Afternoon Break	Dinner Preparations	
6:00 to 7:30	Chores, games, playtime	Vis as needed by parents		Dinner Preparations		
7:15	Dinner, cleanup, prepare for Bed		Dinner, cleanup, prepare for Bed	Dinner, cleanup, prepare for Bed		
	Lights Out - Kids	Lights Out - Kids	Lights Out - Kids	Lights Out - Kids	Lights Out - Kids	
10:00	Lights Out - Parents					

Howard and Susan
Jesse, age 17
Jacob, age 14
Molly, age 11
Hannah, age 7

Susan wrote this on a rainy and rather dreary day in early December, at their farmhouse in the hilly countryside of Kittanning, Pennsylvania.

WE NOTICE THE CONNECTIONS

I meant to keep track today of what we were doing. It was my plan to watch this day and be aware all day long that *this* was to be my real day for this book. But, of course, I forgot this in the whirl of the day, and the day just happened without much thought. I didn't write anything down about it until now and it's after 9:00 PM. The kids are all brushing their teeth and getting ready for bed.

So, what happened today? Can I remember?

But first, who is our family? When is this day?

We have always been homeschooling, and we're just about to have our first son graduate from homeschooling—Jesse's heading for the university next fall. Next is Jacob who is a ninth grader, then Molly is a seventh grader, and Hannah (our "baby") who's now in second grade at home. Our kids have never known anything but homeschooling, and they've all done very well over the years, which is not to say that they always do well in everything each day or that we don't struggle with some areas.

And when is this day? It's in early December, and a rainy and rather dreary day outside. Just the sort of day for staying inside and home-schooling—on brighter, more cheerful days the kids would've played or worked outside more, but today we all were quite content to stay in. And besides, we all felt the need for catching up on things—at least I did. And we were all glad that we actually have three days in a row this week with no outside outings or chores or trips or appointments, and no visitors. Our more usual schedule is a bit more hectic, with lots of folks coming here, lots of going out, and quite a bit of long distance traveling across Pennsylvania on various homeschooling business activities, especially year-end evaluations, achievement testing, and curriculum fairs. We also run a small mail-order catalog, do lots of phone counseling, and have written a few books here and there—we are busy folks! So, we were all grateful for this brief lull of a few days, and planned to get a lot done.

And where do we live? Home for us is an old farmhouse on a 135 acre farm in hilly Western Pennsylvania. There are neighbors a bit up the road and down the road from us, but we rarely see them. Our community is the community of homeschoolers that we know—both in our area and all across the state. And what's our house look like inside? My mother used to say that I decorated in "early kindergarten" because I loved putting children's artwork all around our home—even before I started homeschooling. I've now graduated to at least "early junior high" in my decorating scheme as the kids have gotten older—children's artwork and projects are everywhere on display (there is not much wall space left around here!), along with thousands of books.

We are fortunate to have a whole room we can use for storing our homeschooling supplies (we call it our project room), but we hardly restrict ourselves to that one room. In fact, I can hardly remember a time when all four kids were in the project room at the same time. Jesse might be upstairs reading in his bunkbed or typing on his computer in the office. Jacob is usually found at his computer in the project room. Molly might be sprawled on the sofa reading or on the floor somewhere involved in some new art project. Hannah might be playing up in her bedroom or the finished-off attic, or talking with me in the kitchen as I do dishes, or doing French with me up in my bedroom (that way the tape recorder won't distract the other kids downstairs).

Our house is a bit (well, on many days this is quite an understatement!) tumbled and messy and full of odd collections of things to look at and wonder about. Upstairs in our hallway we have our Bone Museum—a collection of skulls and vertebrae gathered over many years, with everything from baby crow skulls to turtle shells to two cow skulls. And we usually have various piles of stuff from the kids' latest projects lying about—this week it's weavings made on simple looms using recycled cotton loopers from a sock factory.

Our home business that serves homeschoolers has its office on our second floor—a hi-tech room with four computers, a photocopier, laser printer, comb-binding machine, a FAX phone machine, scads of file cabinets, and our stock of books we sell in our small mail-order catalog. My husband Howard is up here most days when he's home, and the kids often find their way into the old easy chair in one corner. The two boys both work for us for at least a short while most days—Jesse is in charge of all our routine mail-order work, and Jacob is in charge of our video loan library. Molly and Hannah earn extra money by doing photo-copying for us, and everyone helps with our regular bulk mailings when our quarterly newsletter goes out, when test score reports go out, and when

Jesse (17), Jacob (14), Molly (11), Hannah (7)

renewal notices go out . . . . And Jesse and Molly especially do their share of phone call answering. They all know about all of our work—they do not have that vague sense of not knowing what their parents do for a living, because we do it all around them and involve them right in it.

But on to this day, early in December . . . .

I awoke a bit earlier than in other recent days and had most of the kids up by just after 7:00 AM. This involves me in cheerfully and loudly announcing at bedroom doors that it's morning—usually I need to do this several times before any kids actually start making the groggy move to the bathroom and showers. I seem to be the only true morning person in the household, although I can be easily thrown off schedule by too many late nights. But today I was more responsible, and we sat down to breakfast by 8:00 AM. Hannah slept in, even though I tried to wake her (she has, perhaps not wisely on our part, gone to bed at the same time as all the older kids all her life, so sometimes needs to sleep in), but the other three were actually all at various tasks by the time I got down-stairs—Jacob probably programming or reading, Jesse reading about the history of Haiti for a research project he's planning, and Molly reading *Zlata's Diary*.

During breakfast I read aloud a wonderful essay called "On Kittens" from a 1940 literature anthology, then read several essays by E. B. White. We ate homemade granola—easy preparation on weekdays. We save a hot breakfast of eggs and waffles for weekends when Howard or Jacob cooks. I made a turkey roaster full of granola Sunday afternoon, just two days ago, along with a batch of whole wheat bread (almost burned).

I asked all the kids for their morning plans as we finished breakfast, and then they set off. I find this little step of asking the kids to think about their day is very beneficial—much more beneficial than my telling them what they should do when. I feel free to make suggestions of course, but I put the responsibility for the rough timetable on them. Jesse chose to practice piano first, Jacob worked on his letter-to-an-author entry for the Books Change Lives Contest, Molly read more of *Zlata*, and Hannah continued sleeping. I found myself with little to do, and so spent some time setting up math work for Hannah to start on when she got up, and also made plans for her French time. The other day we had just begun working to prepare for her first National French Exam (the elementary version—all listening and marking multiple-choice picture answers) by using a practice test, and I wanted to review what she had done yesterday, as some vocabulary was brand new to her.

I stopped to talk with Jacob about his letter for the Books Change Lives Contest, and he let me read it, although he felt it was not working out at all well. I felt he thought it was too similar to last year's entry, and although I assured him I thought it had possibilities, I searched in my mind for other books I could suggest he choose to do instead. He was trying to write a letter to the author of a physics book called *The God Particle*, and much of his writing was similar to last year's entry, when he wrote to the author of the mathematical fantasy *Flatland*. I finally suggested he might want to write to Jonathan Swift, as he'd

Jesse (17), Jacob (14), Molly (11), Hannah (7)

read *Gulliver's Travels* recently and really enjoyed it. He had even given a report on it to our writing club and had written an hysterical burlesque travel tale of his own. He liked the idea right off and started in on revising his piece for this purpose. The deadline for this contest is on Friday, so he doesn't have much time. I'm pleased he is working happily on it—he worked on it on and off throughout the day.

During this time, Jesse practiced piano diligently on his own, with only occasional reminders from me to get back to it, or queries about if he was done already, or should he practice that section of the piece slowly. How different this is from his early days of playing piano when it was *very* necessary for me to be right there with him every minute. They do grow up.

Molly stops reading when finished with her book, and goes to work on her letter to Anne Frank, her entry in the Books Change Lives competition. It's coming very well, and she also works on it on and off throughout the day. Her first attempt is really getting filled in. She asks for my suggestions on what I feel she might still hit on, or places where I think things are awkward or disorganized. She points out the many places where she has made changes herself—where she's added in thoughts, rearranged paragraphs, developed a new idea, etc. She is very receptive to my help, and although the piece is quite personal, she is not overly protective about it but is able to look at it quite dispassionately as a piece of writing that she wants to improve and make as fine as possible. She's figured out how to count up the words in her piece using our computer, and proudly keeps me up on how much longer it's getting throughout the day. Her top limit for this contest entry is 1000 words, and she's getting close now.

Molly also takes time several times in the day to write in her own diary, inspired by Anne Frank. She has always kept diaries of various sorts before—she always liked the idea of a diary—but this one feels very different to her, much more personal and less just chit-chat and niceness. She took a notebook last week (those nice stitched ones with the lined pages and the thick cardboard covers that I remember loving even when I was a girl), and made her own cloth cover. She's putting in photos and mementos also. Again, Molly and all my kids usually set their own times for doing specific tasks, and often choose their own new tasks to do—I don't micro-manage their time during the day, in part because I'm usually quite busy myself.

Hannah has now gotten up and I'm working with her on French. My review idea is an instant hit. She is simply redoing yesterday's part of the exam, re-listening to the tape and marking the multiple choice answers on her new answer sheet. (I had to buy a set of twenty-five old practice tests to have samples to show her—may as well use them!) She is really getting quite good with her beginning French and this exam preparation is very good for us and fun for her. She is thrilled that she now gets every question right, remembering almost everything from yesterday. We chat in French a bit, act things out in funny ways, laugh, and enjoy our time while the older kids are all still working independently on their own projects.

Jesse (17), Jacob (14), Molly (11), Hannah (7)

When finished we move to math time. (Does Hannah ever eat breakfast??? I'm not sure . . . she's not much of a one for breakfast anyway, and not one to ask until it's about lunch time. Maybe she gets herself something at some point . . . .) I've planned to have Hannah do more problems in my newly published book *Math by Kids!* today. She chooses to do all the *easy* problems on the first page in the book, very excited at how quickly she can figure them out. I, at first, thought these problems might be too easy for her, and so a waste of her time, but for Hannah it has real value—she's getting warmed up and confident, and ready to tackle some harder work on the next page. She is really improving in her ability to relate to me orally *how* she goes about math thinking—something I regularly ask her to do, but something that was not always easy for her. She is clearly developing many helpful strategies and "tools" for working out new problems, and she discusses with me today how she now knows how to use scratch paper well—"When I was five or six I didn't know how to use scratch paper, but now I *do!*" She uses it well indeed to keep track of all the steps in a problem, translating word problems effortlessly into symbols and then manipulating them into solutions. She even is able to attack the very difficult problem on Mrs. C's six boys and their three pairs of socks a day for a week—Hannah *knew* that she had had great difficulty in doing that problem two months ago and has often said "I'm *not doing* that problem again! I don't understand it!!!" But today she is ready, fit, and able, and tackles it without too much trouble. Diagrams help, and the barest suggestions from me get her going. I am even amazed at her way of tackling 18 x 7, a calculation that comes up in this socks problem. She writes down seven 18's on her paper, adds all the 10's to get 70 and writes that down. Then she's faced with those seven 8's. I suggest that *maybe* she could think of them as 10's and then subtract, because 8 is almost 10. She immediately sees what I'm getting at. A few months ago she probably would have balked at this type of suggestion and I would have had to back off. She realizes she needs to subtract seven 2's from her new 70, then add that 56 to her original 70, and she has it. She's thrilled. I don't teach beginning math in a traditional "algorithm" way of showing specific rules and procedures and expecting the child to just mimic them thoughtlessly until some later age when maybe it will all become meaningful. Instead I encourage my kids to come up with their own ways of doing calculations and solving problems.

Hannah, later in the day, comes to me to tell me she has been reading and has just finished a *Step-Up* book on American Indians—she's read the entire book all on her own. I don't get to talk about it with her because I'm in the middle of French time with someone else, but I congratulate her and am excited with her for a moment about her accomplishment.

We all talk of kittens and cats a lot all day because of the essay I read at breakfast—and our mother cat Moppet is especially playful with her kitten Butterball all day long, perhaps as a result of all our interest. Or maybe Moppet was listening in . . . after all, the point of the essay was partly that people love kittens but find older, more sedate cats less charming.

Jacob practices juggling during the morning, with rings, bean bags, and clubs, and does a bit of unicycle riding in the house—at 9:00 AM he shows me that he is beginning to learn how to keep basically in one place on his unicycle by going very quickly forward and back. I do a bit of juggling with Jacob in the morning, during a break where everyone else is busy. Jacob tells me I should practice regularly every day, and then I might have a chance of actually getting better. Jacob is one child who clearly knows in his gut the value of working at something regularly, daily. He's that sort of person. He has incredible concentration-on-task when he's learning something new—I still remember when he was six years old and learning to jump rope. He spent two entire days doing almost nothing but trying, and by the end of day two he had it. He doesn't give up quickly. So I spend a few minutes juggling three bean bags with Jacob, and chatting with him informally while the other kids are at their tasks. I leave the breakfast dishes till later.

Jesse moves to work on his Great Essay correspondence course work after piano, and I come up to discuss it with him as he finishes it up. He's not entirely pleased with his effort, but it's a serviceable essay, and I encourage him to get it off in the mail to his teacher. His assignment is rewriting Bacon's essay "On Delays" in a more modern style, using some specific ideas from real life to illustrate his points—and Jesse jokes in his note to his teacher at the top that he has certainly delayed once again in getting his work off to her. He promises himself he will stay on top of this course more from here on in. He took a poetry course from the same teacher last year, and this experience of sending work off to someone else is very good for him just now. He gets feedback from someone other than me, he is learning to complete regular assignments (the deal is that if he doesn't finish by the end of the year, he gets to pay for the entire course from his own money... we're not above little "motivations" like this!) and the work is challenging and rigorous and different from what he might choose to do all on his own. He also just finished a lesson in his college-level Western Civilization university correspondence course yesterday and got that off in the mail—as this is a relatively free and unencumbered week for us, he is taking advantage of it and getting caught up on lots of things that he is behind on.

I'm back downstairs working with the others, mostly Hannah, but when I happen back upstairs at some point, Jesse is working away at reading his Western Civilization text in his bedroom—he's finishing his new reading assignment today, all on the High Middle Ages. I'm learning about his course work through final help and discussion of his essay responses to assignments—in no way do I have the time to read all his material, let alone teach it to him, but it's good to keep in touch as much as I can so that I can share his interests. I do try usually to watch the videos we also purchased on Western Civilization this year (these aren't officially part of his course, but the tapes work very well with his text and are a nice complement to his reading—they are produced by Annenberg/CPB). The videos are a way that all of us can learn from Jesse's course together.

After a quick exercise break for some stair climbing (quick indoor aerobics—remember that it is a dreary, drizzly day outside), Jesse is back at his computer in our office working on his Letters About Literature entry. He is still in the formative stages with this one, but it's much better than a few days ago when I snuck a look at his first draft. I admit to him that I looked at it earlier without asking him and that is okay with him—and I let him know that I can very clearly see that he has made lots of improvements in it since that initial draft. He's decided to write to Eric Hoffer about his book *The True Believer*; he read the book a few weeks back after hearing Howard and me discussing it with a friend (we'd all read it back in college).

There are various usual interruptions during the morning—the mail arrives, which means we all have to look it over and discuss what's come. "A letter from Japan! A letter from The United Arab Emirates!" This last prompts me to suggest that Molly locate that country on a map, which she does—using our living room ceiling maps as her atlas! She just read a wonderful article by a National Geographic Geography Bee winner, and I'm hoping now she will be inspired to study geography a bit more seriously in preparation for our upcoming homeschoolers' Geography Bee in January—she did voluntarily sit down to read the *National Geographic* article on the breakup of the Soviet Union that I suggested to her yesterday (I make *many* suggestions all day to my kids, not all of which are followed up on, by the kids *or* by me . . . . In fact, I often forget what I've suggested—one of the dangers of being a bit spontaneous in my work with the kids.) Molly later tells me that she read a one-page article in *TIME* magazine about Sarajevo—it means more to her now that she has read *Zlata's Diary*, and I think Molly is changing a bit and becoming more interested in world events now.

Molly also tells me about the *TIME* magazine cover article she's read about the dangers of overbreeding dogs—and I mentally chalk that up to biology reading for her. Her science program is more free-form than most areas, and is an area we do not focus on as much as others, but the plan indeed was learning about animal behavior and beginning biology this year, so I'm glad she read this piece. She started out the year planning to read a chapter a week in a biology text book, but that hasn't quite happened . . . . Oh, she's on maybe chapter two and it's December. Ah well. . . . You can't focus on everything. She has read several very good books related to her topic though: Conrad Lorenz's book about the animals in his life, and a book about orangutans in the wild and the people who study them. And we visit our share of science museums over the year and do our bit with nature study and leaf collecting and dissecting milkweed pods. It will have to suffice this year.

After lunch I have French time with Jesse—we planned to go at it for thirty minutes, but I'm sure it stretched into an hour. We work at *French in Action* until we finish the lesson (listening to audio tapes while responding orally to questions and also completing written exercises in grammar patterns in our worktext; we had already watched the video portion of the lesson), and then we go over the little play he plans to do with a friend over Christmas vacation when we have a three-family French Night here. Doing the plays will be fun I think—I got inspired to try them after reading a little piece in a newsletter published by

Jesse (17), Jacob (14), Molly (11), Hannah (7)

the American Association of French Teachers that I get. I am a member of a zillion educational organizations, and although I don't get to read half of what comes into the house from them, I do occasionally get an inspiration and insight, and that makes it all worthwhile. In part I joined the AAFT so that my kids can take part in the National French Exam for a cheaper fee.

Next is French for Jacob and Molly. We first go over their little play they plan to do at our French Night—an adaptation of a cute little story from a beginning French reader that is easy enough for even Hannah to understand and read. Molly will be narrator, Jacob is Henri (a young boy) and Hannah will be Michelle (a cat). Practice goes well, even though Jacob frankly thinks the whole thing is a bit dumb. But he wants to be involved (and we need him to be involved—he has no choice!), so we all persevere. Then it's on to Molly and Jacob's *French in Action* lesson—we've probably been on lesson 7 for a month, but by tomorrow (if all goes to plan) we'll be finished. Molly and Jacob are beginning to work together well—not an easy task for these two middle children who are both very competitive and who have a history of, well, numerous disagreements. Having Molly, who is naturally much better at languages, work with Jacob is much like having Jacob work with Jesse in math—a helpful spur to better achievement. A little competition from the younger sibling helps to move the older to better efforts. We complete the amount of the lesson we had planned to do (this makes it two days in a row we've worked on French—*maybe* we can keep up our momentum!). I planned (mentally that is—I rarely write plans down . . . when I *do* write them down I usually forget to look at them . . .) also to have them practice with the French exam, but we run out of time—it's about 3:30 PM in the afternoon already.

Molly then gets back to her Anne Frank letter. She also got in a brief piano time with Hannah. I plan to have Hannah start lessons with our teacher next fall, when Jesse is off at college (I somehow can't imagine having three kids officially in music lessons at the same time), and right now Molly has taken on the task of teaching Hannah piano herself. She is doing a fine job. She even made Hannah a little practice record book, has an "official" lesson time with her once a week, and Molly is learning to be a patient teacher. Hannah is very proud of her growing playing ability. (Molly started piano lessons at exactly age five—with Hannah I couldn't imagine starting that early!).

Jacob tries out a new vocabulary program on the computer that someone has sent us to review—it seems to Jacob to be mostly an arcade game with a thin veneer of education. Molly also tries it out, and she thinks it's useful. I never see it closer than from the other side of the room. Jacob also spends a bit of time using the French verb drill program that he made for us this fall. Jacob *loves* programming computers (another task that takes lots of time and lots of regular and continual work to learn), and has made many, many games and astonishing math and physics simulations. We rarely buy commercial software, as Jacob can just make us anything we need—and we like the kids to be using the computer actively as a tool, rather than just using someone else's program or game. I sometimes make suggestions for particular programs I think might be

Jesse (17), Jacob (14), Molly (11), Hannah (7)

helpful, like this verb drill, but usually Jacob just continues to come up with his own ideas. He's a self-starter in programming and I mostly just try to stay out of his way. He also enters the annual International Computer Problem Solving Contest (he came in first place when he was in sixth grade)—we are always on the lookout for competitions in areas where the kids have deep interests, as we feel that competing with others usually spurs them on to much greater efforts.

Jacob reminds me that someone needs to think of dinner. I am happy to tell him that I *do* have plans—I'm making pizza, using pie shells I made two days ago on Sunday when I made bread. He helps me make them up—pizza is usually his arena anyway—and we eat at about 6:00 PM. (Our plan is 5:30 PM, so this is close!)

During the last fifteen minutes before supper I read to everyone at the table (we thought those pizzas were ready and had everyone there, only to find the dough in the center was quite doughy yet . . . .) So I read from *TIME* magazine, from an article Jesse had been telling me about. It's about orphanages—I'd just heard a National Public Radio spot on "BOYSTOWN, USA" this morning and we'd already planned that the next video we are borrowing for Friday evening will be the Spencer Tracy movie about Boystown. So I'm interested in this article and so are the kids—and we can compare it to *Oliver Twist*, which we just finished as a family read-aloud last week.

When the pizza is finally ready I start on our new read-aloud book—I've chosen *Great Expectations* by Dickens, another book I've never read. I'd read aloud an article on the book to Jesse during the afternoon—I found it in a magazine called *Imagine* put out by the Center for Talented Youth from Johns Hopkins University. The article actually compared Jane Austen's *Emma* (which the kids know I read this fall, and they've all heard about the basic plot and characters from me) to Charles Dickens's *Great Expectations*, so Jesse and I have a good talk about it, and decide to read the book. I'd never read anything by Dickens before this year, except for *A Christmas Carol*—I faked my way through the abridged version of *David Copperfield* that I was supposed to read in tenth grade English class. I'd always in the past found those long, long Dickensian sentences just too much, but now they aren't so hard. I'm enjoying this move into reading aloud real classic literature, not just kids' books anymore.

After supper we have our regular twenty-minute family cleanup time. This is a real blessing for me, and a *very* regular routine for our not-very-routine family. Even if the house has completely self-destructed in the day (not an unusual occurrence around here) our evening clean-up gets things back in line enough so that I don't feel frantic. All the kids but Jesse have set, assigned, long-term jobs so that there does not need to be lengthy discussion about who does what. Jesse has a "floating" job, he's old enough not to be thrown by doing different tasks each evening.

Right after this, Howard arrives home from the university where he does part-time research work in artificial intelligence. He quickly settles down to an evening chess game with Jacob, a regular routine now for them. Jacob has enjoyed taking part in several chess competitions this year, and Howard has

Jesse (17), Jacob (14), Molly (11), Hannah (7)

started a homeschoolers' chess club so we can have a whole high school level team competing. Howard loves chess, and so this is wonderful fun for him. In fact Howard loves playing all sorts of games with the kids when he has time—which is lucky for the kids, as I have to admit I don't like playing many games anymore; it has to be pretty "educational" to get me playing.

Sometime, I think just before lunch, Jacob worked on mailing out videos. He is in charge of this part of our service business, and he has developed his own computer program to keep track of records, etc. He handles taping and mailing and record-keeping—and gets out about twenty videos today. We pay him for all his work, of course, as we pay all our kids when they do special jobs for us. Jesse usually does the mail for us daily, but I don't remind him today and he instead uses his free time freely—and reads *TIME* magazine.

I also spent a good bit of time today on the phone, mostly during the morning and from 3:00 to 5:00 PM (our official phone answering time, according to our answering machine message). When Howard is home he answers phone calls, or we let the machine take them. But Howard was at the university today and I often did have times today when all the kids were legally busy and I was not needed, so I took some calls. Some are just quick routine calls on homeschooling ("How much is your *Guide to the Law*?") but others are more complex or take more of my time than I'd planned—a new homeschooler needs lots of advice, someone is having trouble with a district over their special needs child, and more. Once I'm actually working with the kids on something (say, during that French time after lunch) I just let the machine take over and I do *not* answer the phone. I'm pleased later in the day that only two messages are left on the machine—sometimes it can seem easier just to take the phone calls as they come than face twelve messages waiting for me at the end of the day. Once, during the official answering time from 3:00 to 5:00 PM, I was upstairs helping go over Jesse's Letters About Literature essay, and asked Jesse if he would take the call. He does, and talks to someone for about five minutes about the books we stock and how to order. He never tells them he is just one of the "kids" in the family, and I doubt the family realizes it. He also does simple phone counseling for minor homeschooling problems at times—he knows when a problem is too difficult and Mom or Dad need to be called in. Jesse probably knows the state homeschool law about as well as anyone in the state, and he has heard us talk with people about these sorts of things for years and years. It just comes naturally to him. I appreciate his help—it's allowed me to keep proofreading over his piece without interruption.

I spend my time after evening cleanup browsing through the stack of books that Howard has brought back from the university library for Jacob on his upcoming Galileo project—I plan to have all the kids enter the National History Day competition program this year with history research papers, and at my suggestion Jacob is doing a paper on the conflict between Galileo and the Catholic church. Jacob loves physics, and has learned quite a bit about Galileo from the video course on physics that the boys use together, so I thought this would be a natural for him. The topic also ties in a bit with the world history learning Jacob has also been doing this year. Howard has borrowed wonderful books for Jacob—one is completely primary source materials, the letters written between Galileo and his friends and enemies about all his controversial findings.

I also spent some time in the early afternoon looking over the Student Guide booklet to this National History Day program—I thought I didn't have a recent copy of their booklet, but found one when looking for something else and fell to reading it instead. We've always meant to enter this contest, but I never before started the kids on it early enough. Jesse is doing a project on Haiti, and has borrowed lots of books also—and I think he spent some time reading one of them during the day sometime. I'm not sure, though—he also started reading Alan Bloom's popular book *The Closing of the American Mind* today, and may have been off reading that instead. Last night, though, he was up with the bedside light on reading until 11:00 PM about Haiti, and was telling me about it as he woke up this morning. I actually try to dissuade Jesse from pursuing the Bloom book *right now* because he does have all these deadlines staring at him.

Getting everyone to bed can take a while around here. Seems my kids are usually not quick about teethbrushing, flossing, and changing to nightclothes—everyone gets talking, gets distracted by something else they still want to do, or in some way slows down the process of getting ready for bed. Ah, well. At some point everyone is ready. Bedtime usually means reading-aloud time, with Howard or with me, although with the kids getting older we're not as regular about that as we used to be. Jesse now often goes downstairs to write in his computer journal before bed, and is often the last one upstairs. Jacob sometimes reads to himself in bed before turning off the light, and Molly and Hannah often read a bit in bed on their own too. There are hugs goodnight and Molly always says a cheerful "see you tomorrow." It's finally reasonably quiet and calm.

Now that the day is finished I take mental note of what we didn't do today. Let's see, Jesse and Jacob didn't squeeze in time for physics or calculus, something they work on together. They are using the *Mechanical Universe* text and videos produced by California Institute of Technology for physics, and several different texts and practice books for calculus. They both plan on taking the AP exams in both subjects this spring and Jacob is actually the teacher for Jesse. The last two days they have had good sessions together, and tomorrow we'll be sure to work it in. Molly didn't get to her algebra lesson either (and we didn't find the notebook she's been diligently working in all year either—just yesterday we discovered it was lost . . . .). But, all in all, it's been a productive day, with lots of interaction and learning and work from everybody. And time out to enjoy ourselves a bit too. It was indeed nice to have a day all at home—socialization is wonderful, but relaxing at home and getting lots of work done is wonderful too.

After supper, just before our clean-up time, I asked to see everybody's charts for the day, as the kids are in charge of keeping their own records. I should be so organized everyday—many times we *all* forget to jot things down and I forget to check. But today we all do it and everyone has been responsible. I

Jesse (17), Jacob (14), Molly (11), Hannah (7)

know, of course, that the mere jottings in our logs bear absolutely no resemblance to our actual day—they couldn't. But it suffices and it keeps us on track and keeps us legal. I could never take the time to write out this sort of narrative every day on what we all do—and even here I'm feeling that I'm leaving things out. I've learned not to expect to write everything down or have something to show for every little natural learning opportunity that comes along. Most of our conversations and musings go on without anyone thinking they should be logged and counted in officially, although we all do joke a good bit about how integrated we're being when we notice the connections between disparate topics. Mostly we just keep talking with each other, keep reading, keep talking about what we're reading, and keep writing about what's most important to us, and sharing our writing. And that's what our days are mostly like.

UPDATE:

Jesse's in his freshman year at the university and is fitting right in, doing very well and loving it. Molly's *Anne Frank* letter was a national finalist winner and was published in a book called *Dear Author*, along with the other finalists. Happily, both Jesse and Jacob passed all of their AP courses.

Jesse (17), Jacob (14), Molly (11), Hannah (7)

Blake and Karla
Ian, age 6
Rachel, age 4

Karla wrote about this cold morning but warm and sunny afternoon in November, from the small city college town near a nice park in College Station, Texas.

WE LIKE IT THIS WAY

Our home is a small three-bedroom house on a nice lot in town, not terribly big, but it backs up to a large field. Directly across the street is a large park. Quite a few people homeschool around here and there are more than eight support groups! The schools leave us alone and so do our neighbors—really nice neighbors—not the sort to try to interfere in our business.

Homeschooling takes place all over the house. It has been at the kitchen table, at a card table in the living room, on the floor of whoever's room is picked up, and both at a table and on the floor of the converted garage that I use as a library. The most effective places have been on the floors and at the card table. The materials are in the library in a cupboard under one of the shelving units. We organize time around chores and meals. The more formal parts of schooling are done between breakfast and lunch, but time on the computer is anytime the children want it.

Usually Ian and Rachel wake up between 6:30 and 7:00 AM. We adults are awakened by the sounds of a cat being chased and the penned up dog barking to join in the fun. I yell "quiet!" and tell everyone to go back to bed. That brings everyone into our room for hugs and a chorus of "but the clock says it's seven and the sun is up!" Compelling arguments since I'm the one who set the rules that the clock must read seven and the sun must be up or it isn't morning. I love cloudy mornings—sometimes I can get an extra fifteen or twenty minutes sleep before they think to check the clock.

Blake, who got in from his early morning paper route around 5:30 AM and went straight back to sleep, gets up and starts breakfast while I get ready for my day. His route gets him up between 12:30 and 2:00 AM. We are all at home asleep so he is careful not to wake us. A large truck arrives from the city with all the sections of the newspaper in bundles. Blake and the other men who do papers, unload the truck and sort out the bundles. Blake moves the bundles for the commercial routes to another area of the business park where he and several other people open the bundles and put the papers together. Blake's route takes him to stores and newspaper machines all over the north part of the town. He usually gets home around 6:00 AM and relaxes and gets his shower—unless he is really cold or tired and then he catches another hour of sleep. Everyone gets up for the morning at around 7:00 AM. Blake is up and awake during the hours I am at school and he goes to bed in the early evening, around 7:00 PM. (We put the kids to bed about the same time.)

The children get themselves dressed and most days they do a fairly good job, so I'm willing to be seen in public with them. Neither child can find their shoes today, so I tell them to look some more. Ian finds his, but all Rachel can locate are a pair she outgrew months ago and her boots. Boots it is for the day.

Breakfast is usually a bit noisy, and since Blake cooks it, we generally get either scrambled eggs or toasted cheese sandwiches. Right after breakfast, I settle down with my computer and Blake begins the school day for Ian and Rachel.

I'm telling about a day that I stayed home and watched Blake teach. Usually I'm off at school myself. I'm a graduate student in Animal Sciences and find it much easier to concentrate on my studies in my office at school. Also, I write up the lesson plans for Blake and sometimes he even follows them. Ordinarily, I leave around 8:00 AM, later if my class schedule permits, but I like to get to school early. I am home again between 3:00 and 4:00 PM. Usually we eat dinner early. I spend time with Ian and Rachel, and then once everyone is in bed, I work on reading, homework or go on-line. Most of my social life is from the computer. It allows me to have adult contact with people who share my interests whenever I have the time to fire up the modem! In Animal Science I am working toward a masters in Animal Breeding, so I am taking quite a bit of genetics and statistics. I want to have a strong grasp of breeding theory to apply to my own horse breeding, and I'd like to work with a breed registry gathering data on the breed. With horses, very little is known compared to what there is to know.

Blake and I both agreed to homeschooling. Of the two of us, I am the more strongly committed. I think that is because I am more certain that the children will learn everything they need to learn. Blake, on the other hand, needs to see more clearly measurable results. He worries that they might get "behind." I have confidence gained from development and curriculum classes. I know they are right on schedule or doing better than they would in public school. I can sit down and talk with them and ask questions and see what they are doing. Blake

Ian (6), Rachel (4)

doesn't like to read up on schooling, so he has only my evaluations. He is so used to the children learning and talking that he expects that all children are where they are in their development.

I have a teaching certificate and by the end of my student teaching I had decided that "no way were my children going to the public schools." Three towns, six schools, and not one was doing anything I couldn't do better at home. We found ourselves schooling the way we do because so much of my education was gotten outside of school. I read anything I wanted about subjects for which I had questions. I realized that my children could do the same. They certainly ask enough questions. Blake's work schedule allowed him to be home in the mornings. I was not going to be there due to my decision to return to graduate school. But Blake didn't feel confident to school without a plan to follow, so I write up the plans for him. We discuss how the previous lessons worked out, who is advancing faster in which subject(s), and how they are dealing with their lessons emotionally. Occasionally Blake will get too ambitious and Ian will get frustrated. Then we have to talk about backing off and letting him have extra time on material with which he is comfortable.

I am still developing a "plan" form. Mostly, we have general goals. I want Ian to know all the names of the letters and their basic sounds. I'd like to see him master most of that before summer. Rachel likes to learn Ian's lessons, sometimes better than Ian does. This causes frustration for Ian, and so we have Rachel working on the educational programs on the computer. She *loves* this computer—much more than Ian does. She will spend hours exploring a program. Her current favorite is a CD-ROM on musical instruments, Microsoft Home-Musical Instruments *Exploring the Amazing World of Music.* So I have the general goals, and I write up a weekly framework, covering which books to use and how many pages I'd like to see finished that week. From there, I'll make a sample day, so if Blake cannot decide what to do, he has a guide. Our biggest problem is getting off the plans. Not that it is much of a problem as we follow the interests of the children. Some weeks, math gets lots of coverage, but most of the other "work" is left for another week. I insist that at least some practice in phonics be included. Other than that, we are looking more and more like unschoolers—enough so that Blake gets worried that they aren't learning anything and even I get nervous. But then Ian or Rachel (or even both of them) will be talking about something, and we'll hear them talk and realize what they have learned. It doesn't happen often enough, but perhaps we are so busy that we miss some of the great moments. I want to finish my schooling fast and get back to schooling them myself. I don't like missing the rewarding moments and Blake sometimes doesn't recognize them.

Math is first. We use *Miquon Math Lab Materials* with Cuisenaire rods, Legos, loose change, and any other manipulative Blake chooses for the moment. We started both children on the first *Miquon Orange Book* and Blake lets them both work the lessons with the manipulatives, but Ian does the book page. This takes anywhere from thirty minutes to several hours. Blake has a way with math three of them stretch out on the carpet while working. The children view it as a game and often don't want to stop. For Blake, mathematics and statistics are as natural as breathing. He brings that joy to the work and both Ian and Rachel catch that enthusiasm. Blake understands the concepts so well, that he can see what they understand and what they are unsure of by the way they respond, so he is able to structure each lesson so that they succeed. He also sees the mathematics or statistics that are inherent in everyday life, and he shows it to them. He teaches them to see numbers as well as letters in their environment so that math is as natural as rain in the eyes of each child.

While they do math, I am either on-line picking up e-mail or writing answers and sending them. I use the computer this way because I must be home in the evenings and in school during the days, and this allows me to have contact with people, to get my messages any time of the day or night, to answer them whenever I am able, and to send my answers at any time. I know that when I return to the computer the next night, my friends will have responded whenever they could and I can then respond back again. I love keeping in touch with people who share the same interests as I have and listening to the conversations between Blake, Ian, and Rachel.

Almost all of our homeschooling is three-way. Rachel tries to do every lesson Ian does. I'm constantly amazed at how much of his lessons she can do. Having his little sister so eager keeps Ian trying to do more. He figures if his little sister can do it, then he most certainly can do *more*. We try to get Rachel on the computer, doing lessons that she needs, and that allows Ian more space, without competition, to practice his letters. Later, we put Ian on the computer to practice his letters and will work with Rachel on prereading language development—mostly reading and talking about what is read.

On this day they completed one lesson in the *Miquon Orange Book*, then moved on to the big workbook. It is one of those "all-of-first-grade-in-one-book" books of worksheets. Ian likes to color so Blake teaches language arts, colors, right and left, big and small, and all the other simple concepts covered in the worksheets, and while Ian colors his pictures, Blake goes over an alphabet coloring book with Rachel and she colors her pictures too. While they are busy, Blake tries to get the dishes washed, some picking up done, and whatever else is terribly pressing.

After the worksheets, Blake tries to get across the street to the park for some physical education. Both children like soccer and, come spring, Ian will be enrolled on the youngest team. I'm pretty certain that Blake is even more excited than Ian. I'm anticipating the day the two are in Scouting and Pony-Club. That will be so much fun! This day, they run around the three backstops and across the outfields to the swings. Some days they do P.E. between the math and workbook segments of the day.

We use workbooks because the children like them. The lessons are fleshed out with readings from various books. A favorite is *What Would Jesus Do?* They really enjoy the lessons on how people ought to treat each other and how that differs from how people often treat each other.

This day, they read about nature and the outdoors from a set of

Ian (6), Rachel (4)

children's books we have. Then they talk about the plants and animals they see and how they grow. Other days they also use Alpha Omega LIFEPACS. Rachel is asked to identify the colors and decides to be cute. So today, green is blue and purple is pink and yellow is orange. She thinks giving incorrect answers is cute. I find it frustrating but Blake patiently corrects her and moves on to the next question.

When they finish all the school work (there isn't much this first year) Ian and Rachel clamor for the computer so Blake puts on their favorite educational software. Today's favorite covers map skills, language development, direction, matching, and memory skills. Some of the other computer programs they like are Sierra Discovery Series *Alphabet Blocks* and *Mixed-Up Mother Goose*, Brightstar's *AJ's World of Discovery* (all modules) and *Early Math for ages 3-6*. Blake is able to finish the dishes and take out the trash before they get tired of the game.

Lunch is nearly always sandwiches and sliced fruit. Blake gives both children big glasses of milk. After the meal, Ian and Rachel go play in their rooms, I head to school to study and Blake does housework. Blake dislikes housework almost as much as I do. He would rather I be able to be home to do the teaching, and I will be as soon as I finish school. Blake is a very involved and nurturing parent and loves being home with Ian and Rachel. He likes to cook and he does very well with what he fixes. His standard response whenever there is a question as to what to fix for a meal is *spaghetti*!!! We haven't had it for breakfast . . . yet. Meals are odd sometimes. But he keeps track of what nutrition is needed and meets those requirements. I've had tuna fish sandwiches for breakfast with a tall glass of milk and enjoyed it. Blake has been asked, "What is wrong with your wife?" by other men who cannot understand why he does so much. Usually, we just say, "We like life this way" and leave it.

Then, Blake lets Ian and Rachel out into the backyard. I return home for dinner, put some dirty clothes in the washing machine, set the table, and we eat. The TV has usually gotten turned on and the news is in the background as we talk. Ian and Rachel fill me in on their day and do all the usual tired children behaviors. We all just relax and enjoy whatever is on the TV or put on a movie. Ian and Rachel miss me and they take turns on my lap after dinner. They and Blake go to bed at 7:00 PM. Sometimes I tell a story or read one. More often, Blake lets the children pick a story and he is talked into reading two or three stories. Blake has to get up for work at 1:00 AM. Rachel usually falls right to sleep, Ian usually keeps a light on and looks at a book or works with his Legos before he falls asleep. I stay up until around 10:00 PM. Part of the time I'm doing e-mail again, part of the time studying. Then I check the doors, fold the last of the laundry, and go to bed as well.

, Rachel (4)

UPDATE:
We decided that with my husband returning to graduate school to finish his degree, and with my part-time graduate studies, that for now we'd accept my parent's offer to pay tuition for our children to attend our local Christian school. My kids love it there and I am very comfortable working with their teachers but I can hardly wait to be finished with school so that I can pull them back out and return to our homeschooling schedule. I still have another year at least, so unless I begin to see my children acting inappropriately, they will stay in this Christian school. I am the library mother for both classes—I get the books together for the unit studies (I'm given the topic and then I choose the books) and they are using the same curriculum I have been using. They follow the general curriculum with each unit as enrichment, where I was doing primarily the units, and using the general curriculum only as a guide. I think I do as much now in gathering materials, but I don't teach it directly. The compromise is working for us, but only because I can really work with the teachers.

On the negative side, I don't get nearly the time with my kids that I have grown to love. I miss the flexibility that homeschooling gave me. I miss being able to cover the entire day of school in a few hours and being free to play and do things together afterwards. It is true that it takes the school several hours more to cover the same material we can do in a short time. However, I cannot say that they aren't getting the same educational quality.

I can see that Ian and Rachel are enjoying their schooling and benefiting from discovering that other adults think and believe the same as their parents. This wouldn't work at all if the school didn't have the same philosophies of education that I have. If anything, they are *more* conservative. I like that, as I believe that loosening up a child's conservativism is much easier than it is to increase it. They finish schooling by lunch time and spend the remainder of the day in music, Spanish, storytime and playtime, with playtime being the lion's share of the rest of the day.

We don't stop learning during the summer just because school lets out. That is when we return to regular homeschooling in the mornings. I won't have my graduate classes this summer, so I'm looking forward to using some of the materials that I haven't had time for this winter. I'm planning to let Ian do a bug collection this summer. Personally, I *hate* bugs, but I think he will get a lot out of it. Rachel is interested in the horses, so I plan to get her out and start her driving my harness horse with me.

I'm still struggling with sadness that I cannot do it all, but I have had to accept that I am not a superwoman. Neither opportunity of teaching my children

Ian (6), Rachel (4)

nor going to graduate school will wait. So this year and next I am doing graduate school and staying involved with my children's schooling. After that, we will have to reevaluate; I want to return to homeschooling even if I haven't finished my degree.

Ian (6), Rachel (4)

John and Valerie
Dorien, age 14
Tyler, age 11

Valerie wrote about their January day from their neighborhood in the old coal and steel city of Johnstown, Pennsylvania.

WORKS-IN-PROGRESS

We lived in a rural trailer park for fifteen years, up until two and a half years ago. We owned our very old trailer, and lived very cheaply. The trailer sat on the edge of a corn field that was surrounded by woods. We routinely saw herds of deer close enough to touch; flocks of pheasants: scores of rabbits and groundhogs; and hawks that used our swing set as a resting place after eating their fill of the incredible variety of birds, and the field mice that frequented our year-round feeders. Once we even saw a stray mountain lion crossing the field at dusk! We were twenty minutes away from our favorite forest hiking trails, and forty minutes from a beloved state park for swimming, picnicking, and hiking. For our family, this was Heaven!

Back at the trailer park, there was always a regular core group of neighbor children of all ages coming and going, riding bikes, skates, or sleds, and an unpredictable number of kids moving in and out of the park, who had to be met, or sadly missed.

Then we moved into a neighborhood in the city of Johnstown, a very familiar place, and only a few blocks from where I grew up. Our very large, irregular yard is right up against the woods, and we discovered that it had been used as farmland for almost fifty years. We're closer to the stores, libraries, and relatives, but pretty effectively isolated by geography and our retiring personalities. The kids, who previously took the hordes of neighbor children for granted, have found it difficult making good friends in this neighborhood but we see a lot more of our large, extended family. We've strengthened our ties to the local library and have strong allies in the librarians. The kids take lessons in guitar and ballet within five minutes of home—something that would have been impossible in our previous location.

The kids have their own bedrooms; their dog Alice; and plenty of room to run, skate, play basketball, badminton, and ride sleds. Despite the lack of kids their own ages, (most of this neighborhood is made up of elderly people), or kids with whom they have anything in common, Dorien and Tyler are on friendly terms with most of the people they see daily.

My husband, when asked how he wanted to have his job described, said: "I am a Peruvian god, whose services are required only once every eleven years for the sacrifices." This is not how he earns his living, however. He is actually a union bricklayer, and an adult masonry instructor at the local vo-tech school. In an ironic twist, most of his income for the past five or six years has come from building schools!

In the matter of raising our purely theoretical children, my husband John and I shared a philosophy on this as on so much else. It is uncanny, really. The children (two perfect ones) would play with simple, natural objects such as walnuts, sticks, and interesting rocks. They would have intense relationships with trees; their constant companions would be figures of myth and imagination; and the music they would prefer would come from the wind sighing in the leaves. This is how seriously muddled a couple of idealists can get.

The children were duly born; two perfect female lumps of clay; three and a half years apart. As the partner with the least marketable skills, I volunteered to undertake their education at home. After all, I already had a fine collection of sticks and rocks. "Oh no!" our families and friends exclaimed, raising their hands in dismay. "Oh yes," we answered firmly, "Home education it is." This is to show that John and I had a Plan, and an unshakable resolve. Our daughters were five and two years of age.

The only parts of the Plan to remain unscathed ten years later are the number of children and the "home education it is." Our daughters, Dorien and Tyler, follow their own paths. Dorien lashes her tail in righteous indignation at the injustices of the world. Tyler is a dreamer, a dancer, an artist, our comic relief, and an explorer in the world of imagination. Neither of them has ever played with walnuts.

We have three types of days in our homeschool, sometimes all three types in one day, (but those days I would prefer to forget): "good," "excellent," and "bad." A typical "good" day starts when we all get up around 7:00 AM, well-rested and good-humored. A typical "bad" day starts inevitably with me shouting and threatening at 8:30 AM or later and everyone bleary from lack of sleep.

On "good" days we watch the ten minute news and weather bites on the TV while eating our toast and cereal, and before sitting down to discuss the day over tea and hot chocolate.

On "excellent" days we exercise after the news and weather, and toast and cereal, and before the tea and hot chocolate and the discussing. As much as I personally hate to move quickly, the blood *rushing* through our veins and careening off our brains makes us all a little keener. "Excellent" days are without a doubt the ones when I've got something special in mind. Many, too many, days are just little soldiers marching across the calendar, marking time. (We homeschool year-round, but take plenty of improvised excursions, writing days, and good-weather breaks, so I have to keep a rough estimate of the required days in my head.) Really good days happen when I wake up around 6:00 AM or so and set to wondering over something that has intrigued me. A chance statement in a book, newspaper, or magazine, or on TV might initiate hours of speculation. Having a rational bent, my preferred reading is in science: *Discover* magazine, *The Planetary Society Report*, *National Geographic*, books by Stephen Jay Gould, Carl Sagan, mystery and science fiction. I enjoy watching nature shows, *NOVA*, and *Star Trek*.

Any one of these can inspire that spark. For instance, the Levy-Shoemaker 9 comet's collision with Jupiter, as covered in the local media, was a black hole of frustration with the maddeningly unavailable science facts, but a supernova of creativity for our speculative fiction. Referring to the catastrophe/survivalist tales so common in science fiction, and reading everything from articles scrounged from the women's magazines in the dentist's office, to the technical reports in the science journals; we imagined all the possible scenarios, and wrote stories, planned long-term survival strategies and argued their accompanying ethical problems, and generally enjoyed a creative frenzy. When the hard scientific data began to be assessed and passed along to the public, we were keenly disappointed at the anticlimactic end to our wild imaginings, and some of us put away our end-of-the-world survival plans with real regret.

At other times, a library book has captured my interest—*Frost Hollows and Microclimates* is one that immediately springs to mind (even now, that title sends little trills along my spine) . . . and frankly, what intrigues me is definitely going to become part of the curriculum.

I should mention that my daughters have become wary of anything that excites my imagination. They see that enthusiasm building and know they are in for some work. Dorien, a mature, intelligent teenager, has found that the path of least resistance is to become excited as well; after all, I am never bored and rarely boring, so in all honesty, she has to admit I can provide some creative stimulus. Tyler, having only recently achieved rationality at age eleven, likes routine, method, and an ordered progression of facts; and fights tooth and nail against any disruption to her plans.

Every day during that rather typical week, first thing, the kids took turns reading aloud from the written-for-children *Frost Hollows*, taking unnecessarily long (so they thought) spells to reread and wonder over key points and microscopically examine the beautiful photographs. I asked them to map the backyard, and identify all potential microclimates. For weeks afterward, this heightened awareness led to triumphant shouts of discovery at yet another border between sunlit and shade-loving plants, at snow-melters and snow-preservers. They wrote a great deal as well.

Dorien (14), Tyler (11)

Then, since I insist on having them write, "Write something," I say, "I don't care if it's a report or a poem or a story." "How long should it be?" Tyler asks, calculating how much writing it is going to take to make me happy so she can get on with her life. "I don't care," I just about always say. "If it's good, you can write haiku; if it's bad, you could write a novel, and you're still going to know it's bad."

I never grade, except theoretically, in a threatening manner and for comparative purposes. What I do is feel a thrill of delight at a good effort and a pang of disappointment at one that's just mediocre. I always share my feelings, clasping them joyfully and dancing them around the kitchen with praise; while sorrowing openly over the poorer efforts. They are never surprised by my evaluations because, being honest, they've already come to the same conclusions.

We've also gotten a lot of really good materials for daily use from PBS: *NOVA*-related teaching guides, and literature tie-ins. I've always found that these packages do inspire active thinking. Unfortunately, our reception of the local PBS channel is very poor, and requires tremendous imagination just to watch the programming. Usually we attempt to watch the broadcast the night before, then wake up the next morning eager to share our theories or express indignation over certain aspects. The printed materials are very good for approaching topics, but we often forego the prepared lessons and tack off in the direction that inflames us the most. A recent documentary on a "wild child" filled us all with overwhelming sadness and outrage. We related the story to animal experimentation, the true story of another little girl, parental inadequacies in child development, and to examples from our personal experience.

Just recently we've gotten *Seek Out Science* printed materials from PBS emphasizing women in science. The materials directed students to seek out, interview, and do a project about their chosen scientist for eventual display in cooperating museums later this year.

All of us shrink in horror from such an undertaking! Interviews? Video or photo presentations? Museum displays?? We shy people *observe*, we do not *participate*; we achieve *private* satisfaction, rather than *public* acclaim. It is a liability John and I have dealt our offspring. That's the breaks.

I suggested that since we actually do know a few scientists, one or two of them women, that we keep them in mind for future reference; or that we choose an admired (though unfortunately deceased) scientist—an option given in the materials. The kids agreed warily. The reading, writing, drawing, and discussing have been productive, fun even. But Mom is going to have to change her stripes and perhaps her skin as well before they will be displaying anything in a museum.

Another great resource that we get our inspiration from is the weekend newspaper. A quick glance through the log entries for newspaper-inspired work shows that their work included oral debates, oral and silent reading, research, and written reports. These creative endeavors are the reason I homeschool. Everything else is required by law and does not interest me much.

Dorien (14), Tyler (11)

Unless our projects have taken up too much time, I try to get math in everyday. Dorien works fairly independently, taking her ninth grade algebra text borrowed from the school district, and the Jacobs' *Mathematical Endeavors* and *Geometry* books into the library to work undisturbed. One third of the way into the algebra text, she informed me that she hadn't a clue as to what was going on.

I have dreaded this moment for years. So far I have handled all the math, science, literature, and social studies with aplomb; but I'd faked my way through high-school algebra way back then with only a faint glimmer of understanding. Now, to my intense surprise and delight, I find this stuff makes actual sense! My dedication to *Star Trek's* Mr. Spock and his models of rational thought have paid off! Together, Dorien and I unpeel the layers of mystery. John had bought a computer algebra program, and he and Dorien spend hours at the keyboard confusing themselves.

Tyler plows stoically on through long division, division by two digits, fractions, and decimals—stuff that knocks birds out of the sky with boredom. She seems to be absorbing most of the concepts. A few years ago she could scare me witless, when after having done multiplication or division, or even addition and subtraction for weeks, she'd get stuck on how to proceed. Her confidence has improved along with her abilities but she wants *me,* conscious or not, in the same room when she's working or the self-doubt kicks back.

We usually wind up the math for lunch, at around 11:30 AM, and take time to play with the dog. I do the laundry, take a shower, and get supper underway before getting them back on track.

Dorien has papers she has to do. The topics of her projects have always been of her own choosing, and I sincerely do not care what subject matter she's chosen, whether in literature, history, or science. Most commonly, and ideally, the projects have involved all three. She researches her own material, takes notes, and writes summaries leading up to what will eventually be the required-length paper. What I deeply care about is that she learns something. I keep asking, "What have you found that's interesting, or that you didn't know?" Often what is interesting and unknown to *her,* is unknown to *me* as well.

After she's done the expected amount of reading and note-taking, Dorien is free for the day and can do what she really cares about, which is handling her massive penpal correspondence. She used to write incredible poetry, and has several 100-page novellas to her credit. Now, all of her energies are devoted to gossiping. Our computer runs well into the evening hours till her father demands that she exit. Everything, from guitar lessons, to food shopping, to eating, to chores, is an interruption in this long distance socializing. She spends her evenings when pushed off of the computer watching favorite TV shows, listening to her cassette tapes and reading the two foot stack of science fiction/fantasy books she keeps beside her bed till 1:00 AM, or till I catch her and give the standard "healthy mind, healthy body, early to bed . . . " speech. This late-night lifestyle is a source of conflict between us; one we argue and compromise endlessly over.

Tyler, works on spelling and handwriting in the afternoons. I assign spelling lists, chapter readings in biographies and histories, and ask for oral and written reports. She especially enjoys reading the biographies. She and John have been on an Amelia Earhart binge for months. They really like her and enjoy sharing fascinating tidbits with each other.

Tyler also writes lyrical poetry and fantasies—long fantasies of sixty pages or more and over long periods of time, in which she unveils motivation for her character's actions. Just lately she's discovered the value of humor in creating effects in writing. And Tyler draws nonstop. Her faces, especially, are haunting and, since she has achieved level six in ballet, the bodies dance across the pages.

John's contribution to all of this has been primarily supportive, with large chunks of concrete aid. As the resident Impressionist art and technology enthusiast, he makes sure we get to the museums and science centers on a regular basis. Most of the history has been at his instigation, as specific bits of it are his passion. All of the computer things have been his contribution—from computer literacy, to basic programming, to word processing, to the educational games like *SimCity*. Neither girl would be able to function without the word processor, as their volume of writing is so high. If left to me, they would still be scratching their poetry in the dirt with sticks.

Is our homeschool a success? I have found that, despite all the good intentions in the world, all the best efforts of well-meaning people, and all the patience of saints, that whatever succeeds or fails is up to the individual child. If they stay up too late, or allow themselves to be bombarded with distractions, or if someone's bad temper gets the best of them, we might as well have stayed in bed. I naively undertook a tremendous responsibility (one that I've grown into), one I do to the best of my abilities, and one that I have found to be personally rewarding; but I do not ever confuse my achievements with theirs, or good intentions with end results.

Both girls are award-winning, published poets. Our literature based reading program, which runs the gamut from the beloved Dr. Seuss through Madeline L'Engle to Charlotte Brontë and Lewis Carroll, has produced wildly diverse, critical readers. Both draw exquisitely. Both are honest and honorable. As Works-In-Progress they are interesting and unusual. What kind of adults they will become is their responsibility. This is all part of the Plan.

ME AND MY NEON
(by Dorien)

wiretips like nerves tingle
under the electric current
the energy of potential
as thought flows
raw from the pen
electricity! brain glows
hot bursts of lightning

Dorien (14), Tyler (11)

sparked from the creative storm
quickly now, the page is brightening
with the fire from the mind
and words, like water stream
almost sufficient
to cool the neon dream

TEDDY BEAR
(by Tyler)

The little girl with pleading eyes
Smiles at what her mother buys
A bear for cuddly favorite times
For dressing up and learning rhymes
Your first sleep-over away from home
And sunny fields in which you roam
The summer nights you stayed up late
In the company of your best playmate
Those happy times have all gone by
And your best friend has lost an eye
Your Teddy Bear's not on your bed
She's in a closet on a shelf instead
You need her when you're feeling bad
To remember the good times you've had
You hold her when you're feeling blue
You know you have a friend that's true
You're all grown up but you still care
For your old friend the Teddy Bear

UPDATE:
There are many things I've learned from the ten years of homeschooling my kids: I'm not terrible in math (and actually have the brains to figure out some pretty difficult things); I have a real interest in the sciences, so much so that I read many current science magazines and books for the pleasure of it; that allowing children to make their own decisions and follow their own path can be as painful to a parent as it is rewarding and is filled with self-discovery for the child; and that we are very different individuals. As important as these things are, the one discovery I've had to make over and over is that, like the Big Bang, the big Plan is ever expanding.

I've discovered that while I've been thoroughly, conscientiously covering all the bases, the kids have been sitting back expecting it of me. Even though I *know* that the more you do for people, the less inclined they are to do for themselves; *experiencing* it has been educational. It's not been easy stepping

Dorien (14), Tyler (11)

back and trusting the kids to work through the difficult stuff without my labored breathing down their necks; it's sometimes impossible to believe that one bad math day or an indifferent, toss-away science report does not mean the end of life on earth. Even if the girls may not do something the way *I'd* like to see it done, I have learned that they will be able to meet their own goals when they have the need or the desire, or will adjust their aspirations accordingly.

The big Plan used to mean trying to get successfully through one project to the next with our wits and self-esteem intact. Then, it meant getting from one year to the next. Now, the big Plan means watching a child move through adolescence to adulthood and liking her for her ground-breaking efforts and not saying I-told-you-so over her failures. Even through the process of getting into college, the ever expanding big Plan is helping to keep it all in perspective.

Dorien (14), Tyler (11)

Keith and Sandra
Kirby, age 8
Marty, age 5
Holly, nearly 3

Sandra wrote about their day on October 21, which was sunny and still (as usual),
at their home between the freeway and the mall in Albuquerque, New Mexico.

OUT OF PINK CRAYONS

5:45 AM:

I woke up and wasn't tired, so I got up to make bread (I have a bread machine that I use for first kneading and rising, and then I bake it in the oven, because it rises better—a problem of higher elevation I believe). I cleaned the kitchen, and then messed it up again looking for a container for wheat germ.

7:30 AM:

My husband Keith left for work. He usually leaves earlier, but had stayed up until 11:00 with Holly who Wasn't Sleepy. Keith works about ten miles from our house as a systems software engineer, doing graphic displays for avionic systems. He helps helicopter pilots see maps inside their helmets and for him it's math problems and a job with good vacation and insurance.

I turned up the furnace and took a shower. We don't have a certain bedtime, nor do we awaken by the clock.

8:00 AM:

I heard Marty and Holly, who sleep together in the bottom bed (a double under a single top bunk), discussing whether to get up. I went and got them so Kirby could continue to sleep. Marty wanted to play tic-tac-toe. I got paper and crayons but he wanted to play it in a wipe-off travel book they have.

Holly played "O" and Marty played "X" and I helped just enough to teach them a little strategy and to keep one of them from winning all the time.

The bread was ready to take out, and I put a chair up so Marty and Holly could see it. It had risen extra high and was puffing out the top—I'd had to open the top of the machine. It was whole wheat sesame seed bread and I put in extra gluten and yeast (that high elevation thing, y'know . . .), so it was way up there, and I turned the machine back to "knead" and they watched it be sucked down into a small lump again. I told them a little bit about yeast, got two round pans oiled, and they helped put flour on the dough as I finished kneading and formed balls. They cleaned up the table and floor.

9:00 AM:

Kirby woke up. A little girl who is a little older than Kirby comes to our house on many Fridays. The kids colored and played games for a while, while I was finishing the bread and getting them dressed in disorganized stages. I wanted to take a loaf of warm bread to a friend of mine whose first baby is nearly due. Also, it had been reported to me that we were out of pink crayons which meant the kids couldn't color Miss Piggy, Babs Bunny, or Kimberly, the Pink Ranger. I figured we'd go to an educational supply store and get pink crayons. On the way, we went to deliver the bread and the kids brought some pictures they'd colored and cut out (made with the Brøderbund computer game *PlayRoom*). How much should a pink crayon cost? The store sells individual crayons for 10¢ each. I wasn't really too surprised to learn that pink wasn't one of my choices. No problem; I got a pack of 64. Oh, and a set of 16 "Gem Tones." And a set of 16 regulars, because they could use two pinks and they always use up black and red, too. And I got one 10¢ crayon, metallic gold. So fine; 97 crayons, and at least two or three are pink. They won't go to waste.

It was nearly Halloween, so I picked up a pack each of black and orange construction paper, and an extra pair of kid-scissors. Meanwhile, the three older kids were playing with puppets and a puppet theater the store has set up, and Holly was playing in the area actually intended for play, where the nice wooden kitchen set is, the baby doll, and the chair and footstool. She was having a great time.

Before I got out of the store I had picked up an Usborne book called *What Makes You Ill?*, a deck of cards called *Explorers Card Game*, another called *Greek Myths and Legends*, and a couple of art books in the Children's Press series *Getting to Know the World's Greatest Artists: Boticelli* and *Michelangelo*. I already own a copy of their Bruegel book, which I bought because it had a copy of "Children's Games," a great painting with all kinds of toys and activities of medieval children. So that crayon ended up costing about $56 but think of all the things that came with it!

I stopped at a local fast food place that has a drive-through and takes checks. While we waited in the shade for food to be carried out, I read the first four pages of *What Makes You Ill?* and made a comedy routine of it as much as I could. The kids were cracking up.

Kirby (8), Marty (5), Holly (nearly 3)

12:00 PM:

When we got home I set the kids up with their food and put on the *Schoolhouse Rock* multiplication videotape. I was eating my burrito in the kitchen, reading a bunch of pamphlets a friend had sent on "Michigan's Little Bavaria" and the biggest Christmas store in the world. I overheard Marty and his friend discussing infinity during a song about multiplying by nine. In a discussion like this, if they seem to know what they're talking about and they're happy with the outcome then I stay out of it. If they ask me to mediate or confirm, I will. If I were actually at the table with them I might've led the conversation a little further, but since they were watching something with music, it would've been more distracting than helpful. If there had been more chicken strips in those lunches, they would have watched more *Schoolhouse Rock*. Just as the parts of speech section started, they were down to the French fries and, one by one, they wandered off to do other things, except for Holly who fell asleep on the couch.

1:00 PM:

Kirby and his friend were playing *Ninja Turtles, the Arcade Game* (a two-player game) on Nintendo. Marty was out front on his roller blades (which he had actually had on since we left the house at 11:00), playing with an old toy that mixes different colors of plastic film to teach color mixing. He came in and declared that purple wasn't a very good color. I suggested maybe he needed more light for it, but he said he had been outside in the sunshine and it still wasn't very good.

1:30 PM:

Marty and our visitor were playing on swings in the back yard.

1:45 PM:

I read most of the rest of the Usborne book aloud until attention was flagging and skimmed the last few pages in a humorous fashion. We'll catch it later. Kirby had started off playing *Gameboy* and I asked him to turn the sound down. A couple of pages later, he was over looking at pictures. Marty was coloring and would skate over and look at the pictures and skate back and color until I turned the page again.

2:00 PM:

Marty started cutting up the black and orange paper to make chains. Kirby wanted to play the Greek Myths card game, but I was typing this book chapter and the table was full of half-cut-up construction paper.

2:30 PM:

Kirby and his friend wanted to put wood glue on the floor in the front part of the garage to catch prowlers. I talked them out of it. They went to finish the *Ninja Turtle* game. Holly was still asleep. Our young visitor's mom should

Kirby (8), Marty (5), Holly (nearly 3)

be here soon to pick her up and Kirby will miss her company, though we have lots of neighbors their age.

We live on a residential street of three-bedroom, single family houses built in 1952, flat-roofed, smaller than quarter acre plots. My husband's family bought this one in the 60s. We have kids next door on each side, and in three of the four houses across from those. Six houses in one small area, with a total of eleven kids from two to nine years old, five boys and six girls. That's quite a deal, and covers the socialization concern pretty well all by itself. My fear that our kids would be the odd ones out was taken care of by the fact that there were two different public elementary schools and two different private schools attended within that small sampling. Each family was unique so our kids weren't outnumbered. The neighborhood is what we all have in common, and for that I'm grateful. Kirby has been writing down the high scores on their *Turtle* games, and he and his friend are discussing scores—thousands and hundreds of thousands, and dreaming of higher and higher scores. We started to play the *Greek Myths* game, but Kirby thought the directions were too complicated and he was afraid he wouldn't be able to read well enough to play it. (I was afraid I wouldn't be able to pronounce all the names myself.) My husband called from work and while I was out of the room they voted to watch *Tiny Toons* instead. It was a parody of *Teenage Mutant Ninja Turtles* and I kind of got into it myself. Holly woke up and one of the neighbors came over.

Our house is the hangout because we don't have carpet and we *own* our home, which makes me less uptight than some of the other moms need to be about who does what where. We have more toys, less order and fewer rules, so kids can play harder and get along better over here. Here's an example: When I bought a discount pack of cheap Power Rangers coloring books, I bought an extra pack and hid it in my office closet. Just a while ago the kids started arguing over two workbooks (which they got out to make use of the 97 new crayons!). I figured it was a good time to pull out the extra Power Rangers books.

3:40 PM:

My husband Keith came home from work. He said, "Kirby, did you tell Mom?" "Tell me what?" I asked, popping out of the office. "Your friends are coming early." "When?" "This afternoon!"

I thought they were coming *tomorrow night*. We met them through the Society for Creative Anachronism, which is a medieval and Renaissance studies and re-creation club in which Keith and I met almost twenty years ago. We and the kids all have enough medieval clothing to last us several days, dishes, toys, musical instruments, calligraphy and arts supplies, medieval cookbooks—it's two dozen hobbies in one. The best thing about it is that we have friends all over the United States, several in Canada, we've hosted visitors from Australia twice, and if we get to Europe we'll have places to stay there. It will be interesting to get to know them better.

Kirby (8), Marty (5), Holly (nearly 3)

4:00 PM:

Holly was wandering around the house with a sucker in her mouth (she found the Halloween candy) and my older two and their visitor were coloring Power Rangers pictures and watching *Animaniacs*.

4:00 to 5:00 PM:

Keith watched *Star Trek* in the kids' room, since they were watching the big TV and coloring. Holly came and cuddled, I went in a few times to lie down and to see whether I'd been writing enough to cover this day.

5:30 PM:

Our young visitor left with her mom. Kirby went to take a shower, Keith helped him wash his hair. Marty and I worked on a black and orange paper chain for a Halloween decoration and watched *Full House* while we glued. Holly wanted to glue too, but wanted to use the bottle instead of wiping it on with her finger from the common "puddle" of glue. I wouldn't let her. I gave her some tape to make a decoration with a scrap of orange paper and she was happy.

Marty found two little pieces of construction paper Holly had glued to the wall in the hallway. If she hadn't already colored all over the wall and it needed to be repainted really badly, I might've cared.

Kirby went over to the home of a neighbor to play video games. He took his Nintendo cleaning kit. Marty and Keith went to the grocery store and the bank. When Holly found out she had been left home with me she wasn't too happy and I told her she could go to the store tomorrow with Dad. She and I were having snacks of melted Muenster cheese on the homemade bread. I don't think Kirby or Marty ate anything but they drank some milk. I supposed when they came back home I'd need to feed them.

8:15 PM:

My friends still haven't shown up. What a bad food day we had! Not a bad kid-stimulation day, though. And it's not quite over. Marty came home and ate peanut butter and jelly.

9:00 PM:

My friends showed up. We sat and talked and joked and my husband and I got to know them, while Holly and Marty colored and read books and climbed in and out of my lap and Keith's. Kirby came home from playing video games at a neighbor's house at 10:00 PM. Marty was playing on the computer—*Playroom* or *Treehouse*, I think, or maybe *Ishido*. The kids asked to get on the computer and play games. We have about a dozen good kids' games—*Treehouse, Back Yard, Treasure Mountain, Math Rabbit*, etc. We took *Miracle Piano* off a while back for a system upgrade and haven't put it back in yet (I want a stand for the keyboard so I can hide it under the desk) and when we do it will seem brand new and get a lot of use again.

Kirby (8), Marty (5), Holly (nearly 3)

One by one the kids said they were tired, and I set them up to go to sleep. I put a tape on for Marty (a story tape we got at a thrift store which is supposed to go with a book but we never had the book), and for Holly (after Marty was asleep) I put on the soundtrack of *The Lion King*.

11:00 PM:
Keith turned in.

11:30 PM:
I stayed up talking and then went to bed.

END NOTES:
Our daily plans are nebulous, and although we might schedule a trip to the zoo or a papier-mâché day (something that takes a clean table and a lot of set-up and no big interruptions), we don't have something scheduled on most days, and we don't "educationalize" trips to zoos and museums and such. We just go, and what we read or see is discussed, but not in a scheduled, checklist way.

There are several ways that I get ideas and resources. I have e-mail friends. I have a few local friends who homeschool but the homeschool scene is too structured for my tastes. I'm a member of the state organization and I get some good ideas from their newsletters. When I was beginning to homeschool, I got reassurance from a friend who has four older children. Her philosophy is that as long as they know things by the time they go on dates or get married, it doesn't matter how soon or in what order they learn them. *Family Fun Magazine* has some good ideas and I have some books on arts and science projects. Nothing has helped me as much as reading *Growing Without Schooling*.

Keith might go several days without any particular homeschool-looking interaction with the kids, but he's good at playing games with them and letting them help him work around the house. When he reads to them he ad libs and the kids think it's fine. When he reads them a book and when I read them the same book, it can be like two different books!

Kirby (8), Marty (5), Holly (nearly 3)

UPDATE:

Since our October day was documented, I've gotten an unschoolers' group going in Albuquerque. It's not so much a support group as a playgroup for the kids and a place where we can hang out with adults and not have to explain why our kids are home during the day, or why we don't use a curriculum. It's refreshing and relaxing.

Except that the kids are older now, everything is the same even to this *amazing* coincidence: Today our kids are working on paper-chain advent count-down projects for our house and a friend's house, and our Friday visitor is here again. Things are definitely still the same at my house!

Kirby (8), Marty (5), Holly (nearly 3)

Randy and Sharon
Amberle, age 9
Nathan, age 7

Sharon wrote this on October 4, from their mobile home in the rural setting of Ephrata, Pennsylvania.

FIFTY CHARACTER TRAITS

Our home is situated in a mobile home park in a rural setting. Therefore, we have both "fresh country air" and many neighbors close by. Our home is fairly large with an extension that adds a separate dining room and third bedroom. We converted the dining room into our school room when we began educating at home. Fortunately, my kitchen is large and we moved the dining table into there. Our "school room" has two old school desks, two large bookcases, three file drawers, a computer, and three drawers of a dresser. Only about 50% of my daughter's school time and 10% of my son's school time is spent in the school room. We have our daily beginning activities together on the living room couch. We do almost all of our reading on the couch. Sometimes the kids prefer to do their math work on the kitchen table.

Randy works in an office as Senior Accounting Supervisor. His job is basically 8:00 AM to 5:00 PM, although he works later when report deadlines come fast and furious. I had difficulty incorporating gym time into my lessons so I gave Randy the Presidential Fitness Program. Providentially, our local bowling lanes offered a twelve week bowling class that we chose for Amberle. We have an outdoor fort with rings, bar, rope, and horizontal ladder that I hope to use for exercises. Randy's main homeschooling assistance is in the form of conflict resolution. If I have a schedule problem, curriculum difficulty, or negative child attitude, he helps me sort it out and resolve it. I do the planning, curriculum, and actual teaching.

7:15 AM:

We're actually all awake! My husband, Randy, has been up for half an hour and he's dressed for work. This means we can all eat breakfast together, an uncommon occurrence. Randy leaves around 7:45 AM; we finish breakfast and I clean up. I send Nathan off to get dressed. Amberle usually comes to eat already dressed, with her bed made.

8:00 AM:

I jump in the shower and am ready to start at 8:30 AM. Wonder of wonders, that is our ideal starting time. While I've been dressing, the kids were brushing their teeth and then roller skating on the porch. Now the three of us settle on the couch for our opening prayers. We go over the Bible School verses for next Sunday. I read Proverb 22 and we each pray for folks in our church from a calendar that's supplied each month. While I'm trying to hold our beginning activity together, the kids are fascinated by the new anole (lizard) across the room. Just watching her little tongue dart out to catch droplets of water from her cage is amusing. (You can see we're easily amused!)

9:05-9:35 AM:

I send my daughter to practice her Casio keyboard. Since we live in a mobile home with no room for a piano, we like having a keyboard. Amberle's grandmother, a former piano teacher, has given her lessons every other week for almost two years. Nathan and I settle on the floor for reading. Since he *loves* animals, I'm having him read the backs of animal flash cards I got for our church nursery because it's fun for him. We've been stuck on lesson 19 of *Sing, Spell, Read and Write* for a while because that lesson presents words that are commonly used but are phonetic exceptions. Nathan is fantastic with logic but this step requires memorization. Little by little he is tucking away more of these difficult words into his permanent memory. But it still frustrates him very much when he cannot decode a word by the rules. I also get frustrated for him because I can see that many of the roadblocks in reading are because of illogical phonetic patterns and I don't know any good way to present them. It is even more difficult because my memorization skills are highly tuned. I usually don't get angry when Nate doesn't remember or understand something. He is very proficient, even advanced, in math and other subjects (history and science) that are oral, artistic or hands-on. We then move to the kitchen table where Nathan must read and write one sentence I've constructed with lots of letter clusters and sight words.

9:35-10:15 AM:

Amberle sits at her desk to work one lesson in *Saxon Math*. Nathan goes outside for more roller skating. Ordinarily I would work with him on his *Miquon Math Lab Materials* at this time, but we have a "deal" today whereby Amberle works hard to finish her math so she can help Nathan with his math lesson. This does not often work out very well. I'll put dishes away now while I wait for the "tutor." It is not quiet in here because my son came in and talks

Amberle (9), Nathan (7)

without pause and my daughter "sings" her math lesson to herself. Would either of them be able to express themselves like this in a public setting? I correct Amberle's *Saxon Math* and send her back to correct the errors.

10:30-10:50 AM:

Nathan and Amberle are working on *Miquon* together. Well, for a few minutes, then Amberle is missing and I'm explaining the instructions to Nate. Then I explain to Amberle that she was not responsible and won't tutor again for a while. Meanwhile, I started a load of delicates and forgot to toss the clothes in (and people at church think I'm so organized). I let the kids skate for ten minutes.

11:00-11:45 AM:

Amberle's fourth grade level requires her to study state history so I've combined it with early American history for two quarters this year. We're reading and discussing *The Light and the Glory* for children. I wrote my own discussion and vocabulary guide during the summer. When I reviewed the texts of *The Light and the Glory* and *From Sea to Shining Sea* before the school year, I supplemented discussion questions in the back of the books with specific questions to reinforce the people, places and events of the time period. Because I was planning to read the texts aloud to the children, I highlighted any words that I thought they might not have in their vocabulary. I made up short definitions for these and gave the lists to Amberle to study. I sometimes quizzed her on these vocabulary words. I also made discussion guides with a few questions for each page of text. We discussed these questions as I read and they were the basis for tests on the material. I planned to cover a chapter a day of history, three times a week. We also worked on a timeline (by Creation's Child) and read about twelve historical fiction books independently or together. We finished one text book each quarter and began our Greenleaf study of ancient Egypt this third quarter. (What a delight!) Nathan sits on the couch with us and I involve him as much as I can.

11:50-12:45 PM:

Nathan plays on his sister's keyboard while I go over an activity in Amberle's language arts. We're discussing the First Amendment's effects on the press. She is thinking as an editor and listing guidelines for reporters. She must also work on an essay rewrite, just for me.

12:45-1:00 PM:

At lunchtime I fix the kids' lunches first, with their help. They eat while I fix mine. They always request a story cassette or a VCR tape. Sometimes I demand silence or soft music but usually I allow them to listen to something. I had read aloud many *Mrs. Piggle Wiggle* stories onto cassettes a few years ago and they request them (too) often. I usually eat with a book by my plate because lunch is a refueling time, in more ways than one.

Amberle (9), Nathan (7)

1:00-1:30 PM:
Both kids are out skating again. I'm habitually beginning lunch when they're finishing so I can read while I eat. It's one of my favorite times of day.

1:30-5:00 PM:
The three of us are out running errands. My regular errands consist of grocery shopping on Tuesday afternoons, a trip to the discount store for toiletries and miscellaneous goods, and the library on Thursday afternoon. We spend about an hour to an hour and a half at the library. I get mail sorted or coupons cut or look for an auxiliary school book I might need. Sometimes I just read the whole time (oh, bliss!). The children look for books to take home and others just to look at while in the library. Amberle reads long books and so she often brings her current book of interest along and reads it in a comfortable chair. We have encyclopedias and many reference works at home and so do not need to do much research at the library yet.
I usually squeeze library, errands, etc., into the schedule before 3:00 PM so that the children have time to play with neighborhood kids before supper, but it doesn't always work that way. When we return from our errands, Nathan feeds his first meal worm to his new anole.

5:00-5:30 PM:
We put things away and get a quick dinner started.

5:30-6:30 PM:
Supper with Dad. This is never a quiet somber affair but full of talk and good-natured teasing.

6:30-8:30 PM:
We pick up a neighbor girl and head out to a homeschool roller skating party. This is our physical education for today, although Randy and I spend more time talking with homeschool friends than skating. He will soon begin to use the Presidential Fitness Program information I gathered.

9:00-9:45 PM:
The kids are changing for bed. Amberle eats an apple for a snack. (Nathan didn't want to finish his leftover lunch.) Randy is working on the aquarium to separate our aggressive shark from our goldfish.

10:00-10:15 PM:
The children are in bed, about an hour later than usual. I'm finishing this diary while Randy works on church responsibilities at the kitchen table.

10:15-11:00 PM:
This is my usual time for some milk and cookies, then Bible reading

Amberle (9), Nathan (7)

and prayer while Randy finishes paperwork.

11:00 PM:
Definitely ready for bed. I feel this has been a productive day and maybe a little better than usual. I could say this kind of life is tiring; however, I believe most families' schedules are hectic and wearying but not nearly as rewarding. Spending lots of time together as a family and working on character twenty-four hours a day are two of the reasons I chose to school at home.

I did not mention our science program because it was not covered on our sample day. We scheduled science for two days a week the first two quarters. I wanted to use a hands-on approach that would excite and interest the children in science. Last year Amberle studied science through a workbook style and she did not enjoy it much or retain very much. This year, I purchased the *Backyard Science* books. I also bought the new teaching guide by *Backyard Science*. The first section of the guide is labeled for grades K-3 and deals with physical, earth, and life sciences. The back cross reference tells you which experiments relate to the different subjects studied. We are recording some of the experiments in a *Science Notebook* by Castle Heights Press. Doing experiments has been more gratifying than studying science from a workbook. For solid definitions and explanations I found my Usborne *Science Encyclopedia* to be top rate. We actually use it as a "text."

This is my second full year of homeschooling, with a half-year before that. I find that academics are the least of my difficulties and that attitudes are the greatest. Therefore, I have striven to encourage good character and positive attitudes by several methods.

First, I compiled a short job list for each child. Morning preparation was first and included dressing, making the bed, eating breakfast, and brushing the teeth. Other chores are commensurate with the age of the child (i.e. the seven-year-old can gather all the trash cans for collection and removal). Each of these chores earns one jewel (small colored beads from a craft store). Cleaning up large areas of clutter earns a jewel and prevents constant scolding. Even musical instrument practice can go on the list to add motivation. Fifty jewels earns a book or other prize.

Second, the children needed to be made more accountable to their father. They tend to take mother for granted and treat her differently than they would an outside teacher. Repeated complaints or whining about the necessity or difficulty of work produces frayed nerves. I made three frowny faces for each child and one smiley face to be posted on the refrigerator. Each negative incident would earn a frowny and three frownies would earn some disciplining from Daddy after work. The children anticipate a positive remark for a smiley face even more than they dread discipline for misbehavior. My children are well liked and very well behaved at church, with grandparents or at a friend's house. We have the usual problem that "familiarity breeds contempt" and spending such a large quantity of time with my children means that they feel comfortable acting

Amberle (9), Nathan (7)

as they feel like, instead of as they know they should with me.

I have compiled a list of fifty character traits which we would like to encourage in the children (and Mom and Dad). The lack of some of these are noticeable during the day and provide an opportunity to go over a corresponding Bible verse and discuss what God wants us to be or do. For instance, if I give Amberle a paragraph to copy and she has several spelling errors even though the words are in front of her, then we talk about accuracy. Our two verses from Proverbs show us that being slack destroys work instead of producing good work and haste makes us too careless to find the right way.

CHARACTER TRAITS

1. Accuracy: getting it right.
2. Alertness: noticing specifics.
3. Attentiveness: listening well with ears and mind.
4. Cautiousness/Discretion: considering the consequences of an action beforehand.
5. Compassion: feeling another's pain
6. Confidence: knowing your abilities and the power of God.
7. Contentment: accepting "now" with thankfulness, peace and joy.
8. Courage: pressing on in spite of danger or persecution.
9. Creativity: being unique and original; not a copy.
10. Decisiveness: able to choose with confidence.
11. Deference: putting another ahead of yourself.
12. Dependability: worthy of trust; not disappointing.
13. Determination: keep on going when the going gets tough.
14. Diligence: hard-working; concentrating on a task.
15. Discernment: able to recognize quality and right.
16. Endurance: not giving up.
17. Enthusiasm: going with gusto.
18. Fairness: treating everyone with equal respect.
19. Faith: able to trust God for the unseen.
20. Flexibility: agreeable with change.
21. Forgiveness: able to release an offense (hurt).
22. Generosity: freely giving of possessions, energy or time.
23. Gentleness: treating others tenderly; a soft soothing touch.
24. Gratefulness: thankful for blessings.
25. Hospitality: making others feel welcome and important.
26. Initiative: a self-starter.
27. Joyfulness: an inner happiness that comes from having the Spirit of God.
28. Loyalty: devoted to another's good (name).
29. Meekness: humility; strength under control.
30. Neatness: an organization that promotes efficiency.
31. Obedience: submitting to an authority's will.
32. Patience: willing to wait in difficulty.

Amberle (9), Nathan (7)

33. Peacefulness: trust in God, which brings calm.
34. Peace-maker: one who prevents or resolves conflict.
35. Punctuality: considering others' time as valuable.
36. Resourcefulness: good steward of gifts.
37. Responsibility: doing the expected task; taking control.
38. Reverence: respectful; giving honor.
39. Security: not fearful; confidence in God.
40. Self-control: able to deny or delay personal desires.
41. Sensitivity: aware of others' feelings.
42. Service: ready to meet the need of another.
43. Sincerity: not pretending; presenting truth of character.
44. Teachableness: able, even open-minded, to receive correction or instruction.
45. Thoroughness: committed to a complete job.
46. Thriftiness: frugal; a saver.
47. Tolerance: seeing differences as positive.
48. Truthfulness: honest .
49. Virtue: purity of thought and action.
50. Wisdom: seeing from God's perspective; applied knowledge

Amberle (9), Nathan (7)

Here are some examples of Biblical verses that I looked up in the New International Version of the *Holy Bible* Book of Proverbs that correspond with a few of the character traits:

ACCURACY
18:9 One who is slack in his work is brother to one who destroys.
19:2 It is not good to have zeal without knowledge, nor to be hasty and miss the way.

ALERTNESS
14:15 A simple man believes anything, but a prudent man gives thought to his steps.
14:18 The simple inherit folly, but the prudent are crowned with knowledge.

ATTENTIVENESS
18:13 He who answers before listening—that is his folly and his shame.
18:15 The heart of the discerning acquires knowledge; the ears of the wise seek it out.
4:1   Listen, my sons, to a father's instruction; pay attention and gain understanding.

CAUTIOUSNESS/DISCRETION
14:8 The wisdom of the prudent is to give thought to their ways, but the folly of fools is deception.
14:15 A simple man believes anything, but a prudent man gives thought to his steps.
22:3 A prudent man sees danger and takes refuge, but the simple keep going and suffer for it.
4:26 Make level paths for your feet and take only ways that are firm.

Bill and Leslie
Adrienne, age 11
Jesse, age 8
Brennan, age 5
Zachary, age 1

Leslie and Bill each wrote about homeschooling during the very cold and snowy middle of winter in the rural forested mountains of Val-Morin, Québec in Canada.

A COMEDY OF WISHFUL THINKING

FROM LESLIE:
    During a radio show, we were recently asked the question: "What is a typical homeschooling day for your family?"Our initial response was, "There really isn't one!" Then I sat guiltily thinking about how other more organized "superfamilies" might manage to tick off an impressive list of educational activities, and not only two or three days a week for perhaps a few hours a day, but *daily* and with an orderly schedule—beginning with the older children being tutored by their father for an hour *before* breakfast, studying geography, history and languages. Following breakfast they would have two hours of formal class time used to teach spelling, grammar, phonics, and arithmetic, to introduce a new topic, assigning work pages and checking problem areas. Before lunch would be physical education/remedial time. In the afternoon, the children would have two hours of quiet, by themselves time followed by a session for music, remedial work and finishing assignments. Next, playtime with neighbourhood children before an early supper. Then a family activity. They would have a review session before bed, leaving a couple of hours of reading, relaxing and conversation time for the parents. . . .
    Meanwhile, back to us lesser mortals. Despite many organizational

strategies and educational plans, our typical day needs to be broken down into two categories: the ideal scenario (WISH) and what actually happens (REALITY). However, each day usually begins with the thought: "Today things will be different!"

WISH: We're up at 7:00 AM, leaving time for the children to dress, have breakfast and clean up their rooms by 9:00 AM, ready and eager to begin our book work.
REALITY: We get up after Dad has left for work and are just beginning breakfast by 9:00 AM, with some of the kids still in pajamas, or worse, still in bed and thinking: "If it's clean-up time, you know what I try to do? I try to lie in bed as long as I can till it's almost over." There is general resistance to anything resembling a work book. Kids disappear into a bedroom to play with an ongoing rainforest creation using all the household plants.

WISH: Since we have a large variety of pets, this provides an ideal opportunity for nature study, complete with a daily log book, sketches and research.
REALITY: I seem to be the only one scooping poop and cleaning cages. However, the kids do provide some assistance by holding the animals while I work.

WISH: The house is tidy, the animals cared for, the dishes and laundry caught up. I have an overall educational plan, prepared unit study topic, and plan-for-the-day that was compiled the previous evening.
REALITY: Both sinks are full of yesterday evening's dishes. The diaper pail is overflowing. The rat cage has an overwhelming odor, competing with the diaper pail. The kids played with friends the day before, making a fort in the living room and using all the spare blankets, towels and clothespins in the house. Their structure is still intact. I start tackling the above, and several hours later as I eat breakfast, I contemplate my plan of attack for homeschooling: "So what are some other fun things we plan to do but never do?". . . "Homeschooling."

WISH: After breakfast, the children and I will spend several hours in productive and pleasant academic work, improving their literary and mathematical skills.
REALITY: My preschooler wants me to make another complicated origami airplane from his favourite book (he has a large collection scattered about the house) as well as play a few rounds of his next favourite alternative, one of our co-operative games. The plane will have to wait till Dad has a day off, but I manage to play a game while nursing the baby. At this point, I realize that it's time to start lunch. After much persuasion and many threats, I convince the kids to sit down with their workbooks while I chop vegetables. The phone rings at regular intervals. Shortly thereafter one kid stomps off in a huff—too much assistance was given, or given in the wrong way. Warning: Don't ever check their problem areas!

Adrienne (11), Jesse (8), Brennan (5), Zachary (1)

WISH: While lunch is cooking, we take the time to practice yoga, tai kwon do, or take the dogs for a walk.

REALITY: I decide that my sanity is more important, so it's time for us to dismantle the structure in the living room. Does housework count as calisthenics?

WISH: After lunch, we have a tranquil together time reading the latest issue of the children's nature magazine and assembling a scale model structure from some ancient civilization.

REALITY: It's now mid-afternoon by the time the dishes are done. The phone hasn't stopped ringing. We're four issues behind in our reading of the kid's nature magazines and we are unable to do the scale model construction when the baby is awake. However, books have arrived in the mail from the library, and the house is remarkably quiet as the kids peruse the new offerings. I decide it's a good time for the baby's nap, and fall asleep myself as well.

WISH: The children play happily outside with their neighbourhood friends, giving me an hour or two of peace and quiet to prepare supper, look over the mail and perhaps tackle that ever mounting pile of things to do or read on my desk.

REALITY: Most of the kids' friends live beyond walking distance, which means driving Dad back to work after lunch in order to keep the car, dropping off the kids at the friends' homes and going back later to collect them. OR, it's our turn to host and the house is (literally) crawling, jumping, resonating with kids. I'm lucky to have enough time and space to reheat leftovers for supper.

WISH: By the end of the afternoon, I would have spent individual time with each child, working on their favourite project .

REALITY: We're all tired and cranky, and everything is now being promised for tomorrow.

WISH: After an early supper, we play some educational games as a family and hold a family meeting to plan events, share feelings and discuss issues. After story hour, where we read the children each a chapter from their books, the children are in bed, asleep, leaving several hours for us parents to enjoy "adult time."

REALITY: We finish supper by 8:00 PM, followed by a steady half hour of trying to pick up the house. The dishes will have to wait for a fresher me tomorrow morning. After the kids' bath, there is a major lake with islands of soggy, discarded clothes to deal with. During story time, the kids wheedle an extra chapter or two: "I won't be able to fall asleep unless I know what happens!" Dad reads until his voice gives out or he falls asleep mid-sentence and cannot be prodded awake. The oldest stays up reading in bed, the second needs company in order to fall asleep, the third is carried to bed and the baby is nursed to sleep. Parents fall asleep at the same time as the kids, if not earlier. However,

Adrienne (11), Jesse (8), Brennan (5), Zachary (1)

tomorrow, things will be different!

We just built our new home ourselves (it took a year and a half) out of squared and dove-tailed hemlock logs on a dead-end road half way up a mountain in Canada's province of Québec. We no longer have neighbours with children—there are only three houses on our stretch of road: one stands empty and the other is the home of good friends. Before moving, for six years we lived nearer the village center, "in the valley" beside the river. As we live in the middle of the forest, I guess you'd call us rural. We are part of a network of homeschoolers in the Laurentian mountains, many of whom are a five to fifteen minute car ride away. We designed our house to suit our family needs. Homeschooling activities are integrated into family life and so take place

Adrienne (11), Jesse (8), Brennan (5), Zachary (1)

throughout the house . . . and often spill into the outdoors. Book work, if any, usually happens at the dining room table. We have an open kitchen-dining-living area. Family meetings happen in the quiet room (which houses our books and rug and pillows). The playroom is where we share family videos once a week and the kids have free rein and can romp as noisily as they like. The kids use their bedrooms to do projects they want undisturbed by younger siblings. Reading takes place in a large sunspace upstairs where we have a couch and the children's collection of books. Bill has a woodworking shop in the basement, so any building projects with wood and nails happen there. Due to a large rock that had to be removed, part of the basement has a ten foot ceiling, where we hope eventually to create a gymnasium of sorts.

Homeschooling is different in every Canadian province, with British Columbia's laws being the most open and accepting. Québec tends to be on the other end of the scale. The law is general and left to each school board as to how it will be interpreted in practice. The actual law states that compulsory school attendance is not required for "a student who is provided, at home, instruction and a learning experience, which, according to an evaluation made by or for the school board, are equivalent to what is provided at school." Our community is fairly supportive, although we don't really talk about it much—only if people ask us questions.

We try as much as possible to let the children determine what they want to do. I feel that if *you* still need the "lessons" for your peace of mind or to meet school board standards, make sure what they "have to" learn is relevant to their lives *today*, not something they will need in the future—they can learn it then. During adolescence there is plenty of time for children to study the specific knowledge and write tests necessary for whatever they choose to do in life, based on the interest they develop from a young age. Our daughter is just approaching adolescence and has only just recently shown any interest in "formal" learning. It seems much easier to let our children play and explore while they're young without imposing "lessons." Later, when they have the interest, discipline, maturity and brain development for abstract concepts (yes, the three R's I would include in that category!), their learning in that area will be very fast and effortless.

There are many resources that my kids like. Nature magazines include *Chickadee, Owl* (Young Naturalist Foundation) and *Ranger Rick*. Co-operative games come from Family Pastimes. Resource books from Kids Can Press include *Let's Celebrate, Science Express, Weather Watch, Science Book for Girls and Other Intelligent Beings, Discover, Cat's Cradle, Owl's Eyes, Super Flyers, Kids Can Crafts Books* (*Friendship Bracelets*), and also the Amazing Series books (*The Amazing Paper Book*). They also uses resources such as *The Usborne Book of Word History* and *The Random House Children's Encyclopedia*. They will spend a lot of time on their own perusing the above two books. This year we have recently started using a program called *Challenging Math* by Michel and Robert Lyons. The kids like it as it involves constant parental participation. Children have to explain how they arrived at their

Adrienne (11), Jesse (8), Brennan (5), Zachary (1)

solutions (often many solutions are possible), they make "errors" on purpose, and generally encourage children to be creative, self-confident and questioning. By far the kids' favorite is learning through toys and games such as *Take Off* (geography), chess, *Scrabble, Passing Time* (telling time), math games from *Family Math*, puzzles with educational themes (solar system, rain forest, dinosaurs, etc.). We don't have a computer, and up until last year didn't have a TV—still unsure about that one!

I kept a log one year, just to allay my fears. I don't keep either a planning sheet or log now. Our newsletter *Québec Homeschooling Association* is province-wide, for home-based education in Québec. It was edited for ten years by a friend who died a few years ago. Another friend and myself took over where she left off, with a few changes: it is now longer and bilingual (English and French). At first the two of us had to write all of the articles or solicit nearby friends. Now we receive contributions from many subscribers so function mostly as editors.

We have a homeschool support group of about twenty families. The first year we met we had a monthly activity and monthly parent meetings with a theme. When attendance started dropping off and I felt I "should" go instead of looking forward to the meetings, we reduced the meetings to three a year. One to plan our calendar of events and the other two to get together to compare notes, meet new families and socialize—but no theme. We have shared many activities and had great fun from interactions within this group.

GO-KART CURRICULUM—Homeschooling with Dad:
by Bill

My training is as a biologist and I worked for the Ministery of Natural Resources for a number of years. Since leaving that, my paid employment has been primarily in the field of woodworking and construction, and my work has included teaching yoga and storytelling. My kids often join me on storytelling engagements—even to schools. Leslie feels we share the homeschooling about 50/50, though being away at work three or four days a week, I feel that she spends more time with the children. I tend to be fairly activity- or even project-oriented with the kids, and what skills we need to complete the project are the ones we learn.

Our initial inclination to homeschool sprang from a distrust of large institutions and many years of being schooled ourselves. We now perceive the advantages as being innumerable. First amongst these is the richness of family life that is created. We don't just spend "maintenance" time with our kids—brushing teeth, eating meals, being chauffeur, and we don't spend just "quality" time with our kids. They get to experience all of us and we all of them. We are each other's main sources of inspiration, support, love and laughter as well as frustration, conflict, tears and pain. We spend too much time together to ignore any of that. We simply have to sort it out. We have to find ways together to make it work. Homeschooling forces everybody in the family to deal with the

Adrienne (11), Jesse (8), Brennan (5), Zachary (1)

issues we have with each other, to resolve our relationships. It is this depth of relationship that I now value most in homeschooling.

We have four children, between the ages of eleven and one. Our approach is very much child-led—our role being to provide resources and activities to allow our children to pursue interests as they arise. It seems clear that any standardized skill testing that would be used as a measure of the success or acceptability of homeschooling automatically distorts, if not precludes, child-led learning. During the week, we keep a record sheet of each day's activities broken down into educational categories. Building a samurai sword might include social studies, art and life skills, or a video night complete with tickets and popcorn could cover math, science, language arts and music. This lets us easily see if there are any subject areas that are being grossly neglected. Part of our weekly family meeting is a review of the past week and a discussion of what we'd like to learn about or do in the coming week. This seems to keep us pretty much on track with each other and with our learning objectives.

We go through cycles of more or less structured book work time, usually instigated by our parental fears that "this can't possibly work" or "they're not learning anything." Most of the time, however, we manage to keep the wolves of doubt at bay and trust that our children will learn and ask to learn all they need as they need to. I'm not sure our children are up to par with their peers in the three R's, but they do play the leadership roles in neighbourhood activities. They are the instigators, the referees, the diplomats; they are sought out as companions. Ultimately, these human and social skills are perhaps the most valuable tools we can help them develop.

Perhaps the greatest amount of our children's time is spent in fantasy play. Using a magnificent collection of toy wild animals, dinosaurs, and horses, the richness of characters and heights of adventure created match the best of mythologies anywhere. Adrienne draws for hours on end, mostly animals. She often chooses a particular subject, such as jumping horses, and will spend two to three weeks drawing nothing but, until she has mastered them to her satisfaction. She is well beyond either of us in her ability and what makes us, at times, feel like she could benefit from a good class or tutor. It's that nasty niggly voice that tells me that some expert, someone more experienced, someone *else* knows what or how would be best for her to draw next. She resists any such suggestions. We respect her resistance; I guess deep down inside I am much more excited to watch the entirely independent unfolding of her creative self unencumbered by any tried-and-true techniques or uninvited influences. When she comes to the point where she cannot create the results she wants, I trust she will ask for the help she needs. When it comes to knowing what comes next, who could possible know better than she herself! Dance is her other passion, pursued with the same intensity, discipline and resistance to outside interference. Her reading took off last fall when she discovered she could read her lady heroine books as much as she wanted, as late as she wanted, by herself. Her math skills grow as she encounters ever more situations in her life where she needs those skills.

Our eight-year-old has a bent for inventing and spent much of last year

Adrienne (11), Jesse (8), Brennan (5), Zachary (1)

devising every imaginable means for launching projectiles. His big interest this past winter was to build a go-kart. Boy, does he know how to hook me, and the other kids too! This soon became a family project. However, as I didn't want a go-kart running around inside the house for a couple of months while we waited for the snow to melt, we all agreed that this would be a long term project. We spent a couple of weeks devoted to designing. The first step was to measure everyone's bodies to make sure they could fit in. Then we discovered we didn't have paper big enough to draw our design on so, we had to make a scale drawing of the side, front, back, and top views, and lastly, the artistic rendering of the dragon's face, flames and claws. There were bundles of measuring, calculating and geometry, the climax being the discussion of how long to make the front axle so that the wheels wouldn't rub on the front bumper! There were equal amounts of dreaming and scheming, extravagant and silly, culminating in water cannons, Ben Hur wheels and ejector seats. That was January.

We then fell into several weeks of collecting materials. Allowances were pooled to buy the necessities: five lag bolts and washers. Everything else was begged, borrowed or scrounged. The building part was almost the easiest. We simply took the measurements off the plan, cut out the pieces, and lo and behold, they all fit together! There were a few unforeseen kinks to be worked out, especially in the steering, but, no, the wheels didn't rub on the bumper. We were through in February.

We moved into sanding, planing, and painting. Between two base-coats and the toothiest, flamiest dragon ever mounted on four wheels, we made it to April. That left us with only two weeks worth of indoor car rallies and crunched toes until the snow banks finally faded enough to risk a few test runs.

We now go almost weekly for our dose of high speed thrills and spills. And while the design doesn't permit bodies of my scale to participate in the breath-taking ride down the road, I know I have shared with the children the thrill and fulfillment of transforming a dream into a reality. I have savored, enjoyed and learned as they have, every step of the way.

Our five-year-old has a definite penchant for the intellectual. There's no Mickey Mouse or fairy tales when he picks books at the library. No siree, it's airplanes, communications, Marco Polo, or stars and the universe. However, at this point, he is still pretty much following his older siblings in awe, this being one of the biggest advantages of homeschooling. The same holds true for our one-year-old, for he is surrounded by a richness of activities that is bound to influence him. It has always seemed to me that schools cream off our children just as they come to an age to really participate in and contribute to family life. Homes generally are left to infants, preschoolers, and a parent—a combination that's guaranteed to drive any of the above to distraction. It is also an environment that no more reflects the real world than does school itself. A home that has children spanning a broad range of ages, fully present, soon begins to generate its own educational dynamic. From modeling to leadership, from underdog to heroine, from devastated to inspired, everyone gets a chance to play all the roles. At its best it is learning and living as it really happens. We don't

Adrienne (11), Jesse (8), Brennan (5), Zachary (1)

feel our children will have to "be prepared to go into the real world" for they have never been taken out of it.

WEEKLY HOME SCHOOL JOURNAL
FOR: Adrienne

DATE	TIME SPENT	ACTIVITY DESCRIPTION	LANGUAGE ARTS	MATHEMATICS	SCIENCE	SOCIAL STUDIES	MUSIC	ART/DRAMA	PHYS. ED	LIFE SKILLS	SOCIAL SKILLS
Dec 6	30 min	discussed credit cards								✓	
	1 hr.	math - multiplication tables.		✓							
	3 hrs.	tobogganing w/ Natalie + Simon							✓		✓
		built campfire								✓	
	2 hrs.	painting - clay + papier-mâché						✓			
Dec 7	1½ hrs	reading - Veronica's passport	✓								
	2 hrs.	making snow flakes						✓			
	½ hr.	reviewing 7x table		✓							
	1½ hr.	housecleaning - cleaned cages.			✓					✓	
	1 hr.	Ranger Rick - cougars			✓						
Dec 8	2 hr.	skating on lake.							✓		
	30 min	reading "Castle" Macaulay	✓			✓					
	30 min	lang arts - antonyms	✓								
	30 min	sentence structure	✓								
	2 hrs.	drawing/more snow flakes.						✓			
Dec 9.	1 hr.	National Geog. - cats			✓						
	1 hr.	practiced part for pageant (fox)	✓					✓			
	30 min	reading "Castle" Macaulay				✓					
	1 hr.	painting - papier mâché						✓			
	1 hr.	reading - Calvin & Hobbes	✓								
Dec 10.	1 hr.	Nat. Geog. Apollo moon mission			✓	✓					
	1 hr.	language arts - penmanship	✓								
	½ hr.	phonics lesson	✓								
	1 hr.	skating on lake.							✓		
	2 hrs.	used jigsaw to cut out sun design						✓			✓

BOOKS READ "Lassie Come Home" - Knight

NOTES Singing carols with ___ family - playing word games "categories"

7X 1 hr. collected cedar boughs + decorated crèche.

Adrienne (11), Jesse (8), Brennan (5), Zachary (1)

UPDATE from Leslie:

This winter, as a result of doing a program called *The Artist's Way* by Julia Cameron which helps you to rediscover your creative and artistic self, I have realized that we as parents need to do our *own* home education, that we need to research our own projects that interest us, pull out long forgotten dreams, dust off those old books and plunge into learning, letting our children be inspired by our example. This takes the focus off of thinking that the process of homeschooling is entirely for our children's sake when, actually, it is a continuing journey that goes on for our whole life. Instead of chasing after my children to get them to do some homeschooling, I tell them the hours that I am available (undisturbed by housework, cooking, or dishes) and that they are to come to me and ask for help on their projects if they want. I remind them when it is their time to be with me.

The most consistent problem I have dealt with is my feeling that I will be unable to meet their needs in terms of money, time, and enthusiasm and that they will not have what they require to meet the world. Just keeping up with everything they want to do is impossible because there is so much they want to do! (I still have interests of my own and find that I must juggle to find time for them.) As the children get older, there is even more that they wish to do and explore, and the questions get more complex and harder to answer. I really wish I could have it all here at my finger tips! (But I don't.) My ultimate goal is to become confident enough that I can scrap the school model and just abandon myself to the process of learning rather than schooling.

Adrienne (11), Jesse (8), Brennan (5), Zachary (1)

Greg and Jo-Anne
Gregory, age 14
Rebecca, age 13
Stephen, age 10
Mary-Beth, age 5

Jo-Anne wrote about this hot day of 24th January, in *midsummer* from Kellyville, the semi-rural suburb of Sydney, Australia.

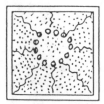

LEARNING HAPPENS IN BURSTS

Tuesday, 24th January—mid-summer, hot 30° C (88° F) day:

7.00 AM:

My husband Greg and I rise and talk about plans for the day. I collect dirty washing from collection points around the house. Greg takes it all to the laundry, puts one load in and another load out on the clothes line, collects the newspapers, and unstacks the dishwasher. In the meantime, I have awakened Rebecca and Stephen warmly. They know that their first tasks are to do their rooms (make beds; put away shoes, clothes, etc.; open blinds), do their daily diary (about the day before's activities, books they are reading, letters received, discussions undertaken, articles read, etc., and Stephen usually illustrates his diary), and then have breakfast. Gregory, who is always up early, has done his diary, room, and eaten his breakfast, and is working on his financial maths with his new financial calculator.

7.30 AM:

Greg Sr. starts work. Greg is a part owner of a technology company that develops special applications software. This gives him the opportunity to be with us at home a great deal of the time.

I tidied the study where we all work at three reasonable-sized tables and

Mary-Beth has two small-sized tables so she can be with us. Yesterday Mary-Beth had out heaps of material for making a material collage on cardboard, numerous craft books (she is always looking for new things to make), glitter, (she likes to glue it to material) and a large jar full of water that has rose petals and crayons bobbing up and down inside and paper with stars on it stuck on the lid. Needless to say, bits of crayon, paper, glitter, and rose petals are everywhere as well as painted bits of wood! Other rubbish has been left by me—the computer manuals; my journals to read, piles of paper, etc., a few of Gregory's textbooks, Rebecca's biology books and Chinese writing, a couple of Stephen's *Capsela* kits and pieces that he was creating yesterday. Now that all is clean I feel I can function a lot better. Greg and I organize the mail from our homeschooling business, fill book orders (only four today), and send out invitations to a BBQ we're having on 5th February.

8.00 AM:
    I start work with Gregory on Chapter 18 in the management textbook by Robbins. Gregory is doing two units this semester on the Open Learning University course towards a Bachelor of Business Degree. He started in December and it is a thirteen-week semester involving assignments and examinations. He has definitely been challenged by doing university-level work, but I have been surprised and delighted at how well he has risen to the occasion. I have been helping him by reading aloud the chapters with him and discussing what is meant by concepts such as "dissonance theory" with practical examples. He left me behind in the maths text sometime back, especially with *Excel* spreadsheets and the financial calculator. However, he has kept himself to schedule with both subjects and assignments, at first planning the hours he would spend on it, and now working until he feels he has completed enough for the day. It is actually summer holidays now in Australia but Gregory really does not want to do the highly stressful end-of-year-twelve matriculation exam in two years, so he has decided to circumvent this by being well and truly into a degree at the time his compatriots are just undertaking their horrendous matriculation year. (Because he has decided to do this himself he is more motivated than I have ever seen him before, and it has been such a pleasure working with him.) We finished this session with Gregory completing the computer-generated questions on the chapter that he did most recently and with Mary-Beth on my knee asking for breakfast.

9.15 AM:
    Mary-Beth is organised, Stephen has been sent to the piano to do his warm-up exercises and Rebecca and I discuss what she wants do to today—some more biology (she is working on the functions and simple anatomy of the brain, shapes of neurons, etc.). She is planning to do two hours of Chinese because her Chinese teacher has left a lot more characters to write out and learn than usual. Rebecca will also plan the German lesson for two homeschoolers she teaches on a weekly basis. She wants to do some running practice later and we are

Gregory (14), Rebecca (13), Stephen (10), Mary-Beth (5)

determined to get some more of a book called *Woman's Perspective* read as Rebecca is starting a University course in March called Gender Studies and she wants to have this book (the main text for the course) read by then.

9.30 AM:
    I adjourn to Stephen who is practicing piano. He works on today's scale (six scales, one a day) major, minor, melodic, contrary motion, triads, and arpeggios. Then he practices his pieces for the day (the *Heller Study in D Minor*, the *Debussy Little Shepherd*, the *Bach Sarabande French Suite #3*, the *Chopin Waltz, Opus 69 #1* and *Kuhlau, Opus 83 #3*). My job was specified by the piano teacher yesterday, "Watch elbows are at least eight inches out from the body, wrist is down, fingers are well-shaped and playing on the pads." As well, I help him by reminding him of the different issues that came up with each piece at the last lesson: "Don't plod on the left hand," "Raise your hand at the finish of the phrase, gentle touch," etc. Stephen believes he would like to be a concert pianist and has no trouble putting in two to three hours of practice a day as well as six to ten hours of lessons a week. His level of personal commitment to task is also quite high, and while he might require a reminder or two about practice, once reminded he heads off with no complaint.

10.30 AM:
    Stephen's other music mentor arrives to teach Stephen composing, harmony and voice leading, as well as history of music. He is a qualified musician and composer himself and has been a real find for us: Flexible enough to approach Stephen's music in a non-linear way and confident enough with himself to be a friend and mentor despite the age gap of thirteen years (and they like to joke around). He encouraged Stephen to write some serialist music last year and it has expanded his vision quite a lot. Stephen is a couple of years ahead of his peers in music and loves it passionately. He also does trumpet, bass and electric guitar, and piano accordion whenever he gets the time. The three older children have a rock band together with Rebecca on drums, Stephen on keyboards and guitar, and Gregory on electric guitar. I sit in on lessons regularly. Today I ask his teacher to break up the hundred bar piece Stephen is composing for four instruments into more manageable pieces so he isn't intimidated. Throughout this interaction and listening to them both at the piano, Mary-Beth and I are knitting a twenty stitch doll's scarf—she slipping the wool over and pulling the stitch off. Soon she'll be able to do it on her own.

    All the while this has been happening, Gregory has been working on his Business Maths unit and Rebecca on her Chinese. Greg Sr. is in his study planning, phoning, balancing and doing all the things that thankfully allow us to do all the things we do. Stephen will proceed with his music lesson until 1.00 PM.

11.20 AM:
    Rebecca and I start on *Woman's Perspective* by Robin Rolland. This is

Gregory (14), Rebecca (13), Stephen (10), Mary-Beth (5)

a really great time for us because we make my bed, then sit on top with lots of pillows (for comfort) and read and discuss the nature/nurture, culture issues, etc. Rebecca reads an enormous amount in a wide variety of areas, so contributes so much to our discussion! For instance, she has read a thick book on the Yanomani people of Venezuela. She is very interested in Aboriginal culture and is widely read here too, so she can discuss more about rites of passage and food collection and tribal law than I can dream of. So it's a real give and take. With so many issues and the fact that this is a university text, after one hour we are quite ready for a break. All this time, Mary-Beth has been making "presents" for us, wandering in and out, asking for sticky tape and admiration and ideas, which are happily delivered (she likes to have Becky and me in the same place to consult at the same time). Gregory even came in about a Maths problem but we sent him to Dad. Just last December, not four weeks ago, I was able to proudly say that I was having no trouble with Gregory's Maths, but this Business Maths with consumer price indices, statistics and spreadsheets has quite thrown me for the moment, though I am planning to put my head around it!

12.30 PM:
     I read my list of phone calls to return. We have an answering machine because, while running a homeschool organisation, I found I could spend my whole life on the phone, so now I strictly limit my calls—none in the "school time" unless desperate, and my darling husband handles the simple ones in amongst his tens of other calls. Then, I check up on everyone. Becky has decided to look at some slides until lunch so gets out her microscope and histology book. I ask Mary-Beth to get out five books from the "animal" shelf. We have thousands of books and I found that I wasn't using them very effectively until a couple of years ago when I had heaps of bookshelves put up in each bedroom and our workroom and then got the kids to help me really sort out every book. So we now have science, history, geography, animal, humour, English, reference etc., books and we have a policy of returning things to their correct shelves. This really helps me when directing the children's reading, too. For instance, I can say to Stephen, "What have you just finished reading?" As is the case at the moment, he is reading a book on the history of the world since 400 B.C., called *Threads of Time*. When finished, if he's happy, I might say, "Well how about you choose something of interest from the science shelf?" If nothing can be found then, of course, he could be sent to the *National Geographic* to look through all the spines until he can find a topic he may find interesting., Of course, he may choose another history-type topic but just the looking expands horizons! I've always been fairly directive of my children's reading and still am. Gregory and I read aloud the Oxford's children's version of the *Iliad* and the *Odyssey* when he was six or seven. Rebecca, on the other hand, read the adult's version to herself last year at twelve years old because at the same age (six or seven) she was interested in a range of other issues, including simplified Greek and Roman mythologies. These included the books *Heroic Deeds of Men—Heroic Deeds of Women* and also books about Egypt, Romans, etc. We

Gregory (14), Rebecca (13), Stephen (10), Mary-Beth (5)

really value reading in diverse areas and each read hundreds of books a year. Gregory certainly has explored World War II thoroughly from the *Rise and Fall of the Third Reich* (Shirer's classic) through a book called *2194 Days of War*. He has read biographies of anyone who was anyone, the minutia of troop movements, technology, spying, armaments, political lead-ups, and the problems and realities of war. Still, while he had this interest, I would send him off on tangents like the *Secret House* (science in the house), *National Geographic*, *Australian Geographic*, biographies of everyone from sports people and musicians to politicians (past and present), explorers, scientists, etc. Therefore, it is a *big* advantage to have him on your team in *Trivial Pursuit* and more importantly, he has read widely enough to be sensitively critical and fairly cynical when he meets with the written word or with people generally. Newspapers (edited for some issues when they were very young) have always played a large part in our house. Lunch time often sees us reading out articles to each other.

Whereas most of Gregory's reading has seemed to derive from the "military-empire" approach including Egyptians, Greeks, Romans and everyone since; Rebecca has taken a more eclectic approach to her reading. L. M. Montgomery, Laura Ingalls Wilder, and Rutger (*Children of the Oregon Trail*) gave her a different insight into North America than Gregory. Her language background (German and Chinese) has sent her to read about Europe and Asia, especially folk tales and traditional stories, and her deep love of people has lead her into literally hundreds of biographies of a humanitarian bent. All of these things lead to "other things." So last year when she found that she was "bookless" for a day she consulted my shelves and decided to "have a go" with Tolstoy's *Anna Karenina*. She found some of it hard going but was very persistent, often you would walk in to find her with tears dripping down. Then, when she finished *Anna*, she marched on to *War and Peace* and finished it—much to our shock and pleasure. In the meantime, of course, she read many other things including a history of Napoleon to iron out how she felt about Tolstoy's view of the French. More than anyone in our house, Rebecca uses *National Geographic* as jumping off points. For instance, a fabulous piece on chocolate sent her into South American history. A picture she glanced at that had a piece of luminous bacteria in it sent her to biology in a big way so that she really plugged away at a matriculation level (year twelve) biology text all last year (when she would have been in year seven at school) and decided to ask for a very good microscope for Christmas and her birthday. Her abiding interest in whales, sharks and the marine environment in general comes from *National Geographic*, and her desire to become a marine biologist is lovingly encouraged by their beautiful pictures and wonderful writers. Last year I remember Becky saying, "Mum, how come *National Geographic never* has a boring story?"

12.30-1 PM:
    I read to Mary-Beth and just talk generally about all the issues she cares about today.

Gregory (14), Rebecca (13), Stephen (10), Mary-Beth (5)

1-1.05 PM:

Everyone's really ready for lunch. This is a real coming together. No matter what, at 1.00 PM we down tools and head to the kitchen! First we make lunch for Greg Sr.—tomato sandwiches and a piece of fruit. Rebecca cut up a watermelon, Stephen cut up an avocado and Gregory put on noodles and grated cheese.

Last night we were privileged to hear Noam Chomsky, the famous linguist who is in Australia on behalf of M.I.T. There are just so many issues to discuss—prejudice, the examples he quoted and the whole history of language development, knowledge and theories. Chomsky is of special interest to me because when my children were born I always intended that, if possible, they would be bilingual. From birth, we have had native speakers of German and Chinese in our house for a couple of hours a week who only spoke in their native language to the children. They were not allowed to *teach,* only to *play*. Both boys have now stopped Chinese but Rebecca is doing it much more formally over the last two years and is doing very well.

The dynamics of lunch time are always changing. We usually discuss things, often as a result of any of the books or newspapers that decorate our kitchen bench. In fact, Gregory always brings the daily papers, the morning mail and whichever magazines have arrived (*Nature, Scientific American, Cobblestone, Odyssey, New Moon, Growing Without Schooling, Mothering, Faces, Calliope,* etc.) with him to lunch and we sit down to a quiet, companionable read and talk period. Some of us might adjourn to other jobs or pleasures such as uncompleted computer games, folding laundry, vacuuming, or preparing for dinner. Today we are putting on a Christmas pudding (despite the fact that it is not Christmas, this is my children's favourite cake) to boil for five hours. Rebecca prepares the fruit for next week's pudding and the boys pitch in to help. We make six dozen sausage rolls to go in the freezer for a party we are having on the 5th of February. We also dice up the meat for tonight's casserole because tonight is athletics training. We leave at 5.20 PM and don't usually get home until 8.00 PM.

2.30 PM:

Everyone is back at work. Gregory is doing his electric guitar homework and practice for an hour. Rebecca is reading the biography *Elisabeth Murdoch* (humanitarian and mother of Rupert) and I am working on my management assignment, having taken on the first year of an MBA course this year. It has certainly made me much more "timetable" aware, and each moment is more precious but I really enjoy the challenge. Rebecca is proud of me and it doesn't hurt any of the children to know I really value education. Learning is something you should be doing all your life and I really work hard at it.

Stephen arrives from his theory study to argue with me about a question on plagal cadences. I have absolutely no idea what the answer is or even what they are. So I do what I do in such circumstances—reread the question out loud very slowly and ask him to explain to *me* what they are asking. Half way through

Gregory (14), Rebecca (13), Stephen (10), Mary-Beth (5)

he'll say (usually), "I know what they want!" I might add that this method doesn't work with everything, but after ten years of homeschooling highly inquisitive children with very diverse interests, I've had to acknowledge that I just cannot explore everything to the level they wish to reach. I have been lucky with the eldest two being very interested in reading, military and general history, planes, biology and people. I've mostly kept up or been ahead. (Becky did sail past me with Tolstoy however). But by the time you get to child three and four and find they are so incredibly different—well, I just knew I couldn't be all things to all people so now I help them with the *method* or the *how to*. This I can still manage. So often I find that even, say, a difficult algebra problem can be quite easily answered by the child if only I tease out the problem and get it identified or review the theory. Anyway this is what is working at the moment and I'm standing by it!

3.30 PM:

Rebecca finished reading and starts Maths. She is working on reviews of last year's work. (The new school year always starts in January in Australia.) Stephen finished with music theory cadences (fifteen minutes) and reading *Threads of Time*, now fronts up for Maths. He is doing all operations with fractions from the textbook. Mary-Beth is writing letters all over a page, pretending they are words and illustrating same for sending to a growing list of people. She has also spent some short time watching a German video tape. I do expect Mary-Beth to entertain herself a fair amount, though am happy to give her some structured work if she's having trouble entertaining herself. Despite the fact that I am often accused of being a "servant" to my children by home-schooling them, I try very hard to make sure this is not the case. They are expected to be as self-motivated and organised as I am.

Gregory asks many excellent questions from his readings, and I can really see that all those hundreds of intelligent books he has read have educated him. He and Rebecca use fabulous language quite naturally—high quality vocabulary you'd really be delighted for an adult to use. He also spells perfectly, punctuates superbly, and has very mature opinions on things. He uses these questions to test his theories on very complex issues of content and format. I know there are no "one best" answers, so there is a wonderful back and forwards argument/banter. Perhaps my only major contribution is grounding the questions in reality (examples from real life) but it is a source of much joy and pride for me. Even more secretly delighting is the fact that this child has never done an English language textbook per se, yet "autonomous," "synonymous," "strategic policies" etc. are all known by him and, until two months ago, he'd rather clean bathrooms than write an essay.

4.30ish PM:

We drift away from our workroom. Everyone relaxes in one way or another. I talk with Greg Sr. about a range of things and basically recuperate.

Gregory (14), Rebecca (13), Stephen (10), Mary-Beth (5)

5.10 PM:
They all get ready for athletics. Greg takes all four children to training at a local park with a number of their friends. It is something they really enjoy.

5.30-8 PM:
I get washing in and then fold it. This is not my usual chore. Mostly the kids are responsible for getting the washing to machine, on line and off again. We share out tasks pretty evenly and often have an hour when all six of us work like crazy and achieve a great deal. We do try to clean up as we go. For instance, as part of lunch and dinner, we would clear up, wipe surfaces, stack or unstack the dishwasher, vacuum the floor, prepare for the next meal. I must admit I am still very much the "director" of these operations, something I find unfortunate, but they are improving, especially with bathrooms. Their bedrooms are always tidy, as this happens before diary writing and before breakfast in about ten minutes every morning.

I return some phone calls and check what we've achieved. I make a weekly list on Sunday of hopeful (though not frozen in stone) achievements for the week. I correct Maths and mark appropriate "redo these ones." Next, I put on tea and some music while I am peeling the potatoes. Then I adjourn to my management essay.

8.00 PM:
The sun has just gone down, a little *too* soon!

8.10 PM:
Everyone is in the kitchen, except whichever child is showering. We're all bopping around to music and chatting, reviewing all the athletics gossip, times, training procedures, etc. This continues over dinner. I often *wonder* or should I say *marvel in awe* through these conversations. Then I consider my "schooled" self at the same age as my eldest and I listen to them speak about the to and fro of the social group at athletics, I am just so pleased with their maturity and comments. They are both extremely well liked and popular but they are continually amazed by the petty back-biting and are very "cluey" about finding ways to stay out of it. I keep telling them it was because they were "desocialized" so effectively as children (I was never much for group things for under eight years old). I really don't know why they are so good at being "immune" to the peer group, yet looking for all intents and purposes like one of the members. They are even really good at identifying trouble brewing (despite never having been in school to "learn" this) and I see them either diffuse it or quietly absent themselves. I know all the experienced homeschoolers said this would happen, but I can tell you it is a real thrill to actually *see* it myself.

9.30 PM:
The kitchen is finished, rubbish out, athletics gear cleaned up, and water bottles refilled. Everyone is already in pajamas (after their showers). I've

Gregory (14), Rebecca (13), Stephen (10), Mary-Beth (5)

brushed Mary-Beth's teeth. She has kissed everyone and is loaded down with her five books (though she has some favourites, I've asked her to get two from the nature shelf and one from the biography shelf—she has picked Queen Victoria). We adjourn to read. Often this task is Greg Sr.'s or maybe each child reads one book (they have their own favourites they like to share with Mary-Beth) and Greg or I read the last two.

Greg and the kids head to a game or a computer or books or something else. We don't watch television in our house through the week despite having three. Greg Sr. is masterful at programming whatever is on, say a series on the history of steam engines or Antarctica. He picks out a list of anything relevant on Sundays and then records them during week. We watch the best shows with no advertisements at the weekend. We might watch a movie or an interview with a scientist. Some weeks there is just *nothing* to watch. TV definitely doesn't play a large role in our lives.

10.00 PM:
    Mary-Beth is in bed, though not asleep.

10.30-11.00 PM:
    Gregory, Rebecca, Stephen, Greg, and I hit the sack. Greg and I will talk, read for a while, etc. If something exciting has happened through the day I will be bursting to tell Greg, "Do you know what Gregory/Rebecca/Stephen/Mary-Beth did/said today?" Philosophically and emotionally Greg is behind us. He provides all the monetary support we need to achieve our learning objectives. He does some of the main support work—the washing and the kitchen for instance (though not his most favourite jobs). This also used to entail walking or burping crying babies or rocking them on his lap while he worked and still entails endless hours or reading and taking them to sport activities, the movies and other big events. He is my "spaceman." By this I mean he has always been there for me when I needed "space," either for my sanity, study, submissions, work, seminars, meetings with officials, etc. He is 150% behind homeschooling and as proud of us as he can be. In the last two years he has taken over the day-to-day phone calls with the ten or twenty people who ring in with enquiries about homeschooling (I am exhausted by this job). However, the advent of University level Maths has seen me push him and his skills to the fore. I feel like I have taken on everything from Astronomy to Zoology at one stage or another. Many issues we've covered I haven't really even had any interest in but I've pushed myself (and often been pleasantly surprised),but University level Maths . . . . And, sweet man that he is, he will listen and question and advise . . . then there is another day soon upon us!

Gregory (14), Rebecca (13), Stephen (10), Mary-Beth (5)

Now, when I look back at all this writing, I am aware that while this is a typical day for us, especially in terms of hours spent and general business, it is also untypical. Two days a week I go out for Stephen's music lessons and take Mary-Beth along. This allows her four solid hours of "Mum-time." · She reads to me and we play number games and place games while I have one ear on Stephen, writing down the notes the teacher is contributing every so often over that period of two hours. They still all have German lessons one afternoon a week. Rebecca has four hours of Chinese on either Saturdays or Sundays. Friends come over and we are flexible enough to just "cancel" everything if we've an opportunity to go and see an exhibition or hear someone speak, etc.

I have always observed that their learning happens in bursts and I sometimes find these times incredibly hectic. Suddenly Rebecca is asking wonderful questions and pushing herself to new heights of information. (The other day she wanted to know more about kidney transplants so rang and ordered information from the kidney foundation without telling me until after the deed was done.) At these times I put my work aside and the child who is bursting might work with me for hours. I also notice that by the end of ten weeks I am really exhausted and so are they. Generally, Australian children have six weeks off school in December and January, our summer, but we find this too long. We tend to take around ten days to two weeks off after every ten weeks. Those "holiday" days however would not be what you would call "veg out" days full of TV and computers. We do always try to be balanced. They do include a good deal more time with friends and swimming and tennis and reading though.

Gregory (14), Rebecca (13), Stephen (10), Mary-Beth (5)

Why did we homeschool? When I am giving talks to colleges, on radio and to prospective homeschoolers, I am really careful to be diplomatic on this issue of schooling. Practically, I think society will always need schools because for so many parents there is no choice. Despite the fact that I went to really good schools and did very well, I can say that we homeschool because, from my experience, schools are a grossly impoverished environment. They are impoverished academically, emotionally, spiritually, and, most important, socially. I feel that home and the family is really the environment where they can best be individually nourished and enriched in a myriad of life's offerings.

Gregory (14), Rebecca (13), Stephen (10), Mary-Beth (5)

Vernon and Cathy
Tim, age 8 (now age 15)
Jason, age 6 (now age 13)

Cathy wrote about a day seven years ago, adding later thoughts, at their home in the somewhat rural area of Quakertown, Pennsylvania.

LOOKING BACK

It has been many years since we first began homeschooling. Over these years I have tried to write a diary or review for each year. Our homeschooling has changed quite a bit. Below are some samples of our practices and thoughts.

We have over three acres of land with a large bank barn. The porch, which my husband added, is useful in warm weather as we put a large picnic table there and usually one end is strewn with text books. It saves us from clearing a table for meals. Usually the kitchen table is our workspace in the colder weather but we also have another table in the living room that is utilized. At times, a card table is erected to provide for extra work space. Beds are excellent places for reading—or the couch in the living room or den. I used to have homeschooling supplies in almost every area of the house.

There were books in the bathroom for potty training and books in the bedrooms. As the children got older, I removed books from certain areas of the house and now have most of the supplies in what we call the den. We have many shelves there. One set of drawers upstairs in the hallway contains art supplies. The kids work everywhere and anywhere.

My oldest son was enrolled part time last year at school so that he could play football, and this year he is enrolled full time. I am relieved and happy with the decision, as is my son. I still grieve at times not having my son at home, but it was an educational decision to have him learn from others instead of learning individually. We did community basketball and baseball last year and are doing it for our second year now. We also participate heavily in church

The boys are involved in a community wood carving club, which my oldest started having an interest in when he was in kindergarten. We usually attend a few meetings a year and Tim will try to participate in a competition in the yearly February mall show. He has won two blue ribbons for youth.

With my oldest in school now, I learn that some students have different learning styles and lying on the bed listening to rock music is acceptable. He did get on high honor roll so who am I to start complaining?

I first found out what I wanted to know about homeschooling from radio programs, other homeschooling families and reading, reading, and more reading. The most helpful insight is to hear about how others do their homeschooling. I share the following day to indicate how our homeschool worked in our earlier years. Vernon is the father and I am Cathy, the "supervisor."

BEFORE BREAKFAST Vernon feeds the animals (chickens, steer and currently a brand new venture—a veal calf). He leaves for his long day at about 6:30 AM. The time before breakfast and before the children wake up is very precious to me. I usually can be found with a large mug (it actually holds a quart) containing luke warm water to "break the fast of the night" as Raymond Moore says. I will then spend time in the Bible or related book or both. Currently I am reading Proverbs and have just finished *A Time For Anger* by Franky Schaeffer. I am convinced I can not reveal truth to my children unless I am daily receiving truth or revelation from the Lord. I am also developing the practice of sitting quietly before the Lord and ministering to the Lord during this time. One way I am doing this is to page through a hymnal and sing hymns to the Lord. If not my daily prayer, than at least my daily attitude is that the Lord's favor may rest upon me and that He will establish the work of my hands, and that He will guide me to teach each child what he needs to know that day. How we need His wisdom!

The boys may sleep in as late as 8:00 or 9:00 AM or later if we have had an especially late night. If they wake up individually, each boy has his own devotions with me followed by his "morning water" which flushes the kidneys and helps the bowels to be regular. Each child would receive either reading or reading instruction until the other child wakes up. We have a strict rule to let everyone get their sleep. Right now both boys are usually waking up at the same time so we use a common devotion book followed by our own system of memory verses. We have made cards with pictures as clues to the verse on the other side. We are trying to learn the references but, after all, the verse is more important, as Tim pointed out to me this morning. I actively learn with them. We review so as to really know them. This system started because I didn't want them just to learn a verse for Sunday School and forget it. Also I wanted to have verses that they could use during the day. Dr. James Dobson gave me the idea with the phrase "inserting the Word in your child's day." We started out with a few Bible verses, and where we haven't gone from there!! If there is a good Sunday School verse, we copy the entire verse and add it to our cards. Sometimes they already know their verse because we have learned it in

Tim (8-15), Jason (6-13)

homeschool. I am thinking about letting each of the boys be in charge of their own Sunday School verses since they can both read. Right now I am not very diligent in helping them learn short parts of verses that will only stay in their heads for a few minutes. I think I will teach a verse instead—"Study to shew thyself approved unto God" (2 Timothy 2:15) and let the Holy Spirit lead them from there. Many times, following their verses, I will share what the Lord has taught me that morning through the books I am reading. Currently, I am sharing the important points from a chapter in *Revival* by Martin Lloyd-Jones, the sequel to *Joy Unspeakable*. I want the boys to see the excitement in my daily learning.

Then we usually move to library books. These are books the boys pick, but right now we are working on a few that I picked to go along with units we are studying. We used library books for a unit on the Pilgrims during the months of November-February. (The Pilgrims lived in February as well as November!) We also used library books to study a unit on skin, which was prompted by our newspapers, *Sharing God's World*. Usually every Thursday after breakfast we do our newspapers. We have been working on a library book on Israel. We have only one chapter to go and I am determined to finish it before the due date. (I finally know where the Gaza strip is.) Israel's recent history is falling into place! At any rate, we usually have at least a half hour of reading or more during the quiet part of the morning.

BREAKFAST can be anywhere from 9-11:00 AM depending on how much reading we do and the time both boys awaken. I enjoy the morning hours to read before the phone rings and while the children are fresh. To enrich the breakfast prayer, I am using some verses from Proverbs that can be used as a prayer to help us to seek wisdom. Many times I will wait to eat until after the boys. This allows me extra teaching time while they are eating. I will read a chapter of a book we are working on, or if I do eat with them, many times I will put a tape in the tape player and eat while enjoying an Old Testament or New Testament story. We started reading a book on China, which I need to get back into. I also try to read to the boys in Spanish at some meals and I read their Sunday School papers to them at this time.

AFTER BREAKFAST we are usually ready for a break from each other and the boys are allowed to have free time while I enjoy a leisurely shower (if the phone doesn't ring) and get dressed for the day. Many times Tim will use this time to call his eighty-nine-year-old great grandmother to check on her. Other times the boys have their favorite fantasy play of "Power Peep." I do not interfere except to put time limits on this activity. On many days we will all meet at the kitchen table for written work. The boys will work on penmanship and math, write letters or work in phonics books. By 11:00 AM we usually break to listen to a radio program called *Insights for Living* by Charles Swindoll. Some days we sort wash while listening to this program. The boys sort into three baskets—white, colored and the really dirty stuff. (I do not sort wash any more!) Another day we match clean socks or cook or bake while we listen to our

Tim (8-15), Jason (6-13)

morning radio program.

Then it is time for "outside activity." Everyday the boys look forward to going out. There is always the barn for those really wet days. On the days I feel good about, we take a walk together. Then there are most of the days when I need to get things done and they are free to roam and play to their heart's content. Sometimes we carry firewood into the house at this time.

LUNCH is usually later for us than most families and the boys will come in saying, "We're hungry," if I haven't called them. So we will be eating sometime between 1:30 and 2:30 PM. We are flexible when we have other homeschooling families in for lunch or if we are invited out. Once again, lunch affords time for more reading and this helps with discipline at meal times.

AFTER LUNCH we're now able to find more time to learn since we are growing out of naps. On some days we might still go for a rest or Jason might read to me from his reading text or an I Can Read library book. Some afternoons we spend time learning to use a computer that was given to us! This is my time to teach them from the manual. They may use it for short periods during their free time. All too soon it's 5:30 PM and time for the boys to set the table and put the dishes away from the dishwasher. We listen to two radio programs at this time: *Children's Bible Hour* and *Stories of Great Christians*. Also many times the boys need another time outside before the evening meal.

THE EVENING MEAL is served shortly after Vernon's 6:00 PM arrival time and we share the evening meal together. We usually read a short section of Scripture suggested by "Keys For Kids" (a devotional booklet) followed by a true life story emphasizing the Scripture passage. The evening meal also allows us to all share books such as *Better HomeSchool* by Bill Butterworth, *Billy Sunday* by Robert Allen, *A View From the Zoo*, by Gary Richmond, and now we are working on *Samuel Francis Smith* by Marguerite Fitch. I started reading from the family book once a week but now we have been able to do it three or four times a week.

AFTER THE EVENING MEAL Vernon will spend time with the boys. Many weeks he will take the boys shopping, which is really a nice break for me as I am not a shopper. Sometimes they will bring the firewood to the house from the barn or read or play games. Vernon is also in charge of industrial arts; he used to be a carpenter. I assign nature study and animal raising to Vern, as those are areas of interest to him.

Mondays are special days in which we go to The Life Quest Nursing Home for a Bible study that we lead. The boys will many times take toys or objects of interest to share with the folks for show and tell. What a receptive, appreciative audience. The boys are now able to help find page numbers and at times hold someone's hand or rub a back to help keep a troubled lady contented and quiet so the rest can hear the lesson. We use a flannel board and colorful

Tim (8-15), Jason (6-13)

figures which both boys and residents enjoy. Monday afternoons are special times to spend at my parents' house.my dad, who has read a bit on home-schooling, pitches right in and teaches the boys such areas as World War II history; he lived through it and can share the emotion. He also does physical education, hunting safety, and is now helping the children start their own coin collection. My mother is a very active member in the DAR (Daughters of the American Revolution) and so enjoys teaching patriotism to the boys. There is now the CAR (Children of the American Revolution). Mom is great for buying the kids good clothes, thus saving me hours and hours of shopping time and aggravation. My parents are also our field trip coordinators I can't skip my grandmother who makes requests for sewing that she can do for me. "I have to have something to do!!" She is a real blessing and we include her in our outings and meals many times. She can teach us so much. Vernon's parents were the ones who introduced us to the *Growing Without Schooling* publication and pro-vide most of the boys' clothes through a very involved hand me down system.

Basically I try to have a teaching attitude twenty-four hours a day and whenever there is a free block of time I do some teaching required by the Commonwealth. The boys are sporadically using *Pre-Math It* and *Math-It*. They usually initiate art by asking for materials or by simply drawing. As I keep a diary type of record of what we are doing, I page through it to see what areas are being neglected and try either to take out a library book in that area or find some game or other means of not letting that area slide. Music time is basically while driving to or from appointed destinations. I have several tapes that were made for me by a senior citizen from our church. They are hymns and choruses that we enjoy or want to learn so we can be seen (or heard) practicing lyrics as "we walk (drive) along the way." It's paying off already. Jason can be heard singing while at work or play. Another man (soon to retire) generously donates his time to teach the boys wood carving. They decided to pursue this hobby after reading a library book in which the main character's father sold wood carvings for a living.

It is impossible to describe all that happens in a homeschool. For example, I almost forgot to mention that a friend stops in at least twice a month to check on our progress. She is encouraging us and we jointly read a book by Charles Colson entitled *Loving God*. We discuss the chapters with the boys. We are also pursuing a chess club. The boys attend a monthly church program and we try to have many families, especially homeschooling families, into our house for meals.

BED TIME usually occurs at the same time for all of us except that Vern and I read in bed. Well, the boys have now also been granted 10-15 minutes to read. Tim has chosen to read the Bible! I shared that another homeschooling family allows their children to read for a half hour and Tim was wanting to do that also until he heard that their bed time was 7:00 PM.

MOTIVATION has always been an important issue for us as we homeschooled. Through the years, I have developed ways to motivate my

Tim (8-15), Jason (6-13)

children. Many parents do not even consider homeschooling due to the fact that they feel they couldn't work with their child nor their child with them. Many have difficulty relating to their children, even in trying to help with homework. (This was written three years after the day I described.)

One day, while reading a newsletter, I was wondering how I could interest Jason in the pages about birds. He happened to come and sit down right at my side. I wondered how to approach the issue. I decided to just page through the newsletter and read it to myself. When I got to the pages with pictures of birds Jason said, "Mom, read this to me." It was so easy! He asked for what I wanted simply by my apparent interest in the article just for myself.

One of the easiest motivational techniques is to see what each child is interested in and pursue this interest in any and all ways. Possibly take out library books on the topic or invest in the material needed. Oh dear, I forgot to buy those sweet potatoes that Jason wanted for a science experiment that he read about in a book. I've been feeling guilty about a lack of hands-on experiments in our curriculum anyway, so I am going to follow his lead in this area. We could call this "delight directed" motivation.

The motivational tool I use to teach reading is to read to the children. I have read aloud the complete works of *Sherlock Holmes* as well as *The Bible* to my oldest. He is voluntarily reading adult books at this time. I can surely state that I had no desire to read the second *Bobbsey Twin* book to my youngest, but I was glad I did, for the next one he picked up and read to himself! He has now read eight more!!

One way to motivate is to have real expectations. I know I can expect my eleven-year-old to go upstairs and clean his room in an hour or two. I need more realistic expectations for my nine-year-old. I started by giving explicit directions and showing him how to clean. Then we moved to cleaning a quarter of his room. We have just moved to expecting him to clean half of his room one day and the other half the next.

Wise use of scheduling can be a motivational tool. I found, for example, that the wash got hung up a lot faster when there was free time scheduled immediately following this chore than when we were going to do workbooks after the wash was hung. Also we have to be ready for the child's creativity in his work. Is there anybody else's child out there who hangs socks vertically, one to the other, and then loops the chain back up to the line? I decided to take a picture. The socks usually dry just the same. That's what you get when you ask an artist to hang socks!

Scheduling also helps when a new unit or subject is introduced. For example, I just started using Winston's *Grammar* with my fifth and third graders. I started first familiarizing myself with the material. Then I let them see the new material. Next was to introduce note-taking to reinforce some of the rules. I pull out Winston's *Grammar* the same time each day and I try to use it regularly each day we are home. One day I deliberately took two days on a lesson because I could tell the boys wanted to get done so they could go outside. I let them play and finished the lesson *well* another day. As I proceeded, I

Tim (8-15), Jason (6-13)

realized I was going to make grammar interdisciplinary and started teaching the Spanish articles along with the English. I know the children are grasping the material because in another setting my oldest observed that a man who was circling words on an overhead projector was doing just like we do in marking certain words on our worksheets.

At times it doesn't seem like we are getting very far, but we plod along making sure we are all understanding. I used this method in teaching cursive this school year. We began in June and finished the lessons suggested in *How to Tutor* by Sam Blumenfeld in February. I will reteach cursive using different workbooks this next summer to help them remember the lessons. It was a real joy to see both boys voluntarily using the cursive to write letters to friends! My oldest even grabbed Blumenfeld's book to use as a reference for letters he forgot. I must say it was a lot easier for my fifth grader to pick up cursive than for my third grader. When I can, I teach subjects together in a one-room-schoolhouse atmosphere. Working and studying together motivates children better than isolated study and work.

At times I like the children to sit in on adult sessions. For example, a man was speaking about the Christian history of our area. I told the boys I wanted them to attend as part of our history course. I offered them a special treat after the hour lecture. This type of motivation is enjoyed by all and helps guarantee good behavior. (It's called bribery.)

Motivation for writing comes from contests, invitations to write for newsletters, or other homeschooling local groups that publish the children's work. I read about children looking for pen pals and my youngest wanted to write to a boy his age. My oldest freely decided to write to a homeschooling friend.

At times, my very presence serves as motivation. I am teaching the boys piano and at times I have one student who will waste time and will refuse to play. By sitting at his side I usually get better cooperation. At times I have sat by his side reading to myself so as not to waste my time while allowing him to waste his. He soon realized he could be doing other things he desired if he complied with my requirements on the piano.

Motivation for neat work sometimes requires that I point out all the numbers or letters that I will not accept and see to it that they are all erased and rewritten. The easier way is to not take the time and let the child get away with sloppy work. I realize I need to insist on neatness and make the child erase and erase until he knows and produces what I am requiring.

There are times when emotional stress or distress will prohibit any sort of motivational techniques. At times like this I realize the child needs support. I am getting better at forgetting my agenda even if the emotional distress is mostly brought on by the child. Recently I had a child who *no way* was going to spell the words I wanted so I picked up a book that was of interest to him and as I started reading he began to snuggle up to me and listen. The issue came up a bit later in the reading, but we got back to the book and the evening was saved. I am learning that a child feels loved when he is read to.

Tim (8-15), Jason (6-13)

May we all be granted wisdom, sensitivity and love as we attempt to motivate our children learning at home.

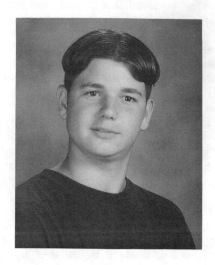 

UPDATE:

Now that Jason has finished sixth grade, I intended to send him part time to school. All of a sudden he decided he wanted to go *full* time. He's currently in a traveling team basketball league and next year he'll be able to try out for the middle school team. It is working out very well for him to be in school and he is learning to get used to a large social life. He is adjusting academically.

We took a trip to Florida but, due to all the work they miss at school, we won't take extended trips. Tim is very well adapted at this point to having all these friends, parties, sleep-overs, etc.

I'm getting used to being at home without homeschooling. Its almost like the empty nest syndrome. They are doing more work at school than they might have done at home. I miss having them here to teach and am now asking the Lord what he will have of me . . . volunteer, work around home or whatever. We now have to deal with the peer pressure of foul language, taunting, ridiculing and other byproducts of public schooling.

Looking on the bright side, things are wonderful at middle school because they are doing so much there that homeschoolers are doing. For example, they are using the interdisciplinary method of teaching, with several teachers getting together on projects. Students get involved in projects that three or four of the teachers have worked on together, and it's easier than what one homeschooling mother can do with an interdisciplinary unit. The school has even purchased large red notebooks for the student that are displayed in the library and each student has a working portfolio in the teacher's planning room.

Tim (8-15), Jason (6-13)

The students and the teachers decide together what will go into the red book to take with them for when they graduate. The district superintendent feels that homeschoolers are on the right track. I am just delighted about these changes and that everything is working out so well for us.

Their grandparents continue to be a help with the boys. They drive them when they each have games on the same night and take them places, as when we homeschooled. They have been supportive throughout our homeschooling years and the support continues now that their grandchildren are in public school. Homeschooling was right for us throughout childhood!

Tim (8-15), Jason (6-13)

Dave and Ruth
Elizabeth, age 5
Tim, age 4
Dan, age 2
Peter, age 1
(and now, newborn Jonathan)

Ruth wrote this in June, when it was warm and humid in the Philadelphia suburban area of Aston, Pennsylvania.

THE BIG HAND'S ON THE SIX

We have a large house. It's one of those poorly built tract homes, but the size is a great blessing—five rooms upstairs and four rooms downstairs (living room, dining room, kitchen, and a room we have left unfinished to be the playroom). The toddler can safely play there with the gate up, without supervision. We have a large yard, though I could wish for a fence. We do most of our homeschooling at the kitchen table—it just worked out that way. We usually do memory work on the living room couch (also where I read to them, most of the time).

Dave and I first heard of homeschooling by reading Mary Pride's *The Way Home* when we were engaged. It sounded a bit strange at first, but it didn't take long for us to know it was for us—it fit in with our philosophy of family. I know this has been an advantage to me—knowing I was going to homeschool even before we had children, and being able to make plans.

Part of our philosophy of family is that parents are responsible for the children's education. Why delegate what you can do yourself? With all the materials out there, it's easier than ever these days. Also, we think that families should be together a lot. Homeschooling families certainly are.

HERE IS A TYPICAL DAY FOR US:

The children are not to come out of their rooms until 7:30 AM (the big hand's on the six). Usually, they sleep this late or later. Since I am an early riser, I've already had some time to myself. I take about five minutes before the children wake up to think through what we'll be doing or to look over a page, but the things we do really don't require advance preparation. Dave takes the train into Philadelphia. where he works in financial services.

My goal is to "start school" at 9:30 AM, but by the time everyone is dressed, breakfast is done, the laundry started, etc., it is usually 10:00 AM or later. No big deal at this point in our lives. The baby goes up for a morning nap/rest. Dan is usually in the playroom with the gate up, though a little bit at a time I'm allowing him to sit at the kitchen table with us to "write." When he starts to distract us, back in the playroom he goes.

We start with devotions: short prayer, Bible passage I pick out, and a Bible song. Many good discussions have come out of this short time.

Then I work with Tim and Elizabeth individually. Usually, the one not being worked with occupies himself at the table quite well Sometimes, he goes up to the computer or wanders into the living room, but they seem to prefer being together. If not, they go to another room to use the computer or play. We do phonics, reading practice, handwriting, writing, and arithmetic.

Ruth Beechick's little books, *The 3 R's*, have really guided me in teaching reading and writing. It's not as hard as we thought it would be and doesn't require special resources and lots of preparation. They both like to write. For handwriting, at this stage, I just want to make sure they don't form any wrong habits in the way they make their numbers and letters. Legibility can wait until their fine-motor muscles mature. As for math, we are using a series of workbooks called *Developmental Mathematics*, but they really learned their math facts by playing computer games. Since they understand the concept of addition and subtraction, instead of using manipulatives, we use a hundred chart (which has always fascinated them).

Earlier this year, Tim sprouted wings and started flying in his reading. I no longer had to teach him any phonics—he taught himself. He now reads at a second grade level.Elizabeth was a bit unhappy that he sped ahead of her, but it was an opportunity for a good lesson. I told her she'll always find someone better than her and someone worse than her in everything. It does no good to compare ourselves with one another.What matters to God is whether we are working hard and doing our best. She seems to have accepted it. It's a good lesson for us all.

Back to the homeschooling routine. Elizabeth gets a short piano lesson. I have been pleased with the Bastien piano primer. I listen and help her play a page. It's my idea, but she enjoys it.

We sit on the couch to read a science or social studies book and to listen to a Spanish tape together. Dan is in the playpen, half participating. All of this "official" homeschooling takes about an hour and a half.

Then I like to take the children outside. I want to make sure the younger

Elizabeth (5), Tim (4), Dan (2), Peter (1)

two children have a chance to be outside sometime during the day. Then lunch happens. Elizabeth can now make peanut butter sandwiches and Tim can load dishes into the dishwasher, but I do most of the serving and clean-up. It takes time—it can take over an hour before everything is cleaned up.

After diapers have been changed and toys picked up (maybe), we start the nap routine. I review their catechism and Bible memory work with them, then Dan gets a story, with the older two always looking on. After he is upstairs, I read them a chapter from whatever book we're in the middle of—currently *Little House on the Prairie*. I believe reading to children is one of the most valuable educational experiences you can give them. I admit, I also enjoy it.

Here is one of my keys to avoiding "homeschool burnout"—nap/rest time. One hour is a reasonable minimum amount of time for them to stay in their rooms. I require an hour and a half, and I know several mothers who require two hours. Elizabeth and Tim rarely sleep. They look at books, write, draw, listen to tapes, record tapes, build with Legos/blocks/Lincoln Logs, play with dolls, trains, etc. It is a valuable time for them and a cherished time for me to sit down and read. I intend always to continue with it in our daily routine.

Theoretically, after nap time, there is time for me to do some housework, but this is often not the case. I am learning to be flexible about this reality. Housework has never been one of my life priorities, anyway. The children keep the toys off the floor as needed. Sometimes Elizabeth helps sort laundry—that's another time-consuming chore that I don't see any way out of. It has to be done once a week, or we run out of clothes to wear. As for vacuuming, dusting, mopping the kitchen floor, and bathrooms—I'm happy if these get done every other week, with quick touch-ups before guests come or as needed in the bathrooms. Things very often get put off "one more week."

I am fortunate that my husband comes home from work early. We eat dinner between 5:00 and 5:30 PM. After dinner we clear the dishes, then Dave reads a chapter from the Bible. Then we discuss it. Everyone who can talk is expected to contribute something—they all do and are proud to, even if it's just mentioning a few words they heard! As you can imagine, we have some very important spontaneous discussions during these times. Then Dave prays and we all pray the Lord's prayer. Then we sing from Psalms and the children participate in selecting them. They are familiar with quite a few Psalms and frequently sing snatches of them throughout the day. We are a singing family! By the time family devotions are done, it has been a long dinner hour, but there is still plenty of time to get everyone ready for bed. Everything generally goes more smoothly when Dad is home. The children's bedtime is between 7:30 and 8:00 PM.

After the children go to bed, I talk with Dave, read the mail, write a letter, make a phone call, read a magazine, whatever needs to be done and is hard to do when the children are awake. There is never any lack of things to do.

I try not to be overwhelmed when I think about all I *could* be doing. There are many, many things that are nice and fun to do, but only a few are essential. I tend to be strict with my children. They are not permitted to say, "I don't want to do this." Rather, I have been guilty at times of pushing them too

Elizabeth (5), Tim (4), Dan (2), Peter (1)

hard, especially Elizabeth. It has taken experience to learn what the limits of their capabilities are and my discipline is far from perfect.

In homeschooling, the parents learn along with the children—character as well as content. I am learning how to manage my children while maintaining a good example of patience. I certainly have my share of bad days. Nevertheless, even with the bad days, I thoroughly love this calling. There is nothing I'd rather be doing. I love this lifestyle, and I love homeschooling. It is so rewarding, and it is exciting to look forward to the things we'll be learning together in the years ahead.

Dave supports us by choosing the computer software for the children. His encouragement, support, listening ear, suggestions, interest, etc., are invaluable. I don't think I could do this without his help in these ways—at least it would be far harder.

HERE IS A LIST OF SOME OF THE RESOURCES THAT WE USE:

Phonics--Ruth Beechik's 3 R's series—*A Home Start in Reading, A Strong Start in Language,* and *An Easy Start in Arithmetic.* I also use her *Teaching Preschoolers: It's Not Exactly Easy But Here Is How to Do It.*

Writing—Ruth Beechik's *You Can Teach Your Child Successfully*
Alpha Phonics here and there.

Reading—readers from bookstore or catalogs

Handwriting—little workbook called *Let's Write,* published by Hayes—as a resource for me.

Arithmetic—*Developmental Math*

Computer Games—*Stickybear Math, Math Blaster, Paintbrush, Tinytap* and *Amy's Primer* (shareware), a USA and world map program, and *Spellbinder.*

Elizabeth (5), Tim (4), Dan (2), Peter (1)

UPDATE:

We have a new baby now! This squeezes the time we have, forcing me to evaluate what is really important and what can wait. I'd rather do less in a day than rush around and snap at the children for being too slow. Jonathan has been such a joy to us all and especially to Elizabeth. She can't get enough of him and I have seen her character markedly mature as she helps with him. Strange as it may sound, I sometimes wonder what I'd do without her help.

Elizabeth (5), Tim (4), Dan (2), Peter (1)

Mark and Sarah
Ben, age 10
Nathan, age 8
Aaron, age 6
Rachael, age 5
Ethan, age 3
Reuben, age 2
Isaac, age 1

Sarah wrote about this cold and gray day in January, when there was no snow in the rural farm town of College Corner, Indiana.

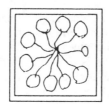

OLDER BOYS HAVE "THEIR BOY"

A DAY AT OUR HOUSE:

We live in rural Indiana, on the southeastern border near a college town . . . Oxford. We did do our academics in a "school room" upstairs between two bedrooms. We still keep all our books upstairs, at least all our resource books, but we do our academics at the kitchen table now. I'm not sure why. It's a little more distracting downstairs because the little ones don't have their toys down there.

Our day begins at the decadent hour of 8:00 AM. Actually Reuben usually enters our room with a resounding slam of the door at about 7:50 AM. I feign sleep, hoping to eke out another ten minutes of quiet before the day begins. I really don't have anything against the sunrise; I just would rather be up to see it than have *it* awaken *me*.

At 8:00 AM Reuben and I sneak out of the bedroom, trying to let Mark, my husband, and Isaac sleep longer. In the kitchen I find Nathan and Aaron already up, dressed, beds made, rooms straightened, and chickens fed. It did take about two years for them to remember exactly what their chores were. (No, Aaron, you need to get dressed before you go out to feed the chickens.) I find that if they have to do their chores before they eat, the chores get done. Food is a powerful tool of coercion in our house.

Ethan comes down now. Sometimes I send him back up to get his clothes, other times he eats in his pajamas. It depends if I have time to help him dress. Today he eats first because there are a few supper dishes left to do. I finish the dishes, make a bottle and oatmeal for the baby, and pour my one cup of whole grain cereal. (I will lose all that "baby" weight yet.) Our breakfast consists of cereal. Cold cereal. I have a hard time facing much of anything in the morning, let alone elaborate meals. As we eat, we sometimes listen to our favorite tape, *History Alive Through Music* or the local classical station. Other times we listen to ourselves chew. This morning we opt for chewing. Rachael comes down at about 8:30 AM, still in pajamas. I send her back up to dress, make her bed and wake Ben. He is just like me and tries to sleep until the last possible minute. "But mom," Rachel cries, "Can't I eat first just this once?" I get asked this about twice a week from someone. "Nope," replies the meanest mom in the world. At least that's what they tell me.

It's 8:45 AM and at last Ben is downstairs. His upstairs work is done and all he has left is to water the chickens before he can eat. The kitchen closes at 9:00 AM for breakfast, so he is right on schedule. Nathan and Aaron have disappeared upstairs without sweeping their assigned floors, so I have to chase them down, and Isaac has awakened and needs his bottle. "Nathan, you have to sweep the living room before you and Aaron can play." "Since when?" he asks, not disrespectfully, but in astonishment. "For about seven months, dear," I reply, shaking my head. Aaron brings down Reuben's clothes and I dress him as soon as Isaac has had enough milk to make him happy. Ethan has brought his clothes down and just needs help with his shirt. He is getting so big! Aaron sweeps the kitchen while Nathan tells me his dream about Batman or someone super like that. "Can I check my mail?" Ben asks, referring to his e-mail. He is quickly becoming enamored with the computer, much to my delight. "Only your mail, then get the clothes from the dryer and sweep the dining room." Ben is very amiable once awake. Hopefully, by 9:00 AM everyone, including myself, is dressed, breakfast is done, and the floors are swept. Usually Isaac is not quite fed, but that can be accomplished while I help the others with lessons. This morning I am the only one not yet dressed so I tell the older ones to straighten the living room while I sneak into the bedroom. (Why all the sneaking you ask? My husband is an R. N. and works nights part-time in a nursing home. He stays up late on his days off so his body doesn't get too wacko.) As I return to the living room, I see that cleaning has degenerated into a free-for-all. "STOP!" I yell. Yes, yell in order to be heard over the ruckus. "We are supposed to be cleaning the living room. Let's go!" I often feel like a drill sergeant. All I need is the whistle and uniform.

The living room, which was only cluttered, not dirty, is straightened in short order. Our next chore is to fold clothes. Clothes were my favorite job until I had seven children. Then they became my nemesis. I finally stumbled upon a system that, hallelujah, is working. I began to notice that I was doing all the

Ben (10), Nathan (8), Aaron (6), Rachael (5), Ethan (3), Reuben (2), Isaac (1)

work around the house and that my older children were capable of doing much more. I came up with the idea that each older boy would be responsible for a younger boy throughout the day. When we would go places, they would be responsible for their charge's coats and shoes, etc. At home they were responsible for getting "their boy's" clothes in the morning and pajamas in the evening. Making each older boy responsible for folding "his boy's" clothes was a natural extension of this. My work load decreased dramatically when we started using this system, and the clothes get folded a lot faster. Rachel is responsible for her clothes and all the washcloths and small towels.   I fold Mark's and my clothes and the big towels. Amazingly, for the first time in years the clothes are caught up on a regular basis.

While the clothes are being folded, I put in a call to the pediatrician to ask about Isaac's cold. Isaac was born with a complex congenital heart defect, and was hospitalized five times within his first seven months of life, undergoing two surgeries. With any other child I wouldn't be worried about a cold, but an infection in Isaac could cause him to go into heart failure. (If you think these days are hectic, last year when Isaac was not in the hospital, he was at home with tube feedings and intravenous antibiotics. Life was really wild then.)

We finish the clothes and get them put away.   Then we either have an exercise time, a singing time, or we spend time   praying. I feel it is very important not just to teach the children to know the Bible, but also to know Jesus and recognize His voice. We sometimes spend time waiting for God, asking Him to speak to us. I haven't seen a lot of fruit from this effort in the younger ones, but the older ones are learning discernment and are developing a listening ear. It is exciting! This morning we worship the Lord with song and pray for a time. Each child picks out a favorite worship song, (yes, Rachael, we can sing the one with the horse) and then we pray. In the middle of prayer the phone rings. Our pediatrician has called back and asks if Isaac has had a change in activity level or increase in temperature. He has no fever and his activity is high so she says to stop worrying and call if anything changes.

Everyone has disappeared upstairs and it's quiet so I quickly check my e-mail. It's empty. Good thing because its 10:00 AM and we really need to start lessons.

Upstairs, I call everyone into the middle room to begin lessons. I won't lie, some days my kids complain, and this is one of those days. I remind them of the generation of Israelites that died in the wilderness because of their complaining. Subtle, eh? The grumbling may not stop completely, but it does quiet down.

Ben works by himself on his language arts and math. I help him a bit, but for the most part he is self-taught. Ben, as I have said, is amiable and self-disciplined as well.

Nathan is a different story. He is a physical enigma. One minute he zips along in his math just fine and the next moment his facial muscles scrunch up. When this happens I need to send him to his bed to relax for about five minutes until he is ready again. Because of his own physical experiences,

Ben (10), Nathan (8), Aaron (6), Rachael (5), Ethan (3), Reuben (2), Isaac (1)

Nathan is very interested in medical things and we think he will be a doctor. Today, however, all goes well as he progresses in his math.

Aaron needs lots of help with his reading as this is his first year of lessons. He is sanguine in temperament and is easy to instruct. He does his math with little instruction and oversight. He enjoys his math drills quite a lot.

Rachael has begged to be allowed to begin reading lessons. ("I'll set the table if I can do three pages of *Alpha Phonics*.") I don't start five-year-olds as a rule, but Rachael really seems to be ready. I start reading with her while feeding the baby his oatmeal. Nathan and Aaron work well until they have a question. Frequently they both try to ask me questions at the same time while Rachael continues to read aloud. Quite honestly, I can lose my temper with this. I remind them to be polite and speak *one at a time*, because I can only hear *one at a time!* I get their questions answered and Rachael and I go back to work.

I haven't mentioned the toddlers. Some days Ethan and Reuben play well. Some days they don't. I find that if I take time out during lessons to wrestle with Ethan, he is much more content. Today he and Reuben play happily for awhile. I realize he needs some attention and I have to ask Rachael to wait while I spend some time with Ethan. A quick wrestle and hug and we're back to work.

Rachel is done and runs off to play with the toddlers. Now Nathan will read to me. We are reading the *Pathway Readers*, second level. And "when Nathan reads, everyone listens." The stories are riveting to the children and provoke a lot of discussion. The kids get very involved with the characters. All right, I like the books too. I even snuck upstairs last night and finished the latest book after writing lesson plans. After Nathan reads, Aaron reads the first level book. After Aaron finishes this and his *Alpha Phonics*, he does his handwriting. Nathan has finished his handwriting and begins his *Daily Grams* for a five minute grammar practice. He likes help with this, even though I am convinced he could do more of this on his own. ("Please, just sit with me while I work.")

All this time, Ben has been giving me work to check. He usually finishes his desk work in a little over an hour and runs off to read. Aaron is finished with his morning work and Nathan and I have only a little left to do. ("Hurry up Nathan, as soon as you are finished we can eat.") I told you food was a great motivator.

By noon we are finished with our morning lessons. As I fix lunch, Ben checks his e-mail again and writes his Grandma a letter. Aaron and Nathan play together upstairs, while Rachel, Ethan, and Reuben play "dog" downstairs. (They even have dog names . . . Rose, Rover, and Keleshane.) Isaac sits in the high chair and throws food on the floor. I sneak into the bedroom to see if Mark is ready to get up. He is and so I add one more meal to the lunch menu.

After lunch, everyone goes upstairs to play, except Ben who returns to the computer. Mark and I sit and talk over tea, deciding what to do this afternoon. Our afternoons are very unstructured. Sometimes we have a school project we are working on, sometimes everyone goes off to play or read. Other times we run errands or go places. We have been involved with several co-ops

Ben (10), Nathan (8), Aaron (6), Rachael (5), Ethan (3), Reuben (2), Isaac (1)

covering topics such as the Civil War, human anatomy and physiology, or Indians, and those occasionally meet in the afternoons. It depends on the particular day what shape our afternoons take. Since I am innumerate, Mark has taken over teaching math to our oldest son, and he sometimes uses this time to work with Ben. Mark also does various experiments with the children in the afternoons, depending on his interests.

Whatever we end up doing, unless it is an out-of-the-house activity, we are generally finished by three. Today Mark is home, so at 3:00 PM he and the children watch some TV. I use this time to read, write, or stare into space.

Dinner is between 6:30 and 7:30 PM, depending on how long I stare. I do all the cooking, by choice, and Mark either plays with the children or works on house projects. The children flit in and out of the kitchen helping me in their own manner. I plan out what suppers I want to make two weeks in advance. I found that usually by 5:00 PM I was either too hungry to think straight and decide on a meal, or I was too tired and didn't care if I ate anything or not. For me to write down the dinners in advance means that we will eat something besides cold cereal or order-out pizza. Some mothers have marveled at my superb organizational skills but, in reality, any organization I possess is a result of necessity.

After dinner we have a mad scramble to prepare for bedtime. The older boys get "their boy's" pajamas and a flurry of table clearing, dish washing, teeth brushing, diaper changing, and pajama putting on ensues. This is often the most tiring part of the day.

Our evenings are also very unstructured. Either we watch TV, depending on what is on, read aloud, play games, tell stories, have "Bible Time," or sit around and talk.

Bedtime is a very flexible 9:00 PM. Our children go through stages of all sleeping in the same room to sleeping as far apart as possible. It takes a while to get them all bedded down satisfactorily. Once they are in bed, Mark and I spend time reading, talking, writing, or watching movies. Mark is a great encouragement to me about homeschooling. He will listen to me talk out how to make my ideals practical. He also gives me balance in understanding our children's behavior. Mark encourages me to take the time to write and delve into my other interests.

I usually fall asleep on the couch at about 11:00 PM, while Mark stays up until around 3:00 AM, trying to maintain that night shift stupor! At 3:00 AM he awakens me and we stumble into bed to sleep until tomorrow's cycle begins.

ONE YEAR LATER:

This year is our sixth year of teaching our children at home. The previous account is actually a day from about a year ago. Many changes have come about since last year including the fact that our children are all a year older. In addition, they have all "moved up" in their grade work, the chickens all died, Mark no longer works nights, I started back to work (I am an R. N. also), and Rachel has become literate. Our days are similar to last year's; we just don't

Ben (10), Nathan (8), Aaron (6), Rachael (5), Ethan (3), Reuben (2), Isaac (1)

sneak around as much.

I have wanted to homeschool since I was in first grade. As a five-year-old, I anxiously awaited the day when, like my older brother and sister, I could climb on the magic yellow bus and go to school. I would play school in our basement where an old, painted-over chalk board hung on the wall. I would look over the primers in our house and pretend to have homework. I was so disappointed when I found that kindergarten was only half a day instead of a full one. No matter, soon enough I would be in real school.

And then the day came when I did begin first grade. I was happy to finally be "grown up," but the joy didn't last long. I don't remember when I started to become disillusioned with school, but I do remember sitting in my classroom early in the year, looking out the window thinking, "All those people out there are living, while we are stuck in this room playing at life."

Soon after, I came up with an elaborate plan to escape. I decided to buy "soundproofing" gas that I would use to spray my classroom rendering it soundproof. Then I was going tell my teacher just exactly what I thought of her and this school business. After that I would trounce out of the room, head held high, never to return.

The actual confrontation took place without the benefit of the soundproofing gas. One day I lost my temper and yelled at some students while on "bathroom break." My teacher came to get me and I yelled and yelled at her, pouring out my frustrations. She handled it well, my mom tells me. I don't remember much except I did get to eat with my best friend at lunch that day. (She was in a different class and we never got to eat together.)

My frustrations may have been vented, but the feeling that I was stuck in prison persisted till I graduated from high school. In fact, the only single day I have ever had where that feeling disappeared was the day I finished my last high school exam. I literally felt a huge weight lifted off of me. I could finally start living.

I didn't know that homeschooling was even an option till I was a sophomore in college and heard a radio program about it. The program was *Options in Education* and one particular night a homeschooling parent was interviewed. His son was studying Russian, algebra, and other things that he was interested in. His father kept stressing that his son could study what he was interested in at his own pace and could participate in "real life" events with his parents. I was sold! This was what I had been longing for my entire schooling career. I resolved that if I had any children this was the type of schooling they would receive.

I did have children. Lots of them. However, when Ben reached the magical age of six and began formal academic instruction, I had no guide to go by except my own experience in public school. Poor Ben suffered through many weeks of rigid scheduling and me worrying that I would fail him. Our schedule followed that of a typical school; math 9-9:30 AM, reading 9:30-10:00 AM, etc. I tried to the best of my ability to replicate a classroom, complete with standard achievement goals. With this type of ideal, pressure followed, which

Ben (10), Nathan (8), Aaron (6), Rachael (5), Ethan (3), Reuben (2), Isaac (1)

quite naturally led to a short temper. Our first year, as you can guess, was far from pleasant. I had no idea that Ben would learn in spite of me, but that is something I would soon find out.

In April of our first year several things happened. I started the month off by getting pregnant. The first few months of all my pregnancies are exhausting and this one was no exception. Soon after I found out I was pregnant, my husband's grandmother came to live with us. She had been badly burned in a house fire and required extensive burn dressings twice daily. My time was soon eaten up with nausea and nursing care, so I ad libbed and called it spring break for Ben. I don't remember seeing much of Ben those few weeks, but when the nausea cleared and grandma was hospitalized, an amazing thing had taken place. Ben could read. Not just sound words out, the vocal equivalent of hunt and peck typing, he could really read.

This entire event, Ben's painless step into literacy, reminded me of my children learning to walk. We played typical baby games with our children to encourage them to walk, but no matter what games we played or what encouragement we gave them, they only walked when they were ready. I saw this phenomena happen with walking, smiling, talking, crawling, sitting, and any number of developmental milestones. And I had seen it again with reading. We had given Ben the tools for reading, phonics and reading to him primarily, and he had read when he was ready. On spring break, no less.

That one incident colored my whole view of teaching. I became a staunch believer in watching my children and waiting for them to show signs of readiness before I pushed them or panicked that they were not learning something as fast as I thought they ought. Since then I have taught three more children to read and have been amazed by how different their timetables have been for learning. Nathan sometimes struggles with his reading at nine. Aaron is doing well at seven and Rachel had reading click for her at the tender age of five. (Actually, Rachel learning to read early had a great motivational effect on Nathan and Aaron. There was no way they wanted their *little* sister to be better than they were. Their reading improved dramatically when she started reading.)

Another area to be considered about our children is their gifts or talents. My children all do well academically. I realize that in the large classroom setting that individual types of giftedness is not appreciated or encouraged. But in the home setting couldn't a parent look at a child's gifts and help that child to grow in them? All of our children have differing talents or gifts. Shouldn't we help them cultivate their gifts to the best of their ability? Some children will be gifted academically, but others will have a hard time with book work. Some will see beauty in every corner, while another has music filling his soul. One runs like the wind, another has a heart to serve mankind. How can we judge one gift to be more valuable than another? And how can we deny our child's gifts and try to stuff him into a box labeled "*Standardized Achievement?*" Tragically, many parents try to do this, just as I did my first year of homeschooling.

So, how has my growth changed the way I homeschool? We are freer in our structure. I still have structure, but I allow more input from my children

Ben (10), Nathan (8), Aaron (6), Rachael (5), Ethan (3), Reuben (2), Isaac (1)

about what they want to learn and how they want to learn it. We still use workbooks, but only the ones my children choose. On the surface, our day looks a lot the same as it did last year, but underneath there had been a major shift as I quit worrying I would fail my children and allowed them to learn and grow according to their abilities.

Our family also had to discover our own rhythm for everyday life. Don't we all know of a supermom, whose children take ballet, piano, art, violin, give puppet shows for neighborhood children, participate in all the support group activities and are excelling academically? Thinking this style of homeschooling must be right, I tried to duplicate it with my own children. We spent last fall racing from one activity to the next, going to every single support group function, and generally exhausting ourselves. As we sprinted through the fall days, I kept thinking breathlessly, "we've lost our rhythm."

As I talked with other mothers and observed their family tempos, I realized that each family has to find its own pace, its own rhythm. All so different. All valid. And all found by trial and error, experimentation, failures and triumphs.

I am beginning to understand that just as each child has his own rate of learning, each family has its own rhythm. There is no one way to homeschool, just as there is no one way to live. Each family will discover its own style or pace, and that is the great beauty of homeschooling. Our children are allowed to become who they were born to be, and we are allowed to become ourselves.

We are fortunate to live in Indiana, a state with very little governmental regulation of, and intrusion into, a families educational choice. Our state only requires that *if* you are contacted by the superintendent of your school district, *then* you have to inform them of the number and ages of your students. Not their names, or your chosen curriculum, or anything else. As a result of living in a state so friendly to homeschoolers I could be very lax in my record keeping, but I'm not. Call me compulsive, but I like to leave an extensive paper trail.

To keep a record of our lessons, I use a teacher's plan book that I buy at the local school supply store. Obviously, I document things such as math and language arts, using text name and page numbers as reference. I also record extras such as fine arts, physical education, and spontaneous learning activities. I include household chores under a heading of Life Skills, as practical skills are a necessary part of any education. Since everyone's favorite complaint about homeschooling is a child's supposed lack of social interaction, I also record most of my children's overnights and play times.

No one has ever asked to see my lesson plan book or proof that my children are being taught or have any social interaction. But if they do ask, I have the documentation to back up my claims about their education.

I mentioned earlier that our son Isaac was born with an abnormal heart requiring extensive medical intervention and numerous hospitalizations. Besides dealing with the emotional heartbreak of having a seriously ill child, there was the difficult balance of maintaining a school schedule, running a home, meeting the emotional needs of a family in crisis and taking care of a sick child. All of

Ben (10), Nathan (8), Aaron (6), Rachael (5), Ethan (3), Reuben (2), Isaac (1)

these are full-time jobs.

After Isaac's birth we had several months when we spent every other day sending our older six children to friends' houses while my husband and I or just I went to the hospital to spend the day with Isaac. On my days home, I would frantically do housework and try to keep up with school lessons. My children suffered with a very irritable mother who felt pulled in too many directions.

After a few weeks of trying to continue schooling I was at my wit's end. As I prayed about the situation, I felt that my children didn't need school at this time. What they needed was me. So, several months early, we quit academic work for the year. When one of the pressures was removed, we all relaxed and our collective irritability levels dropped considerably.

To take that step of giving up on academics for the year, I had to trust that they were not missing out. I had to act on my belief that academics are not all there is to an education. That wasn't easy but, at the time, persevering in academic work could have done more harm than good.

I will say, though, that my children have little fear of hospitals now and have a more thorough understanding of the workings of the human heart than most adults I know. The down time was not a total wash out.

UPDATE:

Amazing how things change with time. This year started with a big change in schedule. Not only did I quit my outside job, but we also decided to scale back on our outside activities and take more time to relax and learn together as a family. We ended up cutting out almost every outside activity except for a writing group for Ben, Nathan, and Rachael. Also, Ben is taking karate and Rachael has begun piano lessons. Our family is more relaxed and we have begun to enjoy school again.

Isaac's health is stable at this point. We did spend last month running almost weekly for doctor appointments for a newly discovered seizure disorder in Isaac, but all that seems to have settled down for now. I was glad we had already opted to scale back when that flurry of doctor appointments began.

School continues for us in a rather normal fashion, but Mark's life has had a major change. Mark has gone back to college to get a degree in history and hopefully he will go to law school in two years. This is a fulfillment of a dream of his and something we are all happy he is getting a chance to do.

Another major change is that we are now expecting baby number eight. Not *all* of those doctor's appointments were for Isaac, after all. Being pregnant only adds to the normal tiredness of any mom of seven children. I am learning what things are essential and what things I can let slide. I have to realize my limitations and not feel guilty when I can't live up to some idealistic standard. (If only I could convince my husband that a clean house was an *idealistic* standard!) The baby is due in five months and I am anxious to see what sort of changes another new baby brings.

Ben (10), Nathan (8), Aaron (6), Rachael (5), Ethan (3), Reuben (2), Isaac (1)

Tim and Tina
Jacob, age 12
Joshua, age 11
Jordan, age 8
Hannah, age 4
David, age 2

Tina described this January day in Temple, Pennsylvania which is a small town with only a bank and a bakery.

TRIAL AND ERROR

There are seven of us living in a tiny town in Pennsylvania.The thriving metropolis includes a bank and a bakery! We are about a mile and a half out of town.They call this mushroom country—because there are many mushroom growers in our area. We have an acre of land that is backdropped by many acres of woods. This is great, for the kids will often go exploring up there. They have often brought home crayfish, frogs and a various assortment of rocks and fossils (science). Tim and I have four boys and one girl.We've been homeschooling for eight years! Before I get into our philosophy of education let me introduce you to ourselves.

Jacob is in the seventh grade, Joshua in the sixth grade, Jordan is between third and fourth grade, Hannah has just turned four and David is two. Tim is the breadwinner in our home. He is a self-employed electrical engineer. He went out on his own shortly after Hannah was born. At first, it was a risk but I am so glad he did this, as he gets so much satisfaction out of his work.

We began homeschooling when Jacob was five.Then, as now, we take it year by year and child by child. In other words, we pray about each child on what and where their education should be. During Jacob's fifth grade when David was born, we felt he should go to Christian school for that year. That was a big adjustment for our whole family. After much prayer, the Lord laid it upon my heart that both older boys would be at home the following year. Tim did not agree with me. That was in June. I did not mention it again but kept it before the Lord. Finally, that July, I felt so burdened that I prayed, "Lord whatever you want I will do. Just give me peace." At the end of August Tim said they would both stay at home. I was full of joy. It was exciting to see how the Lord worked. This past year we both agreed that they should be at home. Basically, we are not your militant homeschooling advocates, however we leave the door open for the Lord to work in our lives and hearts.

When we first began I thought school at home should be done just like they do in the government schools. We signed up with a satellite program. It was not a bad decision to get ourselves familiar with various types of curriculum. I then began to order materials from individual publishers. At this point of our studies everything was strictly bookwork. I should have known there was a better way to learn than "to school" the day I saw how fidgety Jacob was. I looked at him and his head was down on the floor while his feet were up on the desk. "Jacob, why are you so fidgety?" He sat up, threw his head back and said, "It's the electricity zooming through the walls—it's vibrating me out of my seat." Needless to say, I couldn't take a hint. Four years later I decided all we do is bookwork and we are just memorizing facts. There is no real learning going on.

I did a lot of praying and talked with fellow homeschooling moms. By this point the number of homeschoolers had increased immensely. One of the moms told me about the KONOS curriculum. It is a unit study, hands-on learning approach. We dumped our books and tried one unit. This was it! This was the method for our family. Actual learning was taking place and the kids were starting to retain what was read, taught or acted out.

Several people have asked, "Doesn't that approach take a lot of preparation?" I don't know how other people prepare, but I do most of my preparation in the summer. KONOS is divided into three volumes with six units in each volume. We have only used volume one in the four years that we have been implementing it. I choose one or two units for that school year. I'm slow. So far I've only been able to do one unit per year. All of the units revolve around character traits that you would want to encourage in your children. Last year we did attentiveness. They learned how we use our ears and eyes to be attentive. So we made an enlarged version of the ear drum, using lawn chairs with a blanket thrown over the top of them to make the ear canal. At the end of our "ear canal" we had a large canning pot with three items to represent the hammer, anvil and stirrup bones. We secured plastic across the top of it to simulate the membrane. The kids then crawled through the tunnel pretending to be a molecule of air vibrating on the membrane which causes us to hear. Josh rambunctiously rammed through the canal and burst the ear drum. This then promoted a discussion on health and safety involving anything that is stuck into the ear. The lessons then involved the eyes and how to be attentive with them. We went to our farmer's market and talked to the butcher about getting some cow eyeballs to dissect. This sounds very gross. I wore rubber gloves and found the inner eye to be quite fascinating. Now, when the kids suck all the color off of a jelly bean

Jacob (12), Joshua (11), Jordan (8), Hannah (4), David (2)

they say "Hey, this looks just like our retina!" Throughout the rest of the year we learned how American Indians and pioneers were attentive, which led into studying many different frontiersmen and Native Americans. At the end of this unit we had a pow-wow in which we invited several families over to participate. We had bow and arrows to shoot at pictures of animals the kids had stapled to trees in the woods. (Obviously there were many adults to supervise this activity.) We also prepared some food that they may have eaten back then. When the meal was over we built a fire in the fire pit and asked everyone to share what they knew about Indians and their way of life. Some sang cowboy songs, recited poetry, or related the many uses for the parts of a buffalo!

The Bible is our foundation. I select the verses to be memorized for the year along with Bible characters and lessons. All of it is written up in the text. Then I select the people that we will learn about in our history. I like to order Christian biographies whenever I can. But we usually get a lot of our books from the library. KONOS comes with a timeline which is great for visually seeing where the people we are studying fit into the scheme of things. During my preparation I will also cut out the various characters that will be stapled up on our timeline that hangs in our dining room. I then make a list of science and art supplies that we will need for the year. This is helpful because I can often get things on sale or at a garage or yard sale. I like using the KONOS because I teach the same lesson for all three boys in the areas of Bible, history, science, writing, art, music, with some math and language skills. This has taken a lot of the pressure off of me—like dealing with three different history lessons. Now I just teach one lesson at the oldest child's level and the others get what they can. Usually, what happens is that the older two will explain to Jordan what we're talking about, which is good review. Sometimes Jordan has to explain to the oldest one what is going on. For review I like to make up question and answer cards as the unit progresses. One year we made up a game board that looked like the United States. This year, because we are studying medieval times with kings and queens, we made crowns with jewel shapes on them. When an answer is said correctly they get to choose a jewel that was made from construction paper of various bright colors. This has been a fun way to review and we always have a different winner each time. They are learning and remembering.

In the beginning of our school year, which starts in August, I will make up a schedule, which I will post in our school area, but I often have to revise this as the year proceeds. Maybe I've put too much into one day and not enough for the next. I think scheduling is basically trial and error. We have changed so much over the last eight years, not only curriculum but with the number of children in the home. With their various interests and activities that are going on, it gets to be very difficult to be rigid with the scheduling. The order of our day is basically like this: Bible, math, language/writing, snack, Spanish, *English From the Roots Up*, lunch and break, KONOS, project time, then reading which coincides with nap time. When the kids are on break or done with schoolwork they will do a variety of activities—splay basketball, Legos, computer games, or sometimes they will have work to do. In the summer, the one acre of grass we

Jacob (12), Joshua (11), Jordan (8), Hannah (4), David (2)

have needs to be mowed. The older two take turns driving the tractor. Jordan has just learned to use the push mower to do the trim. It takes about four hours for it all to get done. I try to help with the raking if I've been caught up with the housework. During the winter, because we heat with wood, the boys have to carry wood in. Tim often gets wood from various farmers clearing out a lot. In the summer he rents the motorized log splitter and the kids help stack the wood so it will stay dry for the winter.

We try to go to the library every three weeks. I will take in with me a list of people, places and events that we are studying. We will get out twenty to thirty books on the current topic of study. The boys have their own cards and get to choose some books for their pleasure reading. I always try to approve their choice before they check them out so that they are not reading mindless stories. They like mystery and western books the most.

To supplement KONOS in math and language arts we use the *Saxon Math* books when the kids are ready for a math book, which is also something else that I have learned over the years. Jacob has used strictly textbooks for math with very few or limited manipulatives. Gradually I have learned that children learn better with games and songs rather than rote memorizing or drill pages. By the time Jordan, our third, got ready to begin math work, I knew enough to play number games. For example: How many telephone poles can you see on this street? If we changed the baby's diaper four times today how many diapers would we use in four days? We also have *Grandma's Felt Math*, which is exactly that. It's felt shapes of various fruits, geometric shapes, numbers, and the signs for addition, subtraction, multiplication, and division. I'll give them a scenario such as, "Grandma went to the tree and saw how many apples?" They will choose a number and put that many on the tree. "Then a bird came and ate three of the apples. How many were left?" They will take three away and count the remaining apples. This past year I discovered *1-2-3 MATH* by Warren Publishing House. It is full of math games and ideas for young children until they are ready for a math book. I like it because I don't have to think—all the ideas are written down. Many times when one of the boys has finished up his individual work I will have him get this book and choose something to do with Hannah and David, our toddlers. When Jordan was learning measuring, Hannah and David did several of the activities with us. One of them was to get a crescent-shaped log with the flat side down. Then they were to balance a board across the top of the log. They would put a toy on one end of the balance and see how many shoes or rocks would be of equal weight. I'm not sure if at three and two years old the little ones retained any of it, but it sure kept them occupied for a while!

For language arts we use *Learning Language Arts Through Literature,* which also incorporates reading. The language lessons revolve around a work of literature. I have my kids read the book for that week's lesson, but I know of a mom who doesn't. That is one of the advantages of homeschooling! We don't have to do it like every one else. L.L.A.T.L starts the week with dictation, and various grammar lessons are taught using that text. Spelling is also included.

While using the unit study approach, it is easy to incorporate research

Jacob (12), Joshua (11), Jordan (8), Hannah (4), David (2)

and writing projects into our year. Usually at the end of a topic I will assign the boys a paper to do. The length of it depends on their ability. When Joshua was in fourth grade and we studied American Indians and the westward expansion, he dictated his paper to me. All eight handwritten pages of it! Needless to say he wrote his own the following year. For creative writing this year we started using *Writing Strands*. This has been a challenge as well as fun writing. It has brought out the writer in two of the boys. Don't get me wrong—they just don't sit down and write—it is a challenge for them. But the author has a good way of getting the kids to tackle assignments, which builds their self-confidence in their written word.

So that you get the picture of what is going on in our home, I will describe what our house looks like. We have a two story home with no basement or attic. There is a large room above the two car garage that we use as an attic/playroom. Our school room is our dining room. There is a timeline up on the western wall. We have a six foot shaker table with a bench on either long side and a chair at each end. On the wall to the right of the table we have a white marker board and a cork board. On this board we have missionary pictures and notes and also our verse and theme for that unit. This room connects with the living room to make an "L" shaped room. Along with the wood burning stove, we put the six foot, very heavy bookshelf that Tim made out of oak wood into this room. The television is enclosed in a wooden cabinet, which cuts down on the viewing temptation. Periodically I will allow Hannah and David to watch a video. But this tends to distract the boys. Sometimes we will go into our back room, where the couch is, to read. Our computer is also in this room. Hannah calls it the "blue room" for the wallpaper is blue. Our laundry room is at the end of this room, for which I am very thankful that I do not need to go down steps to do the washing. All four of our bedrooms are upstairs. When we first bought this house it was listed as one and a half bedrooms. So now you know what school work Tim does with the kids. Building projects. They rearranged the walls and added two bedrooms and a bathroom to the upstairs. This past summer they built a shed with a wood storage area for our fire wood. The boys will measure and mark two by fours—sometimes the older ones can use the saw to cut them. They learned how to set a foundation and level it. One day all five kids were on the roof nailing down shingles—even David who was eighteen months old. He had a tight grip on that hammer and was so determined to hit a nail that his entire concentration went into it. The kids have helped to do the drywall and plastering, as well as the painting.

Each one of our days is different from the previous one. Basically, we start out the same way. Tim and I are up at 6:30 AM. I make the bed before I go down to make coffee and start Tim's breakfast. This year, Tim has been waking the kids up before he leaves home at 7:00 AM. This has made a big difference in everyone's attitude. We know he can't be with us for the majority of our day but it gives us the assurance that he is interested in what is going on here at the home front. After Daddy goes out the door, the kids go to get their cereal unless I am making them a hot breakfast. The three older ones have to be dressed for the day,

Jacob (12), Joshua (11), Jordan (8), Hannah (4), David (2)

teeth brushed and their faces washed when they come downstairs. We are not real strict about making their beds. We used to be but it seemed that it caused more tension. They tend to do it on their own. At least all of their bedding is *on* their bed. After we eat I go up to get dressed and also to dress the little ones. During this time the boys must clean up from breakfast, which includes clearing and washing off the table and counters. Sometimes the floor will need to be vacuumed depending on how coordinated the smaller ones were with their spoons.

When I come downstairs we are ready to begin. We start with our Bible lesson at approximately 8:30 AM. Sometimes we begin with a fresh section. If so, we all take turns reading. Hannah and David are usually listening for a few minutes then they go to play. If the passage is a story that is familiar, the kids will act it out. They even include Hannah and David. Earlier this year, because we are studying obedience, they acted out Adam and Eve being deceived in the garden. Hannah was Eve and the end table was the tree where the serpent deceived her. At dinner that night she pointed at the table and said to Daddy, "That's where the snake got me to eat the apple." Tim was a little bewildered but understood after the boys explained it to him. Our Bible time can take anywhere from thirty to sixty minutes. We then have a prayer time during which everyone prays for someone's salvation, a missionary, our church leadership, and any governmental concerns that are presently going to affect us. Also we pray for anyone we know of that is sick and then any family situation that may have arisen since the last time we prayed.

After prayer we tackle the math lessons. This seems to be an area that the kids find the least pleasing. To make math more fun I try to give out small rewards for those who get an "A." This might include a sticker or a piece of candy. If they don't balk they will get an extra treat like playing Nintendo for a half hour after school. Because we are using *Saxon Math,* I read the lesson to each child individually to make sure he understands it. I usually start with Jordan. He only needs to do half the lesson per day. If it is a new concept for him, I get manipulatives out to help him. Sometimes it takes a few days. He just started using the *Saxon 54* book. Before that I gave him problems out of the A Beka second grade book that Jake and Josh used. He also has completed the *Weekly Reader* word problem skills book for third grade. While I am working with him, Jacob and Joshua read their book, they read to the little ones, or they'll play a game with them. They usually rotate who does what—that way they don't feel the whole load of toddlers. Once Jordan is settled in at the table I'll read Jacob or Joshua their lesson. Although they are capable of reading it on their own, they seem to retain it better if they hear it while they are reading it. I supervise the practice problems. Then I will throw laundry into the machine if it is laundry day. It works for us to do laundry about every fifth day. When the kids need something done before I get to it they will throw a load in of that color. It is their responsibility to dry and fold that load. The little ones follow me around and help by carrying wash from the washer to the dryer or getting it into the baskets. Hannah likes the task of folding the towels. If I'm not doing wash, I

Jacob (12), Joshua (11), Jordan (8), Hannah (4), David (2)

will get the tape recorder for Hannah and David. We used S*ing, Spell, Read and Write* for Jordan to learn to read, so I taped the alphabet chart on the refrigerator with a sheet of self laminating paper on it, so it stays nice. Hannah likes to push the buttons on the player and tries to sing the song that teaches the sound of the letters. She points at all the letters. Even if her words aren't keeping up, her little finger does and she always grins at the part where it says, "see my smiling face."

After this it is about 10:15 AM at which point we get a snack. Joshua has been diabetic since he was thirty-five months old and it is our habit to eat every two and a half to three hours. If Josh's sugar level is high at this point in the morning then he will need exercise time to bring that level down. The boys will go up into the attic and lift weights. Since we have four boys, we have picked up various weight sets and exercise equipment at yard sales. Sometimes they will just run up to the apple tree five times, which is at the back of our property. Whichever exercise they choose, they do it for fifteen minutes. Then we begin our language lessons if it's Monday or Tuesday. On Wednesdays and Thursdays they do their *Writing Strands*. Fridays tend to be the proofreading and "polishing up that story" day. I will mark their papers with red pencil so that they can make the various spelling, grammar or punctuation corrections. This has been the easiest way to get the most accomplished. They are to finish the week's worth of lessons during those two assigned days. While I am dictating to one, the others will be occupying the little ones. Sometimes Jacob and Josh dictate to each other. A lot of it depends on how content Hannah and David are. Last week during this time slot they were real content to spread sheets of blue typing paper across the living room as a path and then glue them together. They got three glued before the two of them became unglued! Then it was clean up time. I usually try to get them involved in something like coloring or cutting or playing outside since they are at their best and not yet tired. Once in a while I let them wash the plastic dishes that are dirty. Usually I only do this if the floor is in a particularly sad state. Obviously I like to make good use of all that water that runs onto the floor! This has been a fairly easy year as far as occupying them. I think it is because they are older and can play together better than they did last year.

After language arts we do Spanish lessons or Greek and Latin roots. This year I got *Spanish Made Simple*. It has cassettes and very detailed directions for the homeschooling family who is Spanish illiterate! This is an area I feel very inadequate at teaching. But the boys seem to learn it in spite of me. If we're not doing Spanish that day we do the Latin and Greek roots. This is something that is a part of our co-op that meets every other Thursday.

At co-op there are three families that meet. One mom teaches music history, using *Music Smart*. Then the children (eight that are school age) share something that they have written during the two previous weeks since the last time they met. This has greatly improved their writing skills from the standpoint that they now have an audience to hold them accountable. Plus it is rewarding to share their work with peers. After they have all read, one mom introduces two or three new Greek or Latin roots using *English From The Roots Up*. The moms

Jacob (12), Joshua (11), Jordan (8), Hannah (4), David (2)

then prepare lunch. After two years of trial and error, we found that if we each bring something to contribute to lunch, it seems to go much more smoothly. With eleven of them to feed it can get hectic. Whoever's house we meet at, that mom prepares the main dish (for example pizza, hot dogs, or sandwiches). The other two moms tend to bring applesauce or another fruit, and a dessert. When lunch is cleaned up the kids get to play for half an hour. Then I teach art using *Art Smart*. This is a really good art text using themes, time periods, or you can choose to use it by artists. Art usually lasts for an hour or more and then we go home in time to prepare supper.

Back to our day. After Spanish or root review, we get lunch and have a break until 1:00 PM. For lunch we will usually consume some tasty leftover morsels from the previous night's dinner. Or we'll just have sandwiches. We all clean up from lunch and the kids go out to play until it's time to begin again. I will usually pick up or do some laundry if it is laundry day. For us, it has helped to do the washing one or two days per week. I sort, wash, dry and get it upstairs to our bedroom. The boys will carry the baskets for me as I am trying to save my back from breaking. I fold Tim's and my clothing as well as Hannah and David's. The boys have to fold and put their own away after I have sorted it from the rest of ours. This will often take place the day after the washing.

When the kids are called in I put the little ones down for a nap. Hannah doesn't always nap but she must spend at least an hour of quiet time in her room. This time is directly proportionate to the amount of hands-on work the boys need to do. We will tackle the science or history part of our study during the next hour. I give the boys notes and vocabulary words. Sometimes they have projects to do, and when the weather is nice, we go out to the picnic table to work. We are studying obedience and this unit included a science unit on light. This year they did a papier-mâché lighthouse, complete with a working light. This then led to Jesus being the light and the authority. Obedience to various people, as well as situations when we should *not* be obedient, were all discussed. Authorities have included Kings and Queens in our study. We read about Bible people as well as secular historical personalities. Greenleaf Press has been an excellent resource for these people. Indoor projects include the cut-out medieval village and port by Dover Publishing. We are hoping to have a medieval feast reenacted at the end of this school year.

Reading time comes next. This is where the writings of Charlotte Mason have influenced me quite a bit. Her philosophy was to use real live books for the student instead of a predigested textbook of facts. The books pertain to our area of study and are appropriate for their reading level. While they are reading I will lay down for thirty to sixty minutes.

After a refreshing rest, the kids get a snack and usually they go out to play or they will play on the computer. One of our computer rules is that you must do something educational for an hour to get a half hour of a mindless game (of which we only have two). They always grumble and complain but then I remind them they don't need to play it at all. While they are doing this I will get the dishes done and prepare dinner. Tim usually gets home around 5:15 PM. We

Jacob (12), Joshua (11), Jordan (8), Hannah (4), David (2)

eat at 5:30 PM. The boys are on a rotating schedule for dinner clean-up. This gives Tim and me a chance to talk or take the little ones with us on an errand. At 7:30 PM I get the little ones ready for bed and a bath if they need it. After their pajamas are on I will read to them and get them in bed. The older three get to stay up until 8:30-9:00 PM. They belong to the Christian Service Brigade at our church so this is usually the time we work on their badges and verses. I usually am able to get a quiet time in with the Lord after everyone is settled down into their beds.

I do our daily log in a rather unconventional method. I get a blank calendar and write in the dates for that month, I then add the name(s) of people or science activities we study. If we go on any field trips, to the library, doctor or dentist visit I'll have the boys read on the way to and from the office and count them as "school days." I enter these as they occur. I also include any camping or canoeing trip our family goes on.

I am often asked why we chose homeschooling. At first the answer was easy: "Because we couldn't afford private school." Now it seems it has become a way of life for us. We strongly believe that if we are a Christ living and serving family, then the early education ought to coincide with that belief. It is our goal to raise godly young men and a woman that have a Christ-centered life and to be able to put these strong young people into the world to make a difference. That could be in the later high school years or in college. The maturity levels vary with each child, so again it will be a matter of prayer asking for that depth of insight that only the Holy Spirit can give.

"How do you deal with an uncooperative child?" This is a question I am often asked. The kids know when I am tired and just am not the best that I can be if they have worn me down with whining and complaining. This is my fault for not being consistent and that is probably every Mom's goal—to be consistent. When it is time to do this or that and there is no question about it, the child will do it or they will be justly punished. Sometimes they don't get to go on an outing or they will be assigned housework. This tends to work better for the older ones.

Another question I get asked is, "How did you convince your husband to homeschool?" When I first heard about it, homeschooling just seemed right to me. Tim wasn't so sure about it. I had called the Christian bookstore to find out about ordering materials. They didn't have any at the time. However, the woman on the phone knew someone at her church who was homeschooling. I gave her my number and a few days later the homeschooling mom called and we set up a night for three moms to come over to tell us more about it. The dads were also invited. Tim had several questions that night that were answered quite thoroughly. But I think the point was driven home when Tim was concerned that the boys wouldn't get the benefits of public school music lessons. One of the wise moms answered, "Did you take music lessons in school?" His answer was yes. "Well, what instrument can you play?" "None," was his reply. In fact, neither one of us can read music. "Well, how was that a benefit to you?" was her reply.

Jacob (12), Joshua (11), Jordan (8), Hannah (4), David (2)

So, we began school at home on a trial basis for one year. Tim now tells me that he saw such a change in me that certainly we would continue on. What were those changes? I became a more confident mother. I had more structure to our day. The children, as a result of this, were becoming more obedient.

What happens when something needs to be taught that I don't know? Those are my favorite lessons. In fact I am very poor in history. With all those dates and wars, I could never keep them straight. I learn right along with the children. In fact, the year we studied the American Revolution was the year I found out that Paul Revere, The Boston Tea Party, and The Declaration of Independence were all connected and going on at the same time. The kids were astonished at my amazement. I kept reading and sharing things that I discovered and they, in turn, would do the same thing. So I guess my ignorance really sparked some good learning times.

How do we get our housework done? Whenever we get a chance! Basically we do laundry once or twice per week and the bathrooms get done about every seven to ten days. I keep a sponge on the counter for quick wipe ups of the counters in the bathrooms. So if I wash my hands I quickly wipe the toothpaste out of the sinks and surrounding areas. The toilets also get a wipe if they get too bad. Vacuuming gets done everyday downstairs and twice per month in the upstairs bedroom area. We usually do major cleanings twice per year. I wouldn't call it spring or fall cleaning, because it is usually summer or winter before we get to it. I guess when nothing stays put anymore then we rearrange and clean deeper than the surface. The floors get washed twice per month and we all rotate as to who will do what. For example, one does the floor, one does the downstairs bathroom and two will do the upstairs bathroom. We usually make this part of our school day and play learning or review games in the afternoon. One year we even got an elderly woman to come and help with the housework one day a week. At first I felt guilty that I had her come. But then I realized how much of a help she was to us.

Entertaining the toddlers has scared many people from even attempting to homeschool. So, what do we do with these little blessings from God? One homeschooling mom says keep them fed and watered and the day goes much more smoothly. This is true to some extent. Although they need a little more interaction than that, it does help to keep their little bellies full. The hardest time, I think, is when they no longer stay on my lap but are too little to actually content themselves with play. When I am working with one child on math or language, one of the others is to read or play with the little ones. Hannah is now wishing to "do school" too. So I'll cut out pictures and have her glue them onto paper or color them and she gets great satisfaction from this. David is content to play. Sometimes they do climb up onto the table. This is when I realize they just want to be involved in what we are doing. So I'll have them sit with us and explain what is going on. That seems to satisfy them more than telling them to get out of the way. Doing that puts them in tears and often leads to more of a disruption. We have a little table just their size that they will sit at to do play dough (homemade—in case they eat it, at least I know what's in it!) and

Jacob (12), Joshua (11), Jordan (8), Hannah (4), David (2)

coloring. They like to work with stuff we call goop. It's cornstarch and water mixed together to make "goop." Often we'll add food coloring or spices for odor stimulation. This is very messy stuff. I resort to it only periodically, like when I want to get something accomplished with the older ones where the little ones would only frustrate them on their concentration. We have a variety of stories on cassette that they will be content to listen to on the tape recorder. Unfortunately, I have had days end where I think, "Why didn't we get this or that done?" It's usually because I've had to stop someone from crying because of a minor injury or an argument and got side-tracked. This doesn't happen too often but when it does, I try to remember that tomorrow is a new day and try to recover what was lost then. Again, dealing with toddlers is trial and error. What works today may not work tomorrow.

We are also asked "What about socialization?" Well, that is one of the advantages of being at home. We get to choose who our children will socialize with: Peers of their own age, as well as siblings with as much as a twelve year difference. They are often put into situations that they must carry on an intelligible conversation with an adult. We try to do things with other homeschooling families like picnics and museum or zoo trips. Our home is always open and often other families who just need to "get out of the house" drop in. For sports activities our boys have played on the township leagues for soccer, basketball, and baseball. These have been relatively good experiences, although we found that as they got older the scheduling of three different age groups took up seven days of our week. Right now the solution to that problem has been solved by Tim volunteering to coach a boys basketball team for the homeschoolers in our county. The objective is to teach skills and team work. They will play some scrimmage games with the surrounding private schools in our area. Next year we hope to create a soccer team.

When the boys have reached the age of eleven, we have felt strongly that it is time for them to start an apprenticeship-type activity. There are several considerations here. For example, Jacob is very mechanically minded so we wanted something that would further develop this in him. Also, we want them to be with Christian men that are walking with the Lord. We asked a self-employed man in our Sunday school class who is a welder if he would be willing to do this. At first he had Jacob come periodically. Now he is in his second year going steadily once per week. He misses out on co-op, and he also has to keep up on the rest of his studies. Now Jacob is welding and cutting pipe as well as menial tasks such as shoveling out a farmers pig pen before they install the new gate. Josh likes to be with animals and we are presently looking for a farmer or veterinarian for him to apprentice with.

Overall, I think that our homeschooling experience has been a positive one. I hope that telling about some of our experiences and situations will be an encouragement to someone else not to give up but to persevere. Maybe if what you are doing isn't working, don't be afraid to step out and try something new. There is a ton of curricula out there. It can become overwhelming to make those decisions. Borrow from seasoned homeschoolers. And listen to their advice. I

Jacob (12), Joshua (11), Jordan (8), Hannah (4), David (2)

wish I had listened when they told me to just read and play games with our oldest until he was seven or eight. I can't go back but I can learn from that mistake. Most of all, may I encourage you to pray for God to lead your family in what is best—not what others think is best.

UPDATE:

The biggest change for us is that we've come up with a cleaning schedule. We've been doing this for about six months now. We've divided the house into four sections and we have four teams: my daughter and I, Jacob with David, Joshua, and Jordan. They are each on a weekly rotation where they are assigned the section for which they are responsible for any dirt or clutter. We decided together what needed to be done. They clean the surface areas but then I'm able to come in and do deeper cleaning, like dusting the lamp shades. This has really helped and I feel good about it.

We're also steering away from KONOS a little bit, though we're still using unit studies. We are using the *Biblical Principal Approach* from the Foundation of American Christian Education. Basically, every subject is taught through the word of God, including word studies and classical literature that combines with studies of our founding fathers. The way our founding fathers were raised and taught was by using the Bible, so we implement that into *our*

Jacob (12), Joshua (11), Jordan (8), Hannah (4), David (2)

way of life and curriculum. We use actual documents to study events, such as the Mayflower Compact, and not just stories about them. It also stresses the four Rs—Reading, Research, wRiting, and Recitation.

Jacob is now babysitting on a regular basis. Joshua has started his own business selling gift wrapping and cards. Jordan has started a garbage can service where he takes our neighbor's garbage cans to the street and then puts them away after they have been emptied. The neighbors must really appreciate it because he asked for twenty-five cents a week and they've been paying him a dollar a week.

Jacob (12), Joshua (11), Jordan (8), Hannah (4), David (2)

Matt and Susan
Sarah, age 11
Caleb, age 10
Ricky, age 4

Susan wrote this on March 3, which was very cold and snowy, from the edge
between civilization and the wilderness in Chugiak, Alaska.

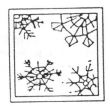

EACH SNOWFLAKE IS DIFFERENT

6:00 AM, Friday
     The alarm is ringing and I just remembered that today is the day I
promised myself I would record our "homeschool day." I hit the off switch and
forgo the snooze alarm option for this morning. Matt is already making coffee
and I know he'll bring me a cup if I just lay here quietly for another
minute—it's our morning ritual. As I lay here thinking about the day, I realize
that one problem I've had in trying to record an average homeschool day is that
during each of the days that I tried to start recording the events, something
would happen and I would think, "Oh, I can't possibly use this day because this
has happened . . . ," but today I have promised myself that no matter what the
day brings, I am going to record the events and write about the day.
     There was the day a few weeks ago when I started to record our day,
only the kids woke up with the stomach flu. Then there were the "science club
days" where we would drive Matt into work and spend the morning doing
errands and I didn't think that those would be good days. The thought flashed
through my mind that this is probably not a good average day either, because I
baby-sit two little girls for the day, but I have banished the thought and am
forging ahead. Having two extra young children to watch during the day does
make school more difficult, but we only do it two days a week, so it isn't a
problem to work around it. Learning to adapt to the needs of two more children
in the household is, after all, a great learning experience.

Matt brings me my cup of coffee and as I sip the strong liquid I peer outside to see what kind of weather we are in for today. It's still dark outside, and will be until about 7:30 AM. At least the days are now getting longer, as those long days of northern darkness can be trying. I'm glad we are heading toward the long days of the midnight sun and blooming tundra. Glancing at the outdoor thermometer I see that it is -3° F and snowing. I smile because just as each snowflake is different, so each of our homeschool days are unique—each day unlike the rest, and yet all consisting of a pattern and adding to the structure of our lives.

Matt heads for work where he is a network systems engineer for corporate sales, and I get ready for the day. Matt has been working hard to start his own computer programming business so that he can work at home and be more involved with the schooling. He is great at organizing and keeping us focused though, and he always takes the time to make sure we are on track! He has always provided me with the encouragement and support I've needed to keep going when things seem hard.

Sarah, Caleb, and Ricky are all still soundly sleeping. I take advantage of the quiet time to have some personal time for myself and check my e-mail. There are some messages waiting for me from homeschoolers around the world. I enjoy the homeschool mailing list I subscribe to and find the opinions and messages as varied as the snowflakes falling outside, yet it's nice to know that there are others struggling with the same problems and questions that I have, whether they agree with me or not! There is a note from a homeschool family in California who is heading up to Alaska this summer for the vacation of a lifetime, and would like a few pointers on what to see. We have a "Home Page," which is a document with text and pictures telling about our family on the World Wide Web. I have "met" more homeschoolers through the computer than I have at our local homeschool support group. The chance to communicate with other homeschoolers around the world has made this winter an enjoyable one. The people and messages have been like rays of sunshine on dark and cold days. I am without a car during the week, and because of the cold weather, we don't get a chance to get out much during these dark winter months of the year, but the Internet has allowed me to "visit" the world from my desktop, and the adult interaction has been a life-line of communication.

6:45 AM:

I hear a truck drive up and this means that the two little girls (three and one year old) I babysit are here for the day. I have baby sat both sisters since they were born for a couple of days during the week. This gives the kids and me fun money to spend, while still allowing us to stay at home. I lay the baby down and she immediately falls asleep. Her sister plays with toys in the schoolroom/playroom while I sit at the computer. We are fortunate to live in a fairly large house with a spacious multipurpose room downstairs that we have turned into our "schoolroom." Matt built each of the older two kids huge oak desks with large plastic laminate surfaces. We have kept the colors light to

Sarah (11), Caleb (10), Ricky (4)

counteract the darkness of winter time and have hung posters of Alaskan animals on the walls. Caleb has a gurgling fish tank on his desk, and the computer is at my desk. The other half of the room contains a couch, toys, books, blankets, and a large floor space (when everything is picked up). This is where I can let the young ones build forts, play, and have their own space.

8:00 AM:

I go in to tell the kids it's time to get up for the day. Ricky bounds out of bed with sparkling eyes and all the mischievousness of a four-year-old. Caleb quietly gets out of bed and plops down on the couch. Sarah will be a bit harder to wake up. I turn on her bedroom light and let her know what time it is. Hopefully I will only have to come down and tell her to get up about two or three more times before she actually stumbles out of bed.

All the kids are awake and at the breakfast table, eating the cereal I have given them. They know what chores are expected of them before we start school, and so I leave them to finish their eating and to get ready for the day. Last year, out of sheer desperation, I printed out chore charts for each of the three kids. Organization does not come naturally to me, and so I have a hard enough time keeping myself on track, let alone the three of them! The chore charts are a way for me (and them) to know what needs to be done. Now, when they come and ask me, "Can I go play, Mom?" or "Is there something I need to do?" all I need to say is, "Well, is your chore chart done?" What a relief for me!

9:00 AM:

I call the kids for school time. We "try" to begin each school day with prayer. We have cards with each family member's name written on them, and every morning we sit in a circle and we each draw a card, then we take turns praying for the person whose name is on the card.

Next, both Caleb and Sarah use *Saxon Math* and I have Caleb do his math first, since that's his least favorite subject. He needs structure and deadlines and it is best if he gets it out of the way first thing. Sarah moves through her school day at full speed, setting her own goals, and thinking up new projects to do. With Caleb, I need to try gently and encourage him forward. With Sarah I need at times to gently restrain her. I find that she pushes herself much harder than I would ever dream of doing, which all simply goes to show what every parent knows—no two children are the same. One of the wonderful things about homeschooling is that I can tailor my approach to suit each child and his or her own unique needs.

Right now I find that one of the best things I can do for both Sarah and Ricky is to let Sarah teach him his numbers and ABC's. She loves doing it, and he responds well to her. To him, it's like a big game that they play together. The other day Sarah laid out glass marbles for Ricky and started to teach him how to add. I almost stopped her, thinking that he was too young, but to my surprise he picked right up on it, and loved the "game" of adding marbles. How precious this time is that we have together as a family. It's moments like these that

Sarah (11), Caleb (10), Ricky (4)

remind me why I'm homeschooling.

While gathering the toddlers, I'm giving Sarah her *Word Building* self test. We use A.C.E. or Accelerated Christian Education for English and *Word Building*. The curriculum comes as workbooks called PACES, in which they write. There are twelve PACES per year per subject. We used to use ACE's science and social studies, but I find we prefer the A Beka and our own resources for those subjects. *Word Building* includes spelling and vocabulary, and there is quite a bit of writing and drill work. I find that when I let them give me the answers out loud instead of writing them down, they respond better to their work. I like to have them do a math lesson and work in their English and *Word Building* PACES every day. It's like our basic three R's, which we can then creatively build on.

A dirty diaper changed and we are ready for a break.

10:30 AM:

Break time. Today is Friday, and so the kids can turn in their "merits" for merchandise in the merit store. Ricky is so cute counting out his merit "dollars" to see what he can buy! For every box checked on their chore charts, I give the kids a "merit." At the end of the week they turn in their charts and I pay them with paper merit bills that we printed out on the computer. Even Ricky has a chore chart with chores ranging from feeding the cat to kissing Mom each day. Ricky buys a hot looking red matchbox car, and Sarah and Caleb combine their merits to buy a video, *Mrs. Arris Goes to Paris.* I take the break time to quickly jot off an e-mail note to my sister, and then it's back to work for all of us.

12:00 PM:

Lunch. Orchestrating lunch time, I turn out peanut butter and jelly sandwiches (except for Caleb who wants cheese), and spoonfuls of baby food to the baby in the high chair. The birch tree outside our dining area window is full of chirping birds who take turns eating the sunflower seeds out of the bird feeder hanging on the tree. There are redpolls with their bright red spots on their heads, chickadees who never stay at the bird feeder very long but quickly fly in and scoop up a seed and then fly away, and the big pinegrossbeaks with their bronze and gray coats. There are even a couple of the bright red pinegrossbeaks here today. The snowfall always brings birds in abundance . . . .

1:00 PM:

Nap time. Our young visitors lie down for a nap and all is quiet. Caleb is practicing his multiplication tables using *Mathworkshop* on the computer. *Mathworkshop* is a computer program on CD-ROM that allows kids to learn, practice, and improve critical math skills by using a fun, interactive interface. The program is recommended for ages six to twelve, but it has such a variety of activities that even four-year-old Ricky finds things to do on it.

Caleb is finished and so we sit down to read aloud and go over a lesson in his A Beka science book. Our local homeschool group has a wonderful

Sarah (11), Caleb (10), Ricky (4)

science club to which we belong, and I have worked out lessons based on what we will be doing at the club for that month. Last month we studied snow and ice and the kids did a number of activities ranging from digging a snow pit to measuring snow depth. We had a gentleman (whose job it is to measure snow) come in and speak to the kids and we had a snow safety day where a person from avalanche control came and spoke with them. The hands-on activities and chance for the kids to get together every other Tuesday are a perfect complement to homeschooling. Science club is high up on the kids' list of favorite things to do and one of my favorites as well. We try to follow up at home with what we have learned and make trips to the library to obtain more books on the subject.

2:30 PM:

We are finished with science and Sarah and Caleb are cleaning up their offices for the day. For social studies and science I try to find something that the kids are interested in and expand on it. Also, with the weather dominating such a large part of our lives here in Alaska, I try and work our studies around the seasons. We also enjoy doing a number of arts, crafts, and sewing projects..

3:00 PM:

Sarah and Caleb are finished with their work for the day. Naps are over and I'm taking a moment to check e-mail. Caleb has a letter from his friend in the Ukraine! We saw a posting on the Internet Usenet from a nine-year-old Ukrainian boy who was looking for an English-speaking pen pal. Caleb responded and we have all had a wonderful time learning about him and his family. Caleb soon realized that he needed to have complete sentences and use very little slang to be understood.

We were sitting and working when we heard a crunching noise. Yuck!! The cat had dragged in a shrew and was eating the head. By the time I got to him, the decapitated corpse was laying on the carpet and Rocket (the cat) was licking his chops. Sigh, I guess it's part of my homeschool Mom duties to dispose of the body.

4:00 PM:

The baby is fussy and so I'm taking some time to hold her in my lap while I work on drawing some graphics on the computer. We all enjoy drawing on the computer and making things to print out. Ricky would print out every drawing he makes if he had his way, but I explain to him that we have a limited amount of toner in the printer and so we need to save printing for special projects. Sarah and Caleb do their own kids newsletter, and I'm not allowed to help them! They use *Creative Writer* and print out copies that we send to relatives and friends. They look fantastic printed on the color printer and they enjoy the results. What better way for them to learn English and writing? Of course, I don't tell them that it is actually schoolwork and that they are learning—they might not enjoy it as much!

Sarah (11), Caleb (10), Ricky (4)

6:00 PM

At this time of year, the end of the day always takes me by surprise. I'm not used to having it be light outside before dinner time and Matt will walk in the door and catch me with no dinner prepared. Since I'm keeping track of the day today, I've already started dinner and cleaned up the kitchen. I can't wait for the long days, sitting outside at 10:00 PM on the porch drinking ice tea with the sunshine flowing over us, working in the garden at 11:00 PM pulling weeds. I'm busy day dreaming while dinner cooks, until I hear the kids cry, "MOOSE in the yard!" Not again. We have had a real problem with moose this year. The front of our house faces the woods, and every winter moose show up to browse on the willow. This year we have had so much snow that the moose are extra hungry and extra ornery. The other day a moose went after our dog, Musky, and was trampling him. I did the only thing I could think of—I grabbed my pots and pans and headed outside banging them at the moose. He stopped and turned to look at me, and then meandered away. I have had to resort to *loaded* pots and pans before to scare moose away, and I've even sung a few bars as my singing usually drives any living thing within earshot far away. Fortunately, Musky was fine, though a little shaken up. I tell Caleb that he can't go outside until we know for sure that the moose is long gone. Moose can be a nuisance, but we do enjoy some of the other wild life. We've had bald eagles flying outside our schoolroom window, a black bear walk down our driveway, and porcupines climb the trees by our yard.

Dad is home and we all chow down on baked chicken and rice with peas. Caleb tells Dad about the moose and Dad heads outside armed with Caleb's sling shot to make sure the moose is gone.

7:30 PM:

While I'm getting the two little ones ready to leave, I'm letting the kids put in a video to watch. Sarah wants to go downstairs and do some typing and Dad goes off to his home office to do some computer programming. In the evenings when I'm tired, there are times when I wonder what on earth I'm doing homeschooling. Then there are the days I know I'm doing the right thing. Last week Sarah and Caleb were sick with the flu bug, and so I told them they didn't have to do any schoolwork and that they could do whatever they wanted to for the day. I was amazed to see that they chose to watch a Discovery channel special about the brain (this won out over cartoons), read books (right now they are reading through the whole *Redwall* series of books), and built a motion alarm and other projects on their electric circuit board. One of my main goals in homeschooling is to make learning a way of life, and not something that just happens in a classroom. To see them choose to do these activities as a natural part of their day was reward enough for all those days when I struggle with multiplication or grammar, or just climb the walls from having been inside all week with below freezing temperatures!

Sarah (11), Caleb (10), Ricky (4)

8:30 PM:

The little girls' dad comes for them and the house is once again quiet. Ricky is exhausted from playing all day, but still dawdles over getting ready for bed. I help the kids get ready for bed, tuck them in, and we say our prayers. The house is silent with them sleeping and Matt downstairs programming. I hurry and do a quick clean-up, picking up all the toys strewn everywhere, so that I can treat myself to a nice hot bath and read my latest issue of *Victoria* magazine.

10:30 PM:

After a nice luxuriating bath, I'm off to bed, wondering if we will have more snow tomorrow, hoping that the moose will not come back, and looking forward to checking my e-mail in the morning.

A NOTE ON HOMESCHOOLING:

The state of Alaska is an easy place to homeschool. Legally, I am allowed to register as a private school and am required to hold school for 180 days out of the year. The children must be tested in the forth, sixth, and eighth grades using any standardized test, and I must teach Alaskan history at the seventh grade level. Beyond that I am free to do as I please. The community is very supportive of homeschooling, and I have yet to encounter anyone with a negative attitude towards it. Most people are very favorably disposed towards the idea, and everyone else simply has the Alaskan attitude that a person should be free to do as they choose and not have the government meddling in their choices.

We first started homeschooling a few years ago when the private school to which we were sending Sarah and Caleb to closed. We didn't want to send them to public school and so homeschooling it was. But now we homeschool because we have discovered the vast benefits of homeschooling. I don't think we would send them back to a school. There are so many personal and academic benefits to keeping the children at home and learning together. The time shared with my children is priceless, for I know them better than any one else and we are learning and growing together. I find that they are often the ones to teach me something, and that in striving together to learn about the people and the world around us, it has given all of us a greater love of learning and respect for each other. I may not have all the answers and there may be gaps in my knowledge base, but I can help my children to learn how to learn as we figure out a problem together, and isn't that what education is really all about? The   kids love homeschooling and, so far, want to continue staying at home to learn.

We also involve the children in AWANA's (much like a Girl Scout or Boy Scout program with a Christian emphasis), church, Sunday school, and make sure that we take time out for them to have a variety of friends over so that they will not feel isolated from kids their own age. I am grateful that they learn their socialization skills from our family unit and these activities, and not from a classroom full of thirty other kids their own age.

Sarah (11), Caleb (10), Ricky (4)

UPDATE:

Over the past year our family made some drastic changes in our lifestyle. Matt quit his job and we started our own home business doing computer programming and consulting. The benefits have been many, but there have also been some adjustments. Now that Matt is home more, he has taken an active role in homeschooling the children. Sarah is learning programming and the kids enjoy being able to have Dad involved. I'm doing World Wide Web publishing as well as helping with the homeschooling. Our house is now our workplace, school, and home!

Due to Matt's involvement and availability, we now have a computer for the kids set up with a full-time networked Internet connection. We are finding the Internet a wonderful resource for research, software, and educational material.

Sarah (11), Caleb (10), Ricky (4)

David and Karen
Joshua, 15
Rachel, 13

Karen wrote about March 14, which was sunny enough to smell the gardenia outside their home, which is in a small neighborhood on the edge of the farmlands of Lancaster, Pennsylvania.

OFF THE MAIN TRACK

Welcome to a glimpse of life at our home. Our family would have been considered typical several years ago: a father who works full time; mom stays at home; two kids, dog, cat, and other animals occasionally; house in the suburbs with two cars. But seven years ago we stepped off the main track to *homeschool.*

It's hard to remember when we began to think of homeschooling. We had talked and prayed about homeschooling as a family since before Joshua, now age fifteen, went to school. David says it was before he was even born. But it wasn't until he was in second grade and our daughter in kindergarten that we became convinced that we had to try this. Actually, it took the Lord to convince me, a professional educator, that the obstacles I saw to homeschooling were, in fact, opportunities for growth in character—*mine.*

Rachel was adamant that she didn't want to go to school, even to kindergarten, but I didn't listen. In fact, both children seemed upset when they came home from school, even though they attended the Christian school where I had taught before they were born and where I continued to be a substitute teacher. This concerned me since I felt I didn't have the patience to deal with these strong emotions all the time. Finally, I realized that they were saving their pent up emotions for me, when they were safe at home.

Another concern was that I knew how well we worked together at home on "homework," NOT! Eventually, I saw that I was giving the school the best of my children. Yet when there was any problem, guess who was supposed to take care of it after school? This brought us to a second realization: bottom line—the job of educating our children is ours. I can give them to the school for most of the day. Then it is my job to fill in any gaps during the short time they have at home.

At the time, the children caught the morning bus at 7:15 AM and returned home at 4:15 PM, ready, of course, to jump right in to their homework (HA, HA). I felt resentful when the teacher sent home "my assignments" because Joshua needed to practice sentences each night. After all, she'd had him all day. Now we want to play.

Finally, we were influenced by our own school experiences. Neither David nor I had ever really fit into the school system, although for completely different reasons. So we both learned more *in spite* of the system rather than *because* of it. Furthermore, I went to college during the early 70's. They taught us about the open classroom. I read John Holt. As a teacher, I knew that the open style of teaching was a classroom management nightmare, but at home?? Maybe it would work.

After all of this thinking and talking, we went back to praying,"What is Your will for our family, Lord?" We knew we had to do it.

As we walked through this process, it became clear that the day-to-day responsibility would fall on my shoulders. David works full time as a manager for a church agency. He has more than enough details to take care of there. David initially was not directly involved in the schooling. He was, however, right there to hold me up when I wavered or fell. He kept us going on the myriad occasions when I was ready to send them to school the next day. He cheerfully did a lot of housework that was no longer getting done. He took off from work for field trips or to continue the schooling when family hospitalizations caused me to be away from home. Even now, he doesn't complain about all of the clutter in the house, especially in the school room and the library. And, in fact, he teaches the children many subjects as he spends time with them.

As the years have progressed, we have learned a great deal. We started out depending heavily on curriculum and spent a good bit of time searching for the perfect materials. Initially, I wrote over forty letters asking for catalogs and information on resources I had read and heard about. Although we associated with an official school the first year, I didn't use the curriculum they provided. After all, I knew how to develop my own curriculum. After the first year, we went completely solo.

During the first years, *I* wrote out the log and made assignments. Just like I had been taught to do. I had my third grade son complete a research paper, properly footnoting the sources he used for his research. The dear supervising teacher kept reminding me, "Karen, you are a secondary teacher and he is in third grade." Soon we moved to using less and less text-type materials. I also began using a checklist of expectations for the week. This takes care of when I would write something for one day but it wouldn't get done until the next. I hated erasing and writing it over so the work would fit neatly in the blocks of the plan book. I believe it is important for there to be some plan in writing. If the

Joshua (15), Rachel (13)

children have to wait for me to tell them what to do, they tend to do nothing while I'm instructing the other. Well, they would build with Legos and draw, but no math or writing.

At this point, the children maintain their own logs, for better or worse. We have arrived, mutually, at a general outline of what needs to be accomplished and they decide when to do it. We try to have time spent in each general area several times a week. Then deadlines arrive and we have to cram to get things done in time. Now, join us for a "real day."

Tuesday, March 14
6:00 AM:
      First alarm ring—oh, yuck. Let's hit the snooze bar.

6:15 AM:
      I guess it's time to get up and start this day. It's always difficult to get up in the morning, but even more so now that my leg is broken and sleeping doesn't go well. So, I get dressed and "walk" (really hop with a walker) into the bathroom.

7:15 AM:
      I'm stationed in the living room, leg up on the recliner, ready to begin the day. When you can't walk, everything takes a *long* time. I'm listening to a music tape, *God is Able,* as devotions, to remind me that God is able to get me through this day. We have discovered that our dear son, who started the bread machine last night, forgot to add yeast. We expected to wake up this morning to a fragrant and delicious loaf of raisin bread. Instead, we have fragrant, baked cinnamon paste.

7:30 AM:
      My husband goes upstairs to wake the children—Joshua and Rachel. He is the morning person in the family. Rachel begins each morning with a blood test and shot of insulin for her diabetes.

7:45 AM:
      Now, what shall we have for breakfast? I think raisin bread is out. Rachel arrives downstairs and inspects the bread. "How did he do it?" she asks as she thumps the brown rock on the counter. Rachel returns upstairs to show her brother the bread. David decides to make pancakes for breakfast. This morning is going very slowly! Rachel remarks that the "bread" is still warm and would make a great hot pad. She offers to put it on my knee. It *is* holding the heat well. We spend a few moments discussing alternative uses for failed bread.

8:00 AM:
      This morning is *still* going slowly! David reminds Rachel to come and unload the dishwasher. This week, cleaning the kitchen is Rachel's job. Joshua is

Joshua (15), Rachel (13)

in charge of the other things like trash, dusting etc. During breakfast we discuss what needs to be done today, and where it will be done. We have two major events that we are preparing for today. First, tomorrow the children will spend the day with four other families, studying world geography together. We are using the curriculum *Mapping the World by Heart* from Tom Snyder Productions. We divided the world into sections, roughly by continent, and each month we cover a different area. This time the kids are drawing maps of North and Central America. They will also find some interesting facts to share with the group. Rachel must finish reading *Treasure Island* for the book discussion that follows, and write a response to the book. We're also getting ready for our homeschool evaluator to come one week from today. AAAARRRGGGHHH! This is not difficult if you keep up really well during the year. Two weeks ago, I realized that I had *not* kept up. Help!!! But I knew I had three weeks to go. So, let's see what projects we might want to finish and/or spruce up to show the evaluator. Then I broke my leg. Well, needless to say, not much work has been done these two weeks to get portfolios and all in order. So that's my main job for this week.

8:30 AM:
   We're winding up breakfast. David has left and Rachel is beginning her map at her father's desk. Joshua is working at the kitchen table. We have a nice room, dedicated to school, with spacious desks for each person. We also have another room called the library, where there are thousands of books. But no one is working at their assigned space???

9:00 AM:
   Rachel finishes cleaning the kitchen. After some general conversation and hugs, the kids go out to hit some tennis balls.

10:00 AM:
   Finally, everyone is working. The kids are in different rooms working on their maps and calling out, "Where is Sacramento?" "Is Phoenix the capitol of Arizona?" Joshua suggests that since scientists say California is going to slip into the ocean, he should not include it on his map. That way the map will stay accurate longer! I am at the computer typing a list of field trips and summarizing our curriculum for the evaluator.

11:30 AM:
   It's time to start cooking lunch. There are no leftovers so Joshua will make macaroni and cheese. Whoops, there is no macaroni, make that *pasta* and cheese. My leg is aching, so it's time to move back to the recliner.

12:15 PM:
   Lunch appears. "What are those blue specks?" Rachel demands. Yes, Joshua did put some blue cheese into the pasta. Sigh. I did say he should use up

Joshua (15), Rachel (13)

the leftover bits and pieces. Actually, it's not as bad as it sounds. As we eat lunch, Joshua discusses his courses for next year. Drivers Ed??? He also speculates on how he will fix up our 1973 Dodge Coronet and register it as a classic car. We call Dad at work to check on his plans. He has a meeting after work, so he'll be home late. Then the kids work at planning and packing their lunch for tomorrow.

1:00 PM:
Today's lunch is over and tomorrow's is packed, so Rachel cleans up the kitchen. Then she announces she is going out for a while. However, when I tell her she must wear shoes (it's mid March, remember) she changes her mind. She goes upstairs, still wishing to go barefoot, and would rather not study geography or read *Treasure Island*. After a short while of being quietly alone, though, she continues with her work.

1:25 PM:
Joshua is dust mopping. It's a beautiful sunny day out and I can smell the new blossom of the gardenia plant.

2:00 PM:
Rachel reports she has finished two more chapters. Yeah!! Now she goes to wash a load of laundry, then back to reading. Joshua is petting the cat, then he gets back to the map. All is quiet . . . maybe this day will be okay.

3:00 PM:
I read the mail and answer several phone calls.

4:00 PM:
Rachel comes down to change over her laundry. She takes a break to look at the koala bears in the new *National Geographic.*

5:00 PM:
Supper arrives. That's *one* advantage of having a broken leg—the church brings in meals. I visit with the dear friend who brought the meal.

5:50 PM:
We eat supper.

6:15 PM:
Dad's home!! Yeah!! And he's earlier than expected. David and the kids go out to shoot baskets.

6:30 PM:
We listen to *Adventures in Odyssey* on the radio while Rachel cleans the kitchen. David and Joshua discuss a computer project. I do some typing at

Joshua (15), Rachel (13)

the computer.

7:10 PM:
Rachel leaves for a step aerobics class. I give up the computer and return to the recliner. I was up for about two and a half hours today. I guess I'm making progress. I'm trying to finish a book order from Scholastic Books.

9:30 PM:
A friend of mine brings Rachel home from her class and visits with me for a while, giving me a chance for some nice adult conversation. Rachel then tests her blood and gets a snack. Finally, we all start to go to bed at around 10:00 PM.

UPDATE:
We are now into our eighth year of homeschooling. I am walking well again and Joshua is learning to drive. While I had a broken leg, Joshua and Rachel learned how to cook an *entire* meal with no adult supervision and to clean the *whole* house, including washing the kitchen floor, cleaning toilets, stripping beds, etc., on a regular basis. And the gardenia died.

Joshua (15), Rachel (13)

Lorin and Cindy
Meredith, age 8
Dana, age 6
Bailey, age 5
Adam, age 3

Cindy wrote about their day of Wednesday, January 4, in the Kansas City
suburbs of Overland Park, Kansas.

THE CURRICULUM WALL

Welcome to the Gideon Academy Homeschool. We consist of a family
of six: Lorin, Cindy (that's me), Meredith, Dana, Bailey, and Adam; plus various
dogs, cats and other small pets as the life-cycle evolves. This has been our first
year of homeschooling, and what an adventure it has been!

The topic of homeschooling first came up in our family before
Meredith began kindergarten.We knew some friends who planned to homeschool from practically the moment their baby (the same age as Meredith) was
born. My husband, Lorin, was all positive and thought it would be no problem
for me to do it. However, I was much more skeptical. I had had three children in
less than four years, and was feeling overwhelmed at the prospect of not getting
a "break" by sending her off to public school kindergarten.

During the three years that Meredith was in public school, she had her
ups and downs. She really didn't seem too interested in academics until several
months into first grade, when she finally caught on to reading. (Our school was
using the "whole language" approach to reading—very little phonics. They have
since "seen the light" of the phonics revolution.) With some phonics practice at
home, she rapidly caught up to her peers, and has since surpassed them. Even so,
it was not always easy for Meredith to get along. In first grade, after a
particularly bad spell, Meredith brought up the topic of homeschooling. She was
having trouble concentrating in her "open-school" classroom (no walls or doors

in any of the classrooms, only dividers). She could hear people sharpening pencils in the library, going in and out of the noisy lunchroom, etc. She asked if I would homeschool her at Christmas break. Still having three non-school aged children at home, and barely keeping my head above the piles of laundry for six people, I know I wasn't ready for it.

Finally, during second grade I was ready for homeschooling. I think God must have placed about five different families in my path that year who homeschooled, and I knew that it was not something weird or freakish. And, probably more important to me, I had another child in kindergarten, and one in preschool, so I was feeling slightly less overwhelmed (though the piles of laundry were growing). Of course, at that point my husband decided that maybe I wasn't "patient" enough to be a teacher. But, when I brought up the idea with the private psychologist who was then evaluating Meredith, and he thought it was a super idea, my husband decided it was an option to be considered.

At that point, I began pursuing homeschooling in earnest, reading everything I could get my hands on. God also was leading four other families from our elementary school to pull out and homeschool some or all of their children at the same time, so I was feeling some "safety" in numbers. Our area has a great support group with over 500 families participating from our suburban Kansas City area. They put on a homeschool seminar that spring, which I found out about at the last minute and squeezed into my schedule. It was about this time that I ran into the curriculum wall. I was clueless as to what to look for, and how to evaluate at what level my child was. A lot of the curriculum for her grade level seemed too easy for her. Since curriculum doesn't come cheaply, I was scared to plunge in and buy something that I was afraid I would be wasting my money on.

As it happens, at that seminar and feeling totally helpless, I overheard someone talking about Sonlight Curriculum, Ltd. They had a booth at the seminar, and after checking it out further, I thought, "I could do it with this curriculum." Sonlight, in their statement of purpose, designed their curriculum with expatriate missionaries and busy moms in mind. Their curriculum is literature based (not many "text books" but lots of novels, biographies and other fun books), and most of the books they use are award-winning books, available at the public library. This helped a lot on the cost. Getting used books, and using the public library has cut down on cost considerably. They use good language arts (Winston *Grammar*, *Wordly Wise*, *Explode the Code*) and math programs (*Saxon Math*), put a big emphasis on writing, and their science is very comprehensive. But the best part about Sonlight is their teacher's manual. On the left side of the page is a basic lesson plan for the week. On the right page is a blank lesson plan where you can fill in what you actually accomplish. The teacher's manual is filled with suggestions on how to homeschool, but doesn't say, "You must do it this way!" There is a lot of latitude for accommodating how quickly children learn, and different learning styles. We are ahead in math and reading, behind in writing. Also, in the upper grades, the teacher's manual gives you ideas for different grade level activities, so more than one child can be

:h (8), Dana (6), Bailey (5), Adam (3)

studying the same history and science, while they keep their grade-appropriate math and language arts.

After I showed my husband the curriculum, he agreed that I could homeschool Meredith for third grade, but I had to do at least a one month trial during the summer so I could make sure that homeschooling was for us. So in May, along with one of my neighbors who also decided to use Sonlight Curriculum, we placed our order. In July our family began "test driving" some of the curriculum that had arrived, and by August we were up to full steam. At the end of August, when I knew that Meredith and I were doing okay with the homeschooling, we sent our letter of withdrawal to our school.

Meredith and I have learned a lot about each other in the ensuing months. I think her personality is finally beginning to blossom under the strict discipline and guidance that we provide for her in the home. If you ask her if she likes homeschooling, she will tell you that she loves it, but she misses being around her friends. She participates in Brownies, 4-H dog club, and is a budding star on the local novice swim team, so hopefully we will be able to make some new friends instead of relying on her old public school friends. In homeschooling we are struggling with the format of the science curriculum, so we are currently investigating the possibilities of her "interning" at a local wildlife center that rehabilitates injured animals for release into the wild as her science instead of the zoology that is scheduled in the curriculum for the rest of the year. We have had Meredith tested, and found she falls within "gifted" guidelines (not unusual for children who might have been considered as having attention problems in public school). Her pace in homeschooling has allowed her to complete third grade math and spelling curriculums in the first half of the year, as well as allowing her to read extra books in history so she doesn't get bored.

As far as a daily format goes, Meredith still struggles some with authority and is a very independent learner. She prefers to try to figure things out for herself first, and then come for help when she can't get it on her own. This works well with math, spelling, history and reading, but we've had to go back and do some extensive "teaching" with grammar and other writing opportunities. The physical act of writing is difficult for her. She has struggled with it for so long that she has a mental block when it comes time to do any creative writing. We have finally decided to let her do all her writing on the computer (except for a short daily handwriting exercise, and any worksheets that need to be completed), and this has helped her attitude. So, recently we have added a short daily stint on *Mavis Beacon* to help her learn touch typing.

Each week I go through our teacher's manual to see what we expect to accomplish and what is happening on the family calendar, and try to create a school week that will allow us to keep moving forward. We try to schedule our holidays to coincide with the public school holidays because our second daughter, Dana, goes to public school.

(Since Dana is thriving in the public school, has had wonderful Christian teachers, and still loves learning, at this point we have not felt the need to bring her home for school. However, we do evaluate this on a continual basis

Meredith (8), Dana (6), Bailey (5), Adam (3)

and are ready to pull her out if we see the need. I think it has helped us to start out and get our feet wet with one student at home instead of two.)

Then I create daily lesson plans for the week based on what is in the teacher's manual, where we are ahead or behind in what they suggest, and what our family calendar is like for the week. During the week, I go through my lesson plans daily, record what we accomplished that day, and write out a check list of what Meredith needs to accomplish the next day. Meredith gets the check list, along with a folder of all the worksheets she needs to accomplish. On her check list, some items are designated "DO WITH MOM" and worksheets that are completed and ready for correcting go into a "TO BE CORRECTED" folder. After they are corrected and we talk about any problems, papers go into a "TO BE FILED" folder, which Meredith files about twice a week. If some things don't get done, I go back and reevaluate where they can be fit in that week, or if they need to be put off until later.

At this point, we are keeping all of Meredith's work. Kansas laws are pretty vague about homeschooling, and homeschoolers have existed in a "live and let live" atmosphere thus far. Our personal philosophy is that we have to do as good or better a job at educating our children than the public school just to have a shred of credibility in the world's eyes. And should some circumstance happen where I can no longer school my children at home, I want to be able to send them to school knowing that they will not be burdened with having to "catch up" to their peers. I think I will probably go through all her work at the end of the year, and keep samples of her best work should I ever need to show it to anyone. We have also administered tests that have also helped me to know where she is in terms of her abilities, and have helped me set some goals for what to accomplish with her.

So, welcome to a day at the Gideon Academy Homeschool. I hope having a peek at the way we do things will help you create a good homeschool atmosphere for your child!

Wednesday, January 4:

6:00 AM arrives and Dad hops into the shower. I roll over and try to catch a few more minutes sleep, but when Dana and Adam peer over the side of the bed asking for breakfast at 6:15 AM, I know it will be hopeless. I ask them to go to the kitchen and wait for Dad to get out of the shower, which will be in "just a minute." At 6:23 AM I finally feel awake enough to join the rest of my family who are eating breakfast in the kitchen.

Breakfast proceeds, with the normal arguments about who ate the last bowl of the favorite cereal, and having to get up six times to refill juice glasses. Dana and Bailey finish eating, and go off to get dressed for school (Dana for first grade, Bailey for preschool). Dad leaves at 6:55 AM for the office. By 7:10 AM, Dana is dressed, and is playing on the computer until it is time to go to school. I get the paper, and sit down in the kitchen with Adam while he finishes his breakfast. This is necessary or he will paint the walls with his oatmeal. I use this time to run through my list of things to do today. Since we are in the middle of a

Meredith (8), Dana (6), Bailey (5), Adam (3)

cold spell, at 7:40 AM I go to warm up the car to run Dana to her school, even though it is only a half-mile from our house. At 7:50 AM I run her up there.

Back home at 8:00 AM, I check to make sure Bailey is ready for preschool—dressed appropriately, hair brushed, etc. She needs lots of supervision when she has specific tasks to accomplish. I also settle a dispute about what she can take to school to share for "W" day. She wants to take Meredith's "Water-Baby," since she bit a hole in her own, and Meredith isn't wanting to share. After convincing Meredith that she will not be able to play with it during school anyway, Meredith relents and Water-Baby gets packed in the backpack. With this argument settled, I sit down with Meredith to begin her math. It's now about 8:20 AM. She has just started this week in *Saxon Math 54*, and I am trying to read the opening portions of the day's lesson with her. She does the practice problems on her own. While she does the practice problems, I read the paper and have my third cup of coffee. Reading the paper is very important to me, so I feel like I can discuss current events with my husband (a politics buff) and be able to tell my children about what is going on in the world. I prefer this to the TV, and the radio is distracting to Meredith. Bailey and Adam are sent to play upstairs so they don't bother Meredith as she works.

Oh no! Bailey's car pool ride to preschool arrives ten minutes early (8:55 AM). I rush Bailey down and out the door. After she's gone, I check on Meredith, who has finished her math and has gone on to the next item on her check list. At about 9:00 AM I put *Beauty and the Beast* in the VCR for Adam, and I jump in the shower. I wish some days that I had the luxury of taking a long shower, but say "someday," to myself. I'm dressed and checking on Adam at 9:15 AM. He's doing fine, and seems interested in the movie, so I go out and check on Meredith. She's doing fine, too, so I check the practice problems she did earlier in math, and mark the ones for correction.

Around 9:30 AM I check on Adam again—still entranced by the movie, and then listen to the public speaking passage Meredith is working on. We are studying the Revolutionary War in history, and for public speaking she is memorizing Patrick Henry's "Give me liberty, or give me death . . . " speech. Memorization comes fairly easy to her, and so far this year she has done well memorizing some Bible passages. The Patrick Henry speech seems a little more challenging, as there are a lot of words and concepts that have to be explained and understood. For example, he uses the phrase ". . . song of the siren. . . ," and Meredith hadn't heard about sirens before. Also words like "arduous," "temporal salvation" and "anguish" (just in the first paragraph!) have given us great opportunities for vocabulary building.

No avoiding housework, so at 9:45 AM I go and do the breakfast dishes. At 10:00 AM I sit down to write a "New Year's Letter," as opposed to a Christmas letter. I haven't found the time the past two years during the Christmas season to do Christmas cards, let alone a Christmas letter. I am going to try to write a New Year's letter instead. It makes more sense to me, but we'll see if I actually get it sent out. In the middle of writing, Meredith tells me she's ready for her spelling test, so I try to give her spelling test while I write the letter.

Meredith (8), Dana (6), Bailey (5), Adam (3)

I could see on her check list sheet that she had thought she didn't need to study her spelling words. Well, she did poorly. I told her she would have to study the next day, even though there was no school scheduled. She would get a retest on Friday. She agrees, and moves on to her next item while I continue working on the letter.

At 10:30 AM, I put on a new movie for Adam, then answer a phone call. At 10:40 AM Adam decides he wants to play outside, so I get him bundled up for the outdoors. This lasts about ten minutes, and he wants to come in and have hot chocolate the exact minute I get on the phone again to set a vet appointment for the dog. I make the appointment, and get him undressed, but no hot chocolate since lunch time is approaching. He crawls back under the covers in my bedroom to finish watching the movie we had put on earlier.

Now it's time to read science with Meredith. We are doing zoology, and using an Usborne book with lots of great pictures, along with a more "text" oriented book that is teaching some basic scientific facts like classification. The Usborne books are wonderful—lots of great pictures and information, but I think next year we will be looking for a more traditional approach in the science area. We finish up science around 11:15 AM, and I go to finish my New Year's letter and check my e-mail. Meredith starts some new work on her check list.

At 11:45 AM Bailey arrives home and I begin lunch preparations. Meredith goes on break until 1:00 PM. She only has one or two things left to do at this point. (Meredith is a big animal lover, and likes to watch the old *Lassie* reruns at 12:30 PM. Those are such wholesome shows, I can hardly find a way to say no to her.) Lunch is served at noon, and at 12:20 PM I do the lunch dishes. After the dishes are done, I start putting away some of the holiday decorations. I hate this, as I need to go through a lot of the boxes and throw away some old broken light strings, etc., but I just don't seem to be able to get a long enough period of time to focus on projects like that. Chances are good that the cleaning out won't get done this year. . . .

Around 1:20 PM a friend who does floral arranging comes over to help me decide on a floral arrangement to hang over my fireplace. Since we both do craft shows together, she gives me a pretty good discount, and I trust her taste. It turns out she has something in her car that works just right for a great price. So I get it, and put it up where I just took down a star from a nativity set. Well, it won't look too empty until I can get the regular stuff back up there. . . .

Nap time arrives at about 1:30 PM for Bailey and Adam. They fight it, and truth be told, they could both probably live without it, but *I* need the break , and it gives me some good time in the afternoon either for myself or for working with Meredith if she needs some concentrated Mom-teaching time. Today she doesn't, so I continue to work on packing up the Christmas decorations. When she's done, she plays for a while on the computer, watches some TV, and plays in her room. While she's doing that, I record the day's accomplishments in our log, and work on an outline for next week's lesson plans.

Here I will interject that we became a "computer family" a little over a year ago. Our public school became a technology school, installing a large

Meredith (8), Dana (6), Bailey (5), Adam (3)

computer lab for grades K-3, and one computer for each three students in the classroom for grades 4-6. We decided that if they were going to make computers an integral part of the educational experience, we probably needed to have one at home so they could use it for practice. Lorin is a computer technical specialist, and our our computer is taken up by educational games for the kids. We love all the Learning Company Programs—*Math Rabbit, Reader Rabbit, Treasure Mountain, Super Solvers Outnumbered, Super Solvers Midnight Rescue, Super Solvers Spellbound,* and the *Student Writing Center. Super Solvers Outnumbered* has a good "practice" feature, which was invaluable for Meredith to learn her math facts. Written time tests were totally frustrating for her, and Mom wasn't ever being "fair" when we tried to do flash cards. It put the burden squarely on her shoulders, where she likes it. We also like the Edmark House Series for the younger kids—*Bailey's Book House, Millie's Math House,* and *Sammy's Science House.* Even Adam, who just turned three recently, can operate these programs, which are mostly point and click. There's always a lot of laughter when they're using one of the House Series. This Christmas, we were also given a gift subscription to the online service that my parents have, and now I am hooked on that. I usually check in on the homeschool bulletin board at least once a day. I find I always seem to have *something* to say, or need advice from *somebody!* I also like desktop publishing, and did a newsletter for the youth at our church for awhile. Lorin is the caretaker of the computer, and several times (though not so much recently) I had to call him at work to ask him why something wasn't working the way it should. Because of his responsibilities at work, he has an Internet access account, and he spends a lot of his free time "surfing the Net."

Around 3:00 PM I pick up Dana from public school. When we get home, we have snack time, then Meredith and Dana go and deliver the Girl Scout cookies to the neighbors who have ordered them. That takes from about 3:30-4:30 PM. They pick up a neighborhood boy along the way, and bring him home to play when they are done delivering cookies. After nap time, Bailey and Adam have inside play time as it is quite cold outside.

While the kids are playing and delivering cookies, I get dinner started. Meredith has swim team practice from 6:00-7:30 PM tonight, so we are eating a casserole that will cook while I run her to the pool (about a twenty minute trip each way). Tonight I come home and eat at 6:30 PM with the rest of the family. Then Meredith will eat when she gets home from practice. Some nights when Lorin gets home in time to watch the other kids, I will stay at practice to watch, and then eat with Meredith when we get home. I leave around 7:00 PM to go pick up Meredith. While I'm doing that, Lorin does dinner chores with the kids, makes sure Dana has any homework done that needs doing, and gets them ready for bed. When I get home with Meredith (usually around 8:00 PM), I get hugs and kisses from the younger ones, and Lorin herds them up to bed. We try to make bedtime a "quick" experience. Usually no stories or fun stuff. Just prayers, tucks in and lights out. I think that's a function of us being worn out by the time bedtime rolls around. We're ready for some peace and quiet—adult time. Once Meredith eats dinner, it is usually pretty close to her bedtime.

Meredith (8), Dana (6), Bailey (5), Adam (3)

Tonight she came in and watched television with us for about ten minutes, and went to bed at 8:30 PM, which is her normal bedtime. She is allowed to read from 8:30-9:00 PM, and then turn out the lights.

After Meredith goes to bed, I worked a little on the computer, then watched television with Lorin until about 11:00 PM. Other nights I may have to make a run to the grocery store or do other errands. Lorin and I wish we had more time to spend with each other when we're awake.

Lorin is encouraging of homeschooling, but doesn't really participate in the daily process. I make most of the curriculum decisions, keep the daily records, and keep Meredith motivated. He wants occasional "reports." and does ask all the kids what they learned that day during dinner. Again, we are very committed to doing a better job than the public school, so even though Meredith is far ahead of the regular schedule, he always appears to be uneasy when we take a day off so that I can work. I have a small gift/craft business which I started a couple of years ago, and October-December is extremely busy for me. I would make a few things—whatever would strike my fancy this week—and I bought other things wholesale. I rent booth space in an antiques and collectables mall and (before homeschooling) I would put in fifteen to twenty hours per week. Since homeschooling began, I've only been able/motivated to put in two to five hours per week. During the holiday season, we took off a week in October, three weeks in November, and ten days in December from what the regular public school schedule is. He was very uncomfortable with that, even though I keep pretty meticulous records to show how we are advancing. I must admit, my business is suffering, too. I did okay this year, mostly because I had my fall/Christmas season pretty well underway when we began homeschooling. But I haven't done any paperwork since July, and with tax season upon us, I feel under tremendous pressure in my business. I have decided that I will go on at least a year's sabbatical with my business starting in the spring, as I begin preparing for the next school year. (We do not depend on my business for additional income. In the past it was mostly a creative outlet for me, but I am finding that most of my creative energies go into homeschooling.)

One area I'd really like to work on is what to do with the little ones during school. Too often I find myself using the television as a babysitter while I get things done with Meredith. We don't have too many other neighborhood kids their ages, and I don't feel ready to invite other kids into the home during the school day, as it might distract Meredith. Preschool helps a lot for Bailey, and Adam will go to preschool two days a week starting in the fall.

I also gave up my morning Bible Study group this year. Meredith can be trusted for a couple hours by herself, but I don't feel good doing it on a regular basis. I am going to the adult Bible Study on Sunday mornings now instead of teaching a class during church. I really feel like I need that regular "feeding" time each week, and I am trying to be more consistent in having a daily Bible study time, though it didn't make it in the schedule for January 4.

As we begin to consider homeschooling for next year, I am fairly confident we will be doing it again. Since we found out that Meredith would

Meredith (8), Dana (6), Bailey (5), Adam (3)

qualify for the gifted program at the public school, I have considered putting her back in. It is a one day per week program where the kids are pulled out of their regular school and given a full day's worth of enrichment activities in the areas where their strengths lie. We had a chance to visit the program recently and I was was not impressed. They don't do much more than we are able to do here at home. And since we have a good public library system and homeschool support group, I feel like I can get all the enrichment materials I need without too much trouble or expense. I also have kept a good relationship with our public school principal, and she has helped me interpret tests, has shared the regular grade curriculum, and has obtained workbooks for me as I have asked her. Bailey is slated to begin Kindergarten in the fall. The Kindergarten teacher at our public school is a Christian, and I will have a long discussion with her before we make a final decision. Dana is a big question mark, too. She does well at public school, and I really don't have a big problem with her returning, but the second grade curriculum teaches a whole unit on Halloween (several weeks of material) so we are unsure of what to do about her. When we ask her opinion, she has no desire to be at home, though we will of course make any final decisions.

On the whole, I would grade homeschooling at our house a B+. Though we didn't formulate any written goals for our first year, I feel like we've accomplished many things. One was getting to know our oldest daughter again. In some ways, I miss my children terribly when they're at school for so long each day (even though, because of sheer numbers, they wear me out quickly!). I think we have also been able to identify some real strengths in Meredith that went either unnoticed or unexplored in public school. I don't think she would have been identified as gifted or been able to forge ahead in her math studies in public school. I'm also not sure if she would have been able to get the individual attention she needs in her writing skills in public school. She is also more able to ask probing questions. Because our learning styles are so similar, I feel it is fairly easy to communicate. On the down side, I'm not sure I'm a very fun teacher. Because of her independence, I have allowed her almost to self-teach so far. But again, for the first year, I feel like we've accomplished a lot. I can start working on fun now that I know that I can do the job. I also feel a lot of pride in the fact that I can teach my own child. When I talk to other parents, they say "I could never do that because. . . ," I feel like I can honestly say, "Well, that is exactly why I am doing it." Why should I expect a public school teacher to have the patience to teach my child if I, her parent, can't do it? I always like dealing from a position of knowledge and strength about my child, and homeschooling has restored a lot of that knowledge of who she is, what she can do, and what it will take for me to be a parent, and later a friend. For our first year, we are doing above average, but there are some significant things we could work on.

UPDATE:

Meredith ended up finishing her entire year's curriculum by Easter so we did quite a few "projects" and a lot of reading until the end of spring. We started schooling for half days in July and then full days in August. Meredith

Meredith (8), Dana (6), Bailey (5), Adam (3)

and Dana had a chance during that time to attend a "pioneer" camp, where they spent time as settlers from the year 1850, which blended in nicely with our studies of U.S. history from the time of the westward expansion through about World War I.

Our big change is that the other two girls are being taught at home also this year. We are still using Sonlight as the basis for our studies, particularly in history/reading. I found that I could keep all the kids studying the same curriculum and adapt it for each grade level. We are being much more "loose" though, and will go off on tangents or do projects on our own.

For Dana, first grade was almost entirely review for her in the public school until about March. When she hit new material then, she was taken aback that the work was no longer completely easy. Now that she is at home, she has a lot more stimulation and consistency from the time she gets up to the time she goes to bed, which we hope will give her a positive learning experience.

Shortly after I wrote about my day, Bailey asked me to read her a book. I was very busy and told her to read it herself. When she became upset because she couldn't read yet, I told her I would teach her to do just that! I think I lucked out in the curriculum I chose—*Teach Your Child to Read in 100 Easy Lessons*. By summer, she was reading easily at a first grade level and, since she started school at home this fall, she has begun reading easy chapter books. I was very excited!

Overall, I feel much more laid back this year—not so tied to a teacher's manual. I have gotten my husband more involved too. For science we are studying anatomy and then supplementing with some hands-on experiments. He has taken over the hands-on experiments, and when I was called to jury duty this fall, the kids voted him an excellent substitute teacher.

We have started doing report cards in an effort to help them to be more accountable for accuracy in their work They both are members of sports teams and must maintain good grades in order to continue with sports, and they have!

I also feel less isolated this year. Along with a friend, I started a "cluster" group of people who live near me. We have fifteen families with more than forty children in the group! We plan field trips, events, classes, and even talent shows to bolster our learning experiences. Everyone shares in the work and planning so it doesn't fall all to one person. I have also joined our church choir and orchestra (I play flute). This is about the only guaranteed "me" time I have during the week and I guard it jealously. I think last year's pulling back was necessary but I'm really glad it's over.

Some days, I will admit, I would love to send my kids off to school for seven hours. But I really believe that through all the struggle and self-doubt, things in our family would probably be a lot worse if we had continued in public school. I really believe that we are growing and learning to love each other and learn from each other, the way God meant it to be for families. I can't wait for my son (now four years old) to be able to join us in two years. He's enjoying his time at preschool but he will be another interesting challenge when we add him to our "puzzle."

Meredith (8), Dana (6), Bailey (5), Adam (3)

Harry and Jane
Jennifer, age 11
Michelle, age 9

Written by Jane on hot and sunny May 23, where there are farm fields with horses, but few houses, in East Hanover, Pennsylvania.

CRAZY QUILT IN THE MAKING

The idea of a patchwork quilt of homeschoolers' days is a warm, comforting family idea. We have two girls, Michelle and Jennifer.Their grandmother has just made them each a patchwork quilt that was very individualized. The quilt reminds me of my mother-in-law, her day and her life. The work is well planned before it is begun and the work is ordered and organized. I've read of many homeschooling families who also are well planned and organized ahead of time. I thought about our homeschooling day in the metaphor of quilts, and we're definitely making a "crazy quilt!" No two days are the same, no two patches are the same shape or size. There are related patches and there are memories behind each patch. Homemade items, close-knit families, and traditions are part of our homeschooling family. Ours is not a story quilt where everyone who looks at the quilt can read the finished story. I think all quilts are beautiful, warm, comforting and crafted with love. Our homeschooling quilt is held together with a backing of family, filled with love and is our own unique design.

MONDAY, MAY 23—hot and sunny:
Our day starts as usual with the girls and me awakening on our own. After getting dressed, each one gets her own cereal and clears the table after eating, rinsing her own dishes. Daddy was first up as usual, but he didn't leave for work at 7:00 AM as usual. First, he fed the baby bunnies we rescued from certain death. (The mother rabbit was killed and two of the litter had

already died.) Then Dad started studying for the final exam he's taking this evening. He is working toward his Masters in Business Administration.

Jennifer makes sure her pet rabbit, Lovey-Dove, has food and water, and lets him out of the cage. He has free run of the dining room as long as he behaves. Lovey does like to nibble on books and hates papers on the floor—he tries to pick them up in his teeth and throw them. I tease that I'm the only teacher who would accept the excuse, "The bunny ate my homework."

Michelle starts working on Brownie craft activities. Jenny helps with suggestions. There has been a lot of rivalry lately, so this cooperation is encouraged. While they're working, I put dinner into the crock-pot. Monday is gymnastics day and we will be away from 3:00 to 7:00 PM. While working in the kitchen, I'm interrupted several times to give an opinion or show how to do the next step. Michelle makes an egg carton and pipe cleaner flower arrangement with the stems anchored in a butter tub filled with glue and mixed beans. The troop will be walking over this evening to give their arrangements to Veterans. Michelle and I review her Brownie things-to-do list and discuss when we might work on another activity. We have a Brownie things-to-do list because of a special troop arrangement this year. Michelle has been with this troop from Daisies. However, because the meetings are held on Mondays, in the middle of her gymnastics team practice, the Girl Scout Council suggested we register with the Council and participate in Council events. Michelle's leader is also kind enough to send a letter home after each missed meeting, telling her what they have done, pages to read and fill in, and materials and instructions for crafts they made at the meeting. In order to get the *Try-It* patches, Michelle will have to do the assignments on her own.

I finish getting dinner into the crock pot, and Michelle and I work on more Brownie activities. Jennifer practices her piano lesson and songs for Tuesday evening's choir. Then the girls watch *Square One* and *Where in the World is Carmen Sandiego?* This was a daily event two years ago but this year they have watched only a few episodes. Jennifer learns very well from TV and video, as it is visual and auditory combined. Jenny is a visual and kinesthetic learner.

Our first trip out occurs when Dad leaves for the college library for quiet study time. The girls and I drive to the Township Building, where we plant the marigolds Michelle raised from seeds (another Brownie Service Project). We stop at the Brownie leader's house to drop off the flower arrangement and a note about a *Try-It* patch that Michelle has earned at home. *The Brownie Handbook, Try-It Book,* the *Junior-Girl Scout Handbook* and the *Badges and Signs* book were major resources for the past two years. For instance, Jennifer was participating in the gifted program at the local public school and one day they discussed types of government. We followed up by going to the township building and getting information on our township's form of government. Then Jennifer used her Jr. G. S. *Badges and Signs* book and worked to earn the Junior Citizen Badge. Jennifer is a very creative, independent learner. She frequently sets up projects and lessons for Michelle using *Try-It* requirements. Michelle

Jennifer (11), Michelle (9)

earned thirty-two of the possible thirty-five Brownie patches. Jenny also helped with crafts at the Brownie meetings.

After we get home from the Brownie running around, I pick up the mail and read an article in the *Pennsylvania Homeschooler* issue. It happens to be Nancy Lande's article about the book she wants to write. I am excited and inspired and decide I will write, and so start writing about our day. But, as usual, I don't have time for my projects in the middle of the day. I fix a quick lunch while Jenny feeds the baby bunnies. Jenny and Michelle practice a science fiction play Jenny wrote this morning. (When did she do that?)

During lunch we practice "grilled cheese fractions." We had enough bread to make five sandwiches. How do we share them equally? After some paperwork and discussion, it is decided that everyone gets ten sixths or one and two-thirds sandwiches. Food is an excellent teaching resource. Why spend money for textbooks, workbooks and hands-on kits? Paper, pencils, small candies and bite-sized cookies are excellent for addition, subtraction, multiplication, and division. Every five problems, the student is allowed to "eat the answer." Sandwiches, pizza, pie, cake, and large candy bars are great for fractions. If we cut our pizza into one inch slices and Michelle eats two of them, what fraction of the pizza did she eat? If Jennifer then eats one fourth of the pizza, what fraction have they eaten altogether? If Mom eats another one fourth of the pizza, what fraction of the pizza will be left for Dad?

After lunch, Jenny works on her final project for our water unit. This unit was planned to last through the summer, then Native Americans of Pennsylvania in the fall, the human body in the winter, and then flowers this spring. Well . . . we're finishing up our water unit. Instead of the research report I had assigned, Jenny is researching and putting together a water exploration kit to share with other kids. It includes simple science projects, word searches, crossword puzzles, jigsaw puzzles that she made, and simple craft projects. Having just read an excellent juvenile fiction book, *My Name is Brain, Brian*, I accept a hands-on project in place of a report. I have seen the encyclopedias spread across the living room, seen the researching and noted the planning stages of her project. The girls each have a folder to put together as their unit. This includes a list of books read, videos watched, field trips taken, notes on science projects and original projects. After lunch I take a few minutes to jot down the morning's activities in the log book. I find that after getting them to bed in the evening, if I jot down what was accomplished in the afternoon and evening, log books can be kept up to date with little effort. If I skip these few minutes and try to catch up after several days, it takes a lot more thinking and I probably miss some things. On the bottom of each day, I draw a small square. If no learning activities were done, it's left blank. If I can count approximately three hours of activities, I put a diagonal line in the box to symbolize a half day. If five or more hours of work and learning occurred, I put an "X" in the box. At the end of each month, I can run through my log and count up the number of "school days." When buying log books, I insist on one that includes space for Saturdays and Sundays, as we accomplish so much on the weekends. It also reemphasizes my

Jennifer (11), Michelle (9)

philosophy of learning, that it does not occur 9:00 AM to 3:00 PM Monday through Friday, from September to May. Learning opportunities arise at all hours, days, and time of the year—seize the opportunities. I feel sorry for kids who do not read an exciting new book, just in at the library, because, "It's summer, I'm not in school and I don't have to read."

Soon, it's time to grab bags, books, and supplies and head out to the gym. Jennifer and Michelle are both on the level 4 team, which practices two and one half hours on Mondays and Wednesdays. Since I am at the gym anyway, and gymnastics gets more expensive as they move up in skills, I started working at the gym as a secretary about three years ago. The girls are in their practice while I'm working so it is a way I can work part time without taking time away from homeschooling. Occasionally, if I have to work past their class time, they bring along the book they are currently reading, a math workbook, a pad and pencil to write a letter to a friend or relative, or something else that they can work on quietly and independently. Today I am able to leave when their class is over—I promised the Brownies I would bring something to their meeting. We drive home and pick up the baby bunnies. Michelle, Jenny, and I take them to the Brownie meeting and talk about how the girls found them. We explain that we took over their care because we knew for certain the mother had been killed. Usually, if the babies had been discovered alone, we would have left them alone. It is possible the mother might be out getting food, and baby animals are always better if left to nature than when humans take over. We also tell them we started feeding cow's milk to the bunnies with an eyedropper and how we went to the pet store and were told that cow's milk is too high in fat and protein for bunnies and that they would die. We bought kitten milk replacer—a powdered milk formula that you mix with warm water. Jenny explains how she researched and found out when bunnies open their eyes, when they develop their fur and other facts, and was able to determine the age of the bunnies.

Finally, we get home and get ready for bed. Since it was about ninety degrees today and the girls had gymnastics, they each get a quick, cool shower. Jenny feeds the baby bunnies while Michelle is showering. Then off to bed. The girls have about a half hour of quiet reading time. Jennifer is reading *The Pushcart War*. Michelle is reading *Anastasia On Her Own*, about the sixth one she's read in the Anastasia series. I finish up log books for today, have my shower and then early to bed for me for a change. I am a night owl and frequently read a book on homeschooling or learning styles, or do some writing until long after midnight. This has been a long day, but the girls treated each other like fellow human beings and much learning occurred. Hectic, happy, homeschooling.

HOW AND *WHY* THINGS WORK AT OUR HOUSE:

After the children were born, I spent a great deal of time reading, from many different sources, on methods and philosophies of child raising and education. Some of the books I read on child education were those written by John Holt. Of specific influence were his ideas on "unschooling" which state

Jennifer (11), Michelle (9)

that children only learn when they are prepared and interested in learning. Thus learning only occurs during these "teachable moments." Another part of this unschooling philosophy is that, when children are interested in learning about a specific topic (such as math), they should be allowed to explore this topic until their interest wanes, rather than being told to change to learning another topic (such as spelling).

As the children grew, I began to look for these teachable moments. My husband, Harry, tells me that, as I looked for these teachable moments, the children learned that if they wanted my attention, all they needed to do was ask me to teach them something. As a result, by generally following John Holt's unschooling philosophy, Jennifer could read a newspaper by the time she was four, and later could tell you details of the nesting habits of the bluebird, though without the background of general geography.

Our homeschool curriculum is largely built around this unschooling philosophy. We tend to keep track of daily hours of education rather than number of school days. We also homeschool seven days a week, 365 days a year. This flexible scheduling allows us to take advantage of a wide variety of educational opportunities that supports the interests of the girls, though the result is often a schedule that is more than a little crazy.

The girls started pre-gymnastics when Jenny was five. I stayed at the gym and watched their one-hour class. As both girls became involved and started moving up into pre-team, we spent more time at the gym and spent more money on expenses. I offered to work as a secretary during class time to cover the cost of the classes. Peak periods, such as end of the year and starting up registrations at the beginning of the year, require a lot more hours. The girls may stay with a friend, come along and read, do "schoolwork," or help me with paperwork. Now that Jenny and Michelle are on a more advanced team, expenses add up quickly. With only one income in the family, my working at the gym allows the girls to continue something they enjoy and are good at.

My volunteer activities were undertaken to support the interests of the girls. These include being coordinator of our homeschooling group, leader of our *Math Olympiads* team, tutoring a friend and her children in math, being co-president of the Team Parents Association at the gym, working at a Riding Association and parents group of Energy, a performance arts group, where Jenny often performs..

These activities came up one at a time over the years. First was the homeschooling group. A friend and I started a local group. Our first meetings were scheduled, topics planned and prepared, snacks served, etc. Very few attended as everyone was busy with activities—music lessons, soccer, gymnastics—and a free night could not be found. So our group became very informal and flexible. In April, I make phone calls and find who wants to participate in *Book It!* and then order materials. They are distributed in September at our annual picnic, for which I ask another mother to be responsible.

In March or April, we have our *Book It!* pizza party. Most years I have planned this but this year I have asked a friend to be in charge. There are three

Jennifer (11), Michelle (9)

families who organize and run a small writing club (actually we do have two writing clubs).

This year I took over our homeschoolers' *Math Olympiads* team. The woman who ran it last year had three girls and the youngest moved up to *MathCounts* this year. The program is too good to miss, so I offered to lead the group. Next year Jennifer will be in *MathCounts*, so we are discussing starting this group in our area, also.

My husband, Harry, finishes his Master's this year. He told me he'd like me to finish my degree and get a teaching certificate (in case I ever have to work). This past summer, I started college classes part time.

This semester Harry has class on Monday evenings while the girls and I are at the gym; my class is on Thursday evenings. Harry is usually in charge of dinner and getting the girls ready for bed by the time I get home. We have to take turns working on papers at the computer or at the library. I frequently read my text, study, or write in my reflective journal for class while the girls are working independently.

Our family is able to be involved in so many things because we believe in the family as a unit. We all contribute for the best of the family. Harry and I both cook, do laundry, grocery shop, etc., depending on who is available and who has more days till their exam or paper is due. Jenny and Michelle help with laundry, dishes, meals, and other things; they know if they help me, it will free up some of my time so that I can take them places they want to go, work at the gym so they can continue on the team, etc.

I believe in not doing things for children that they can do themselves. Jennifer and Michelle sort, fold, and put away laundry, unload the dishwasher, help set and clear the table, help plan and prepare meals, help make grocery lists and shop, clean their rooms, and help straighten the living and dining rooms. Sometimes the girls help wash the car and clean the windows, plant and water the garden, weed and harvest the garden. Jenny is learning to drive the tractor and cut the grass. For schoolwork, they organize their day's work, record work in their log book, and plan a unit in a required subject. For meal chores at breakfast, on the days we go out early, each gets her own cereal, toast, peanut butter, fruit, juice, etc. On days we're home in the morning—pancakes, waffles, French toast, or muffins are for breakfast. Michelle loves to cook.

On the days we're home most of the day, we have lunch. On Mondays and Wednesdays we're out from 2:00 PM to 7:00 or 8:00 PM for piano and gym, so we have dinner at 1:00 PM. On Mondays and Wednesdays we have a light supper when we get home. On Mondays Harry has class and I cook but on Wednesdays Harry's home, so he has a meal ready when we get home. On Thursdays I have class and have dinner at 4:00 PM. Harry has dinner when he gets home. Jenny and Michelle can eat either time and that affects who cooks. I may eat leftovers and Harry cooks for the three of them or I cook for three of us and Harry eats leftovers.

We don't have a specific daily schedule—every day is different. We do tend to sleep late compared to many families. We have many late evening

Jennifer (11), Michelle (9)

activities and have found that trying to keep an early-to-bed, early-to-rise daily routine and then throwing in a very late night makes everyone cranky.

Michelle and I may get up between 7:30 and 8:00 AM. Jenny tends to sleep later. If we have a morning outside activity, I may wake them earlier.

On gym days we get home between 7:00 and 9:00 PM. Tuesdays, when we go to the church handbell choir, we get home at 7:30 PM, with a friend who stays till about 9:00 PM. Thursdays (my class night) I get home at 9:30 PM. If the girls have a gym meet on Saturday afternoon or evening, it may be 10:00 PM before we get home. With a quick supper or snack, getting ready for bed and reading time, lights out might be at 11:00 PM.

I am a night owl, so once the girls are in bed, I may do some writing, plan *Math Olympiads* practice, read for class or relax with recreational reading. Goodnight from a grateful homeschooling mother who goes to sleep warmed by the crazy quilt—always in the making by my own homeschooling family.

UPDATE:

I'm now teaching creative math problem solving strategies to home-schoolers. I'm teaching fourth through twelfth graders, including *Math Olympiads* and *MathCounts* teams.

We have had to drop Girl Scouts because they meet in the middle of gymnastics practices. All of their hard work has paid off and Michelle's gymnastic team placed first in the state finals this year.

Jennifer (11), Michelle (9)

Brad and Betsy
Justin, age 11
Sean, age 8

Betsy wrote about this hot and sunny September day in the small rural Jola village in Senegal, Africa.

WAITING CONSTRUCTIVELY

Just a few words of introduction to give you an idea of who we are in our family and what we are doing living in an African village. Our family consists of myself (Betsy), my husband Brad, and our two sons. Justin is in the sixth grade. Our younger son, Sean, is in the second grade.

We are with Wycliffe Bible Translators and we have lived here in Senegal for over ten years. My husband is from Lancaster, Pennsylvania, so that is where we spent our last furlough, and where we call "home" in America. We are missionaries working on a translation project among the Jola people of southwestern Senegal, in the village of Sindian. It's just north of Bignona, about fifty kilometers from Ziguinchor, for anyone with a map! Our work here is to translate the Bible into Jola and to put into writing the spoken stories long told by villagers.

We have a home in the village that we built (not a grass hut), but we live simply. Our home is made of what we call "mud brick" walls—actually a combination of various amounts of cement and mud mixed and sun-dried. We have a tin roof, as do many people in the village. We have no plumbing, but we have a septic well so we have several drains (in the kitchen and shower, as well as a bucket-flush toilet). There are no stores in the village, not even an outdoor market, so we depend on a market town which is twenty kilometers away. We go in once or twice a week to get our fresh vegetables and other supplies (sugar, flour, etc.) and also our mail.

The boys have been homeschooled since kindergarten, although Justin attended a public school briefly, and a Mennonite school during one furlough year in Lancaster. I started homeschooling Justin when he was five. I taught him at home because I knew we would be living a fair amount of our time in the village, and we never considered sending him to a boarding school as an option. But I was not convinced I actually could teach him! I used Calvert curriculum for the first two years, because many missionaries use this (and have for many years . . . since the "old days"). I think this was a good way to start, because each day was planned out for me and I got an idea of how to organize my time. However, early on I found there were many other things I wanted to do with my son (like have Bible, French, etc.).

We were in the States for furlough his third year, and I attended a Homeschool Curriculum Fair and decided I could not only teach, I could put together a program for us! I have been doing that since, but it is a *major* hassle doing that from overseas. For resource and project ideas, I read several homeschooling journals and book catalogs in my "spare" time, of which I find I have very little (for some reason!!).

There are no other foreign families in our village. There are two American families in the market town whom we see occasionally. It's kind of lonely at times, not having any support other than each other in our homeschool here, but the Lord knows each of our needs and supplies *all* of them!

The village of Sindian is quite large for the area; population is around 2,000 people. But it doesn't seem really big because there are actually fourteen neighborhoods, which are fairly well separated. Community life really is based either on family ties or on age/work groups. We are tied in to our neighbor's family: Brad has the head of the family's name, I have his wife's name. This gives us an instant "in" to the whole Jola relationships system. Our sons have names of close friends.

From childhood, everyone is part of a group made up of his/her peers (these are separate according to sex). As children, you play together; as young people, you socialize and begin to work together; as adults, you work together. We, as a family, have many acquaintances. Our closest contacts are with people either in our neighbors' extended families, or for me especially, the ladies' work group that is my age.

JUST TWO WEEKS INTO THE SCHOOL YEAR, it's September 19:

Has it been only two weeks?! This year, as usually happens, we were settling in at home as we started school. We arrived in our village home just a few days before. But after ten days of school, the routine was beginning to fall into place, and things "felt" more or less under control from my point of view.

Our school days (Monday through Friday) start at 7.00 AM. This time of year it's pretty light out by then, which makes it easier to get up. After two days of rain this week (we're at the tail end of the rainy season), today starts out clear. No candle at the breakfast table. Not having electricity has its challenges, but also its benefits—I, for one, like candles! As far as life without electricity goes, sometimes it's kind of a hassle (like when it's really hot!) but generally

Justin (11), Sean (8)

you get used to it. My first kitchen was in a mud hut in Cameroon, so I have never gotten used to using electric appliances. Even in the States, I tend to mix things by hand and shy away from gadgets. We do have a solar collection system on which we can run our computers, and an occasional fan. We also have a gas stove and refrigerator . . . so we aren't all that deprived.

The boys are to be up and going by about 7.15 AM. Each has his chores to do, and helps to get breakfast on the table. Our boys do household chores like: setting and clearing the table; helping with food prep (peeling vegetables, grating cheese, baking); washing dishes; making their beds and keeping their rooms and toys organized (more or less!); sorting and folding laundry; emptying the garbage; and helping with the water supply (filling filtered water bottles). Saturdays we often will have a family project like cleaning out our storage closet and the boys work with us. They get an allowance and will occasionally do an extra job and be paid for it. I would say they are usually very cooperative and do their jobs well—it's just kind of taken for granted. Occasionally there's a question as to *who* will do something, but it's usually settled amiably.

As I have a friend also helping with housework, there isn't a lot of cleaning to be done. We have to kind of make an effort to have the boys do jobs, because it's expected that (being foreigners) they wouldn't have to work. People are amazed when they see the boys or Brad helping in the kitchen, or whatever. They aren't offended . . . at least the women aren't. They think it's a great idea! I suspect the men probably think Brad is very unliberated though. The village children have work responsibilities from an early age, so they are used to work. The young ones help with child care for the babies, the older ones help around the house or in the fields.

We eat at 7.30 AM. Breakfast is usually oatmeal or yogurt and bread (the yogurt and bread are homemade—no stores in the village). Lately we've had a bad batch of sugar . . . even Dad agrees, "It makes the yogurt taste funny." We opt for oatmeal today. After we finish, we have our family devotions. Dad reads from Matthew 13 (we're reading the Gospels right now). We pray for missionary friends in Burkina Faso (they homeschool, too). Each day we try to pray for one of the families we get prayer-letters from, or for one of our supporting families. We have an album with pictures and prayer updates to help us be familiar with these folks. We then find Burkina Faso on the World Map (National Geographic Society) hung in the hall, and compare its location in Africa to ours (western coast) and to Zaire (we prayed for friends there earlier in the week). Some mornings we listen to the BBC (British Broadcasting Corporation) world report. We've named this the "Bad News," because they really seem to focus on all the world's trouble spots (as American media does). We do find it a bit more international in flavor than VOA (Voice of America) though, and it's one of our few links with current events.

We start our school time between 8.30 and 9.00 AM. I really try to start each day with a time in the Word. I find that when we don't commit the day to the Lord and start in His Word, we often have attitude problems and conflicts

Justin (11), Sean (8)

during the morning. This week we are reading verses about planting, trees, fruit, etc. as a tie-in with our science unit. Each boy has memory work for the week—either a Bible verse or a poem, which we review. Then we have our reading together time, which is one of our favorite times. Even Justin, who is in sixth grade, enjoys being read to! We are on the seventh book in the Laura Ingalls Wilder series.

Our school room is the boys' bedroom. Each has a desk and between these, I have a card table. With the beds and clothes shelf, it's pretty tight space-wise, but we manage! We have a window right over my table, which gives us enough light. Screens keep out most of the bugs! Some days our parrot joins us, and sits of the window bars. He is usually very attentive but sometimes begins to eat the screen, at which time he is invited to leave! Our own attention wanders at times to the field and trees behind the house . . . we keep the binoculars handy, in case we see an unusual bird.

This morning's schedule depends on the weather. In our social studies unit, we are learning about Senegal and, more specifically, about the ways of the Jola people among whom we've lived for several years. Our focus this week is natural resources and agriculture. In science, we are doing a unit on plants. So we integrate the two by planning a visit to our neighbor's compound where we can learn how Jolas farm. The Jolas are farmers, so land is *farmed*. Right around our house, there are fields which are planted with millet, corn, sesame, etc. in the growing season. Outside the villages there are the rice fields. In the past, the Jolas have been wet-rice farmers, so their fields look like paddies. The years of draught have meant a gradual shift to dry-rice, which grows like wheat. They also grow peanuts as a cash crop. Land is very precious and probably the most common reason people have disputes! We don't personally have a garden, although we could if we were in the village for long enough at any given time. Water tends to be considered quite valuable so, although I love flowers, I wouldn't have many, because they would be considered a waste of water. We do have a beautiful bougainvillea bush on our porch that doesn't need to be watered.

We also plan an interview with another neighbor on how Jolas divide and use their land. Yesterday was our day for these visits, but it rained all day, making the farm visit unrealistic. So, *if* today's weather stays nice, we'll try again. In the meantime, we learn once again to be flexible—a worthy lesson in itself. I set a tentative time to go visit (11.00 AM) and send a message to let them know.

The first hour, I get Justin started on his language arts and math work, and then I work with Sean. This year I am encouraging Justin to work more independently. He chooses this morning to write up the interview questions for our visit later this afternoon.

As I find I need concentrated time with Sean, especially for his language arts, having Justin do his own thing works out well . . . usually. Both boys are learning appropriate ways and times to interrupt, and to wait patiently until a convenient break to have their question answered. Waiting constructively is a goal (fits into the "uses time wisely" slot that used to be on our elementary

Justin (11), Sean (8)

report cards). Finding something else to work on if you're really stuck, or working out your problem yourself are two options . . . sitting and staring into space are discouraged! We often are all three at our desks, while I am working with one or the other of the boys. I don't think it's right for the other one (who is working alone) to be constantly interrupting with every question that pops into his head. Often, if a little thought is given to the question, the asker answers it himself. So, when a question is asked, I say, "Could you please wait a minute until we are at a good stopping place? Try to figure it out yourself in the meantime." If it turns out to be a major problem and I am really concentrating with the other boy, I'll suggest that the asker take out a book or work on another assignment for a few minutes until I can help him. Their natural response is to just go out and play, but I try to encourage them to do some other activity/assignment. It is very gratifying for me that, after this kind of approach for a few years now, they actually do start something else on their own. I don't want it to sound like I never answer questions though. With our eight-year-old, especially, he often just needs a word spelled, or directions read. His brother will sometimes help him if I am working on something else.

Although I have been pleased with how this approach of having Justin work on his own is going, one of the most stressful things for me as I teach is juggling the two grade levels, and keeping each boy occupied. I find the difference between second and sixth grade such that there's not a whole lot we can actually do together. Even though we work in the same unit, Sean needs more help and attention usually or Justin needs more extensive explanations (while Sean gets bored). I do try to have chances where they can learn from each other, but I still find this hard.

With Sean, I am using a combination of several language arts programs. His needs right now are in improving reading and decoding skills so I am finding the *Writing Road to Reading* method a helpful guide. We have a spelling and grammar course (with workbook) for specific exercises. One thing that has surprised and amused me is that Sean loves to do workbook pages. I initially shunned this type of "busy-work." He attended a mission school for a week last year, and was thrilled with *all* the pages he got to do each day . . . so much for creative teaching styles! We have just gotten a workbook full of all sorts of pages (called *My Second Grade Super Workbook*) that we'll begin using. I fit in other skills (alphabetizing, penmanship, dictionary use, etc.) using the week's spelling list and the books we are reading as resources for examples and exercises. Sean is to read for fifteen minutes alone each day, and he keeps a record of what he reads (calendar practice). Then he reads out loud to Dad or me later in the afternoon. I find I don't read nearly as much *to* him as I did to Justin when he was younger, and I regret this.

Each Thursday we have a spelling baseball game (our version of a spelling bee, with second and sixth grade words). Each boy takes a turn being up at bat, spelling words from his week's list (or previous words). He gets two "strikes" (mistakes) or can make up to three runs before it's the other's turn. Each correctly spelled word moves him one base (we have a baseball game board and

Justin (11), Sean (8)

each has a player piece). Third base words are harder. When he reaches home, that's one run. Each week is an inning and we keep a running total for nine weeks, which will then be a game. I try to keep the competition factor low key, but it is fun to get those runs! I keep track of the words they have spelled (and for Sean, *how* he misspelled them), for future practice and review. This game is good preparation for their weekly written spelling test, on Friday.

By the time we finish up Sean's language arts and the spelling game, it's time for Sean's break. He takes from fifteen to thirty minutes. Justin and I go over work he's done, and any questions he has. He shows me the language arts assignment he's worked on. I am using the Bob Jones University (BJU) spelling text with him, and also *English for Christian Schools* for grammar. He uses the *Learning Grammar Through Writing* book as well. For writing, he uses the *Learning Strands* and *Learning Language Arts Through Literature* texts. We get his spelling list from words in our reading, or words he has misspelled.

We also go over his math. Anything new or confusing in his math work is discussed, and I give him his assignment. He has a note pad on which he notes each subject's assignment for the following day, or longer term projects and when they are due. Justin's math course is a regular sixth-grade text, but we do take each Monday to work on other things. We use the *Figure It Out* problem solving series, and the *Math By Kids!* problems.

Well, 11.00 AM rolls around and it's still sunny out, so off we go to the neighbor's. I am touched that he has gone to the trouble of setting up his plow (which had been put away for the season) to show us how he hitches up the oxen and uses it. His boys yoke up the two oxen, and we see how they are driven to plow the straight furrows, up and back down the field. Although it's a simple plow (like the Amish use), it is advanced technology for around here. Most people are simply too poor to afford the oxen or the plow. The traditional hoe, used by the majority of villagers, is made of a sturdy branch with a sharpened iron point attached to it. There are actually two types, and we learn today which is traditionally Jola, and which was introduced by a neighboring people group. The boys sketch the tools, watch as we are shown how the seeds are carefully planted (one by one), and Justin takes a few pictures.

We then visit their garden, kind of a "kitchen garden." The regular fields are outside the village limits, and often quite a long walk away, but many families keep a garden in their compound also. We are impressed with all he has planted in a relatively small area (approximately 20 feet by 15 feet). With his permission, we take a sample of various leaves to use in our science lesson tomorrow (papaya, tomato, ocra, manioc . . . for leaf type classification).

Before we leave, we carefully thank both the father of the compound and his son, who is the one who actually showed us everything. We also leave a small pack of (store-bought) cookies for the kids—a small token of thanks for their time and help. As we show this level of interest in our friends' customs, people are very receptive and helpful. The extended family, each doing his job around the compound while were there, seems to get a kick out of our style of "school."

Justin (11), Sean (8)

Back at home, the morning's lessons end with a Jola language class with Brad. We are trying to have both French and Jola lessons, so the boys can feel comfortable in either (French is the official language of Senegal). The man who helps Brad with translations and works in our home each morning pitches in for help with pronunciation (Brad is still learning too) and making good sentences. We have been working with the Jola for ten years so our language ability is relatively fluent. The boys tend to lose their Jola when we are away from the village but pick it up again when we go back. The younger children in the village speak *only* Jola, so our eight-year-old really learned a lot just by spending time with them during our recent stay. Justin also speaks French (as do village boys his age) so he tends to use a combination of Jola and French. We speak Jola all the time when in the village. We also speak French, as that is the language of business and government work here in Senegal.

We usually finish our morning work between noon and 1.00 PM, when we eat lunch. Our neighbor cooks for us on weekdays, and we eat the typical Jola meal of rice and sauce, seated around a large bowl. This frees me from meal preparation and clean-up.

I feel good about the morning because we got in our farm visit. We scheduled the land-use interview for the afternoon, and that goes well also. Justin asked his questions in English, Brad translated into Jola and then explained the response back into English. I am just really pleased we can take this opportunity to learn about the lives and customs of the people around us. Justin is doing research using various sources on Senegal's natural resources and agricultural products. I believe that the type of "real life" experiences we had today, though are valuable and special. I am happy that we are able to supplement our regular curriculum with activities, events, and learning gained by our unique experience of living in a different culture. And I'll say again that our interest shown in their lives means so much to them.

We spend time with the Jolas in the village each day, although we also tend to value our privacy. When we first moved to the village, we decided to build (rather than rent or live with a family) because we feel it's important to have our family life also. Our house is kind of outside the village, so we aren't right in the middle of lots of people, which we like. We are right on the paths to the fields and village gardens though, so we get plenty of interaction!

Usually, I rest after lunch. The boys do any independent work they've been assigned. We have a rest time after lunch until about 3.00 PM. This has always been our family custom, and in Africa it is common for people to rest in the heat of the day. I come from a long line of nap-takers. I actually sleep during my rest time. Brad often has his time with the Lord . . . the kids read or play quietly. Justin works all afternoon some days, and relaxes or reads other days. He has been my *big* challenge as far as keeping a supply of books available . . . he devours books whole! Luckily, he doesn't mind rereading favorites (many times). We have no access to a library while in the village, except the books we bring with us from the States. When we are in the city, we can use the mission school library—a real treat! If you are as dependent on good books as I am in

Justin (11), Sean (8)

your teaching, you may wonder how we manage without the library . . . I wonder too!! Sean, on the other hand, is *out* the door as soon as he finishes his few assignments and his fifteen minutes of reading (book of his choice).

Then there's the whole area of fine arts, which I fit in here and there during the week. I usually incorporate the art component into whatever projects we're doing for science or social studies. This week we did a lesson on calligraphy and each boy wrote his week's memory verse in calligraphy. For music this fall we have started a study of the history of music, with music in Bible times. We discussed Old Testament examples of song and dance, learned some Psalms we put to music, and illustrated instruments used at that time (another art lesson).

Our work day usually ends around 6.00 PM. In the early evening when it cools down a bit (from the mid-90's to the high 80's!), the boys and Brad usually play soccer. Our physical education program is pretty informal. I feel it needs more structure but I have a hard time getting it organized. Brad supervises it and he prefers to keep it informal . . . a good game of soccer (the national sport in most African countries) or baseball. We then spend time outside, either visiting friends or taking a walk. This is the best time of day because it's cooler.

We don't eat dinner until around 7.00 or 8.00 PM. After dinner, the boys and Brad read together, and then they take their showers. Then the boys go to bed around 9.00 PM.

The Jolas, like most Africans, really live outside. The women in the villages cook outside (unless it's raining, when they go into their cook-house). All eating and socializing are done in the courtyard. In the evenings, the family eats outside and then sits around until quite late (around 11.00 PM). Brad often goes over to the courtyard after the kids are in bed and sits with them. He reads them stories in Jola. Very few of the people are literate in Jola yet, and they love to listen to the stories that have been put into small books.

That's about it for a day in our homeschool life!

General Resources and Curriculum:
1. Scope and Sequence Resources:
    Teaching Children, by Diane Lopez
    What Your . . .Grader Needs To Know: 2nd and 6th grade, by E.D. Hirsch—A note about this relatively new series now available for grades 1-6: I have found them *very* helpful. Justin sits and reads them in his leisure time! They are helpful for all the "main" subjects, and a good resource for fine arts also.
2. Language Arts
    Justin: *Learning Language Arts Through Literature* (we're finishing up the Orange text and will do the Tan text)
    Writing Strands, The National Writing Institute (we're doing levels 3 & 4)
    Sean: *The Writing Road to Reading,* Spalding Method
    Letterland Phonics, Reading and Spelling

English From the Roots Up, Joegil Lundquist
3. Science: we use the Silver Burdett and Ginn science curriculum.
4. Math: we use the Open Court, *Real Math* curriculum.
5. Social Studies, Geography, History: we do unit themes and draw from many resources.

UPDATE:

We've had a good fall in our school times . . . our study of Senegal led us through learning about the government (present and past ones, including traditional and colonial), the history (back to Paleolithic times) and describing the Jola culture, as we see it all around us.

Ordering and getting our books each year has become a big headache. So I am about to go back to a set curriculum package, to cut down on the number of sources I have to order from. We are going to use Sonlight Curriculum, which is made for families teaching overseas.

Justin (11), Sean (8)

Ron and Janet
Christopher, age 8
David, age 7
Emily, age 2 1/2

Janet described the hot and muggy day of August 3, in the outer suburbs east of Pittsburgh, Pennsylvania.

HOMEMADE BLUEBERRY PANCAKES

We live in the outer suburbs on a quiet dead-end street. I'd rather live in the "rurals," but my husband is a city boy, so we've compromised. But we do live two minutes from a big park with trails and lots of trees, and sometimes we have deer in the backyard. Plus, in five to ten minutes I can drive to farms and road-side produce markets, so that is nice.

It's 7:05 AM on Tuesday morning and I wake up to the calling of Emily. I am too tired to deal with her yet. Maybe if I just ignore her she'll go back to sleep. I intended, as usual, to get to bed earlier last night so that I could wake up at 6:00 AM perky, refreshed, and rejuvenated. Before the children would arise I would have some personal quiet time. Then at 7:30 AM they would wake up to the cozy aroma of homemade blueberry pancakes wafting through their bedroom door just like Ma Ingalls would have made. Instead, here I lie an hour late, tired, groggy, and puffy eyed. Sigh. Oh well, I'll do better tomorrow.

I'm pulled back from my reverie by the decidedly more insistent call of Emily, and I call back that Mommy will there in a minute. I drag myself out of bed and stumble to my bedroom door wondering what awaits me. Hooray, we hit the jackpot this morning! Emily and I dance around as I sing out what a good girl she is, and isn't she getting so big, and Mommy is so proud of her potty training.

This gives me a bit of renewed energy that I decide to put to good use. It's important for me to have at least a few minutes of time for myself in the morning before I have to start the day, or I get kind of cranky and discouraged. Emily is already up, but I decide to take her into the game room with me anyway as I exercise while watching the "Today" show. It isn't easy to watch a two year old, follow world news, and stay within your target heart rate zone all at the same time. To keep Emily from wandering through the house unsupervised, and to keep her off my exercise bike while I am riding it, I set her down on a comfortable chair with her blankie and some books I keep just for this purpose. Thankfully she is still sleepy and is kept occupied for twenty minutes or so.

Around this time the boys start to roll out of bed. At this point they are fairly self-sufficient at breakfast (except, of course, for those rare Ma Ingalls days). About the only thing I have to do is casually supervise. For instance, if I didn't monitor the situation, I'd have seventeen half-opened cereal boxes in the cupboard because my kids seem to think cereal isn't exciting unless it's been opened today. Oh well, I tell them, you'll just have to suffer with twenty-six-hour-old Cheerios today and hopefully you will survive the trauma to tell your grandchildren about it.

At 8:00 AM we try to have a pick-up time. This includes clearing off the table and doing dishes, making beds, picking up toys, books, clothes, etc. from around the house, brushing teeth, and getting dressed. Some days when the boys do this so quickly and cheerfully, I nearly faint. Realistically, though, most days I have to remind them several times. We also have an afternoon pick-up, usually around 4:00 PM. This way I don't feel obligated to pick up all day long, and the boys know they are eventually responsible for helping to keep some order.

The boys have a check list on the refrigerator where their various chores are listed along with the days of the week in a graph form. When they have done a chore, they put a check on the graph. At the end of two weeks they count their checks and get money for their work. It has worked pretty well for a few months now.

Today is going to be housecleaning day. Normally Monday is chore day, because that way cleaning gets out of the way early in the week. But yesterday was one of those days when I was glad to get the dishes done and the beds made. I am really proud of myself, however, because yesterday I did most of the laundry for the week and now I don't have to do it today! Each boy is given an assignment such as dusting or vacuuming, and when they are done, they mark it on their graph. This teaches them responsibility because if they don't mark down their work, we won't know to pay them for that job. Emily basically helps by putting her dirty clothes in the hamper, "helping Mommy," and staying out of trouble while we work.

The boys also alternate doing a week of dishes with a week of helping with laundry. Some of this work is done independently and some is done along with me, depending on their ability and our moods that day. Doing dishes together affords a one-on-one opportunity to talk and catch up on things. To help them sort laundry, I have a row of laundry baskets on my basement floor marked for various loads such as jeans and dark socks, or underwear and white towels.

Christopher (8), David (7), Emily (2 1/2)

Today we are good and get our work done by 10:30 AM. We take a fifteen minute recess before school work. On other days we try to start school around 9 AM; the operative word here being *try*. It doesn't always work, but it is a goal I shoot for.

We are fortunate in that we have a nice size school room upstairs with a tile floor for easy clean up. Mothers always love this room when they first come to our house. Actually, it is just a large bedroom that we have converted to a school/play/kids room. The boys share a smaller bedroom, but we have found it is worth the sacrifice. We have a table with two chairs, a couple of used children's desks, art supplies, stackable plastic boxes for toys, books, seashell collections, etc., a play area for Emily's toys, maps and a globe, a clock and calendar, a tape player and kids' tapes, time lines and educational posters, artwork displays, a word processor, (we're working on saving for that computer), *GeoSafari* and *MathSafari*, office supplies, games, Legos, a basketball hoop, and an assortment of other things. This isn't to say that the rest of the house is off limits for reading and playing. But it is nice to have one room where most of the things are kept. It helps us keep organized and helps me keep my sanity a little.

I try to have the boys do their least favorite and/or most difficult subjects early in the day. Mondays and Fridays are journal writing days. This way they can write about their weekend on Monday and their week on Friday. They get a bit grumpy if I make them do it everyday.   I don't make a big issue of spelling during journal or creative writing.

While David works on journal writing, I keep Christopher busy independently with *Daily Grams* by Wanda C. Phillips. They don't take too long, he's learning something about grammar, and he doesn't seem to mind doing them. Then while I am doing math with David, I have Christopher go downstairs for twenty minutes of silent reading time. Today for math David is learning problem solving skills in the *Figure It Out* Book 1 by Sandra R. Cohen. I like these books because they are interactive between parent and child, they let you use manipulatives (today we used toy cars), they don't take too long, and they are kind of fun. I try using different math learning experiences for variety. We do math games such as *Muggins*, perhaps some real-life learning experiences like doubling a recipe at dinner, *MathSafari*, and flash cards. The boys even each have a typical "grade appropriate" workbook—the kind with pictures of empty clocks, word problems, and periodic reviews. They aren't particularly stimulating, but some days when I am especially frazzled it is nice to know I can just send a child off to do something on his or her own. I try to make them a little more special by giving stickers (quality wildlife or realistic dinosaur stickers) for correctly finished pages.

During all this time, Emily (bless her little heart) plays on her toy piano while the boys are trying to write in their journals. Then she wants to "culete" in her coloring book on the exact spot where I am trying to note something in the log. She takes a crayon and draws on some of David's work, at which time he gets upset and I am called upon to negotiate before it gets too ugly. She has been singing, loudly dumping blocks, crying when she can't have what the boys have,

Christopher (8), David (7), Emily (2 1/2)

and stopping to say, "Hi, how are you?" every few minutes. Finally, sometime after 11:00 AM I take the time to really focus attention on her. I realize she is still in her pajamas, has two unmatched shoes on the wrong feet and has never had her teeth brushed. Oh well. I pick her up and give her a hug and figure it is so close to lunchtime now that I might as well wait until afterwards to brush her teeth.

Christopher is done reading and wants me to know he is soooo hungry he is going to fall over if he doesn't get food immediately. I tell him I'll make lunch in less than an hour but he can have a plum in the meantime. Suddenly he isn't quite so hungry, but he thinks he could manage to eat a few cookies. I pause, knowing I should say no, but I give in just to have a few minutes of peace with David while he does his oral reading. But as Christopher runs down the stairs, miraculously full of energy for someone starving, I yell down that he can only have two cookies and he better clean up his mess when he's done.

David is improving in his reading but still needs lots of practice. I try to have him read ten minutes silently and twenty minutes orally every school day. Today he is silently reading *The Best Read It Yourself Book Ever* by Richard Scarry. He likes this book and reads a little longer than usual. He is reading orally *The Little Engine That Could* by Watty Piper. Although it is a "little kids' book," it has some surprisingly advanced vocabulary. As he gets tired out before his time is up, I don't push him to finish. Emily is *too* quiet so I go to check on her. She is busy going through my purse checking for old pieces of gum and mints among the hairballs.

It is lunch time and I am discouraged because there was so much more I wanted to accomplish by then. We eat leftovers from last night's dinner, although the boys plead for peanut butter and jelly sandwiches. I swear they would eat that every single day if I let them. After lunch I have to do some errands. I hate doing errands on school days because they always end up taking so much longer than I had anticipated. Yet I always seem to be going somewhere and am forever reevaluating how I can stay home more. I'll think about it later.

I admit I am weak in the subject of music. This isn't due to a lack of interest but rather a lack of time or organization or resources or something. Last year I bought what appears to be a really neat game: *Music Maestro* by Aristoplay, but we only played it once or twice. Why does that happen? Anyway, once again I realize it has been days since we have had any decent kind of music lesson, so while in the car we sing along with the *Kids' Songs* tapes by Nancy Cassidy. They are really cute and come with humorously illustrated books. As far as I know, there are four such sets and we have all of them. They come in handy for trips in the car and rainy day doldrums. I have also found PBS has some really worthwhile musical programs that we have enjoyed.

Since Christopher didn't get to do any math yet today, I give him some mental math problems to figure out while we are riding around. They are on the order of: If you have a 40¢ coupon for cereal and Store A sells it for $4.00 with double coupons and Store B sells it for $3.50 without doubling the coupon, which store has the better buy? We do that for a while, and then stop by the park

Christopher (8), David (7), Emily (2 1/2)

on the way home to play at the playground. We also take a short hike, where we discover a large hole at the base of a tree trunk. A few minutes later we spot a ground hog and are delighted to see that he goes into the hole we saw earlier. We discuss this for a while and then head back for the car.

By the time we get home it is after 3:00 PM. I had intended to do a science project today from *Blood and Guts* by Linda Allison. It is a Brown Paper School Book and has fun and quick experiments. But the prospect at this point makes me sigh deeply, so I tell the boys school is over for now and they can go play while Emily goes in for a nap.

First they ask me if they can go watch TV. Absolutely not, I tell them! It is the end of August and a beautiful day and they aren't going to spend it inside vegetating when summer is winding down, blah, blah, blah. Obediently they go outside and end up building a village with pine needles. We have devised a method of monitoring TV viewing that seems to work for us. It is based on a ticket system. They are given so many tickets at the beginning of the week, each counting for a half hour. Each time they watch a program they put in the appropriate ticket(s). When the tickets are gone, there is no more TV until next week. And to encourage less TV viewing, they can redeem unused tickets for cash at the end of the week. This cash is kept in a fund to be used for a fun outing such as a trip to the Science Center or a game of miniature golf. And once in a while we have found it helps to have a no-TV week.

I start thinking about dinner. I used to love to cook when we were first married. But after the kids came along, I grew less enthused. I think that's partly because most things remotely interesting to an adult's palate seem to bring on an automatic gag reflex in children. But it's going on 4:00 PM, and as I stare blankly into the foggy recesses of my freezer hoping for inspiration, I realize I am going to have to do something. Suddenly I remember I have thawed chicken breasts in the refrigerator and all is saved. I bread and bake them with some spaghetti sauce and cheese and they end up resembling a variation of Chicken Parmigiana.

Everyone is happy and dinner goes along fairly uneventfully. There are the usual little tiffs like who sits where, who gets what plate, who ate the least zucchini. One of the boys informs me, with his mouth full of food, that Emily has bad manners and don't I think I had better do something about it. When someone spills grape juice, poor Dad's patience finally runs out and he firmly orders both of the boys from the room. They each plead they were the innocent party. When all is cleaned up and peace and order return, Christopher is informed it is his turn to do dishes. Instantly he begins to lose his skeleton and crumble to the floor. But when he is told he will go directly to bed without a story if he doesn't march right in there and do them, he recovers and manages to get them done.

After playing a while more, it is time for baths. Each boy wants to go first in our house because the last one has to dry the floor. Christopher goes first, but forgets to put his dirty clothes in the hamper before David gets a bath. Naturally, David, as a faithful town crier, informs me of this omission

Christopher (8), David (7), Emily (2 1/2)

immediately.

Baths are finally over, Daddy reads   *The Monster at the End of th*
(published   by Golden Books) to Emily while tucking her in, and the boys anc
curl up in my bed to read a couple of chapters from   *On the Banks of P*
by Laura Ingalls Wilder. After that, the boys go off to bed. They have to come
down repeatedly to say good night, that they are thirsty, and to ask us when we
are going to bed. At first we are patient, but eventually forbid them to come
down again.

All is quiet. I catch up on some reading, fill in my log, and finish up a
few odds and ends. Ron and I turn in, and as we lie there, I tell Ron about my
day. I suspect he is falling asleep, so I ask him to repeat what I just said. He
attempts something and I appreciate the effort. As I am falling asleep I notice it
is 11:48 PM. I had intended to get to sleep earlier tonight so that I could wake up
tomorrow morning, perky and refreshed, ready to make blueberry pancakes. Oh
well, I'll do better tomorrow.

OUR HISTORY:

A few years ago I heard about homeschooling from a friend who was
going to teach her daughter at home. I admired her noble effort, but I honestly
thought it was kind of a weird idea. Who in the world would want their kids
around all of the time with never a break? I personally was looking forward to
sending mine off to school so that I could finally have the day to pursue other
interests. Plus, I figured my conservative husband would never go for the idea. If
I even suggested it, he'd probably assume it was just some harebrained
inspiration that I'd lose interest in quickly. So, imagine my shock, when he was
the one who suggested we look into it after he had heard about homeschooling
through someone else. We decided to give it a try.

I remember at first being very overwhelmed by it all! There seemed so
much to learn, and I worried about everything! Would I be able to cope when the
new baby (Emily) arrived? What if I couldn't teach my kids everything they
needed to know? Could we afford it? Would they end up as socially backward
Boo Radleys, unable to relate to all the Jems and Scouts of the world?

I don't do anything small, so it was with my usual tunnel vision that I
tackled homeschooling. It was rocky at first, and more than once I felt so
stressed that I wanted to chuck the whole thing. But other times it went really
well and I felt good about what we were doing. Christopher spent kindergarten
and first grade at home.

Then we moved during that next summer, and I decided it was time to
send him to school. He spent second grade and David spent kindergarten in
public school. It was a really tough decision, but one I think we needed to make
at the time. We had gone through a lot of stressful events that year not even
involving homeschooling, and I just felt burned out. Plus the boys were very
curious about public school and expressed a desire to try it.

At first I felt like we had totally failed and "gone over to join the other
side." But in time I viewed it as a sabbatical. For our family, it turned out to be a

Christopher (8), David (7), Emily (2 1/2)

good thing. The boys realized that all the things they had wanted to experience didn't turn out to be particularly amazing, and they missed being at home learning with Emily and me. And I came to feel a lot more confident about what we were doing at home.

I remember a turning point for me was one day when I realized that I had been homeschooling for negative-based reasons: I didn't like public schools, I didn't approve of the values they would be taught and also learn from other children, schools were full of crime and drugs, etc. Those were all valid and good reasons, yet they hadn't been enough for me. But now I wanted to homeschool them also for *positive*-based reasons: *I* wanted to be the one that saw them experience the joy of learning. *I* wanted to be there to share all those precious moments, and I was missing them. That was when I decided it was time they came home again.

We are a lot more low-keyed the second time around. As time goes by, our homeschooling style becomes less structured and more learner-led. It has taken time for me to gain confidence in my children's abilities to learn by themselves and for my children to realize it is "Okay" to learn that way. Some things I am definitely involved with, but now I try to guide rather than interfere and to provide opportunities for independent learning rather than structuring everything they do. Homeschooling is a process much like parenting. You never reach a point and say, "Now. . . I have arrived! I finally have this thing down pat." There is always more to learn, things to change and refine.

My husband is a real gem. He is a kind and spiritual man, very patient. He finds time in his busy schedule for the children, playing ball or reading with them. He helps me with the dishes and laundry sometimes, and the cleaning. They are my jobs, but when he sees I am getting especially behind or frazzled, he does step in to help. He doesn't do a whole lot in the way of "official" homeschooling. I think he always intends to do more, but it doesn't quite materialize very often. Yet the support and encouragement are definitely there for myself and the children.

Christopher (8), David (7), Emily (2 1/2)

UPDATE:
Since I first wrote this, there has been another change. Our "school" room is no more! It has become bedroom number four instead. The boys just wanted to have their own rooms more than we needed a schoolroom. Plus, we do our learning all over the house anyway. We still have certain areas set aside such as art centers, Lego areas, and bookshelves. I try to make things accessible and kid-friendly without having chaos and pandemonium. Some days it works, and other days I just eat chocolate.

My log-keeping has become more simplified. One thing that I personally don't feel comfortable with is that I feel compelled at times to teach "for the log." This is because although a week may have been wonderfully productive in some areas, another subject such as Health may only have been taught once that week or not at all. It can tend to look like there are gaps and I can feel obligated to hurry up and force some learning just so that the log is nicely filled out. Everyone has their own method, and I figure whatever works is fine. Some people like keeping a detailed log to stay organized, to satisfy their particular school district, or even for sentimental reasons. But the law doesn't require the keeping of a detailed log, and personally I always felt distracted and bogged down keeping one. My evaluator and school district are satisfied with samples of work, a chronological reading list, and an attendance record. It has worked out much better for us, freeing us to learn more spontaneously and not so much for the log.

Christopher (8), David (7), Emily (2 1/2)

Matt and Leslie
Jesse, age 11
Benjamin, age 9
Bethany, age 6
Jordan, age 3

Leslie wrote this on the cold, rainy, and windy day of November 1, at their church parsonage in rural Markleysburg, Pennsylvania.

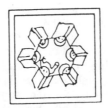

CHARMING CLUTTER

The alarm rings for Dad, Jesse, and me at 6:15 AM. I discover that somehow Jordan has migrated to my bed. It is cold, dark, and raining and my turn to drive Jesse around on his morning paper route. Jesse stumbles upstairs to help count, roll, and bag newspapers. We remark on how few rainy days he's really had on his paper route since he started in April. We get the papers delivered without much conversation while Jesse hops out of the van to slip them between people's doors. I hope the car doesn't break down, as under my coat I'm wearing pajamas and fuzzy bear slippers! Jesse has learned a lot about dealing with the public from his job. Collecting money from customers, which he does by himself, requires real perseverance, as any paperboy knows. But Jesse is saving up for a computer—the best one he can buy, so he sticks with it.

We're home by 7:00 AM. Jesse reads the comics and I skim the rest of the paper while Dad showers. Bethany wakes up a little after 7:00 AM, scared of the thunder and lightning. She cuddles with me for a few minutes then asks if she can have some tea. I ask Jesse if he will get it while I shower and dress. Then I try to have a few moments of relative peace so I can read the Bible and pray. We've been working on memorizing Luke 6:46-49 about the house built on the rock. I reflect that the rock we are to build our lives on is obedience to the Word of God, not just the hearing of it, and I wonder how we are doing in this area. Our kids "hear" so much.

Jordan and Ben are up by 7:40 AM. This is a little early for Ben but it's hard to sleep through the storm. Jordan has an insistent question first thing: "Can I eat brefkiss in my Snoopy shirt?" I reassure him. We cuddle for a few minutes, then Jordan and Ben run downstairs to Jesse's basement bedroom, from where I hear shrieks and house-shaking thumps. All four kids are playing on Jesse's bunk beds. It's early so I don't mind.

At 8:00 AM (we usually aren't punctual about this) I call everyone to breakfast—orange juice and bagels with cream cheese. After this, Pastor Matt leaves for his church office, which is a block away. I remind the kids to get busy on their "morning jobs," which consist of bed making, room straightening (hah!), dressing, and personal grooming. I run down to the basement to check on the laundry (there is always a load in process) and discover my whites are pink. I fish out the culprits (a pair of red socks) and rewash with bleach. Then I'm back to the kitchen to mix up some bread dough and set it to rise in the oven. The dishes are piled in the sink but are left unwashed (sigh!). I have to prod the kids about their room straightening. I glance in our bedroom/computer room/ sewing/junk room and think glumly that I could use someone to straighten up *our* room as well! Unfortunately, as I am something of a perfectionist, my cluttered house *bothers* me a great deal! This probably has something to do with expectations I set for myself as the pastor's wife in the church parsonage. We aren't *supposed* to be messies, are we?

By 8:45 AM all are dressed, although for Jordan this means underwear and his beloved Snoopy shirt. He has an aversion to long pants. Jesse is drawing a large picture of sailors landing on a beach, gathering coconuts and water. Ben is on the couch, playing with Legos. Bethany is dancing around the living room and singing. She practices her beginning piano book. I have heard three kids now on this particular book, and wonder if Bethany is the one who will actually go beyond it. She shows real interest and ability in music. We have sung two-part duets at many a mother-daughter banquet.

I announce it's Bible time. Jordan bounces around me and begs for his "tractor movie" (a half-hour video from the library retelling *Mike Mulligan and his Steam Shovel*). I tell him not until after Bible time, if he's good. A little bribery may work here. We use David and Mary Baker's *Bible Study Guide For All Ages* and have been pleased with it. We pick and choose from the many drills and activities, and we like its emphasis on reading the actual words of Scripture and staying with a character for a long period of time. The time line adorns our kitchen (adding to the cluttered look) and the maps are in the hall. Today's chapter is 2 Samuel 17, about David and Absalom. Jesse coolly and easily reads his portion. Bethany and Ben both want to read a long portion and I try to divide it up in a way that will make them both happy. Bethany, a first grader, loves to read, but the Bible is still slow going for her. I give her a couple of well-chosen verses. Ben, ever competitive, loves to correct her. I remind him to let *me* do the correcting after giving Bethany time to try to sound out the name (Ahithophel?!). Jordan is not particularly cooperative, hoping for some attention. We show him David in his Bible story book and let him hold the pictures for some drills.

Jesse (11), Benjamin (9), Bethany (6), Jordan (3)

Jordan likes Bible time mainly because we are all sitting on the floor or on couches in the living room, and we are easy targets because it is easier to draw our attention. We find in our chapter that Ahithophel hangs himself, which leads to a discussion of suicide. Is it breaking the sixth commandment? The kids say yes. Jesse asks how "Thou shalt not kill" relates to war. We have visited a pacifist Christian community nearby, so this led to an interesting discussion on the differing views on this issue.

We always close Bible time with prayer and today Ben runs out to the kitchen to get some missionary prayer cards. We have enjoyed getting to know missionaries and their children, and the kids are good about writing to their friends overseas and praying for them. Ben passes out a card to everyone (there is some arguing about who gets who) and we all take turns praying for ourselves, each other, and our missionary friends.

It's 9:15 AM. I draw the kids together to talk briefly about their daily plans, assignments, expectations. We put in *Mike Mulligan* for Jordan in the basement and the rest of us gather at the dining room table. We are getting ready for an upcoming "Geography Fair" with our homeschooling group—about six to ten families spread over a sixty mile rural area. Bethany has chosen to study India again. (She did it in kindergarten too! She has dreams of becoming a missionary nurse to India, so she is intensely interested in the country.) We pick a different aspect of the country—animals of India. So Bethany works on a drawing of an Indian elephant. She does a remarkable line drawing from a model of a plastic elephant. I talk with her about the background—filling the page, making the horizon part way up the page with the sky meeting ground. She draws and colors. Palm trees, grass, and a sunset appear. She is pleased with her work.

The boys, meanwhile, are working on writing thank-you's to the newspaper office for our recent field trip there. Jesse has to redo his as there are problems with handwriting, spelling, and capitalization. He fusses but complies. Ben has had the foresight to write in pencil, so he can make his corrections on the same copy. Next, Ben has been working on an article about our field trip for our monthly family newspaper. He is struggling with the organization of the piece, mostly because he will write a sentence and say, "There! Is that enough?" And I tell him he must write more. He is uninspired and mopes. We talk together about what happened first, next, next, and last, and I allow Ben to dictate the rest of the piece. He now has his paragraphs numbered in story order and can proceed to his final copy. Jesse, meanwhile, is writing a chatty letter to his aunt, describing Jordan's antics. I read it and smile. I tell him it's a good letter. Bethany is still working on her picture that will be included on a large poster. All are singing silly little songs during their work, probably inspired by Bethany's verse earlier.

Jordan has been playing with Legos in the basement but he comes up now. He's hungry for one of his six daily meals. I feed him buttered bread fresh from the oven, then run down to put in another load of laundry.

Jesse is studying Spain for the geography fair and he begs to work on

Jesse (11), Benjamin (9), Bethany (6), Jordan (3)

his bullfight model. I tell him not yet. I am concerned that bullfighting is all he wants to know about Spain. So Jesse works instead on a map of Spain. We talk about how isolated the Iberian peninsula is from the rest of Europe by the water and the mountains. Jesse likes maps so does this pretty eagerly. Jordan is up again. He spins our globe for fun. He points. "Here's the ocean." Spins. "Here's the other ocean." We praise him. I ask him where the land is and tell Bethany to find North America for him. She points to the United States and tells him we live there. Jordan says. "No. Only boys can live there—girls live over there," pointing to Russia. Jordan gets on my lap and hugs and kisses me. "My mommy. You can't have her." Then he fusses and begins to mess up the others' writing. I ask Bethany to please play with him in her bedroom where she has her doll house. They go. I ask Ben to start the final draft of his newspaper article. He is very resistant, saying his brain is dead. I tell him he *must*—I do hate the role of the constantly coercive mother/teacher. During this little power struggle, Jesse pulls out some candy, a paper route tip. All appear instantly to beg and clamor. I say they must wait until after lunch.

It's math time for Jesse, and he knows it. He asks me if he can do an activity on the geoboard before I can find which *Saxon 65* lesson he's on . . . it's #125. We started *Saxon 65* in his fifth grade year, after Bob Jones third grade math (he did third and fourth grade in one year). He likes the Saxon program, but this has not been an easy year for math. We are slowing down and trying to do a Saxon lesson three times a week and another math activity *(Figure It Out,* geoboard, story problems, etc.) the other two days. I find an activity from a geoboard workbook that requires computing the area of right triangles that I think is appropriate and he begins it on his own.

Ben is still fussing over his article. I tell him no swimming unless he's done. He dramatically falls off his chair as if wounded.

Jordan comes back out from Bethany's bedroom and draws a picture. He is learning to put eyes in his circles and lines for legs and arms coming out of his heads. I praise him, then hand him a pair of scissors and a used orange envelope. He cuts bits of paper off and makes them fall on the floor, saying, "Look Mom, it's snowing leaves!" This delights him for 15 minutes—a very long time! It is well worth the mess on the floor.

Meanwhile, Bethany and I have started on her BJU first grade books. She is using the reading, phonics, vocabulary, handwriting, and spelling books. We are experimenting with math—using lots of manipulatives and making up activities with numbers. She is using the BJU math book 2 as well. She is a willing and eager student .

Matt has come home for lunch. Time to scrounge in the fridge. At least there is fresh bread. All of us eat it with a hunk of cheese or tuna salad. We have apples and milk too, and Jesse magnanimously doles out his treat—a piece of candy to each sibling. Jordan is looking out of the big picture window at the wind sweeping the oak leaves down the street in huge gusts and screaming with delight, "Look! The leaves are racing!"

Ben does his math—without being asked! It is BJU grade 3. He brings

Jesse (11), Benjamin (9), Bethany (6), Jordan (3)

his page out for my inspection. It is well done and I praise him. We work a little on reading thermometers together. He observes the temperature outdoors in Fahrenheit and Celsius, then begs for art. I say not yet, hoping to get a little picking up out of him. Jesse is still working on his geoboard activity, while Bethany does her handwriting page. Matt takes a few minutes to read the paper. Bethany is working on multiplication of the "six tables" with some stamps torn into rows of six or less. Ben has straightened up a little and now works on his art—a detailed pencil drawing of a clipper ship. I take some time to explain right triangles to Jesse. I once again talk about being careful. He does his page over. Bethany reads a library book, *1-2-3-A-A-choo!* to herself. She can often be found curled up with a book these days, and I think I am just as excited as her to see her reading so well.

It is 2:00 PM. Now I sound the trumpet call: Time to get ready to go to town. Everyone must *pick up*, get their swimsuit and towel, *pick up*, find library books, *pick up*, get their shoes and socks on, put their books away, and get in the car. They move too slowly for me, as I am feeling rushed. The boys are dawdling—*wasted time!* Matt takes a break from the computer to help and finally everything is packed. All record their library reading after frantically gathering books. There is, I am afraid to say, some last minute *shouting* to get them going (Why can't they be a little more *self-motivated?* Are they too dependent on my prodding? I hate having to *make* them do everything . . . .)

At last we are in the van and after Ben prays for safety, we begin the twenty-five minute trip to town. A disadvantage of our rural area is the distance to anything. We try to consolidate trips and, at this point, go to town Tuesdays and Saturdays. An advantage is the beautiful mountain scenery. We comment on the status of the fall leaves as we go, noticing there are only a few still clinging to the trees in the mountains. I suggest to Jordan that he try to fall asleep, which he promptly does.

Soon we arrive at the public library and return our twenty books. We quickly look up India, Spain, bullfighting, and Switzerland (Ben's chosen country) on the computer. Jesse gets another quick lesson on Dewey decimals, as he can't find his books. The librarians know us well, as they do the other homeschoolers in the area, because we check out so many books. We have enjoyed developing a relationship with the librarians, and they have asked our homeschooled children to write book reviews for a library pamphlet and a local magazine. Why us? Because we're the only ones who will *do* it! So we chat for a few minutes before taking off. Once back in the car with our twenty-five new books, we head for the Y.M.C.A. across town. We have just taken out a year's membership after finding out that pastors and their families are half price. Hurrah! A dream for years. We try to swim twice a week when we are in town. We hurriedly change into our swimsuits and head for the pool. Bethany is working on bobbing, floating, jumping in, doggie paddling. She calls me to witness every little amazing advance in her abilities and I praise her. I have strapped a couple of floaties to Jordan's back and he takes off—as unstoppable in the water as on land. The older boys are playing water basketball, diving for

Jesse (11), Benjamin (9), Bethany (6), Jordan (3)

rings, and horsing around in the deeper end. I ask them to take turns watching Jordan and Bethany while I swim twenty laps, playing with the little kids between laps. I reflect that it probably doesn't count if it's not all at once! But this is as good as we can do today. If Matt is with us we take turns with the kids so we can do our laps all at once. We stay in the water until the lifeguard kicks us out. The kids love the hot showers and want to take their time—but Bethany has to be in the gym for gymnastics class soon so I rush her to get her in her leotard. I dress Jordan and get Bethany over to her 5:00 PM class. Jesse and Ben decide to run a mile on the indoor track. I spot a homeschooling friend whose little girl is in Bethany's class and we sit together for a rare opportunity to chat and catch up. Jordan plays with her younger daughter on the mats. We eat hoagies I have brought from home (this is *very* rare; we almost *always* have dinner with Daddy at home).

The temperature has dropped. It's 36° F cold and blowing. I ask the kids if they can handle going to the grocery store. I'd rather head home but since the store is so far from home we must go when we're in town. They are still hungry and say yes, hoping for more food. I shop, kids in tow. It's now 6:45 PM. We all pile in the van for the ride home. I hate driving up the mountain at night in freezing rain. We all pray for safety. On the way home we sing together in the car. We are working on some of the rounds and harmonies in the Lester Family *Homestyle Harmonies* tape that they love. Our kids occasionally perform singing in public so we try to keep working on songs. We play a little Mozart too. The ride home passes quickly and at 7:15 PM we are home! Matt helps unload the groceries while the boys hang out our suits and towels. I chat with Matt about his day and mine. Matt wonders aloud where to find hostesses for meals for his upcoming prophecy conference speaker. I check the calendar and volunteer for a couple of nights. I check the answering machine—someone on the mountain is interested in homeschooling and wants to talk—can I call her back? I am our support group leader and a secondary program evaluator so I get a fair number of these calls.

The kids have all their new library books spread all over the living room floor and are reading the picture books first. After a while they head to the basement to play "Bullfight." It's 8:00 PM. Matt and I talk some more then I pick up *World* magazine. At 8:20 PM I remember Jesse hasn't practiced his trumpet so we call him upstairs. He listens to our request, then runs back downstairs. After all, he's the matador. They need him. We read and talk a little more. Then we realize it is 8:55 PM. Five minutes until bedtime! We get Jesse upstairs and make him play. We help him practice a couple of minutes more, then send him to bed. Then I tuck Bethany in. We talk for a few minutes and pray together. She's tired, but Jordan has napped in the car and is full of energy. He tells pointless knock knock jokes, to which I must respond: Knock, Knock. (Who's there?) Jock Jock. (Jock Jock who?) Jock Jock, I'm riding on the sky! (or, I'm on the train, etc.). I try to laugh at the punch lines. Then the questions start: "Mom, why do little boys have bikes? Mom, do girls have belly buttons too? Mom, when I grow up, will I be a baby . . . or a jaguar or a mommy?"

Jesse (11), Benjamin (9), Bethany (6), Jordan (3)

I am trying to fill in the day in my daily journal. I have kept up with this throughout the day but now check for anything we missed. Matt has done the dishes, bless him. Finally, Ben comes to me at 10:00 PM to tell me he just read three chapters of *Farmer Boy* in bed. He knows I'll be pleased, even though it's past his bedtime. He wants to be tucked in. I think, with a pang, that Ben has probably gotten less attention today than the others. He is just more content to play on his own and is more quiet than the others. Now I try to spend a few moments with him at his bedside. At this time of night, what's important to him is important to me. Ben gazes fondly at his model airplanes and ships and asks, "Which are more dangerous, ships or planes?" I venture my opinion, but add that when it's your time to go, it's your time to go. We are in God's hands, I remind him. Ben says sleepily, "I hope my time's in a million years." He thinks a minute and adds. "In a million years I'll be a million and nine." He sighs. "I wish I were grown up. You get to do more things." Still looking at his ships, he says, "I wish I lived in sailing ship days." We kiss and pray together then I leave him to his thoughts. Meanwhile, Dad prays with Jordan and puts him in bed.

We head to bed ourselves, and see there is folded and unfolded laundry all over the bed. Matt cleans it up while I get ready for bed. It's 10:30 PM now. Time to drop off to sleep. Tomorrow, it's Matt's turn to help Jesse with the newspapers!

AFTERWORD:

We have no such thing as a "typical" homeschooling day in our household, but this is a day, anyway! Our program varies from day to day according to what else is happening: My husband Matt usually takes Mondays off and helps a lot with Jordan on that day. Our family field trips often happen then, and Ben has Cub Scouts in the evening. Tuesdays we are currently going into town in the late afternoons for a seven-week gymnastics class for Bethany

Jesse (11), Benjamin (9), Bethany (6), Jordan (3)

and Wednesday mornings Matt and I have the privilege of teaching release time religious education to the fourth and fifth grades of the local public school. We bring all our children of course, and usually I lead a song time with my guitar, Matt does a review game and a Bible story, and I teach a chapter of a visualized missionary biography. We use Child Evangelism Fellowship materials and feel it is time well spent sowing seeds in the hearts of these children. We have done this for years and our kids are pretty good about going. Jesse can't wait to teach a story. Wednesday night is family night at our church, so we all go. This year I am directing the children's and youth choirs on Wednesday nights. Thursdays and Fridays are mostly academic days. In the spring and fall there is baseball or soccer to contend with on these days too. Matt enjoys coaching soccer as it is a good change of pace from church responsibilities. Jesse has his trumpet lesson in town on Saturdays, so we also try to swim and run errands. I have a guitar student or two, and sometimes tutor English or Spanish for an hour a week.

Sundays are a busy day for us, as we are all fully involved in the life of our country church. Less church involvement is not really an option for us, so we choose instead to involve the kids in many of the things we do in our ministry. They are a part of it all, whether it is nursing home visitation, Good News Club, or choir practice. I want them to grow up with the sense that they are missionaries for Jesus wherever they are, and that other people are important because they matter to God.

Having said that, I will admit that I am constantly struggling with the use of my time. I try to balance my church responsibilities carefully, but do run out of time. What goes is the housework and I battle frustration and feelings of inadequacy in this department. The kids are responsible for their bedrooms and they can wash dishes (although, if in a rush, I usually do it as I am faster), clean bathrooms and fold most of the laundry. Our phone rings often, as Matt has no secretary. An answering machine has helped some and many people try not to call in the mornings.

We have a fairly eclectic academic program. I find that what works well for us is to have a period of time (say, three weeks) when we are all very involved in a unit study, and then we go back to a little more structured approach in language arts for a few weeks. We started out with all Bob Jones texts, but now we use the library more than anything else and our program is literature based. We use *Saxon Math* for the older grades, *Learning Language Arts Through Literature* (based on Ruth Beechik's work), and *Science in the Creation Week*. I like the BJU *Heritage Studies* texts as a springboard for further studies. We try to do a lot of the social studies and science together, using library books and, of course, we write about everything. We write a newspaper each month, we write letters to friends and relatives, we write stories (we have a lot of unfinished ones, though), and we write book reviews, plays, etc. Some of our kids take to writing more easily than others. Jesse can write volumes easily and has several unfinished books, and Bethany is eager to put her newly acquired writing skills to practical use. Once Ben has a good idea he does fine, but he needs encouragement getting that inspiration. I still occasionally allow him to dictate,

Jesse (11), Benjamin (9), Bethany (6), Jordan (3)

as his ideas flow more freely then.

Our kids have done well academically and I love being with them. I have been sobered, though, by how much our children learn from us that is unintentional. With all day to be with them, our influence upon them is so powerful. Many times we have seen ourselves mirrored in our children's attitudes and responses. Homeschooling can reveal the best and worst in us, but I am thankful for the mirror of God's Word and a loving crucible—our home—in which to help each other become more like Christ.

Jesse (11), Benjamin (9), Bethany (6), Jordan (3)

People often ask, "What's a typical day like for a homeschooling family?" When homeschooling mother Nancy Lande asked this question, she got enough material for a collection of essays by 30 families around the U.S. and abroad. These detailed accounts let you be a fly on the wall and observe how families handle chores, mealtimes, following up on a child's interests, balancing the needs of older and younger children. Several families come from a schooled-at-home perspective, others are more free; use these stories to pick and choose what you want for *your* homeschooling experience.
—*John Holt Bookstore*

This book lets us sit at the kitchen table or back porch to watch how each of 30 families approaches "training up a child in the way he should go." Many of the featured families are from various parts of the country, with one from Africa and one from Scotland (I could just hear the Scottish accent as I read this account). The journals are as varied as the people who wrote them; a chronological log, a short story, a comedy. The common thread is that these homeschoolers have opened up a day in their life to share with us. May we glean the good ideas presented here and incorporate them into our own schooling.
—*Rainbow Resource Center*

There is nothing better to give you a clear picture of the flexibility and variety you can find in homeschooling.
—Debra Bell, *The Homeschool Resource Center*

Patchwork . . . is your chance to peek into the styles, habits, and schedules (or lack thereof) of many, many home educators without the fear of burning bridges. Beginning homeschoolers will revel in these essays! You'll be amazed at the myriad methods of homeschooling that *work* and you'll see that the possibilities for making your *own* homeschool fit *your* family are endless. Old-timers will find refreshing ideas and you'll undoubtedly develop a sense of kinship with all these others who are also traveling an unusual path in their familial educational pursuits.
—Alison Moore Smith, *Bright Spark*

Have you ever found yourself, in the midst of your homeschooling adventure, wondering how in the world other families manage their days? . . . The stories are warm and real and refreshing . . . See how families cope with toddlers, out-of-home obligations, in-home businesses, field trips, interruptions and even a few "ideal" days! Look over their shoulders as they keep their daily logs, plan meals, deal with illness, crazy work schedules, pet problems and computer problems. You'll find much laughter and encouragement, and lots of great ideas!
—Wendy Orth, *Mass. H. O. P. E.*

I wish we'd had this at the time we started . . . It would have given us so much more confidence in what we were doing and trying to achieve . . . Some stories will strike an instant rapport with you; with others you will say, "I couldn't possibly do that!". Yet others will give you fresh ideas to try in your quest to educate; or still yet, save your sanity when you realize that you're not the only one still in nightclothes halfway through the morning! Buy this book, and dip into a spare moment (ha!)—it will keep you interested for a long time.
—Jean Smith, *Ed-u-cate On-line World Wide*